Intelligence: From Secrets to Policy, Fourth Edition
Mark M. Lowenthal
October 2008. Paperback. 330 pages. ISBN 978-0-87289-600-0

Intelligence veteran and best-selling author Mark M. Lowenthal details how the intelligence community's history, structure, procedures, and functions affect policy decisions. The fourth edition highlights recent developments in reforms, ethics, and transnational issues.

The Technical Collection of Intelligence
Robert M. Clark
July 2010. Hardback. 294 pages. ISBN 978-1-60426-564-4

Technical Collection offers a succinct, logically organized, and well-written overview of technical collection, explained at a non-technical level for those new to the field. The only book to comprehensively examine the collection, processing, and exploitation of nonliteral intelligence information, including laser, acoustic, and infrared signals; non-imaging optical intelligence sources; and radar tracking and measurement of aerospace vehicles. A full-color interior design features an array of high-quality graphics.

Structured Analytic Techniques for Intelligence Analysis
Richards J. Heuer Jr. and Randolph H. Pherson
March 2010. Spiral-bound Paperback. 343 pages. ISBN 978-1-60871-018-8

Heuer and Pherson turn decades of experience toward formalizing a set of 50 robust analytic techniques for use in intelligence analysis. This ready reference showcases the step-by-step processes that externalize an individual analyst's thinking, enabling it to be easily shared, built on, and critiqued by others. Such a structured and transparent process, combined with the input of subject matter experts, can reduce the risk of analytic error. The easy-to-use handbook design includes tabs, a two-color interior, and lay-flat spiral binding.

Intelligence Analysis: A Target-Centric Approach, Third Edition
Robert M. Clark
September 2009. Paperback. 309 pages. ISBN 978-1-60426-543-9

A collaborative, target-centric approach to intelligence analysis allows for horizontal, networked solutions while better meeting customer needs. Includes discussions of framing effects, human terrain models, cyber collection, computer network exploitation, and more. A new section on the "defense analysis challenge" clarifies the relationship between the analyst and the customer.

ORDERING INFORMATION

Teaching at a college or university? Order exam copies today by e-mailing collegesales@cqpress.com or visiting college.cqpress.com.

For information on discounts on orders of 5 or more copies, send an email to bulksales@cqpress.com.

For individual orders visit our website at college.cqpress.com and enter C0INT and have your order shipped for only $5 (U.S. and Canada only)!

INTERESTED IN JOINING THE PORTFOLIO?

Our suite of intelligence resources is rapidly expanding. If you are interested in writing a book for intelligence training, please contact acquisitions editor Elise Frasier at efrasier@cqpress.com.

The Technical Collection of
Intelligence

ROBERT M. CLARK

The Technical Collection of
Intelligence

ROBERT M. CLARK

CQ PRESS

A Division of SAGE
Washington, D.C.

CQ Press
2300 N Street, NW, Suite 800
Washington, DC 20037

Phone: 202-729-1900; toll-free, 1-866-4CQ-PRESS (1-866-427-7737)

Web: www.cqpress.com

Cover and interior design: Debra Naylor
Composition: C&M Digitals (P) Ltd.

☻ The paper used in this publication exceeds the requirements of the American National Standard for Information Sciences—Permanence of Paper for Printed Library Materials, ANSI Z39.48-1992.

Printed and bound in Canada

14 13 12 11 10   1 2 3 4 5

Library of Congress Cataloging-in-Publication Data

Clark, Robert M.
The technical collection of intelligence / Robert M. Clark.
    p. cm.
Includes bibliographical references and index.
ISBN 978-1-60426-564-4 (hardcover : alk. paper)
   1. Intelligence service—Technological innovations—United States.
I. Title.

JK468.I6C53 2010
327.1273—dc22

2010019424

Brief Contents

Contents

Figures and Tables

Figures

Tables

Preface

The purpose of this book is to explain technical collection of intelligence information at a nontechnical level. Technical collection represents perhaps the largest asymmetric edge that technologically advanced countries such as the United States and its allies have in the intelligence business. Other countries can do as well or even better in human intelligence (HUMINT), given the relatively open societies in the United States and Europe. Most countries have similar access to open source collection—the openly available material that includes the Internet. Many countries collect communications intelligence (COMINT), but technical collection requires a sophisticated technological infrastructure and a need for the intelligence that it produces. Increasingly, major powers are making the investment in satellite-based imaging systems, but most do not yet invest in the wide range of technical collection assets that the United States uses.

The Technical Collection of Intelligence discusses how technical collectors work and are used in the collection of intelligence. It will be of value to:

- managers of technical collection assets who must work cooperatively across collection "stovepipes"—a term widely used in the United States to refer to the specialization and compartmentation practices of collection organizations

- all-source analysts who need to understand the potential and limitations of such assets in order to task them intelligently and use the results in solving analytical problems
- customers of intelligence who need to understand the capabilities and limitations of these assets when the collection results are cited to support intelligence conclusions
- recruiters for the intelligence community who bring in the talented people who develop these systems

This book is intended to serve these readers as a reference. It also is designed to be a textbook for a graduate-level course on technical intelligence collection. It covers terminology and important issues in collection performance and its utility for intelligence.

Definition of Technical Collection

Technical collection is defined and discussed in this book as the collection, processing, and exploitation of *nonliteral* information—that is, information in a form not used for human communication. It does not discuss the all-source analysis of such information. That subject is covered in a companion book, *Intelligence Analysis: A Target-Centric Approach*.[1]

Many definitions of technical collection are broader than the one used here. The deputy director of national intelligence for collection defines three types of collection: HUMINT; open source; and technical collection, which includes cyber collection and all components of signals intelligence (SIGINT)—that is, COMINT, electronic intelligence (ELINT), and foreign instrumentation systems intelligence (FISINT).[2] But HUMINT, open source, and COMINT collection are mainly concerned with *literal* information—that is, information in a form that humans use for communication. The primary sources of literal information for intelligence are well covered in other books. Literal information sources also can use highly sophisticated technology— COMINT in particular. But the basic product and the methods for collecting and analyzing literal information are generally well understood by intelligence analysts and the customers of intelligence.

Technical collection is less well understood, and in fact is often misunderstood by HUMINT, open source, and COMINT collectors who need to collaborate with the technical collectors. Nonliteral information usually requires special processing beyond the translation and analysis of collected literal information, and it is important to understand the nature and limitations of that processing.

The delineation between literal and nonliteral intelligence has become more significant because of the increasing demand for credible and timely information. Intelligence must be precise, accurate, and timely, especially when used to support modern military operations. The literal information sources—HUMINT, open source, and most COMINT—rarely meet these three requirements. In contrast, many of the important technical collection "INTs," especially imagery intelligence (IMINT) and ELINT, routinely meet the standard. Technical collection is becoming more important for all national intelligence services because, as British writer Michael Herman notes, customers assume that "textual sources cannot be counted upon, certainly not in near real time."[3]

Technical collection as defined and discussed in this book has different names within intelligence organizations, depending on the organization and the specific field being discussed. Much of it is often called measurements and signatures intelligence (MASINT) in the United States and allied countries. The term *MASINT* also encompasses a number of acronyms that identify unique sources, such as:

ACOUSTINT (collection of acoustic signals)

IRINT (collection of infrared signals)

LASINT (collection of laser signals)

NUCINT (collection of nuclear debris and radiation)

OPTINT (collection of nonimaging optical intelligence)

RADINT (radar tracking and measurement of aerospace vehicles)

Some classes of technical collection have specific names, such as advanced geospatial intelligence (AGI), electronic intelligence (ELINT), geospatial intelligence (GEOINT), or imagery intelligence (IMINT). These terms are a convenient shorthand, and some of them are used in this book to describe subsets of technical collection. They are widely used in the United States and allied intelligence communities, so the reader needs to understand what they mean. But many of them are not helpful and simply promote confusion and overlap of responsibilities, especially in the U.S. intelligence community. Many of these names derive from political and bureaucratic rather than physical considerations.

Terms like *AGI* and *GEOINT* are not helpful in describing collection. GEOINT in any event is not a collection "INT"; it is a type of all-source analysis, and all intelligence organizations—including national level, military support, and law enforcement intelligence—do geospatial analysis.

In summary, the United States and many other national intelligence organizations are structured by what we call *INTs*, which are often used to create what are called *stovepipes*, but the educational process is ill-served by using these organizational divisions to structure learning. In this book, many of these terms are subsumed under the term *technical collection*, which has some unifying themes:

- collection of nonliteral information, as noted previously
- measurement of a signature
- associating a signature with a person, feature, or object and identifying changes in the state of the person, feature, or object (for example, by geolocating him, her, or it)

It can be argued that the term *MASINT* covers this definition. But many processes in what are traditionally called *SIGINT* and *IMINT*, in fact, involve the measurement of an object or signal and the development of an identifying signature. For example, imagery interpretation often involves both measurement of objects in an image and identifying unique signatures of objects in an image.

Organization of the Book

The book begins with a discussion of the fundamental idea of a signature. It then continues with a discussion of the sensors and platforms (aircraft, satellites, ships, and ground sites) that are used to collect signatures for intelligence purposes.

Most of the signatures collected for intelligence are from the electromagnetic (EM) spectrum, which includes the optical spectrum, and are collected remotely using a technique called *remote sensing*. After an overview of remote sensing concepts, the techniques and systems used for remote sensing in intelligence are discussed in depth.

The book devotes the next several chapters to discussing how sensors work. Technical collection of signatures involves using radar, radiofrequency

(RF) receivers, lasers, passive electro-optical devices, nuclear radiation detectors, and seismic or acoustic sensors. These instruments gather measurements (such as radar cross-sections, radiant intensities, or temperatures) to characterize military operations and tactics; to assess missile, aircraft, and propulsion systems performance; to monitor research, development, testing, and production facilities; and to understand cultural and economic activities, environmental effects, and naturally occurring phenomena.[4]

A separate class of sensors operates outside the electromagnetic spectrum. These collection sensors usually operate at short range and sense acoustic, magnetic, or nuclear signatures. These non-RF sensors are discussed in subsequent chapters. The sensor chapters provide specific examples of sensors used in technical collection and discuss the fundamental limitations and tradeoffs that are inherent in any technical collection sensor.

Some technical collection does not involve sensors at all. Instead, the signatures are obtained by collecting physical objects and equipment (usually referred to as *materiel*) or samples of substances (usually grouped under the heading of *materials*). This field of collection is discussed in the chapter on materiel and materials collection and exploitation.

The final chapter discusses the management of technical collection. A number of studies in the United States have investigated the organization of technical collection and addressed the need for better interaction among the different INTs that are covered in this book. The 104th Congress directed a study, "IC21: The Intelligence Community in the 21st Century," that recommended consolidating technical collection and exploitation activities (SIGINT, IMINT, and MASINT) into a technical collection agency.[5] This book does not directly address the merits of such an agency, but the final chapter does focus on the substantial management challenges of technical collection.

All statements of fact, opinion, or analysis expressed are those of the author and do not reflect the official positions or views of the Central Intelligence Agency or any other U.S. government agency. Nothing in the contents should be construed as asserting or implying U.S. government authentication of information or Agency endorsement of the author's views. This material has been reviewed by the CIA to prevent the disclosure of classified information.

Acknowledgments

Many people throughout the U.S. intelligence community have provided wisdom that I have incorporated. I cannot name them all, but I appreciate their help. I am especially grateful to reviewers within the U.S. intelligence community who have contributed their time to improving the text, including Gary W. Goodrich, former Associate Deputy Director of Science and Technology, CIA; Timothy T. Green, Lieutenant Colonel, United States Army and faculty, National Defense Intelligence College; Erik A. Kleinsmith, Senior Program Manager, Lockheed Martin Center for Security Analysis; Bob Mirabello, Senior Faculty Member, The Intelligence and Security Academy; and Edwin Urie, Johns Hopkins University, and two other anonymous reviewers. Special thanks go to my wife, Abigail, who contributed extensively to the book's readability and understandability. I also want to thank Elise Frasier, Acquisitions Editor, and Joan Gosset, Senior Production Editor at CQ Press, for managing the process, and Kerry Kern for shaping the finished product.

Robert M. Clark
Reston, Virginia

NOTES

1. Robert M. Clark, *Intelligence Analysis: A Target-Centric Approach*, 2nd ed. (Washington, D.C.: CQ Press, 2006).
2. Office of the Director of National Intelligence, "An Overview of the United States Intelligence Community for the 111th Congress," 2009, www.dni.gov/overview.pdf.
3. Michael Herman, *Intelligence Services in the Information Age* (New York: Frank Cass Publishers, 2001), 57.
4. Clark, *Intelligence Analysis*, chapter 6.
5. U.S. House of Representatives, Permanent Select Committee on Intelligence Staff Study, "IC21: The Intelligence Community in the 21st Century," June 5, 1996.

Acronyms

ACINT	intelligence collected from underwater sound
ACOUSTINT	intelligence collected from sound in air
AEOS	Advanced Electro Optical System
AFMIC	Armed Forces Medical Intelligence Center (now the National Center for Military Intelligence)
AGI	advanced geospatial intelligence
ALCOR	ARPA Lincoln C-band Observable Radar
ALTAIR	ARPA Long-range Tracking and Identification Radar
ARL	Army Research Laboratory
ARM2000	Automated Requirements Management 2000
BMD	ballistic missile defense
BW	biological warfare
CBW	chemical and biological warfare

CCD	charge-coupled device; coherent change detection
CCS	collaborative collection strategies
CDAA	circularly disposed antenna array
CIA	Central Intelligence Agency
COMINT	communications intelligence
CW	chemical warfare; continuous wave
D&D	denial and deception
DARPA	Defense Advanced Research Projects Agency
dB	decibels
dBW	decibels above or below one watt
DCI	Director of Central Intelligence
DF	direction finding
DHS	Department of Homeland Security
DNA	deoxyribonucleic acid
DNI	Director of National Intelligence
DoD	Department of Defense
DSP	defense support program
ECM	electronics countermeasures
ELINT	electronic intelligence
EM	electromagnetic
EMP	electromagnetic pulse
EMR	electromagnetic radiation
EO	electro-optical
ERS-1	European remote sensing satellite
FDOA	frequency difference of arrival
FIRCAP	Foreign Intelligence Requirements, Categories, and Priorities
FISINT	foreign instrumentation systems intelligence
FLIR	forward-looking infrared

FM	frequency modulation
FOV	field of view
GEO	geostationary orbit
GEODSS	ground-based electro-optical deep space surveillance system
GEOINT	geospatial intelligence
GMTI	ground moving target indicator
GPS	global positioning system
GRAB	galactic radiation and background experiment satellite
GRD	ground resolution distance
GSD	ground sample distance
GSM	global system for mobile communications
HEO	highly elliptical orbit
HF	high frequency
HPM	high power microwave
HSI	hyperspectral imaging
HUMINT	human intelligence
IC	intelligence community
IC-MAP	Intelligence Community Multi-intelligence Acquisition Program
ICARS	Intelligence Community Analysis and Requirements System
ICBM	intercontinental ballistic missile
ICM	Integrated Collection Management
IED	improvised explosive device
IEEE	Institute of Electrical and Electronics Engineers
IFOV	instantaneous field of view
IIR	intermediate infrared
IMINT	imagery intelligence
IMS	International Monitoring System
IR	infrared

ISAR	inverse synthetic aperture radar
ITU	International Telecommunications Union
IUSS	integrated undersea surveillance system
JCMT	joint collection management tools
JSTARS	Joint Surveillance and Target Attack Radar System
KGB	Komityet Gosudarstvennoy Bezopasnosti (Committee for State Security)
KIQ	key intelligence question
LEO	low earth orbit
LFM	linear frequency modulation
LPI	low probability of intercept
LWIR	long wavelength infrared
MAD	magnetic anomaly detector
MANPADS	man-portable air defense system
MASINT	measurements and signatures intelligence
MATTS	Marine Asset Tag Tracking System
MEO	medium earth orbit
MHz	megahertz
MRS	MASINT Requirements System
MSI	multispectral imaging
MTI	moving target indicator
M_v	visual magnitude
MWIR	mid-wavelength infrared
NASA	National Aeronautics and Space Administration
NCMI	National Center for Medical Intelligence
NGA	National Geospatial-Intelligence Agency
NIC-C	National Intelligence Coordination Center
NIE	national intelligence estimate
NIH	not invented here

NIIRS	National Imagery Interpretability Rating Scale
NIPF	National Intelligence Priorities Framework
NIR	near-infrared region
NOAA	National Oceanic and Atmospheric Administration
NORAD	North American Aerospace Defense Command
NRO	National Reconnaissance Office
NSA	National Security Agency
NSRP	National SIGINT Requirements Process
NTM	national technical means
NUCINT	collection of nuclear debris and radiation
ONIR	overhead nonimaging infrared
OPIR	overhead persistent infrared
OPTINT	collection of nonimaging optical intelligence
OSRMS	Open Source Requirements Management System
OTH	over-the-horizon
PDD-35	Presidential Decision Directive 35
PHD	phase history data
PRF	pulse repetition frequency
PRI	pulse repetition interval
QRC	quick reaction capability
RADINT	radar intelligence
RCS	radar cross-section
RDT&E	research, development, test, and evaluation
RF	radiofrequency
RFI	radiofrequency interference
RFID	radiofrequency identification
RMS	Requirements Management System
R/V or RV	reentry vehicle

SAM	surface-to-air missile
SAP	Special Access Program
SAR	synthetic aperture radar
SARS	severe acute respiratory syndrome
SBIRS	space based infrared system
SECAR	surface-wave extended coastal area radar
SIGINT	signals intelligence
SIR-C	a SAR carried on the space shuttle
SLBM	submarine launched ballistic missile
SNR	signal-to-noise ratio
SOI	space object identification
SOSUS	sound surveillance system
SPOT	Satellite Pour l'Observation de la Terre (French imagery satellite)
SWIR	short wavelength infrared band
TDOA	time difference of arrival
TEMPEST	name given to a process for shielding electronics equipment to suppress emissions
TIRA	tracking and imaging radar
TRADEX	Target Resolution and Discrimination Experiment radar
TT&C	telemetry, tracking, and commanding
UAV	unmanned aeronautical vehicle
UHF	ultra high frequency
USI	ultraspectral imaging
UV	ultraviolet
VHF	very high frequency
VLWIR	very long wavelength infrared
WMD	weapons of mass destruction

1. Signatures

Signatures are created from the measurement of the strength, intensity, or state of some physical or chemical entity over space, time, and/or frequency. Measurements can be made, for example, of an object's dimensions, temperature, signal strength, or atmospheric pressure, all of which are physical quantities. Another type of signature is a chemical signature, which measures the presence (and often the quantity) of chemical compounds or elements in a sample. Perceptions of color are, in fact, rough measurements of the intensity of light as a function of frequency.

In this book, a signature is defined as nonliteral information resulting from technical collection. A *pattern*, in contrast, is the result of analysis (frequently of signatures). It is important to distinguish between the two, since the two concepts often overlap and the distinction can be subtle at times. Again, most technical collection produces signatures. Analysis, either of a single source or of all sources, identifies patterns.

- The geospatial pattern of operations of a criminal, for example, is sometimes described as a signature or, in law enforcement terms, a *modus operandi*. But this really is a pattern identification that results from analysis, not from technical collection.

• A series of aircraft maneuvers creates a pattern that indicates something about the aircraft's condition or the pilot's intent. But this maneuver pattern is not a signature—although the maneuvers might be identified by a series of signatures obtained from a radar.

To illustrate the difference between a signature and a pattern, consider a classic intelligence example: the identification of facilities being built in Cuba at the time of the Cuban Missile Crisis.

Figure 1-1 shows the U-2 aircraft imagery of an SA-2 surface-to-air missile site taken over Cuba in 1962.[1] This image shows a combination of signatures created by earth scarring and the presence of certain vehicles that creates a unique pattern. Analysts readily identified the site because it was laid out in what analysts call a "Star of David" configuration that matched that of SA-2 sites in the Soviet Union. The complete pattern involves the imagery signatures of six missile launchers surrounding an imagery signature of a target-tracking radar.

It can be difficult to distinguish the difference between a pattern and a signature, and there is a certain amount of overlap between the two in practice. But it is an important distinction to make in this book; this text is concerned primarily with the collection, processing, and exploitation of signatures, not the analysis of patterns.

There are many specialized techniques for obtaining signatures, most of which focus on specific classes of targets and provide specific intelligence answers. Most either use specially designed sensors or specially processed raw data from conventional SIGINT and IMINT sensors. As noted in the preface, in the United States many of these techniques are lumped together under the name of measurements and signatures intelligence (MASINT)—a term that embraces a diverse set of collection and processing techniques. Others are designated as SIGINT or IMINT.[2] The range of techniques is very large, and new techniques are constantly being added. This is a fast changing field of study.

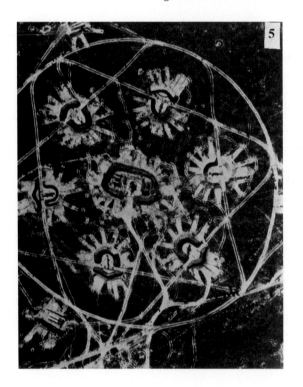

FIGURE 1-1 SA-2 Site in Cuba, 1962

How Signatures Are Used

In order to be usable for intelligence purposes, a signature must be associated with a person, object, or process. Often in intelligence, collectors want to locate a specific person, object, or process in space and time, and the signature is used for this purpose. Following are some examples of the use of signatures in law enforcement, as well as in national and battlefield intelligence.

A number of signatures are used to identify persons and to track their movements. Fingerprints are signatures based on the intensity (darkness) of coloration in a two-dimensional space. They have been used for decades to identify individuals. More recently, techniques such as biometrics have been used for the same purpose. To identify individuals, forensic scientists measure the bonds in the 13 parts of the DNA molecule that vary from person to person and use the data to create a DNA profile of that individual (sometimes called a *DNA fingerprint*). There is a negligible chance that another person has the same DNA profile for these 13 DNA regions (except for cases such as identical twins).

Trace measurement of a chemical produces a signature. Trace measurements of Krypton-85, a radioactive gas, are a signature that Plutonium-239 (a fissionable material used in nuclear weapons) is being produced at a facility. Traces of phosphorus oxychloride in an industrial effluent can be a signature that indicates chemical warfare agent production.

For monitoring missiles, weapon proliferation, arms control, and treaty compliance, signatures are used to identify and track nuclear, chemical, biological, and advanced conventional weapon systems. Technical collection allows target identification from a safe distance based on target features that are difficult to conceal, such as rocket plumes and the biological or molecular composition of chemicals and biological agents. Signature collection techniques like multispectral thermal imaging (discussed in chapter 5) provide valuable insights for identifying trace gaseous emissions, such as those produced by nuclear or chemical weapons whether in production, storage, or employment. Signatures are used to characterize environmental features that have intelligence value—including surface temperatures, water quality, material composition, and pollutants.[3]

Signatures are used by today's smart weapons systems to detect and positively identify surface targets while a weapon is in flight.[4] But technical intelligence collection is needed beforehand to obtain the characteristic signature of the target.

Technical collection can render many modern concealment and camouflage methods ineffective. Based on a signature, commanders can distinguish a specific opponent's equipment on the battlefield for highly selective targeting. Battlefield commanders can use technical collection to track friendly forces in the battle space. In addition, radar systems can remotely measure the shape of an object like a tank, missile, or warhead to help commanders determine specific models or types.[5]

Signatures collected on the environmental conditions present before, during, and after a test event (for example, of a ballistic missile or a nuclear detonation) are useful in interpreting the test results.

Signatures are usually the products of multiple measurements collected over time and under changing circumstances. They often reflect dynamic changes in a target or event. For example, the radar, infrared (IR), and acoustic characteristics of an aircraft in flight will change predictably as the attitude, power level, and flight configuration of the aircraft changes. These signatures can be used to identify specific targets or events or discriminate among them when they are again encountered.

Signature Libraries

Technical collection has little value unless there is a *signature database* or *signature library* that associates the signatures with a specific person or class of objects. With this, when a signature is identified, it can be associated with a specific person, phenomenon, object, or class of objects.

A major continuing task in intelligence is the construction of the necessary signature databases to the needed level of fidelity. Many collection systems can obtain signatures in real time (within seconds). But detecting a signature is insufficient; massive signature-collection libraries are needed so that signature identification can be performed in real or near-real time.[6] For a technical collection system to make rapid and accurate identification on the battlefield, these libraries are critical.[7] Many existing signature databases are out of date, since they contain data recorded by older, much lower fidelity sensors. In some cases, such as chemical-agent detectors, the number of signatures of interest keeps changing, so a library requires constant updating. A library of existing molecular structure signatures is still being assembled, and new chemical compounds are constantly being created.

Electromagnetic Spectrum Signatures

The most important signatures that are collected in intelligence come from sensors that operate in some part of the electromagnetic spectrum. Such sensors are discussed in chapter 2.

An electromagnetic (EM) signature is created by the interaction of EM energy with matter (material solids, liquids, and gases), as illustrated in Figure 1-2. EM sensors function by receiving either reflected or emitted energy. When a wave of EM energy from a source such as the sun or a radar transmitter interacts with matter, the incoming (incident) radiation can be reflected, refracted, scattered, transmitted, or absorbed. EM energy striking a rough object (such as a rock or bare earth) or a diffuse object (such as a cloud of water vapor) is scattered in many directions or absorbed. Some energy also may pass through the object. Energy striking a smooth reflective object, such as a metal plate, will mostly be reflected.

Sometimes, as Figure 1-2 indicates, EM energy is absorbed by an object and stimulates the emission of energy at a different frequency. Ultraviolet light, for example, will cause some materials to fluoresce, or emit visible light. Many people have observed that white clothing will glow in the dark when illuminated with long-wave ultraviolet light (known as "black light"). The glow is due to fluorescence of the chemicals used in detergents.

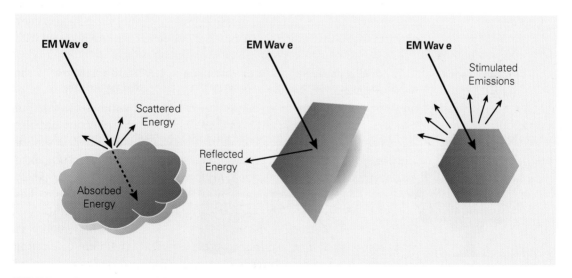

FIGURE 1-2 The Interaction of EM Energy with Matter

Fluorescent pigments find intelligence uses in paints, plastics, and coatings for identifying items or people and for secret writing, among others.

Furthermore, objects emit EM energy both naturally and as a result of human actions, as suggested in Figure 1-3. All matter (solids, liquids, and gases) at temperatures above absolute zero emit energy, mostly in the thermal (infrared) regions of the spectrum, as discussed later in this chapter. Lightning strokes and auroras generate very strong radiofrequency (RF) and optical signals. Radioactive substances emit gamma rays. Many creatures emit energy in the optical bands due to chemical reactions, a phenomenon called *biofluorescence*. Fireflies, plankton, and a number of ocean creatures fluoresce.

Man-made objects emit EM energy both intentionally and unintentionally. Communications equipment, radar, and building lights all intentionally emit RF or optical energy to serve our purposes. But a wide range of man-made objects also unintentionally emit EM energy as a consequence of their functioning—like the truck in Figure 1-3, which emits RF noise from its spark plugs and infrared (IR) energy from its hot engine. As discussed throughout this book, these natural and artificial emissions create a signature that can have intelligence value.

The utility of remote EM sensing derives from the fact that when EM energy is reflected and/or emitted from solid, liquid, and gaseous materials, it is modified by those materials. This modified energy constitutes a signature that is unique to the material. Reflected and emitted radiant energy can thus be used to obtain a signature that is unique to a particular material or object.

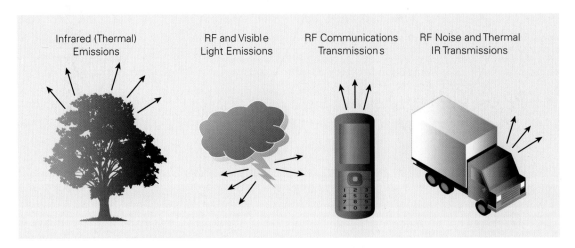

FIGURE 1-3 Natural and Artificial Emission of EM Energy

Most sensors used in remote sensing for intelligence operate in some specific part of the electromagnetic spectrum. The spectrum is described in terms of frequency or wavelength and typically is thought of as having two parts: the RF spectrum and the optical spectrum.

THE RADIOFREQUENCY SPECTRUM

Figure 1-4 shows the part of the radiofrequency spectrum that is used for remote sensing in intelligence. The RF spectrum continues into lower frequencies (off the left side of the figure), but intelligence collectors are primarily concerned with the part of the spectrum shown here. Note that the spectrum is divided into named bands; these will be discussed in later chapters. The spectrum also continues upward in frequency (to the right), but the continuation is the optical spectrum, discussed next.

Signatures are collected in the RF spectrum in two ways: by passive sensors that collect RF energy emitted by the target, and by active or passive

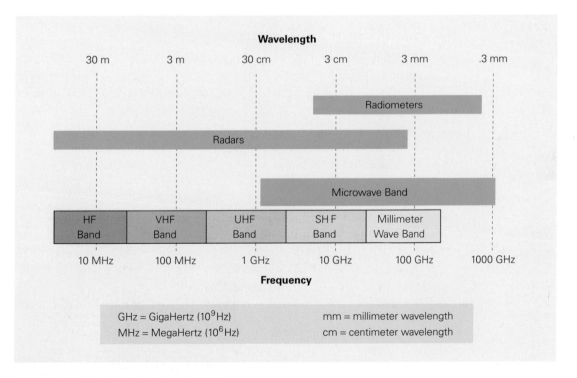

FIGURE 1-4 The Radiofrequency Spectrum

sensors that collect RF energy reflected from the target. Passive RF sensors collect a wide range of natural and man-made emissions, including:

- intentional emissions, such as communications and radar signals
- RF emissions incidental to human activity, such as auto ignition noise
- natural emissions, such as lightning discharges (which are not usually of intelligence interest, being basically noise)
- thermally generated emissions (which also are noise, but are used in imaging)

Most of the reflected RF energy collection is done by radars, which transmit in fairly narrow bands within the RF spectrum. Radars are discussed in chapters 6 and 7. In a few cases, reflected RF collection is done without a radar transmitter, and these special cases are discussed in chapter 8.

Both emitted and reflected RF signals provide signatures that allow intelligence analysts to draw conclusions about the targets from which the signals were emitted or reflected. These signatures are discussed in some detail in chapters 6–8.

THE OPTICAL SPECTRUM

Figure 1-5 is a continuation of the spectrum from Figure 1-4 to higher frequencies (shorter wavelengths). This part of the EM spectrum is called the *optical spectrum*; the sensors used here are fundamentally different from those used in the RF spectrum.

In the optical spectrum, it is customary to refer to a part of the spectrum by wavelength (usually in micrometers, commonly called *microns* and abbreviated μm) rather than by frequency; the frequency numbers are so large as to be cumbersome and are described in terms that are difficult to comprehend, such as terahertz and pentahertz.

The optical spectrum is represented in Figure 1-5 as being composed of energy bands, each having its own name or designation. The band boundaries shown in the figure are commonly used, but there is no accepted standard either for the number of bands or for their boundaries. Astronomers, for example, divide the infrared band into three very broad bands (near, mid, and far infrared) extending from 0.7 to 350 microns.[8] The definitions shown in Figure 1-5 are used throughout this book, since they are more convenient for discussing intelligence applications.

Typically, optical sensing for intelligence purposes makes use of energy in a wavelength range from the ultraviolet to the infrared portions of the

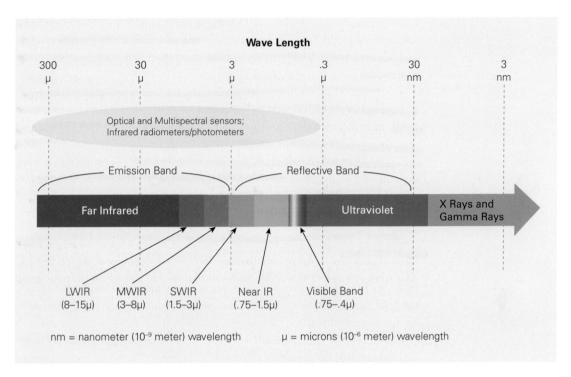

FIGURE 1-5 The Optical Spectrum

electromagnetic spectrum. Therefore, most optical sensors function in some part of the region from the ultraviolet through the long wavelength infrared (LWIR). Note that the visible part of the spectrum, extending from about 0.4 µm to about 0.75 µm where the eye and most sensors function, occupies only a small fraction of the overall optical spectrum.

As Figure 1-5 indicates, the optical spectrum also is divided into two regions based on the nature of the signature obtained. Within these two regions are specific bands that have distinct signature characteristics.

- The *reflective band* comprises the UV, visible, near-infrared (NIR), and short wavelength infrared (SWIR) bands. These bands are called "reflective" because sensors operating in them normally work in daytime only, sensing energy reflected by the sun. The NIR and SWIR bands are therefore known as the *reflected infrared* bands because they rely on the infrared part of the solar radiation reflected from the earth's surface. Some night vision goggles operate in the NIR band using an IR illuminator. Though the NIR band is called reflective, there also are important emissions in this band that have intelligence significance. For example, sensors in the NIR band can detect rocket plumes, ship lights, or factory lights at night to signal that the factory is operating.

- The band extending from mid-wavelength infrared (MWIR) through long wavelength infrared (LWIR) into the far IR band is called the *emissive band;* in contrast to the reflective band, sensors in this band do not depend directly on the sun's illumination. Within the emissive band, the MWIR and LWIR bands are often called the *thermal infrared* bands. Sensors in this band depend on the fact that all objects above absolute zero emit energy somewhere in the emissive band; the hotter the object, the more energy emitted and the shorter the wavelength.

Many signatures of intelligence importance in the optical band are *spectral signatures*. The interaction of EM energy with matter can cause the emission of energy in specific parts of the spectrum shown in Figure 1-5; this resulting signature will be unique to the matter that emits the energy. Spectral signatures therefore can be used to identify individual materials, alone or in mixtures.

Gases, for example, generally produce spectra by emitting radiant energy on being heated by some external source of energy. This could be the sun or an external source such as that encountered in a chemical production process. When heated by the sun, gases produce spectra in the MWIR region, about 2.5–5.5 or 6 μm. Production processes are more likely to produce signatures in the LWIR region, about 7–14 μm. These signatures are discussed in chapter 5.

POLARIZATION OF EM WAVES

A key signature component of an EM wave is the wave's *polarization*. All electromagnetic waves, RF or optical, are polarized, meaning that the electric field vibrates in some direction. Polarization is an important concept in intelligence because it can be used to obtain unique signatures in both radar and optical imaging as well as in ELINT. The concept is introduced and explained here, and it will be revisited frequently throughout the book.

Radiofrequency signals that are deliberately transmitted have a definite polarization and can be defined as one of three types shown in Figure 1-6. The wave can be *linearly polarized*, meaning that the electric field vibrates back and forth in a straight line. It can be *circularly polarized*, so that to an observer the incoming electric field seems to spin like the second hand of a clock (but far faster). Or it can be *elliptically polarized*, so that the electric

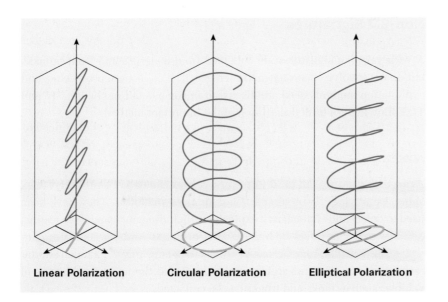

Linear Polarization   **Circular Polarization**   **Elliptical Polarization**

FIGURE 1-6 Types of Polarization

field spins, but the electric field vector is longer (meaning that the field is stronger) in one direction.

In addition to these three polarization types, the polarization has many possible orientations. A linearly polarized wave may vibrate up and down (vertically polarized), side to side (horizontally polarized), or at some angle in between. The type of polarization and the orientation can be used to tell something about the emitter.

Naturally emitted EM waves have a different type of polarization than deliberately transmitted waves. They are likely to be randomly polarized, meaning that the polarization changes constantly. The best-known example is sunlight. But sunlight that bounces off a flat surface—water, for example—is horizontally polarized and we perceive it as glare. Sunglasses can be designed to pass only vertically polarized light, filtering out the horizontally polarized glare. They do this because they have many fine vertical lines that pass vertically polarized light and eliminate horizontally polarized light. To determine the effectiveness of your sunglasses, hold them slightly in front of you and look at a bright reflective surface through the lenses; then, keeping your eyes on the surface through the lens, rotate the lens 90 degrees. The reflective surface should become brighter, as the lens passes rather than filters the horizontally polarized reflected light.

Non-EM Signatures

A wide range of signatures are collected from materials and from humans but do not involve electromagnetic sensing. The collection, processing, and exploitation methods used are discussed in some detail in chapters 10 and 11. Following is a brief description of the important methods.

ACOUSTIC

Acoustic signatures are used in technical intelligence to identify and track ships, submarines, land vehicles, and airborne platforms. They have been used to detect and characterize explosions, including nuclear device testing. Sound waves can travel intercontinental distances underground or underwater, so acoustic signatures can be collected at long ranges. At much shorter ranges, sensing of sound in air can be done, and the unique signatures of vehicles such as tanks and trucks can be collected.

NUCLEAR

Nuclear signatures are the physical, chemical, and isotopic characteristics that distinguish one nuclear or radiological material from another. These signatures allow researchers to identify the processes used to initially create a material and may allow identifying the source of the material—a critical issue in the field of intelligence.[9] The shape and size of uranium particles, for example, provide clues about the origin of the material.

Radioactive materials emit one or more types of radiation, such as alpha particles (helium nuclei), beta particles (electrons or positrons), neutrons, and gamma rays. The specific combination of particles and rays emitted, along with the intensity of each type, constitutes a signature that allows identifying the radioactive source material. The amount of radiation emitted from a given sample can sometimes be used to tell when the material was produced.

In the aftermath of the 9/11 attacks, concern has increased about the possibility of "dirty bombs" (explosives that disperse nuclear material) being used as a terrorist weapon. This concern has led to the proliferation of nuclear sensors at ports and borders. The challenge for such sensors is that they must distinguish between the signature produced by a nuclear device or nuclear material and the signature of legitimate goods, some of which naturally emit a low level of radiation.

CHEMICAL

Chemical signatures are widely used for environmental monitoring and in law enforcement. For example, the presence and source of water pollutants can be determined by water sampling and remote sensing to detect specific pollutant signatures. Similar techniques can be used for air pollution monitoring. Law enforcement uses remote sensing to detect chemical signatures in the air that indicate the presence of illicit methamphetamine laboratories.

In intelligence, chemical signatures are used mostly to identify effluents from factories to determine what processes are being used in the factory. The most common requirement is to characterize suspect facilities that may be producing weapons of mass destruction. Such characterization relies heavily on the ability to identify the signatures of chemical effluents from these facilities. A gaseous diffusion plant that is intended to enrich uranium produces several effluent signatures; uranium hexafluoride and its decomposition products all have unique chemical signatures. A nuclear fuel reprocessing plant produces a wide range of effluents, each of which has a unique signature that can help identify the plant's purpose.[10] Nerve agents that are produced for chemical warfare purposes also produce effluents that have unique signatures and indicate the specific agent being produced.

BIOLOGICAL

The primary intelligence concern for biological signatures is identifying the microorganisms that cause disease. Both intelligence agencies and public health services worldwide devote considerable effort to cataloging these signatures because they permit the source of a disease outbreak to be tracked. The 2001 biological attack using anthrax in the U.S. postal system provides an example of the value of detail in signatures. The anthrax bacteria used in the attacks were identified as coming from a specific strain, the Ames strain, which only existed in specific laboratories, including the U.S. Army biodefense laboratory at Fort Detrick, Maryland. Using this knowledge, FBI investigators were able to zero in on a suspect at the laboratory, Dr. Bruce Ivins, who later committed suicide just before being arrested.[11]

The focus of intelligence interest is on biological warfare (BW) agent manufacture or use, and the ideal would be to remotely sense either. In the case of a BW agent release, medical responders need to know of the release immediately. But remote sensing of biological agents depends on the existence of a signature that can be remotely sensed, and for most agents no such signature exists. Biological agents are usually colorless and odorless. As a result, no equipment currently can provide real time biological agent detection and identification. Detectors can immediately indicate the presence of a biological agent by capturing samples, but the samples must be collected, taken to a lab, and then cultured to identify the pathogen. The whole process can take several hours.

BIOMETRIC

Biometrics is the science and technology of measuring and statistically analyzing biological data. Its importance in intelligence and operations, especially for law enforcement, immigration, and customs agencies, is in identifying humans. All humans have a number of biological characteristics that uniquely identify them, and these are included in the term *biometric signatures*. Fingerprints and DNA are two well-known signatures. The retina and iris of the eye also are signatures unique to an individual. The most useful signatures in intelligence are those that can be identified at a distance—facial characteristics and scent and voice biometrics are some of the currently useful ones.

Summary

Most technical collection involves obtaining and analyzing nonliteral information in the form of signatures. A signature is created by measuring the strength, intensity, or state of some physical or chemical entity, over space, time, frequency, or all three. The analysis of signatures often results in the identification of a pattern that has intelligence value.

In order to be useful for intelligence, a signature has to be associated with a person, object, or process. This usually includes locating the signature (and therefore the person, object, or process) in space and time.

Signatures find wide uses in intelligence. They are used, among other things, to identify and track persons and vehicles, assess industrial processes, monitor treaty compliance, target smart weapons, defeat camouflage, and interpret weapons test results.

An essential component of technical collection is the signature library that associates signatures with a specific person, object, or process. Increasingly, these signatures need to be accessible by military and law enforcement operational units in real time.

Most of the signatures used in intelligence come from the interaction of electromagnetic energy with matter. When a wave of electromagnetic energy interacts with matter, the incident radiation can be reflected, refracted, scattered, transmitted, or absorbed, and the nature of this interaction creates the signature. Objects also radiate energy either naturally or as the result of human actions, again creating a signature. The EM spectrum divides broadly into two regions—the radiofrequency spectrum and the optical spectrum. The sensors used, and the phenomena sensed, differ significantly in these two regions.

A key signature component of an EM wave is the wave's polarization. All electromagnetic waves, RF or optical, are polarized, meaning that the electric field vibrates in some direction. Polarization is an important concept in intelligence because polarization can be used to obtain unique signatures in both the radiofrequency and the optical regions of the EM spectrum.

A wide range of signatures are collected from materials, equipment, processes, and humans but do not involve EM sensing. Technical collection is used to obtain acoustic, nuclear, chemical, biological, and biometric signatures.

NOTES

1. Photo from the Dino A. Brugioni collection at the National Security Archive.
2. Robert M. Clark, *Intelligence Analysis: A Target-Centric Approach*, 2nd ed. (Washington, D.C.: CQ Press, 2006).
3. J.J. Szymanski and P.G. Weber, "Multispectral Thermal Imager: Mission and Applications Overview," *IEEE Transactions on Geoscience and Remote Sensing*, 43, no. 9 (September 2005): 1943–1949; Jeffrey L. Hylden, "Remote Sensing of Chemical Plumes (17)," Pacific Northwest National Laboratory, April 2001, www .technet.pnl.gov/sensors/macro/projects/es4remchem.html.
4. Don Atkins and George Crawford, "Reprogramming Brilliant Weapons: A New Role for MASINT," *American Intelligence Journal,* 17, nos. 3 & 4 (1997): 45–46.
5. John L. Morris, "The Nature and Applications of Measurement and Signature Intelligence," *American Intelligence Journal,* 19, nos. 3 & 4 (1999–2000): 81–84.
6. Zachary Lum, "The Measure of MASINT," *Journal of Electronic Defense* (August 1998): 43.
7. Steven M. Bergman, "The Utility of Hyperspectral Data to Detect and Discriminate Actual and Decoy Target Vehicles," Naval Postgraduate School, Monterrey, CA, December 1996: xiii–xv.
8. NASA definition of near, mid and far infrared bands, 2009, www.ipac.caltech. edu/Outreach/Edu/Regions/irregions.html.
9. "Identifying the Source of Stolen Nuclear Materials," *Science and Technology Review*, Lawrence Livermore National Laboratory, January/February 2007: 13–18.
10. Jack Allentuck and James R. Lemley, "Open Skies and Monitoring a Fissile Materials Cut-off Treaty," Brookhaven National Laboratory Report #BNL-61355, July 9, 1965.
11. "New Details on F.B.I.'s False Start in Anthrax Case," *New York Times*, November 25, 2008, A23.

2. Electromagnetic Sensors

Electromagnetic sensors, as the name implies, receive and process energy from some part of the electromagnetic spectrum—either the radiofrequency or the optical spectrum. When mounted on satellites or aircraft, EM sensors can obtain information about the earth's surface or activity on or near the earth's surface at very long ranges. A great deal of this remote sensing is done for civil applications—environmental and resource management studies, weather forecasting, and so forth. In intelligence, remote sensing from air or space focuses on mapping the earth and locating and tracking the movement of man-made objects. It also includes the reverse—observing the movement of airborne or spaceborne objects (aircraft, ballistic missiles, or satellites) from the earth's surface.

Remote sensing is often described as electromagnetic sensing or spectral sensing. It is important in intelligence because EM waves can be collected at great distances, depending on such factors as the strength of the signal, the noise entering the sensor, and the sensor's sensitivity. But the categorization "remote sensing" is not always an accurate description of how EM sensors are used in intelligence. EM waves also can be sensed well at short distances. At short ranges, EM sensors find many intelligence uses because they can sense very weak signals, including unintentional emissions. The challenge often is to get the sensor into close proximity without being discovered.

Tying remote sensing to EM sensing misses an important point: non-EM waves can be sensed at remote distances under certain conditions. Acoustic signals can travel through the earth, water, or the atmosphere and be sensed at distances of hundreds or even thousands of kilometers. These signals also can have intelligence value, and they are discussed in chapter 10. This chapter and the next few, however, focus on EM remote sensing.

Overview of Collection Sensors

EM sensors divide into two general classes: active and passive. Active sensors (radars) transmit a signal and then interpret the signals that are reflected off the target. Passive sensors exploit natural emissions or man-made signals or use an alternative illumination source, such as the sun. Most passive sensors operate in the microwave or optical bands. Some remote sensors used in intelligence create images, and some do not. Each class and frequency band has unique advantages and disadvantages. And each class encompasses several specific sensor types, each of which has advantages and disadvantages.[1]

For detection reliability, a sensor should operate under all weather and light conditions. But at the higher frequencies in the spectrum, moisture and clouds tend to decrease the sensor's effectiveness by reducing the amount of energy the sensor receives. The tradeoff is that at higher frequencies the resolution of the sensor generally improves.

Figure 2-1 shows the relationship among many of the remote sensors discussed in this book. These sensors can be characterized, as the figure indicates, as obtaining signatures in the spatial dimension, by measuring spectral characteristics, or by measuring the intensity or state of an electromagnetic signal. Sensors that measure a single characteristic are shown in the corners of the triangle

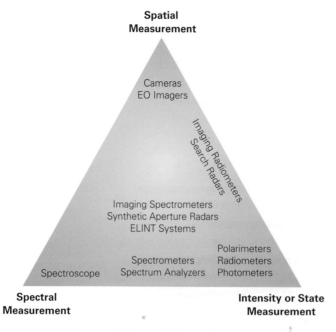

Spatial Measurement

Cameras
EO Imagers

Imaging Radiometers
Search Radars

Imaging Spectrometers
Synthetic Aperture Radars
ELINT Systems

Polarimeters
Spectrometers   Radiometers
Spectrum Analyzers   Photometers

Spectroscope

Spectral Measurement

Intensity or State Measurement

FIGURE 2-1 Classes and Types of Remote Sensors

in Figure 2-1. Some sensors measure two characteristics simultaneously and are shown along the triangle sides. A few sensors measure all three characteristics and are shown in the center. This section provides a brief introduction to the sensors identified in Figure 2-1. The following chapters provide more detail on these sensors and describe how they are used in intelligence.

SPATIAL MEASUREMENTS

Cameras produce a film image that permits an image interpreter to geolocate objects of intelligence interest and to measure the objects' dimensions—provided that the interpreter knows the scale of the image. Black-and-white photos were used in intelligence for many years. Additional signature information was obtained about the objects in a photo when color imagery became available. Film cameras mostly have been replaced by *electro-optical* (EO) *imagers.* The EO imagers used in intelligence are basically sophisticated versions of the digital cameras now widely available. EO imagers have become the standard for obtaining spatial measurements in intelligence. They have a number of advantages over film cameras, one of which is their potential for recording intensity as well as spatial information.

INTENSITY OR STATE MEASUREMENTS

Measurements can be taken of the intensity of energy received (called a radiometric measurement) or of the state of the target object (for example, a polarization measurement). All electromagnetic signals must have some minimum level of intensity in order for a sensor to detect the signal; this is known as a *detection threshold.* But not all sensors measure the intensity of the signal. Following are some that do.

- *Radiometers* are passive sensors that receive and record the electromagnetic energy that is naturally emitted from objects. The term is commonly used to refer to sensors in the microwave and millimeter wave bands, but sometimes it is used to refer to infrared sensors. More commonly, optical radiometers are called *photometers.* A photometer measures the intensity of incoming light in some part of the optical spectrum. It is, in effect, an optical radiometer.
- *Polarimetry* is the measurement of the polarization of EM energy, and a polarimeter is used to make these measurements. Optical polarimetry is often called *ellipsometry.* It is extensively used in astronomy to characterize distant stars and galaxies. In intelligence, this measurement when used with radar is called *radar polarimetry,* discussed later.

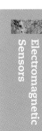

An *imaging radiometer,* as Figure 2-1 indicates, obtains both the spatial and intensity signatures of an object. It forms, in effect, a "radiometric map." Imaging radiometers operate mostly in the thermal IR and microwave bands.

Radar stands for radio detection and ranging. Radar systems are active sensors that provide their own source of electromagnetic energy. Most radars emit microwave radiation in a series of pulses from an antenna, while the antenna moves its main beam to search a volume of space. When the energy reaches a target, some of the energy is reflected back toward the sensor. This backscattered microwave radiation is detected, measured, and timed. The time required for the energy to travel to the target and return back to the sensor determines the distance or range to the target. A radar therefore obtains both spatial and intensity signatures—spatial, by measuring the round-trip travel time for a pulse and the direction in which the radar antenna's main beam was pointing when the pulse was transmitted; intensity, by measuring the strength of the returned signal.

Because radar provides its own energy source, it can produce images day or night. Microwave radar is able to penetrate through clouds and most rain, making it an all-weather sensor. Radars also operate in the millimeter wave bands and in the optical bands using lasers as the transmitters, but weather adversely affects these bands.

SPECTRAL MEASUREMENTS

The simplest type of spectral sensing device is a *spectroscope,* an optical device that splits incoming light according to its wavelength. A prism is the simplest type of spectroscope. A *spectrometer* is a spectroscope that also measures the intensity or polarization of light over different wavelengths in the electromagnetic spectrum (from gamma rays and X-rays into the far infrared). It typically is used in intelligence to identify materials (for example, chemical effluents or factory emissions). *Imaging spectrometers* are the most useful type in intelligence because they obtain an image of an area while measuring the spectral characteristics of each object in the image.

A *synthetic aperture radar* (SAR), as Figure 2-1 indicates, obtains spatial, spectral, and intensity measurements. This allows processing to obtain several types of signatures that have intelligence value. Because of their importance in technical intelligence, SARs are discussed in detail in chapter 7.

Electronic intelligence sensors also obtain spatial, spectral, and intensity measurements. They use *spectrum analyzers* (the RF equivalent of the optical spectrometer) to record the distribution and intensity of the signal across the RF spectrum. Most ELINT systems also obtain spatial measurements (usually determining the location of the signal in a process known as *geolocation*).

TEMPORAL MEASUREMENTS

One important measurement category not explicitly shown in Figure 2-1 is that of temporal measurement. All the remote sensors shown in Figure 2-1 can operate over time, and intelligence is very concerned about the changes in signatures over time. Changes in the spatial measurement of an object often indicate target motion; changes in the spectral or intensity measurements usually result from target activity, and specific changes may constitute a signature that indicates a certain type of activity. For example:

- When a nuclear reactor is operating, the heat causes a shift to higher frequencies in the infrared spectrum of energy emitted from the reactor building, and the intensity of infrared radiation increases as well.
- When a radar changes operating modes, the change often is observed as a change in the spectral signature (a frequency or bandwidth change) or as a change in signal intensity.

Measurements in the time dimension allow *change detection*, a key concept that is revisited in several later chapters. Change detection is a powerful tool in intelligence. Increases in thermal infrared emissions from aircraft engines indicate that the aircraft has recently been in operation; similar increases from ships tell whether the ship is about to get underway.[2] Road and surface building construction, changes in rock and soil composition, and excavations all can be observed as changes in imagery over time. Digital processing of successive images can subtract the features that have not changed between images, allowing the imagery analyst to identify the features that have changed.[3] Radar offers even more sensitive means for observing small changes and is discussed in chapter 7.

Sensor Performance

A perfect sensor would look in all directions continuously, across the entire spectrum, with no limit on its resolution or sensitivity. All its measurements, moreover, would be accurate. Stated another way, it would have perfect spatial, spectral, intensity, and temporal coverage and would resolve all of these to any desired level of detail and desired degree of accuracy.

Of course, such a sensor does not exist. All sensors are the result of compromises. This section discusses the performance characteristics that have to be traded off, with some of the major tradeoffs discussed in the following section. Both optical and RF systems have similar performance limits, but because they came from different physical or engineering disciplines, they tend to have different names.

COVERAGE

The coverage performance of a sensor is determined by its coverage in four categories—spectral, spatial, intensity, and temporal.

Spectral. All sensors cover a defined part of the EM spectrum. RF sensors have a defined *bandwidth.* Optical sensors have a defined *spectral coverage.* The sensor has not been designed that can cover the entire electromagnetic spectrum. Radio receivers are used in the RF band to detect radio waves; detectors are used in the optical band to detect photons. Both radio waves and photons are forms of EM energy, but they behave differently and must be detected differently.

Spatial. All sensors are able to look at a defined volume of space. RF sensors have a defined *beamwidth.* Optical sensors have a defined *field of view.* Beamwidth or field of view is determined by the size of the aperture and by the frequency of the transmitted or received signal. A laser, of the sort used as a briefing pointer or carpenter's level, has an extremely narrow beam because the frequency is very high. A telescope has a relatively narrow field of view for the same reason. A TV antenna that receives local broadcast television has a relatively broad beamwidth. A dish antenna used to receive satellite TV, although smaller than a local broadcast TV antenna, has a relatively narrow beamwidth because it operates at a much higher frequency.

It is especially desirable in imaging to obtain spatial coverage over a wide area, and there are two ways to do this. The first approach is to image one small area at a time, and so over time to build up a complete picture of a large region. The second approach is to image the entire region nearly simultaneously. The latter method is very difficult to do, but it has special value in intelligence, and imagery analysts call it synoptic coverage.

Intensity. All sensors have a range of intensity that they can receive; the range is defined by two thresholds. The lower threshold is a point below which incoming EM energy is considered "noise" and above which it is considered a "signal." An incoming signal that is too weak falls below this threshold and cannot be detected. The upper threshold is the point where the signal is too strong, so that it saturates the receiver or, at some level of intensity, burns it out. The operating range of intensity for a sensor lies between these two extremes of detectability and saturation and is called the sensor's *dynamic range*. The idea of dynamic range is familiar to anyone who has listened to a cheap audio system. If the volume control is set too low, the very soft notes of music disappear; if the volume control is set too high, the loud sounds become distorted.

For intelligence collection, the lower detection threshold needs to be as low as possible because signals are often very weak, for two reasons. First, the sensor often must be located far from the signal source. Second, even when the sensor can be located close to the source, the signals themselves are often very weak. The limitation on lowering a sensor's lower threshold is noise from external or internal sources. As the threshold is lowered, more and more noise "spikes" or interfering signals appear above the threshold and are mistaken for the desired signal. These spikes are referred to as *false alarms*. As an example, an optical sensor could in theory detect a single photon—the smallest possible quantity of light—from a target of interest. But the sensor would also detect a large number of photons from objects near the target, and noise within the sensor itself would make it almost impossible to identify the one photon coming from the target.

Depending on the application, the threshold can be lowered to allow more of these false alarms, known also as "false positives"—noise that is mistaken for a desired signal. Alternatively, if the threshold is raised, the risk increases of getting more "false negatives"—desired signals that are discarded as noise. There are several techniques for lowering the threshold (reducing the false negatives) while not increasing the false positives. One is to use several sensors simultaneously and compare the received signals. Another is to use one sensor but to repeatedly collect the signal over time to eliminate false positives.

Temporal. In intelligence, the ultimate wish would be to have *surveillance*, defined as the continuous or near-continuous observation of a target area. For many sensors and the platforms that carry them, currently the best that can be obtained is *reconnaissance,* defined as periodic observation. The choice between the two usually involves tradeoffs in other types of coverage or in resolution, which is discussed next. For example:

- An emplaced sensor, such as a surveillance camera focused on a street, can provide continuous coverage (assuming some illumination source at night and excluding times when vision is blocked by fog). But such a camera can only cover a very small geographical area.

- An aircraft can provide continuous coverage of a much larger area but only for a relatively short time by loitering; it eventually must return to base for refueling.
- A low earth orbit satellite, discussed in the next chapter, can observe an even larger area, but it can only cover a given spot on earth for about eight to ten minutes; and, because its sensor is typically farther from the target than the aircraft sensor, its resolution suffers by comparison.
- A geostationary satellite, also discussed in the next chapter, can provide surveillance of a large area of earth, but its distance from earth lessens the ability of its sensors to detect weak signals.

RESOLUTION

The same four categories discussed above—spectral, spatial, intensity, and temporal—also describe resolution. Four types of sensor resolution are important in EM sensing.

Spectral. The ability of a sensor to distinguish among energies of varying wavelengths emitted by or reflected from a target is known as *spectral resolution*. The amount of information that can be derived from a sensor increases as a function of spectral resolution, as does the level of information available to the analyst. High spectral resolution is important for intelligence purposes in both the RF and optical bands:

- In the visible spectrum, panchromatic (black-and-white) imagery allows one to simply detect objects. If the image has good spatial resolution, an analyst can also identify the objects. As images of the same scene are added from different parts of the spectrum—for example, red, green, blue, and near IR—the analyst can make more detailed assessments of the object. Adding still more images of the scene from the IR spectrum allows highly detailed assessments—for example, identification of a specific gas being discharged from a smokestack.
- In the RF band, spectral resolution (often called *frequency resolution* in the RF band) allows a passive sensor such as an ELINT sensor (discussed in chapter 8) to distinguish among possible emitters of a signal—to identify a certain type of radar system, for example. Higher frequency resolution might allow the same ELINT sensor to identify the specific transmitter. A radar receiver with high spectral resolution can determine the movement of a target by measuring the Doppler effect.[4]

Spatial. The ability of a sensor to separate two objects spatially is known as *spatial resolution.* It is measured differently depending on whether the sensor is obtaining an image or not. The term *resolution cell* is used to define spatial resolution in all forms of imagery and in nonimaging radar, but the meaning in imagery is somewhat different than the meaning in nonimaging radar. The basic meaning, in all cases, is this: two separate targets located in the same resolution cell cannot be told apart.

- Radar conducts measurements in three dimensions. Conventional nonimaging radar is used to locate a target in a volume of space, so the term *radar resolution cell* is used. Such a cell has two parts: *angular resolution* (which describes the limit on a radar's ability to distinguish targets in azimuth and elevation) and *range resolution* (which describes the limit on ability to distinguish targets in distance from the radar). The resulting radar resolution cell is therefore a volume of space.
- In imagery, whether optical, radiometric, or radar, the resolution cell refers to the size of the target area that corresponds to a single pixel in an image. Stated another way, spatial resolution is a means of specifying the ability to visually resolve objects in the scene. The length of one side of a resolution cell is called the *ground sample distance* (GSD). For an image having a 2-meter GSD, a resolution cell in the image is 2 meters square. The greater the GSD or the size of the resolution cell, the poorer the spatial resolution, and the more difficult it becomes to resolve and recognize objects on the ground. Good spatial resolution—the ability of the sensor to distinguish small objects—allows the identification of specific vehicles, for example. With poor resolution, the objects are blurred or indistinguishable.

Images where only large features are visible are said to have coarse or low resolution. In fine or high-resolution images, small objects can be detected. Intelligence sensors, for example, are designed to view as much detail as possible and therefore have very fine spatial resolution. Commercial satellites provide imagery with resolutions varying from less than 1 meter up to several kilometers.

Intensity. Often called *radiometric resolution*, intensity resolution is a measure of the difference in signal intensity that can be detected and recorded by a sensor. The finer the radiometric resolution of a sensor, the more sensitive it is to detecting small differences in reflected or emitted energy. A sensor with a high radiometric resolution will recognize very subtle variations in energy at a given frequency or wavelength, such as the difference between two types of trees or the presence of camouflage in an image.

Temporal. *Temporal resolution* is the span of time between collections, and it can have different meanings. It can refer to the time that elapses before a collection asset can sense a target for a second time (often called the *revisit time*).

- A video camera offers good temporal resolution; it constantly refreshes the scene it views, so it revisits a scene many times per second. In effect, it conducts surveillance of an area.
- An RF receiver used in SIGINT tunes rapidly through a band, often revisiting a particular frequency several times per second. The antenna, however, may have to be aimed at a different volume of space periodically to cover other targets of interest.
- An air or space search radar scans through a specific region of space as slowly as once every ten seconds and as rapidly as several times per second.
- A typical imaging satellite at low altitude might circle the earth 14 to 16 times a day. Its temporal resolution, or revisit time, would be about 90 minutes—the length of time before it can again look at a particular target.

Temporal resolution also can refer to separating two closely spaced events in a signature. A radar signature can change very rapidly as the radar changes operating modes. An ELINT receiver that is monitoring the radar must be able to detect these changes. An optical sensor that monitors for nuclear blast detection must be able to identify the unique pattern of two light bursts in rapid succession that characterizes a nuclear burst.

ACCURACY

In many areas of intelligence, the issue of precision versus accuracy comes up, and the distinction is an important one. A signature measurement can often be expressed with a high degree of precision, but precision is irrelevant without accuracy.

- *Precision* is defined as a measure of the detail in which a quantity is expressed. Precision is used to describe the number of significant digits used to store numbers (for example, geographic coordinate values). Decimal digits are typically used to express precision; precision in mathematics refers to the number of digits that are used to express a value. In computer and digital communications, precision refers to the number of binary digits (bits) used to express a value.

- *Accuracy* describes how close a measurement is to the true value of the quantity being measured. It is the criterion used in evaluating the quality of information.

It is important to understand the distinction because it is too easy to confuse the two and be misled. An RF sensor may measure the signal strength of a received radar signal, and from that measurement it can be determined that the radar is transmitting with a power of 60.0 dBW (an engineering expression for 1,000,000 Watts)—a very precise number. But the sensor often is in error by as much as three decibels (dB), which translates to a measurement accuracy of 50%—that is, between 500,000 and 2,000,000 Watts. In this example, the precision of expression is misleading. It tends to make the intelligence customer believe that the measurement is accurate to one-tenth of a dB instead of 3 dB.

The spectral, spatial, intensity, and temporal categories discussed above also apply to accuracy.

Spectral. *Spectral accuracy*—the measure of the accuracy with which a sensor can determine the frequency or wavelength of a signal— is important in SIGINT and in spectral and radar imaging. Fine grain measurements of the signal spectrum are used to identify specific emitters, as discussed in chapter 8. In optical sensing, spectral accuracy determines, for example, whether a chemical compound can be identified using hyperspectral imaging.

Spatial. The accuracy of a sensor's location of a target is known as *spatial accuracy*. It is vital in pinpointing the location of a target, especially one that is to be attacked by precision weaponry. In general, optical imagery provides the most accurate location of a target because the location of known objects in the image can be used to estimate the location of a target. The location of the imaging platform when the image is taken can be important for obtaining spatial accuracy, and the global positioning system (GPS) is used extensively to determine the exact location of sensor platforms. The French SPOT imaging satellite, for example, has a spatial accuracy on the order of 30 meters.[5] Spatial accuracy is harder to achieve in SIGINT, where the term *geolocation accuracy* is used to describe the sensor's performance.

Spatial accuracy is also important in determining the visual signatures of objects. Any missile, for example, has a unique set of dimensions at some level of measurement accuracy. If a sensor can only measure those dimensions to within 1 meter, then it is unlikely that the missile signature can be uniquely identified. A sensor that can measure those dimensions to within a millimeter is highly likely to come up with a unique signature.

Intensity. The degree to which a sensor can resolve differences in intensity is known as *intensity accuracy.* It is important in determining the power output of a source. An infrared sensor can detect the emissions of hot gases from a power plant. But the temperature of the emissions, derived from the intensity measurements of the IR signal, can indicate how much power the plant is generating. In ELINT, the strength of the signal collected from a radar can be used to determine the radar's output power. In radar, the strength of a radar return can be used to tell something about the target. A large metal target such as a Boeing 747 typically will have a strong return signal; at the same range, a small remotely piloted vehicle made of plastic and fabric will have a very weak return signal.

Temporal. The measurement accuracy of a signal's arrival time at a sensor is known as *temporal accuracy,* which is important in obtaining spatial accuracy. For images taken from an aircraft or satellite, the timing of the image is important because the platform is moving constantly. But timing the imaging event to within a second is more than adequate for most purposes. In contrast, for systems that receive radiofrequency signals (for example, for radar and ELINT), the timing must be far more accurate *and* precise. Timing the arrival of a signal is critical in geolocating the source. A radar measures range by accurately and precisely determining the time between transmitting a pulse and receiving an echo from the target. As discussed in the section on ELINT, geolocating an emitter depends on accurately and precisely measuring the arrival time of the signal at different points. The GPS, in addition to geolocating a platform, provides a timing reference that intelligence sensors can use to precisely determine the time when an image is taken or a signal arrives.

PRECISION VERSUS ACCURACY

Precision and accuracy are terms used in both collection and analysis of intelligence. While the words have the same general meaning in both arenas, the descriptive terminology used to express them differs significantly. In analysis, it is very difficult to quantify either precision or accuracy.

Precision is used in the analysis process to express uncertainty, the variability of analysis, or the amount of random error that exists in an analytical process. These are called *estimates of likelihood.* Because analytical judgments are not certain, the U.S. intelligence community uses probabilistic language to reflect the community's estimates of the likelihood of developments or events. One way to do this would be to give a percentage probability between 0% and 100%—in which case, the precision would far exceed the accuracy of the estimate, since our ability to make accurate estimates of future events is never that good. Instead, a national intelligence estimate (NIE) uses the following terms for precision in describing the likelihood that an event will occur:

- Terms such as *probably, likely, very likely,* or *almost certainly* indicate a greater than even chance.
- The terms *unlikely* and *remote* indicate a less then even chance that an event will occur; they do not imply that an event will not occur.
- Terms such as *we cannot dismiss, we cannot rule out,* or *we cannot discount* reflect an unlikely, improbable, or remote event whose consequences are such that it warrants mentioning.[6]

In analysis, accuracy means the degree to which information sources are believed to be free from mistakes and errors. A 2007 NIE uses the following terms to indicate the accuracy of judgments:

- *High confidence* generally indicates that the judgments are based on high-quality information, and/or that the nature of the issue makes it possible to render a solid judgment. A "high confidence" judgment is not a fact or a certainty, however, and such judgments still carry a risk of being wrong.
- *Moderate confidence* generally means that the information is credibly sourced and plausible but not of sufficient quality or corroborated sufficiently to warrant a higher level of confidence.
- *Low confidence* generally means that the information's credibility and/or plausibility is questionable, or that the information is too fragmented or poorly corroborated to make solid analytic inferences, or that there are significant concerns or problems with the sources.[7]

To illustrate the difference between precision and accuracy in analysis, consider the human source nicknamed "Curveball," who provided false intelligence about the existence of an Iraqi biological warfare (BW) program prior to the U.S. invasion of Iraq in 2003. Curveball provided highly precise details about the existence of the program and the location of the BW facility, but his information was highly inaccurate.

Tradeoffs in Sensor Design and Usage

As noted previously, all electromagnetic sensing involves tradeoffs in both sensor design and usage. The tradeoffs are normally among resolution, coverage, and accuracy.

RESOLUTION TRADEOFFS

The same four types of resolution—spatial, spectral, intensity, and temporal—have to be traded off in the design of a sensor. For high spatial resolution, an optical sensor has to have a small pixel size. However, as noted previously, this reduces the amount of energy that can be detected as the area of the ground resolution cell within the pixel becomes smaller. The result is reduced radiometric (intensity) resolution—the ability to detect fine energy differences. To increase the amount of energy detected (and thus, the radiometric resolution) without reducing spatial resolution, the wavelength range detected for a particular channel or band would have to be expanded. Unfortunately, this would reduce the spectral resolution of the sensor. Conversely, coarser spatial resolution would allow improved radiometric and/or spectral resolution. Increased temporal resolution always comes at a cost in one of the other three types.

COVERAGE VERSUS RESOLUTION TRADEOFFS

Collectors want to obtain the greatest possible coverage—spectral, spatial, radiometric/intensity, and temporal—with the highest possible resolution, because coverage allows them to collect as many target signatures as possible, not missing important ones, and resolution allows them to better discriminate between similar signatures that come from different targets. So, global synoptic coverage with high resolution is desired in all four categories. The trend is for improvements to occur in all these categories as technology advances. However, at any given level of technology, improvements in one category usually come at a cost in some other category. Consequently, all sensor designs are compromises.

There are tradeoffs between spatial, spectral, radiometric (intensity), and temporal resolution that must be taken into consideration when engineers design a sensor. Imaging sensors can cover a large area of the earth quickly. They can do this because they can have a very wide swath width, allowing the sensor to search a wide area in one pass. But in doing so, they must trade off between swath width and resolution. Generally speaking, the finer the resolution, the less total ground area can be seen. Good resolution is essential for detecting observables on the surface. However, sensors that have wide swath widths generally have poor resolution, and sensors with good resolution usually have small swath widths. As an example, a NOAA-18 weather satellite sensor covers a large swath of the earth (more than 1500 km across), but its best resolution is on the order of 15 km—sufficient for obtaining global temperature maps but not useful for most intelligence purposes. In comparison, current imaging satellites, such as France's SPOT and Israel's Ofeq satellites, have swath widths measured in a few kilometers but with spatial resolution on the order of 1 meter.[8]

Similar constraints and tradeoffs exist for passive RF sensors. A larger antenna aperture allows the RF sensor more sensitivity and also permits it to better separate objects in space. But the result is a narrower beamwidth, so the spatial coverage suffers. For SIGINT sensors, wide bandwidth (spectral coverage) is desirable. But either the detectability of weak signals (intensity coverage) or the revisit time to a specific frequency (temporal coverage) has to suffer as the spectral coverage increases.

Another type of tradeoff occurs when the operating profile of a sensor platform is changed. An aircraft or satellite can be moved farther away from the target area to provide better spatial coverage, but both sensitivity and resolution tend to suffer.

So far, this discussion has focused on the compromises for a single sensor on a single platform. There are other ways to get global synoptic coverage, but they can be expensive. Multiple sensors can be put on a single platform or more platforms can be put up. Chapter 3 describes how a number of satellites can be placed in orbit to provide global coverage; the required number increases at lower satellite altitudes.

ACCURACY TRADEOFFS

The primary limit on sensor measurement accuracy usually is defined by the need to digitize the sensed signal. Even if a sensor can measure to a high degree of resolution, the signature has to be converted to digital format for communicating it to a processing center. Both RF and optical signatures have to be digitized.

Digitization for imagery means that the levels of intensity in a pixel have to be converted to digital form (digitized) for storage and transmission from an aircraft or satellite, and subsequently for storage and retrieval from signature libraries. The number of binary digits used to describe a pixel determines the intensity resolution. The larger the number of data bits, the greater the radiometric resolution will be (that is, the number of levels of intensity that can be discerned or recorded by the sensor). Image data are generally displayed in a range of gray tones, with black representing a digital number of 0 and white representing the maximum value (for example, 255 in 8-bit data). The maximum number of brightness (intensity) levels available depends on the number of bits used in representing the energy recorded. If 4 bits are used to record a pixel, there can be 16 distinct values of intensity— enough for a poor-quality black-and-white picture; at least 9 bits per pixel are needed, giving 256 values of intensity, to obtain good signatures.

Another factor that can limit sensor performance is the bandwidth of the communications channel. This is a significant constraint for satellites, but it also can affect airborne sensors and clandestinely emplaced sensors that must communicate data to a remote receiver. The price of greater coverage or higher resolution is that the subsystem for digitizing and communicating the sensor output becomes more complex. At the other end of the chain, bigger signature libraries are required.

There is a large difference in the level of detail discernible as the number of bits is increased from 2 to 8. But at some point, as bits are increased, little or no change is noticed. When this point is reached, storage space, or communications bandwidth, or both, are being wasted by increasing the number of bits used to represent a pixel. The goal is to use enough bits to capture all details of intelligence value, but no more.

Sensor Suites

The previous sections have noted that there is no such thing as a perfect sensor. All sensors involve tradeoffs. Improving one type of resolution inevitably degrades another type if coverage and accuracy do not change. Better coverage usually means worse resolution and vice versa. Improved accuracy means that some other desired performance parameter becomes worse.

This all applies, though, when talking about a single sensor. There are two basic ways to overcome the imperfect sensor problem; both involve using multiple sensors.

One can deploy a number of platforms (satellites, ships, aircraft or ground sites, all of which will be discussed in chapter 3), each carrying a sensor, to provide better spatial, spectral, radiometric, or temporal coverage.

One can also put multiple sensors on a single platform, each sensor optimized for a specific purpose so that they complement each other. One sensor might provide high spatial resolution, another might provide excellent spectral resolution, and a third might provide a broad area of coverage. The continuing advances in sensor technology have provided smaller and lighter sensor packages that make it easier to put multiple sensors on a single airborne or spaceborne platform. Some examples of multisensor platforms (which will be discussed in the following chapter) are:

- The USNS Observation Island, which carries two radars: an acquisition radar provides good spatial coverage (searching for and acquiring targets); a tracking radar provides good spatial and spectral resolution and measures target parameters with high accuracy.
- The Global Hawk unmanned aeronautical vehicle, which carries both an imaging radar and an optical imager that complement each other very well: the imaging radar can function in spite of clouds or fog, and has good spatial coverage; the optical imager can obtain images having high spatial resolution.

Obviously, both techniques can be combined, as well—deploying multiple sensors on multiple platforms. The Maui space surveillance site, also to be discussed in chapter 3, has a number of optical sensors housed in separate domes. Some provide excellent spatial coverage and are used for sky searches, while others provide excellent spatial resolution and are used for obtaining images of satellites. Within a single dome, several sensors may use the same optics—some for obtaining high radiometric resolution, others for obtaining high spectral resolution.

Another example of multiple sensors on multiple platforms is the satellite constellation that was operated by the European Space Agency (ESA). ESA launched ERS-1 in 1991 and ERS-2 in 1995. The two satellites were designed to complement each other in spatial and temporal coverage. Each satellite carried a combination of four (ERS-1) or five (ERS-2) sensors, including a synthetic aperture radar and an infrared radiometer.[9]

Summary

Electromagnetic sensors can be either active or passive. Active sensors (radars) transmit a signal and then interpret the signals that are reflected off the target. Passive sensors exploit natural emissions, man-made signals, or energy reflected from the target, usually reflected solar illumination.

Technical intelligence sensors are used to obtain several distinct types of signatures. They can collect spatial signatures, as a camera does. They can measure the intensity of energy received (called a radiometric measurement) or the state of the target object (for example, a polarization measurement). They can obtain spectral information, such as a spectroscope does in the optical spectrum and an ELINT receiver does in the RF spectrum. And they can measure the changes in all these signatures over time. Many sensors perform several of these measurements simultaneously.

A perfect sensor would look in all directions continuously, across the entire spectrum, with no limit on its resolution or sensitivity. All its measurements, moreover, would be accurate. Stated another way, it would have perfect spectral, spatial, intensity, and temporal coverage and could resolve all of these to any desired level of detail and any desired degree of accuracy. Such a sensor does not exist. All sensors are the result of compromises or tradeoffs in three areas of performance—coverage, resolution, and accuracy.

The coverage performance of a sensor is determined by its coverage in four categories—spectral, spatial, intensity, and temporal. No sensor can cover the entire EM spectrum. Sensors can observe only a defined volume of space at any instant. Two thresholds limit a sensor's ability to detect a range of intensities: detectability of weak signals and saturation caused by strong signals; these thresholds define the sensor's dynamic range. Continuous temporal coverage (surveillance) is possible, but many sensors can only conduct reconnaissance, defined as periodic revisits to the target.

The resolution performance of a sensor defines its ability to distinguish separate features in a signature, whether spatial, intensity, spectral, or temporal. It includes separating targets spatially, for example, in an image. Resolving fine details in signature intensities can help, for example, to detect camouflage in an image. Spectral resolution allows a sensor to distinguish among energies of varying wavelengths emitted by or reflected from a target. Temporal resolution can mean revisit time between looks at a target or it can mean separating two closely spaced events in a signature.

The accuracy of signature measurement establishes the uniqueness of the signature. Spatial accuracy can mean accuracy in locating a target or in measuring its dimensions. Intensity accuracy is important for determining the power output of a source such as a radar. Spectral accuracy permits identifying specific emitters of an RF signal or identifying specific chemical compounds. Temporal accuracy is needed for accurate geolocation of a target.

Any sensor, as noted above, has to compromise between resolution, coverage, and accuracy. Within each of these, the sensor also will have a compromise between spectral, spatial, intensity, and temporal performance. In general, improving any one of these results in degraded performance for another. The solution for many technical intelligence collectors is to use a suite of sensors on a single or multiple platforms, where each sensor is optimized for a specific performance area and where the sensors complement each other.

NOTES

1. Robert M. Clark, *Intelligence Analysis: A Target-Centric Approach*, 2nd ed. (Washington, D.C.: CQ Press, 2006), ch. 6.
2. Joe Lees and Robert Mott, "Change Detection for more Actionable Intelligence," *GPS World*, January 1, 2006, http://www.gpsworld.com/gis/security-defense/change-detection-more-actionable-intelligence-5389?page_id=1.
3. Jeffrey T. Richelson, *The U.S. Intelligence Community*, 5th Ed. (Boulder, Colo.: Westview Press, 2008), 194.
4. Doppler effect, or Doppler shift, refers to a change in the observed frequency of an acoustic or electromagnetic signal emitted by or reflected from a moving object, when the object and the observer are in motion relative to each other.
5. Spotimage, "Spot Satellite Technical Data," www.spotimage.fr/automne_modules_files/standard/public/p445_3a1cd2cb59b76fc75e20286a6abb7efegeneral-features.pdf.
6. National Intelligence Estimate, "Iran: Nuclear Intentions and Capabilities," November 2007, www.dni.gov/press_releases/20071203_release.pdf.
7. Ibid.
8. Spotimage, "Spot Satellite Technical Data"; David Eshel, "Israel Sustains its Space Superiority with 5th Successful Recce Satellite Launch," *Defense Update*, www.defense-update.com/analysis/analysis_110607_space_israel.htm.
9. European Space Agency, "ERS Overview," updated February 25, 2008, www.esa.int/esaEO/SEMGWH2VQUD_index_0_m.html.

3. Collection Platforms

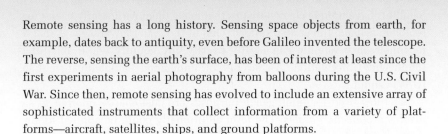

Remote sensing has a long history. Sensing space objects from earth, for example, dates back to antiquity, even before Galileo invented the telescope. The reverse, sensing the earth's surface, has been of interest at least since the first experiments in aerial photography from balloons during the U.S. Civil War. Since then, remote sensing has evolved to include an extensive array of sophisticated instruments that collect information from a variety of platforms—aircraft, satellites, ships, and ground platforms.

Remote sensing platforms can be used in intelligence for surveillance or reconnaissance. The difference between the two is the dwell time on the target area; *surveillance* is defined as continuous dwell, while *reconnaissance* is a dwell for a relatively short period of time, even a snapshot. Since low earth orbit satellites can see a given spot on earth for only a few minutes at a time, this platform can only be used for reconnaissance. All other platforms discussed in this chapter—aircraft, ships, submarines, and ground stations—can be used for either surveillance or reconnaissance.

Since the resolution and accuracy of sensors improve as the sensor gets closer to the target, it is desirable to place the collection platform as close to the target as possible. And when collectors are only interested in collecting data from a single target at a fixed location, that is possible. For example, video surveillance cameras can be positioned to focus on entryways to monitor specific areas and can obtain enough resolution to identify people. At distances of 1 meter or less, the iris and retinal scan devices discussed in chapter 11 can provide very precise (and accurate) recognition of individuals.

But when the sensor is moved closer to a target area, the potential coverage area shrinks. Most targets of intelligence interest, and especially people, are mobile. To continue the surveillance camera example, the camera can identify individuals but cannot track their movements outside the immediate area. As noted in the previous chapter, all sensors have to deal with this tradeoff problem of coverage versus accuracy and resolution, so intelligence services like to use a wide range of platforms: some platforms can get close to the target for high accuracy and resolution, and some offer wide area coverage.

The discussion of platforms will begin with those that routinely provide global coverage: satellites.

Satellites

Satellites provide the bulk of the remote sensing used today in intelligence. Satellites have unique characteristics that make them particularly useful for remotely sensing the earth's surface. One of the major advantages is that a reconnaissance satellite can legally overfly any country while obtaining intelligence information. An aircraft or unmanned aeronautical vehicle (UAV) cannot.

Satellites used for intelligence purposes are customarily referred to as *overhead collection assets*. The term additionally could be applied to aircraft, which also collect imagery and signals intelligence from overhead (and some writers do include aircraft in the definition), but over the years the term *overhead collection* has acquired an understood meaning: collection from satellites.[1] Another term for satellite collection that will be revisited in this book is the euphemism *national technical means* (NTM), which is still used occasionally. The term had its origin in the Limited Test Ban Treaty of 1963, where the signatories used it in agreeing that they would not interfere with one another's satellite collection capability.

The two most important things to understand about satellites are: (1) how different orbits function, and their relative advantages in intelligence collection; and (2) the constraints imposed by the space environment.

ORBITS

The path followed by a satellite is referred to as its *orbit*. Satellites are constrained to move in defined orbits. They cannot "hover" over a point on the earth (and thus provide surveillance) except in a geosynchronous orbit, as discussed below. In all other orbits, satellites move with respect to the earth and can provide reconnaissance. This can be an advantage in geolocating targets using RF sensing, to be discussed in chapter 8.

Satellite orbits are matched to the capability and objective of the sensors the satellites carry. The type of sensor carried and the mission of the satellite determine the type of orbit chosen. Orbit selection can vary in terms of altitude (satellite height above the earth's surface), orientation, and rotation relative to the earth. Four orbital regimes are commonly used to collect intelligence. Figure 3-1 illustrates the four.

- *A low earth orbit* (LEO) satellite orbits between 200 and 1,500 km above the earth's surface. Earth imaging satellites and some SIGINT satellites typically use this orbit, since closeness to the target is most important. Satellites in LEO orbit circle the earth in about 90 minutes.
- A *medium earth orbit* (MEO) satellite typically orbits at 10,000 to 20,000 km above the earth. At these altitudes, satellites need some protection from

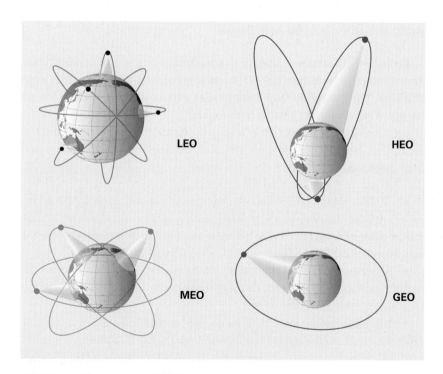

FIGURE 3-1 Main Satellite Orbit Types

the high-energy particles in the Van Allen radiation belts, but they orbit above the high intensity radiation of the lower Van Allen belt. A major intelligence advantage of the MEO satellite is survivability: it is more difficult for opponents to locate and attack than LEO satellites, and the orbit provides better sensing capabilities than the GEO or HEO satellites (see below) can deliver.

- A *highly elliptical orbit* (HEO) satellite is placed in an orbit in such a way that it will spend the greatest amount of time over a specific area of the planet. Thus, if a HEO satellite is launched to provide communications or collect intelligence in the arctic region, its orbit would be configured so that it spends the bulk of its time in orbit above these latitudes. The *apogee* (highest altitude) is typically around 35,000 km, and the *perigee* (lowest altitude) is typically around 500 km.

- A *geostationary* (GEO) satellite orbits the earth in an equatorial orbit at an altitude of 35,800 km, where its rotational period is equal to that of the earth's rotation (24 hours). The result is that the geostationary satellite turns with the earth and remains over the same fixed point of the planet at all times. This allows the satellite to conduct surveillance, observing and collecting information continuously over specific areas. The fixed nature of a geostationary satellite with respect to a given point on the earth makes GEO satellites highly useful for surveillance.

Figure 3-2 illustrates a side view comparison of these four orbit types, drawn to scale. Note that the MEO orbits are shown as two distinct orbit altitudes. The reason for this separation is explained in the discussion on the space environment, later in this chapter.

All these satellite orbits have a specific *inclination* that is measured in degrees. A satellite's inclination describes the angle of the orbit measured from the equatorial plane.

- A GEO satellite, for example, must move at the same speed as the earth's rotation in order to maintain its fixed position over the earth. Therefore, it has approximately a zero degree inclination, so that it travels over the equator eastward (in the direction of the earth's rotation).

- Satellites in a *polar orbit* have a 90-degree inclination; they cross the equator moving directly north or south and cross over the poles. Figure 3-3 shows a satellite in a polar orbit.[2]

- Satellites having more than 90 degrees inclination are in a *retrograde* orbit; they move in the opposite direction from the earth's rotation. The most extreme example of a retrograde orbit is that of a 180-degree inclination satellite (which moves along the equator westward).

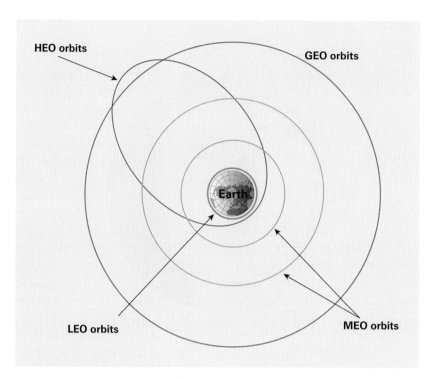

FIGURE 3-2 Side View of Orbit Types

GLOBAL COVERAGE

It is important in most intelligence applications to have global coverage, which is usually supplied by a LEO satellite in a *near-polar orbit*—so named for the inclination of the orbit relative to a line running between the north and south poles. A near-polar orbit would be slightly inclined from the ground track shown in Figure 3-3. Many LEO satellites are in near-polar orbits, in which the satellite crosses the equator at a different point on each pass, traveling northward on one side of the earth and then toward the southern pole on the second half of its orbit. These are called *ascending* and *descending* passes, respectively, as shown in Figure 3-3. The near-polar orbit is designed so that the orbit (basically north-south), in conjunction with the earth's rotation (west-east), allows the satellite to cover most of the earth's surface over a certain period of time.

As a satellite in a polar orbit moves around the earth from pole to pole, its east-west position would not change if the earth did not rotate. However, as seen from the earth, it seems that the satellite is shifting westward because

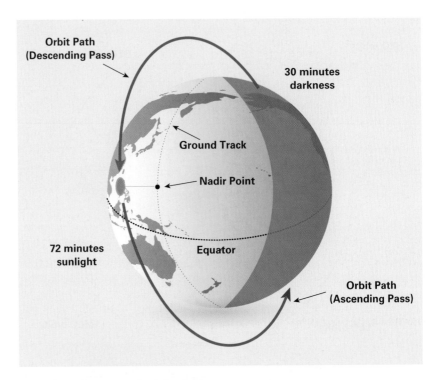

FIGURE 3-3 Geometry of a Polar Orbit

the earth is rotating (from west to east) beneath it. This apparent movement allows the satellite swath to cover a new area with each consecutive pass, as shown in Figure 3-4 (which also illustrates a retrograde orbit).[3] The satellite's orbit and the rotation of the earth work together to allow complete coverage of the earth's surface after the satellite has completed one complete cycle of orbits.

Starting with any randomly selected pass in a satellite's orbit, an *orbit cycle* will be completed when the satellite retraces its path, passing over the same point on the earth's surface directly below the satellite (called the *nadir* point) for a second time. The exact length of time of the orbital cycle will vary with the satellite's altitude and inclination. In Figure 3-5, 14 orbits occur before the satellite begins to repeat its orbit cycle.

The interval of time required for the satellite to complete its orbit cycle is not the same as the *revisit period.* Using steerable sensors, a satellite-borne instrument can view an area away from its nadir before and after the orbit passes over a target, thus making the "revisit" time less than the orbit cycle

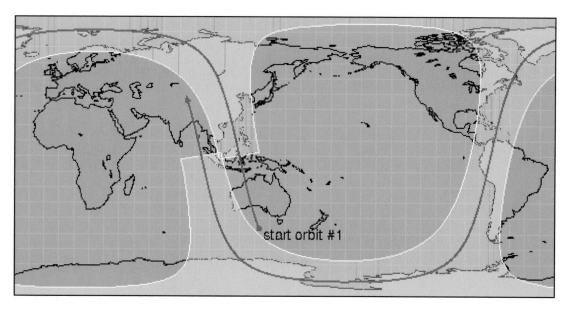

FIGURE 3-4 Ground Path for Global Coverage

time. The revisit period is an important consideration for a number of monitoring applications, especially when frequent imaging is required (for example, to monitor a rapidly developing crisis situation). In near-polar orbits, areas at high latitudes will be imaged more frequently than the equatorial zone, due to the increasing overlap in adjacent swaths as the orbit paths come closer together near the poles, as illustrated in Figure 3-5.[4] For this reason, reconnaissance satellites may operate at lower inclinations, providing increased lower latitude coverage but no polar region coverage. An example is the Israeli series of reconnaissance satellites called Ofeq (Hebrew for "horizon"). These satellites have a retrograde orbit at 144 degrees inclination, phased so as to give optimal daylight coverage of the Middle East. An Ofeq satellite makes a half-dozen or so daylight passes per day over Israel and the surrounding countries, whereas U.S. and Russian imaging satellites only get one or two passes per day over the same area from their higher inclination orbits.[5]

The discussion to this point has been about coverage of the earth by a single satellite. And, as noted, a single LEO satellite can cover the entire earth about twice per day. To get more frequent coverage, more satellites have to be deployed. In intelligence, it is highly desirable to have synoptic coverage—that is, to leave no important target area unmonitored. But doing

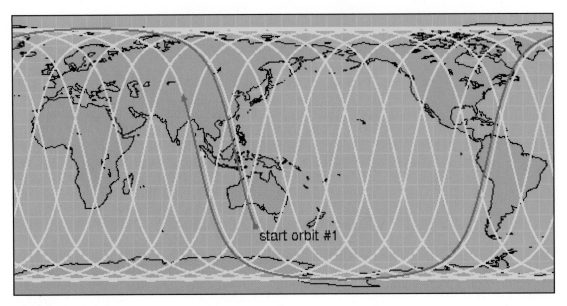

FIGURE 3-5 Earth Coverage of a Sun-Synchronous Orbit

this takes a lot of satellites. Figure 3-6 illustrates the coverage problem for a hypothetical constellation of satellites in a circular orbit at 4,000 km altitude, 90 degrees inclination (that is, a polar orbit), where the coverage is defined such that the minimum angle of elevation from the target to the satellite (known as the *grazing angle*) is 20 degrees.[6] Note that it takes more than 12 satellites to obtain continuous coverage at the equator, while a two-satellite constellation has very large gaps of more than two hours between coverage passes. At higher latitudes, fewer satellites are required because the satellites pass a given point at high latitudes more frequently than they pass a given point at the equator, as noted previously.

SUN-SYNCHRONOUS ORBITS

One specific near-polar retrograde orbit—the *sun-synchronous* orbit—is widely used for intelligence collection as well as for civil remote sensing. A sun-synchronous orbit is designed so that the satellite passes over a given point on the earth at approximately the same time every day. At LEO altitudes, a sun-synchronous orbit is approximately 98 degrees, which makes it a near-polar retrograde orbit. The satellite passes the equator and each latitude at the same time every day. For example, the satellite's

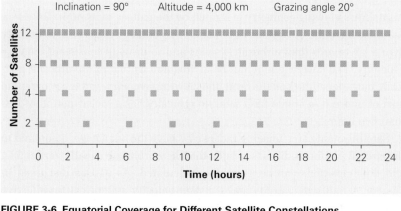

FIGURE 3-6 Equatorial Coverage for Different Satellite Constellations

sun-synchronous orbit shown in Figure 3-5 might cross the equator 28 times a day, crossing northward (ascending pass) at 3:00 a.m. local time and crossing southward (descending pass) at 3:00 p.m. local time. The orbital plane of a sun-synchronous orbit must shift eastward approximately 1 degree each day (365 degrees per year) to keep pace with the earth's revolution around the sun.

A sun-synchronous orbit usually has the ascending pass on the shadowed side of the earth, while the descending pass is on the sunlit side, as illustrated in Figure 3-3. Imaging sensors that collect reflected solar energy only image the surface on the sunlit side, when solar illumination is available. In contrast, active sensors that provide their own illumination (synthetic aperture radars, or SARs) or passive sensors that record emitted (for example, thermal) radiation can also image the surface on the shadowed side of the earth.

A sun-synchronous orbit covers each area of the world at a constant local time of day, called *local sun time*. This means that sun-synchronous satellites pass over any given latitude at almost the same local time during each orbital pass. Thus they collect images at about the same local sun time during each pass, so that lighting patterns remain about the same from day to day. It is important for imagery interpretation that the light conditions be consistent during a specific season over successive years or over a particular area over a series of days. Typically, the time of day of the overpass is selected to help in interpretation. A given target area is best imaged during the mid-morning or mid-afternoon, when the shadows from objects such as towers, vehicles, and buildings are available and of sufficient length to aid in imagery analysis.[7]

SATELLITES AS IMAGING PLATFORMS

A satellite's viewing geometry is limited by the pattern of its orbit. However, satellites have the advantage of being able to collect imagery more quickly over a larger area than airborne systems and to provide consistent viewing geometry. The coverage may not be as frequent as that of an airborne platform, but—depending on the orbit, the viewing geometry, and the geographic area of interest—a single LEO satellite typically has a revisit period of less than two hours.

Satellites that carry imaging radars also have the advantage, compared to the aircraft platforms discussed later, that their orbits are usually very stable, and their positions can be accurately calculated. As will be discussed in chapter 7, platform stability and constant velocity are critical for effective operation of synthetic aperture radars.

SATELLITES AS SIGINT PLATFORMS

Satellites have several advantages for conducting SIGINT. They can cover a large area of the earth in a very short time. While LEO satellites cannot dwell on a target area, their movement across the earth allows them to quickly geolocate the source of a signal. GEO satellites can dwell on a target area indefinitely, and HEO satellites can have a relatively long dwell (on the order of ten hours) near apogee. The disadvantage of both HEO and GEO satellites is that, being relatively far from their targets, they require large antennas and even then cannot readily pick up weak signals.

THE SPACE ENVIRONMENT

It is stating the obvious to note that space is a hostile environment. Humans venture into space only after donning protective clothing and equipment. Satellites also require extensive protection; some possible orbits would face such a hostile environment that they are not used.

In all orbits, satellites face the threats posed by penetrating objects, such as micrometeoroids and space debris. In some orbits, satellites also must deal with high-energy charged particles, radiation, and hot and cold plasmas (a plasma is an ionized gas; if the gas particles are moving very rapidly, and thus have a high energy level, the plasma is described as hot).

The radiation belts, known as the Van Allen belts, encircle the earth and contain particles trapped in the earth's magnetic field. The inner belt contains highly energetic protons. The weaker and less stable outer belt contains energetic electrons. The radiation in these belts can degrade electronic components, especially the sensors onboard a satellite. Sensors designed to sense photons or radio waves also respond to energetic particles passing through them. The effect over time is a gradual degradation until the onboard devices finally fail. Another problem caused by both energetic particles and the hot plasma in the earth's magnetosphere is internal charging—the buildup of an electrostatic charge on the spacecraft that can cause onboard electronics to fail.

Furthermore, the radiation belts are not uniform, and they possess unique features that have to be considered in designing orbits for collection platforms. One of the best known of these features is the South Atlantic Anomaly, a region in space above the South Atlantic Ocean of dense high energy protons and electrons that disrupt the functioning of the charge-coupled devices used in imaging satellites.[8]

Figure 3-7 illustrates the four orbit types discussed earlier. Note that the two MEO orbits are designed to avoid both radiation belts (as is the LEO orbital regime). HEO orbits, however, move through both radiation belts, so satellites in these orbits need additional shielding from radiation effects.

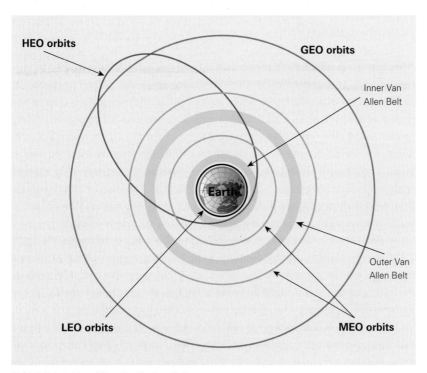

FIGURE 3-7 Van Allen Radiation Belts

Another hazard of the space environment is the combination of space debris, micrometeoroids, and dust that can damage or destroy a satellite. Space debris is an increasing threat as more satellites are placed in orbit along with launch-related debris. Ground-based optical and radar systems can monitor the near-earth space environment to warn against objects above about 1cm in diameter. But at the high collision speeds of orbital objects, a much smaller micrometeoroid can do substantial damage.

Space debris has become much more of a problem for LEO satellites in recent years, largely as a result of two events. On January 11, 2007, China conducted an antisatellite weapons test that created a massive debris cloud at LEO altitudes. On February 10, 2009, a Russian satellite collided with the Iridium 33 commercial satellite, creating an even greater debris cloud.[9]

Some spacecraft also have to deal with problems posed by the earth's shadow. A typical LEO satellite spends close to one-third of its time in darkness. Since most satellites rely primarily on solar cells for power, this means that the LEO craft has only about two-thirds of the power that is available to a HEO or GEO satellite.

Aircraft and UAVs

Airborne platforms have a number of advantages—flexibility, ability to surveil an area, and ability to get close to the target. Getting close to the target can be a particular advantage when using optical sensors, which cannot see through clouds. Unlike a spaceborne optical sensor, an airborne sensor may be able to get close enough to the target to be below the cloud cover. Furthermore, the airborne optical sensor offers a dramatic improvement in image quality compared to a spaceborne sensor. Commercial spaceborne sensors such as GeoEye have demonstrated a resolution of 1.3 feet per pixel (resolution cells and pixels are discussed in chapter 4). Commercially available aerial photography has demonstrated the ability to provide imagery with a resolution of 1.5 inches per pixel—a tenfold improvement in image quality.[10]

When developing and testing new collection sensors, airborne platforms have many advantages over satellites. They can serve as testbeds for new designs, and after each flight be brought back to the ground so that the problems can be corrected. The sensors are accessible for maintenance on a regular basis. If the sensor design needs modification, that can be readily done. But once a sensor is launched on a satellite, none of these things can be done—except at great expense. For these reasons, sensors intended for eventual satellite use often are first tested on aircraft. Finally, because of the harsh space environment discussed previously, spaceborne sensors must be certified as "space qualified"—meaning that they must pass much more stringent environmental testing than airborne sensors.

Airborne platforms have two significant disadvantages. First, they cannot legally overfly what intelligence organizations describe as "denied areas" (areas where overflight is prohibited by international law). Second, aircraft are vulnerable to counter-air weaponry. (While satellites are susceptible to the emerging threat of antisatellite weapons, such an attack on another country's satellite would violate international law.) The vulnerability issue has increasingly led to the use of unmanned aeronautical vehicles in place of manned aircraft. UAVs are just as vulnerable as aircraft to attack, but the loss of a UAV does not mean the loss of a pilot. UAVs typically have a smaller radar and optical signature, which provides them some protection from being detected. But power for radar sensors may be limited on aircraft and even moreso on UAVs.

As sensor carriers, airborne platforms have additional drawbacks. Some sensors cannot tolerate vibration or turbulence. Imaging radars, for example, have special problems on aircraft. SAR imagery is affected by variations in velocity and other motions of the aircraft, as well as by environmental (weather) conditions. In order to avoid image artifacts or geometric positioning errors due to random variations in the motion of the aircraft, the SAR must compensate with sophisticated navigation/positioning equipment and advanced image processing (discussed in chapter 7).[11] Generally, these are able to correct for all but the most severe variations in motion, such as significant air turbulence.[12]

Although airborne radar systems are susceptible to such platform motion problems, they are flexible in their capability to collect data from different look angles and look directions. By optimizing the geometry for the particular terrain being imaged, or by acquiring imagery from more than one look direction, they can obtain intelligence information that would be difficult to obtain for a satellite-borne radar (for example, by looking into an open hangar door). An airborne radar is able to collect data anywhere and at any time, as long as weather and flying conditions are suitable.

A current example of an airborne platform is the Global Hawk UAV, shown in Figure 3-8. It provides military commanders with near real-time, high-resolution intelligence, surveillance, and reconnaissance imagery.[13] Global Hawk carries an electro-optical imager (discussed in chapter 4) and a synthetic aperture radar (discussed in chapter 7).

Global Hawk can range as far as 12,000 nautical miles at altitudes up to 65,000 feet (19,812 meters), flying at speeds approaching 340 knots for as long

Collection Platforms

FIGURE 3-8 Global Hawk UAV

as 35 hours. During a typical mission, the aircraft can fly 1,200 miles to an area of interest and remain on station for 24 hours. It is currently being used to provide battlefield surveillance in places like Iraq and Afghanistan, but it also can provide strategic intelligence.

Global Hawk is a relatively large, long-range UAV. While it has performance advantages over smaller UAVs, it is relatively expensive. The trend is toward the proliferation of small, short-range UAVs. Small UAVs are increasingly being used for battlefield intelligence and law enforcement intelligence. They commonly are the size of model airplanes, and their size is decreasing. UAVs currently under development are dragonfly-sized and carry video cameras that can be used for intelligence collection.[14]

Aerostats

Aircraft, UAVs, and satellites all have one major disadvantage: single platforms are unable to perform continuous surveillance of a target area. (The one exception is the geostationary satellite.) The aerostat, which is defined as a lighter-than-air vehicle that can remain stationary in the air (including blimps, dirigibles, and tethered balloons), does not have this disadvantage. Most aerostats are tethered, but free-flying aerostats (usually called *airships*) are able to either maintain position for extended periods or move around as the mission requirements dictate. The U.S. military has used tethered aerostats for surveillance in Iraq.[15]

Aerostats can carry radar, optical, or SIGINT sensors, or any combination. Since the 1980s, the U.S. Air Force (USAF) has operated tethered aerostats, carrying the nickname "Fat Alberts," to provide radar coverage of the U.S. southern border in order to detect drug-smuggling aircraft.[16] The standard tactic for the smugglers is to fly below ground radar coverage; ground-based radars have very short ranges (about 10 kilometers) against low-flying aircraft. An aerostat-borne radar can extend this detection range to hundreds of kilometers.

The U.S. Air Force (USAF) is developing a high-altitude airship for surveillance and intelligence use. The proposed airship would reportedly be capable of operating at 65,000 feet altitude and staying aloft for ten years. Using its onboard radar at that altitude, the airship would be able to monitor targets of intelligence interest over a region the size of Iraq.[17]

Ships and Submarines

Ships are advantageous for remote sensing in that they have longer loiter times and more power than aircraft or satellites. However, as with the vibrations of airborne platforms, a ship's instability can limit the performance of onboard sensors, especially in rough seas.

The USNS *Observation Island*, shown in Figure 3-9, is an example of a shipborne intelligence collector.[18] It carries the Cobra Judy radars permanently mounted aboard the ship. The ship's primary mission is to collect detailed radar signature data on strategic ballistic missiles to verify compliance with international arms control treaties. A secondary mission is to collect data for U.S. missile development and theater missile defense systems testing. It monitors and collects data on foreign ballistic missile tests, complementing the Cobra Dane Radar System, which is described later in this chapter.[19]

Submarines have an advantage over ships in their ability to conduct clandestine intelligence collection. They are often able to approach another naval vessel, foreign port, or test area without detection and, by raising a periscope or periscope-mounted antenna above the water surface, collect visual or signals intelligence. Submarines also can collect underwater acoustic signals or deploy leave-behind sensors. During the 1982 Falklands war between the United Kingdom and Argentina, Britain deployed five of its nuclear attack submarines about 20 kilometers off the Argentine coast. The boats had been fitted with passive detection devices that could detect Argentine radio and radar transmissions. The submarines used these devices to track Argentine ships by their radar transmissions. The submarines also monitored radio traffic from Argentine air bases onshore. When radio traffic

FIGURE 3-9 USNS *Observation Island*

FIGURE 3-10 German SIGINT Ship

indicated the launch of an air strike, the submarines were able to transmit a warning to the task force commander via satellite link in time to alert the combat air patrol. This early warning gave the British fleet about 45 minutes to prepare for the Argentine air raids. The British submarines for the most part were able to operate undetected by staying submerged with only the SIGINT antennas above the sea surface. Some of them were occasionally detected and attacked, but none were damaged.[20]

Another example of a ship used as a collection platform is Germany's *Oste*, shown in Figure 3-10.[21] This SIGINT ship is capable of collecting ELINT and COMINT with an on-board capability to do technical analysis of collected signals.

The ship's design includes a very tall mast, illustrating one of the challenges of operating SIGINT from ships or submarines: These systems can only collect out to the line of sight. To extend the line of sight and consequently the detection range, the antennas need to be placed as high up as possible. The design also demonstrates another feature that is common to SIGINT ships: many of the SIGINT antennas are concealed, in this case by radomes—the smooth structures located just forward of the SIGINT mast.[22]

The challenge of getting better detection range in shipborne SIGINT can be solved, to some extent, by operating a tethered aerostat platform, as previously discussed, from a ship. Beginning in the late 1980s, the U.S. Army and the U.S. Coast Guard began operating a small fleet of leased commercial vessels with tethered aerostats to detect and monitor boats and airplanes suspected of drug smuggling. The aerostats carried radars that functioned in much the same way as the "Fat Albert" radars discussed earlier.[23]

Ground Sites

Ground sites are used for remote sensing of aircraft, ballistic missiles, and satellites. Radar and optical sensors can be used both for locating these objects spatially and for collecting signature measurements for object identification. Some ground-based platforms used in intelligence are mobile, but the most important ones are fixed—and therefore have the disadvantage of having a fixed coverage area. Offsetting this disadvantage, fixed sites are very stable platforms with precisely known locations (in order to precisely locate something, you have to know precisely where you are). Two important examples are the Maui Space Surveillance System and the Cobra Dane radar.

MAUI SPACE SURVEILLANCE SYSTEM

Figure 3-11 shows the Maui Space Surveillance System, an optical site that combines operational satellite tracking facilities with a research and development facility. It is located at the 10,000-foot summit of Haleakala Mountain on

FIGURE 3-11 Maui Space Surveillance System

the island of Maui, Hawaii. The mountaintop location is well suited for both astronomical telescopes and optical facilities used for space surveillance. The high elevation means that the site is usually above cloud cover, and it also reduces the distortion in viewing caused by the atmosphere.

The telescopes there track man-made objects to GEO altitudes and beyond, and they collect optical signatures to use for space object identification. The site has several telescopes that accommodate a wide variety of sensor systems, including imaging systems, photometers, infrared radiometers, and low-light level video systems, which are discussed in subsequent chapters.[24]

COBRA DANE

The Cobra Dane radar is a technical collection sensor located on the island of Shemya, Alaska. The phased array antenna shown in Figure 3-12 is 29 meters across. The radar's primary mission is to track and collect signature data on foreign intercontinental ballistic missile (ICBM) and submarine launched ballistic missile (SLBM) test launches to the Kamchatka impact area and the broad ocean impact areas in the Pacific Ocean. The signature data collected by Cobra Dane support treaty monitoring and technical assessments of foreign ICBM performance.[25]

Cobra Dane illustrates one way of dealing with the tradeoffs among coverage, resolution, and accuracy discussed in chapter 2. In this example, the

FIGURE 3-12 Cobra Dane Radar

radar has a requirement to acquire, accurately track, and obtain detailed signature data on ballistic missile reentry vehicles. This requirement for high spectral, spatial, intensity, and temporal accuracy and resolution led to the design of a ground-based, high-power phased array radar having a fixed orientation (that is, a fixed boresight). As a result, its spatial coverage is constrained; it can detect and track objects in a sector that is 120 degrees wide in azimuth and centered on the Kamchatka impact area. The radar's location and spatial coverage is acceptable for the radar's primary mission. But it limits the radar's utility in its secondary mission of tracking satellites; only satellites with inclinations between 55 and 125 degrees can be tracked.[26]

BATTLEFIELD SURVEILLANCE

Radars and SIGINT systems that scan the skies, such as the Cobra Dane radar and most air defense radars, have no special requirement to be situated high above the ground. But radars and SIGINT systems that must scan the earth's surface or detect low-flying aircraft need as much altitude as possible. As with the SIGINT ship in Figure 3-10, and the aerostat radars previously discussed, increased height equals increased detection range. Aerostats often are impractical for use in battlefield areas, as they are easy targets for opposing counter-air systems. The solution has been to develop battlefield surveillance systems that can raise their antennas when operating. The Saab Giraffe shown in Figure 3-13 illustrates the use of this design approach in a radar designed to detect low-flying aircraft and helicopters.[27]

FIGURE 3-13 Giraffe Battlefield Surveillance Radar

The Giraffe illustrates another advantage of battlefield surveillance radars—they have to be mobile, both to move with the front and to avoid being targeted for attack—a point that will be revisited in chapter 8.

Summary

Technical intelligence relies on an extensive array of sophisticated instruments that collect information from a variety of platforms—aircraft, satellites, ships, submarines, and ground stations. Two issues about platforms are to protect them, so that they can survive in a hostile situation, and to make them clandestine, to allow them to collect intelligence without the opponent being aware of the collection.

Remote sensing platforms can be used in intelligence for surveillance or reconnaissance. The difference between the two is the dwell time on the target area; surveillance is defined as continuous dwell, while reconnaissance is a dwell for a relatively short period of time, even a snapshot.

Some platforms operate close to their intended target, providing high resolution and accuracy but sacrificing spatial coverage. Some operate at great distances to obtain spatial coverage or to protect the platform from hostile action, but they sacrifice resolution and accuracy to do so.

Satellites provide most of today's intelligence. A satellite can be used for observing the earth or for observing other satellites. Satellites have several unique characteristics that make them particularly useful. One of the major advantages in intelligence is that a satellite can legally overfly any country to get intelligence information. An aircraft or unmanned aeronautical vehicle cannot.

Satellites used for intelligence purposes are customarily referred to as overhead collection assets. The term could be applied as well to aircraft, which also collect imagery and signals intelligence from overhead. But over the years, the term *overhead collection* has acquired an understood meaning: collection from satellites.

Satellites operate in four types of orbits. Closest to the earth are the low earth orbit satellites that complete a single orbit in less than two hours at altitudes below 1500 km. Most imaging satellites and some SIGINT satellites use this orbit. Medium earth orbit satellites, at altitudes between 10,000 and 20,000 km, are more survivable because they are more difficult to locate and attack. Highly elliptical orbit satellites have an apogee near 35,000 km and a perigee near 500 km, and they normally are used to provide medium-term reconnaissance of high latitude and polar regions.

Geostationary satellites appear to remain at a fixed point above the earth at 35,800 km and are useful for continuous surveillance of about one-third of the earth's surface.

LEO satellites used for intelligence collection usually follow near-polar orbits, wherein the ground track moves westward during each succeeding pass in a retrograde orbit to provide global coverage. Imaging satellites frequently use a retrograde orbit that is sun-synchronous, meaning that the satellite crosses the equator at the same local (sun) time each day.

Ships have an advantage for remote sensing in that they have longer loiter times and more power available than aircraft or satellites. However, a ship's instability can limit the performance of onboard sensors, especially in rough seas. Submarines have additional advantages in their ability to conduct clandestine intelligence collection. They are often able to approach another naval vessel, foreign port, or test area without detection, and by raising a periscope or periscope-mounted antenna above the water surface collect visual or signals intelligence.

Aircraft and unmanned aeronautical vehicles are heavily used for electronic reconnaissance, where they can operate near (but not overfly) hostile territory. UAVs have the additional advantage that they do not have an onboard pilot, so they can also conduct imaging operations over hostile territory. Fuel constraints limit the time they can remain in the target area. In contrast, aerostats (unmanned balloons) have the advantage of very long loiter times and can conduct radar or SIGINT surveillance of a given area.

Ground sites range in size from very large fixed facilities used for radar and optical surveillance of space and ballistic missile activity to the mobile battlefield surveillance radars and SIGINT systems and the unattended sensors or small clandestine facilities used for close-in sensing.

NOTES

1. Albert D. Wheelon, "Technology and Intelligence," *Technology in Society*, Vol 26, April–August 2004: 245–255.
2. Figure from www.centennialofflight.gov/essay/Dictionary/SUN_SYNCH_ORBIT/DI155.htm.
3. Figure from www.newmediastudio.org/DataDiscovery/Hurr_ED_Center/Satellites_and_Sensors/Polar_Orbits/Polar_Orbits.html.
4. Figure from www.newmediastudio.org/DataDiscovery/Hurr_ED_Center/Satellites_and_Sensors/Polar_Orbits/Polar_Orbits.html.

5. "Ofeq," Israeli-Weapons.com, www.israeli-weapons.com/weapons/space/ofeq/OFEQ.html.

6. Figure derived from U.S. Patent 5931417, "Non-geostationary orbit satellite constellation for continuous coverage of northern latitudes above 25° and its extension to global coverage tailored to the distribution of populated land masses on earth," published August 3, 1999.

7. Canada Centre for Remote Sensing, "Tutorial: Fundamentals of Remote Sensing Image Interpretation & Analysis," www.ccrs.nrcan.gc.ca/resource/tutor/fundam/chapter4/02_e.php.

8. Sharma Jayant, Grant H. Stokes, Curt von Braun, George Zollinger, and Andrew J. Wiseman, "Toward Operational Space-Based Space Surveillance," *Lincoln Laboratory Journal*, 13, no. 2 (2002): 328.

9. Paul Marks, "Satellite Collision 'More Powerful than China's ASAT Test,'" *New Scientist*, February 13, 2009, www.newscientist.com/article/dn16604-satellite-collision-more-powerful-than-chinas-asat-test.html.

10. Eric Lai, "In Satellite Photo Resolution Race, Who's Winning?" *Computerworld*, October 24, 2008, www.computerworld.com/action/article.do?command=viewArticleBasic&articleId=9118079&intsrc=hm_list.

11. Zheng Liwen, Lv Xiaolei, and Xing Mengdao, "Imaging Method of UAV High Squint SAR," *Heifei Leida Kexue Yu Jishu* (December 1, 2007): 431.

12. Canada Centre for Remote Sensing, "Tutorial: Fundamentals of Microwave Remote Sensing," www.ccrs.nrcan.gc.ca/resource/tutor/fundam/chapter3/09_e.php.

13. Description from U.S. Air Force Web site "Air Force Link," www.af.mil/factsheets/factsheet.asp?fsID=13225. Photo credited to www.DefenseImagery.mil (photographer, TSGT Jack Braden).

14. "The Fly's a Spy," *The Economist*, November 1, 2007, www.economist.com/displaystory.cfm?story_id=10059596.

15. Julian E. Barnes, "Spy Blimp: Air Force Planning Giant Airship," *Chicago Tribune*, March 13, 2009.

16. U.S. Air Force, "Tethered Aerostat Radar System," U.S. Air Force Fact Sheet, August 2007, www.af.mil/information/factsheets/factsheet.asp?id=3507.

17. Barnes, "Spy Blimp."

18. Photo from the U.S. Navy, Military Sealift Command, www.msc.navy.mil/inventory/ships.asp?ship=133&type=MissileRangeInstrumentationShip.

19. Raytheon Corporation, "Cobra Judy Radar System," www.raytheon.com/capabilities/products/cobra_judy/.

20. "The Falklands Radio Line," Strategy Page, December 4, 2007, www.strategypage.com/htmw/htsub/articles/20071204.aspx.

21. Photo from Wikipedia Commons, File:A52_Oste_.jpg.

22. Flottendienstboot OSTE-Klasse (423), (in German), accessed at www.marine.de.

23. U.S. General Accounting Office, Report #GAO/NSIAD-93-213, September 10, 1993, www.dtic.mil/cgi-bin/GetTRDoc?AD=ADA271225&Location=U2&doc=GetTRDoc.pdf.

24. "Air Force Maui Optical & Supercomputing Site," U.S. Air Force, www.maui.afmc.af.mil/. Photo from NASA, Johnson Space Center, Orbital Debris Program

Collection
Platforms

Office (Photo gallery, www.orbitaldebris.jsc.nasa.gov/photogallery/photogallery .html).

25. Missile Defense: Additional Knowledge Needed in Developing System for Intercepting Long-Range Missiles, U.S. General Accounting Office [GAO-03-600], August 2003. Photo from www.DefenseImagery.mil (photographer, Sgt. Robert S. Thompson).

26. E. G. Stansbery, "Growth in the Number of SSN Tracked Orbital Objects," NASA Report presented at the 55th International Astronautical Congress of the International Astronautical Federation, the International Academy of Astronautics, and the International Institute of Space Law, Vancouver, British Columbia, October 4–8, 2004, http://ntrs.nasa.gov/archive/nasa/casi.ntrs.nasa.gov/200600 22013_2006009640.pdf.

27. Photo courtesy of Dimitrije Ostojic.

4. Optical Imaging and Radiometry

Optical imaging systems are usually called *electro-optical imagers* because the incoming optical signal hits a detector array, where it is converted to an electrical signal for transmission and storage. Electro-optical imagers are attractive because they can cover large areas of the earth's surface, with spatial resolutions sufficient for obtaining useful signatures and performing imagery interpretation. They provide a target signature in the form of a target's location plus identifying features (that is, features that allow the identification of a type of terrain, building, aircraft, or ship). A particular pattern of building and equipment layouts might identify a complex, for example, as a weapons test range or a nuclear fuel reprocessing plant. Note that the pattern is not a signature. As discussed in chapter 1, the pattern identification is the result of analysis of a combination of signatures (building and equipment layouts).

As noted above, optical imaging can provide both the location of a target on the earth's surface and a signature of the target. Continuous imaging (surveillance) also can provide information about target movements. Optical imaging systems also can provide spectral signatures and intensity or state measurements for a more complete and useful signature. These measurements are increasingly important in intelligence usage. Such spectral imaging is discussed in chapter 5.

Optical System Basics

The optical sensors used in remote sensing are, for all practical purposes, telescopes with cameras attached. They operate as illustrated in Figure 4-1, which shows the basic function of a telescope. At the left, light from two distant objects arrives at the telescope from two slightly different directions. Because of the relatively great distance to the objects, the light rays from each object are essentially parallel when they arrive at the telescope. The optics focus the incoming energy at a point called the *focal point*. Two dimensions of a telescope (or of any optical system) define its performance: the size of the aperture and the focal length.

Aperture. The light from each object is collected by a circular aperture having diameter D; in this example, a lens of diameter D focuses the light into images of the two objects at the focal plane. (Sensors used for remote sensing in intelligence mostly use a concave mirror to do the focusing instead of a lens, because lenses become very heavy as the aperture size increases.) As the diameter increases, the amount of light that can be collected also increases, and therefore the sensor's sensitivity increases. The amount of light collected by a circular sensor is proportional to D^2.

Focal Length. The focal length, F, of the sensor is defined by the distance between the aperture and the focal plane.

The above discussion assumes a perfect optical system. The resolving power (or resolution) of an astronomical telescope is a measure of its ability to distinguish fine detail in an image of a source. Optical aberrations due to the telescope design or flaws in the manufacture and alignment of optical components can degrade the resolving power, as does peering through the earth's turbulent atmosphere. However, even if a telescope is optically perfect and is operated in a vacuum, there is still a fundamental lower limit to the resolving power it can achieve. This is known as the *theoretical resolving power*. The limit is related to the distance s in Figure 4-1. If s is too small, the two images overlap and cannot be resolved.

To get the best possible image that the optics will permit, the image in the focal plane needs to have as much spatial resolution as possible. What this means is that the separation s between the two sources at the focal plane must be sufficient to detect both sources.

To keep s as large as possible, the optical sensor must have a large focal ratio, known to photographers as the *f number*. This is defined as the ratio of

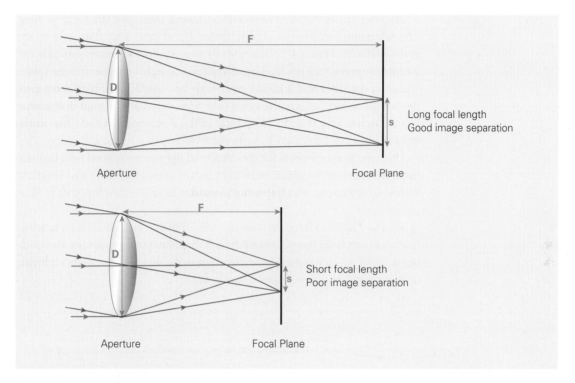

FIGURE 4-1 Optical Sensor Components

the focal length of the telescope to its diameter, that is, f = F / D. The idea is illustrated in Figure 4-1. As the focal plane is moved away from the lens, the focal length F increases and makes the separation s larger. The f number increases, image separation is better, and the telescope has better resolution. But as F becomes larger, the lens must become thinner to keep the focus, as shown in the figure. (In a reflector, this is done by making the mirror less concave.)

Better separation, though, comes at a price. The tradeoff for larger f is that while resolution improves (better image quality), there is less light on each pixel. A camera using an f number of f16 produces a better quality image than it does when using f2, but at the price of 64 times less light on each pixel. Anyone who has used a zoom lens on a film camera may have noticed this effect; the image becomes darker as you zoom in and the f number increases. (This effect is hard to see in a digital camera; the electronics compensate for the decreased light.)

Another tradeoff is that longer focal length decreases the field of view. The telescope can resolve objects better, but it sees a smaller area at any given distance. Figure 4-2 illustrates this constraint. To appreciate this difference, suppose you are looking at a scene through a cardboard tube that is 1 inch in diameter and 1 inch long (f = 1). You would be able to see a great deal of the scene. Now replace that tube with one that is 1 inch in diameter but 20 inches long (f = 20). Very little of the scene would be visible, as the field of view has been significantly narrowed.

One way to compensate for the decreased light on each pixel is to increase the lens diameter to admit more light (while increasing the focal length to improve resolution). The following illustrates how this developed over time:

• The National Reconnaissance Office's 1960s vintage Corona satellite had a 24 inch focal length and a 6.8 inch diameter lens, producing an f number (F/D) of 3.5.[1] The small focal length gave it a wide field of view and wide area coverage, but its resolution was poor.

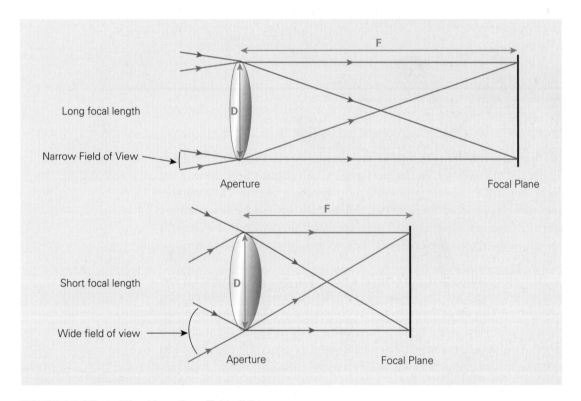

FIGURE 4-2 Effect of Focal Length on Field of View

• The optical sensor in the current GeoEye satellite has a 13.3 meter focal length and 1.1 meter aperture, giving a much better f number (F/D) of 12.[2] The long focal length gives good resolution, but the field of view is very narrow and its images cover a relatively small area.

The other way to compensate for the decreased light on each pixel is to improve the sensitivity of the detector. In old cameras, this sensing unit was photographic film. Film cameras that required high resolution or needed to function at low-light levels used a more sensitive film known as high-speed film; it produced good photographs at higher f numbers. In modern cameras and intelligence sensors, the detector is a flat matrix of tiny light-sensitive solid-state devices called a *focal plane array* (so called because it is placed at the point where the telescope optics focus incoming light energy—the focal plane in Figure 4-1). Most such sensors use a *charge-coupled device* (CCD) for the focal plane array. Current generation CCDs are much more sensitive than the highest speed film. For comparison, the Corona camera used high-speed film and provided an image resolution of 8–10 feet.[3] The digital camera in the current GeoEye satellite, with its better f number and more sensitive CCD detectors, is able to produce images with .41 meter resolution.[4]

If the focal plane array detects visible light, it requires no special cooling. Such devices are relatively cheap to build. But increasingly, optical sensors used in intelligence and earth resources sensing operate in both the infrared and the visible parts of the spectrum. At the lower frequency (longer wavelength) part of the infrared spectrum, the detectors in the focal plane array must be cooled in order to make them more sensitive. Cooled focal plane arrays are much harder to build and more expensive.

Basic Imaging Geometry

Having detailed the basics of an optical system in the discussion above, this section covers the basics of imaging with optics. The distance between the target being imaged and the type of platform plays a large role in determining the detail of information obtained and the total area imaged by the sensor. Sensors located far away from their targets typically can view a larger area, but they cannot provide as much detail when compared to sensors that are close to the target. Figure 4-3 illustrates the *field of regard,* which is the limit of what an intelligence collection satellite might see. The field of regard is the total area that a collection platform is capable of seeing by pointing the sensor.

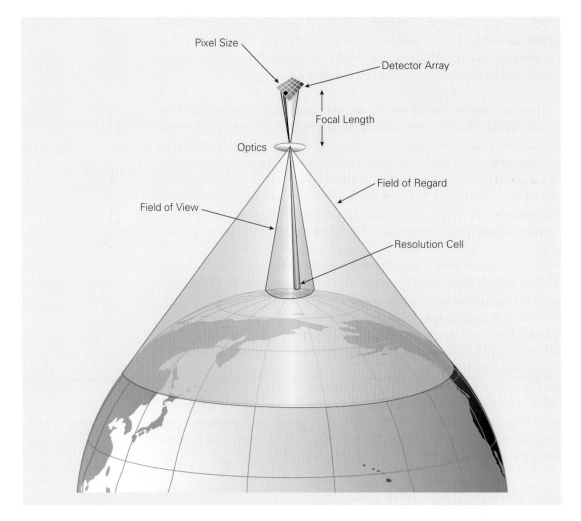

FIGURE 4-3 Sensor Field of View and Field of Regard

There are some basic differences between what a sensor can see of the earth when on an intelligence collection satellite (such as France's SPOT or Israel's Ofeq)[5] versus when that same sensor is on an airplane. A satellite can see a large part of the earth's surface, an aircraft much less. The collection satellite potentially can observe a sector anywhere in a whole province or country at a given moment, but its sensor cannot distinguish fine details. An aircraft-mounted camera could read the license plate on an auto or recognize an individual when the aircraft overflies an installation, but the aircraft camera could only view the immediate area around the installation.

The detail discernible in an image is dependent on the spatial resolution of the sensor (that is, the size of the smallest possible feature that can be detected). Spatial resolution of passive sensors (the special case of radar sensors will be discussed later) depends primarily on the sensor's *field of view* (FOV). The FOV is the angular cone of visibility of the sensor, measured in degrees, as shown in Figure 4-3. It determines the area on the earth's surface that is "seen" from a given altitude at one particular moment in time. The size of the area viewed is determined by the FOV and the distance from the ground to the sensor—the farther the sensor is from the earth, the larger the area that is viewed.

Optical sensors that look out into space function in the same way as earth-looking sensors. The field of regard is the hemisphere limited by the horizon; the field of view is determined by the telescope design.

Pixels and Resolution Cells

Figure 4-3 illustrates two other important concepts—that of the *resolution cell* and the *pixel.* Most remote sensing images are composed of a matrix of picture elements, or pixels, which are the smallest units of an image. In a digital camera—and most electro-optical sensors used in intelligence are digital cameras—a pixel is defined by the size of the detector elements in the camera. Image pixels are normally square and represent a certain area on an image.

Each detector element receives light energy from a defined area on the ground called the *resolution cell.* For a feature to be detected, its size generally has to be equal to or larger than the resolution cell. If the feature is smaller, it may not be detectable; the detector will average the brightness of all features in that resolution cell. However, smaller features may sometimes be detectable if their reflectance is so strong as to dominate within a particular resolution cell.

As an example, if a spaceborne optical sensor has a spatial resolution of 10 meters, then when an image from that sensor is displayed at full resolution, each pixel represents an area of 10 meters × 10 meters on the ground. In this case the pixel size and resolution are the same.

Therefore, the pixel size and resolution correspond; a camera's resolution cannot be better than the pixel size. However, it is possible to display an image with a pixel size different from the resolution. Satellite images of the earth often have their pixels averaged to represent larger areas, although the original spatial resolution of the sensor that collected the imagery remains the same.

Black-and-white cameras show the intensity of visible light in a pixel; color cameras also give some indication of wavelength in the pixel, but they do not measure the intensity of different wavelengths.

Types of Electro-optical Imagers

Three types of imagers are used in remote sensing. Many electro-optical (as opposed to photographic) remote sensors acquire data using *scanners,* which employ a sensor with a narrow field of view that sweeps over the terrain to build up and produce a two-dimensional image of the surface. Scanners can be used on both aircraft and satellite platforms and have essentially the same operating principles. Two such types of electro-optical imaging scanners are used in intelligence: cross-track scanners and pushbroom imagers. Figure 4-4 shows a comparison of these two types. The third type shown in the figure, a framing camera, is not a scanner.

CROSS-TRACK SCANNERS

Cross-track scanners, also known as optical-mechanical or "whiskbroom" scanners, use a scanning mirror that projects the image of a surface resolution element onto a single detector. A cross-track scanner images the earth, back and forth in a series of lines perpendicular to the direction of platform movement, as shown in Figure 4-4. Each line is scanned from one side of the sensor to the other, using a rotating mirror. As the platform moves forward, successive scans build up a two-dimensional image of the earth's surface.

The *instantaneous field of view* (IFOV) is the angular region seen by a single detector in the sensor (shown as the small black region in Figure 4-3). The IFOV of the sensor and the altitude of the platform determine the ground resolution cell viewed, and thus the spatial resolution. The angular field of view is determined by the sweep of the mirror, measured in degrees, and that angle determines the width of the imaged swath. Airborne scanners typically sweep large angles (90–120 degrees). Satellites, because of their higher altitude, need only to sweep fairly small angles (10–20 degrees) to cover a broad region. Because the distance from the sensor to the target increases toward the edges of the swath, the ground resolution cells consequently become larger and the images become distorted at the edges.

The cross-track scanner is a simple design; therefore, it is easier and cheaper to put on a satellite than the other two types. But the length of time

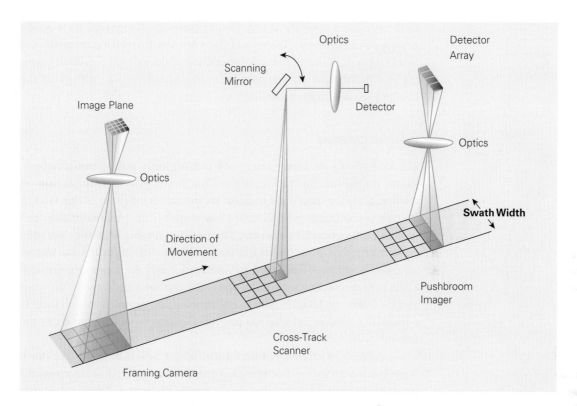

FIGURE 4-4 Classes of Imaging Systems

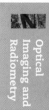

that the sensor "sees" a ground resolution cell as the rotating mirror scans (called the *dwell time*) is generally quite short. The result is that the cross-track scanner has relatively poor sensitivity and, therefore, poor spectral and intensity resolution.

PUSHBROOM IMAGERS

Instead of a scanning mirror, some imaging systems use a linear array of detectors located at the focal plane of the image, which move along in the flight track direction, as indicated in Figure 4-4. The forward motion of the platform allows the imager to receive optical signals from successive strips of the earth and to build up a two-dimensional image, perpendicular to the flight direction.

These systems are called *pushbroom imagers* because the motion of the detector array resembles the bristles of a broom being pushed along a floor.

Each individual detector at any instant measures the energy for a single ground resolution cell. The size of the detectors therefore determines the pixel size and, in turn, the spatial resolution of the system. A current example of a pushbroom imager used in intelligence is the one carried on the French Pleiades imagery satellite.[6]

FRAMING CAMERAS

The most widely used sensor in remote sensing today is the *framing camera,* shown on the left side of Figure 4-4. This sensor will be familiar to most readers, since the hand-held cameras sold in stores today are of this type. A framing camera uses conventional camera optics and an array of detectors located in the camera focal plane. The framing cameras originally installed on aircraft and reconnaissance spacecraft used photographic film, but almost all framing cameras now used in intelligence rely on a detector array of CCDs. The more detectors in the array, the smaller each detector becomes and the better the imagery resolution becomes. But as noted earlier, there is a tradeoff: a smaller detector has less light striking it, and consequently the sensitivity becomes worse.

An example of a framing camera design is that carried by the Global Hawk UAV. It has a 10 inch reflecting telescope that provides common optics for two framing cameras—one operating in the visible band and one in the infrared band (3.6–5 microns). At its best resolution (called the *spot collection mode*), the camera can collect 1,900 frames a day with frame size 2 × 2 km. It can locate targets to within 20 meters circular error of probability (meaning that 50 percent of target locations will be accurate to within 20 meters). The camera can also operate in a wide area search mode, covering a swath up to 10 km wide at lower resolution.[7]

Each type of imaging system shown in Figure 4-4 has distinct advantages and disadvantages. The framing camera provides an image that covers a large area in one "snapshot," but it requires technologically sophisticated planar arrays of small, sensitive detectors. The cross-track scanner can use a single very simple detector, but its overall sensitivity suffers because it spends little dwell time in each of the cells shown in Figure 4-4. The pushbroom imager is a compromise: it allows more dwell time in each cell than the scanner and is less complex than the framing camera.

Framing cameras and pushbroom imagers are probably the most commonly used imaging systems today. Which one works best depends on the mission requirements. If the system is intended to take a series of images of known target areas, then the framing camera is better; it can provide the most detailed image of the target area because of its higher sensitivity. If the system must map very large areas of the earth, then the pushbroom imager is more effective. Spectral imagers, discussed in chapter 5, also tend to use pushbroom imagers because a separate linear array of detectors is used for each spectral band.

Image Processing

In today's world of advanced technology, where most remote sensing data are recorded in digital format, virtually all image interpretation and analysis involves some element of digital processing. Digital image processing may entail numerous procedures, including formatting and correcting of the data, digital enhancement to facilitate better visual interpretation, or even automated classification of targets and features entirely by computer. In order to process remote sensing imagery digitally, the data must be recorded and available in a digital form suitable for storage on a computer. Several commercially available software systems have been developed specifically for remote sensing image processing and analysis.

To get an image that is useful for intelligence, at least two processing functions have to be carried out: preprocessing and image enhancement.

Preprocessing involves making radiometric or geometric corrections to the image before the information of intelligence value is extracted.

- Radiometric corrections include correcting the data for sensor irregularities and unwanted sensor or atmospheric noise and then converting the data, so they accurately represent the reflected or emitted radiation measured by the sensor.
- Geometric corrections include correcting for geometric distortions that occur as the sensor looks at different angles from the vertical and then converting the data to real world coordinates (such as latitude and longitude) on the earth's surface.

Image enhancement is done solely to improve the appearance of the imagery to assist in visual interpretation and analysis. Three types of enhancement are frequently used to help interpret imagery: contrast enhancement, spatial filtering, and edge enhancement.

- Contrast enhancement involves increasing the tonal distinction between various features in a scene so that the features are more prominent.

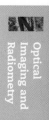

- Spatial filtering is used to enhance (or suppress) specific spatial patterns in an image to emphasize the interesting parts and eliminate the uninteresting parts of the image.
- Edge enhancement is commonly used in processing images for intelligence. Features of interest to the imagery analyst often have sharp straight edges that are not common in natural features, and edge enhancement highlights these features.[8]

The most widely used type of imagery in intelligence is panchromatic imagery from the visible spectrum, collected by an aircraft or satellite platform. Such imagery depends on the presence of an illuminator such as the sun, as discussed in chapter 2. This imagery is described as reflective sensing or reflective imaging because it relies on the reflection of energy from the target. Hand-held cameras do reflective imaging; in low light levels, a flash attachment provides the illuminating energy.

Most images based on reflective sensing are taken in the visible band, but reflective sensing also works in the ultraviolet and the near-infrared bands; objects reflect energy strongly in those bands. Increasingly, imagery from outside the visible band is used in intelligence because it reveals information that simply is not available in visible band imagery. Much of this imaging is done by multispectral sensors, which are discussed in chapter 5.

The processing of imagery that includes nonvisible bands presents special challenges. A camera may be able to obtain images in the nonvisible part of the spectrum, but unaided eyes cannot see those parts. Therefore, a major challenge of such imagery is to somehow represent the nonvisible part in the visible spectrum so that it can be exploited and analyzed. The solution is to use *false color*. A commonly used technique for an image that must include the near infrared band is to shift all colors in wavelength approximately 0.15 microns to a higher frequency (shorter wavelength) part of the spectrum. The result is that a green object is depicted as blue, a red object as green, and an infrared reflection as red. Blue objects cannot be depicted and appear black. Another technique is shown in Figure 4-5, a false color image taken by NASA's Terra satellite.[9] This image of a copper mine in southeastern Arizona was created by combining the visible green, near infrared, and short wave infrared band images. The copper deposits, which reflect strongly in the near infrared band, show as a bright blue. The moist areas in the southern part of the image reflect strongly in both of the infrared bands and show as purple. While false color allows an imagery analyst to analyze the image, customers of intelligence do not like it as much as visible imagery since it is harder to understand the image without training.

FIGURE 4-5 False Color Image

Image Exploitation

After processing, exploitation is the next step in converting imagery into intelligence. This conversion is done by trained experts, who were formerly known as photo interpreters. The advent of digital imagery and the increasing complexity of the exploitation process led to a name change for these professionals. They are now generally called imagery analysts, and the product of their work is called imagery analysis.

Many signatures exist in the world of conventional electro-optical imagery and are used routinely by imagery analysts. Imagery analysis often relies on identifying a unique signature. Most liquid natural gas tanker ships, for example, have above-deck gas storage domes that uniquely identify the ship as a tanker. Many facilities, such as nuclear power plants, possess unique signatures because of the functions that must be performed at the facility— reactor cooling structures, for example.

IMAGERY INTERPRETATION SCALES

The value of the signature obtained in a given image is critically dependent on the quality of the image. Imagery analysts rely on some type of imagery

interpretation scale to tell them how useful an image might be for identifying unique signatures and patterns.

For decades the U.S. intelligence community has used the *National Imagery Interpretability Rating Scale* (NIIRS) to quantify the interpretability or usefulness of imagery. The NIIRS was developed to provide an objective standard for image quality, since the term *image quality* can mean different things to imagery analysts than to optical engineers. NIIRS ratings thus serve as a shorthand description of the information that can be extracted from a given image.

The need for the NIIRS arose from the inability of simple physical image quality metrics, such as image scale or resolution, to adequately predict image interpretability. Complex metrics do not communicate useful information about the image quality to imagery analysts. Table 4-1 is a summary version of the U.S. imagery rating scale.[10]

TABLE 4-1 Description of NIIRS Rating Scale

NIIRS value	Description and Examples
0	Interpretability of the imagery is precluded by obscuration, degradation, or very poor resolution.
1	Detect a medium-sized port facility or distinguish between taxiways and runways at a large airfield.
2	Detect large hangars at airfields or large buildings (for example, hospitals, factories, and warehouses).
3	Identify the wing configuration (for example, straight, swept, or delta) of large aircraft. Identify a large surface ship by type (for example, cruiser, auxiliary ship, or noncombatant/merchant). Detect trains or strings of standard rolling stock on railroad tracks (not individual cars).
4	Identify large fighters by type. Detect an open missile silo door. Identify individual tracks, rail pairs, control towers, and switching points in rail yards.
5	Distinguish between aircraft by the presence of refueling equipment (for example, pedestal and wing pod). Identify radar as vehicle-mounted or trailer-mounted. Identify air surveillance radar on ships. Identify individual rail cars by type (for example, gondola, flat, or box) and/or locomotives by type (for example, steam or diesel).
6	Distinguish between models of small/medium helicopters. Identify the spare tire on a medium-sized truck. Identify automobiles as sedans or station wagons.
7	Identify fittings and fairings on a fighter-sized aircraft. Detect details of the silo door hinging mechanism on launch silos and launch control silos. Identify individual rail ties.
8	Identify the rivet lines on bomber aircraft. Identify a hand-held surface-to-air missile. Detect winch cables on deck-mounted cranes. Identify windshield wipers on a vehicle.
9	Differentiate cross-slot from single slot heads on aircraft skin panel fasteners. Identify vehicle registration numbers on trucks. Identify screws and bolts on missile components. Detect individual spikes in railroad ties.

For a given optical system, the NIIRS values get higher as the collector gets closer to the target. To illustrate typical NIIRS performance, the Global Hawk UAV can deliver NIIRS 6 visible imagery at its normal operating altitude in its wide area search mode. The infrared sensor at the same altitude can deliver NIIRS 5 imagery.[11]

SIGNATURE LIBRARIES

Panchromatic imagery is limited because only spatial measurement (height, length, width, and shape) can be made on panchromatic images. Some indication of intensity is present because bright objects will appear white in the image and dim objects will appear black. Therefore, a crude sort of signature can be obtained, but the resulting signature libraries are fairly simple. These libraries were compiled over many years in the form of "imagery interpreter keys"—books that contained images of, for example, specific types of tanks, airplanes, ships, and buildings.[12]

An example of a signature library data set is one based on "cratology," which is defined as the study of the size and function of shipping crates observed in photography. The size and configuration of a shipping crate often will indicate what is inside. Imagery analysts in the past developed substantial libraries of information on weapons crates down to the size of ammunition boxes. Using the libraries, an analyst could identify the type of ammunition or artillery shells by measuring the box used to ship them.[13]

Cratology has been used for many years to identify movements of military hardware. An early example of cratology success occurred at the beginning of the Cuban Missile Crisis in 1962. On September 28, imagery analysts observed crates on the deck of a Soviet ship bound for Cuba; the crates were uniquely designed to ship IL-28 medium bombers. This report, along with reports of ballistic missiles being stationed in Cuba, led to a U-2 flight in October that brought back pictures of the ballistic missile sites under construction.[14]

More recently, during August 2006, a U.S. reconnaissance satellite reportedly observed crates being loaded onto an Iranian transport aircraft near Tehran. Based on the dimensions of the crates, U.S. intelligence analysts reportedly concluded that Iranian C-802 Noor antiship cruise missiles were being loaded onto the aircraft. According to the press report, the identification set off a chain of diplomatic action that kept the missiles from being delivered to Hezbollah guerrillas who were fighting Israeli forces in Lebanon.[15]

Optical
Imaging and
Radiometry

Stereoscopic Imagery

Soon after aerial photography began to be used in intelligence, it became apparent that an imagery analyst could obtain more useful detail from a three-dimensional image than from the 2-D image provided by conventional photography. To create a 3-D illusion of depth in a photograph, a *stereograph*—a combination of two photographs of the same scene taken from slightly different angles—must be created using a stereo camera. At short ranges, this can be done by a camera with dual lenses. In aerial or satellite photography, stereographs are created by taking two successive images of the same ground area with suitable spacing; the two images are called a stereo pair. The slightly different perspectives of the two images mimic stereoscopic vision. One angle records the scene from the perspective of a viewer's left eye and the other from the perspective of the right eye. Stereographic imagery can efficiently display the distribution of the physical, biological, and cultural components of a given landscape. Natural and man-made features all have different identifying signatures that are more readily recognized in 3-D than in 2-D imagery.

During World War II, many countries began to obtain 3-D imagery using stereographs in aerial reconnaissance. Camouflaged weapons and structures were difficult to see in conventional aerial photographs, but aerial stereographs enabled military personnel to see through the camouflage and recognize hidden features that only stereoscopic vision could reveal.

To appear as a single 3-D image, the two stereograph pictures must be placed side by side and viewed through a *stereoscope,* a device that simultaneously presents the left photograph to the viewer's left eye and the right photograph to the right eye. The stereoscope consists of two lenses that can be adjusted along a slide bar to be as far apart as the viewer's eyes; the lenses are placed in a raised mount (on collapsible legs) that is positioned about six inches above the central region of the stereo pair. The brain receives each image separately and integrates them into a single 3-D image. The stereoscope has been largely replaced by modern digital imagery and signal processing; most stereographs are now created and displayed electronically.

Video Tracking and Surveillance

Airborne video cameras are increasingly being used by both law enforcement and military units for conducting surveillance of developing situations on the ground or at sea. UAVs provide excellent platforms for these steerable video cameras. For intelligence purposes, such airborne surveillance allows analysts to establish connections between known and unknown targets, determine the time history of those connections, and identify new targets. Airborne video is effective in tracking terrorist or insurgent movements, dealing with proliferation, and monitoring activity at borders and ports.[16]

In typical video surveillance activity, the airborne platform constantly monitors an area and feeds data to the ground for real-time analysis. Most cameras used in video surveillance today have a field of view that is fairly small in order for the camera to have good resolution, which is needed for a good identification of the target and to establish a target signature. The challenge often is to track moving targets over an extended period of time. As the target moves around in the scene, it will sometimes be hidden by buildings or trees. The target has to be reacquired when it emerges. Increasingly this requires automated tracking of the target, followed by using its signature to automatically reacquire the target when it emerges from cover.[17]

Newer video surveillance designs can view a wide area at high resolution. The concept is to use multiple cameras and to optically merge the separate images from them to provide both a wide field of view and high spatial resolution. Such sensors, with a capability to view in both the visible and infrared spectrum, offer the possibility of nonstop surveillance. One such sensor, developed by the Lawrence Livermore National Laboratory, has demonstrated the capability to provide continuous, real-time video imagery of an area the size of a small city with a resolution fine enough to track 8,000 moving objects in its field of view.[18]

Radiometers

The previous sections of this chapter focused on imaging of reflected energy. The other type of imaging used extensively in intelligence relies on radiometry. When used to form an image, it is called *radiometric imaging*; when done in the infrared band, it is specifically called *thermal imaging*. Radiometry does not depend on the presence of an illuminator. It depends on receiving natural energy emissions from a warm target.

As noted earlier, all objects at temperatures above absolute zero emit radiofrequency energy. As the target becomes hotter, both the strength and frequency of emissions increase; very hot objects (for example, a lamp filament or rocket exhaust) radiate in the visible range. Anyone who has seen iron being heated first to red-hot and then to white-hot temperatures has observed the phenomenon of spectral radiation as a function of temperature.

If heated beyond white-hot, the iron can reach blue-hot temperatures. Vehicles or factories that are in use tend to radiate more strongly and at higher frequencies than when idle. The presence of such "hot spots" on a vehicle or building allows conclusions to be made about the nature and status of that vehicle or the use of that building.

Different objects radiate differently. Rock, earth, seawater, and vegetation all have different emission patterns, known as *emissivities*. The concept of emissivity is important in understanding the infrared emissions of objects. Black objects, for example, absorb energy far more rapidly than white objects, as any owner of a black auto knows. Black objects also radiate energy more rapidly than white objects. A perfect emitter is called a *blackbody*. Emissivity is a property of an object that describes how its thermal emissions deviate from the ideal of a blackbody. Two objects at the same physical temperature will not appear to be the same temperature to an infrared sensor if they have differing emissivities.

These three facts—that all objects above absolute zero radiate electromagnetic energy, that energy strength and frequency increase as temperature increases, and that different objects radiate differently—are the basis for radiometric sensing. Sensors that detect and measure the thermal energy are called *radiometers* or *radiometric sensors*.

Radiometric sensors take advantage of the emissivity phenomenon to obtain information about ships, aircraft, missiles, structures, and the environment (the natural background). These passive sensors receive and record the electromagnetic energy that objects naturally emit. The radiometer records the natural energy that is emitted in the infrared or microwave bands by heated objects. Radiometers can be either microwave or IR sensors, and they can be imaging or nonimaging.

MICROWAVE RADIOMETERS

The microwave radiometer records the natural energy that is emitted in the RF band by heated objects. As with IR radiometers, the warmer the object, the more energy it radiates. A good microwave radiometer has an intensity resolution of 1 degree Celsius (that is, it can sense temperature changes of 1 degree Celsius). However, the radiometer typically must view the target for a long period of time, as compared to other types of sensors, and therefore it will have a comparatively poorer search rate at its maximum sensitivity. Microwave radiometers can operate as either imaging or nonimaging.

Microwave radiometers normally use cross-track scanning, as shown in Figure 4-4, but an antenna is used in place of optics. In place of a detector,

FIGURE 4-6 Comparison of Visible and Radiometric Imagery

microwave radiometers mostly use a very sensitive RF receiver, while detectors are increasingly being used in the millimeter wave part of the band.

While microwave radiometers have poorer spatial resolution than IR radiometers, they have a substantial advantage for intelligence use. IR radiometers cannot penetrate clouds, haze, fog, and precipitation. Microwave radiometers can, but their performance can be degraded by precipitation. Many microwave radiometers are designed to receive millimeter wave energy, which provides better resolution than lower frequency band radiometers. As illustrated in Figure 4-6, though, it is not as good as a visual image.[19] The better resolution of millimeter wave radiometers comes at a cost, however, as they are more severely affected by moisture and by atmospheric gases such as oxygen than are microwave radiometers operating at lower microwave frequencies.

INFRARED RADIOMETERS

Infrared imaging radiometers, sometimes called *thermal imagers,* detect emitted radiation in only the thermal portion of the IR spectrum. Remote sensing of energy emitted from the earth's surface in the thermal infrared (3 µm to 15 µm) is different from the sensing of reflected energy. Thermal sensors essentially measure the surface temperature and thermal properties of targets. They use photo detectors sensitive to the direct contact of photons on their surface to detect emitted thermal radiation. The detectors are cooled to temperatures close to absolute zero in order to avoid the noise created by their own thermal emissions.

The temperature resolution of current sensors can reach 0.1°C. For analysis, an image of relative radiant temperatures (a *thermogram*) is depicted in gray levels, with warmer temperatures shown in light tones and cooler temperatures in dark tones.

Optical
Imaging and
Radiometry

Imagery that portrays relative temperature differences across the image is sufficient for most intelligence applications. Actual temperature measurements may be made, but they require accurate calibration and measurement of the temperature references and detailed knowledge of the emissivity of the target, geometric distortions, and radiometric effects. If actual temperature is needed, the sensors employ one or more internal temperature references for comparison with the detected radiation, so they can be related to absolute radiant temperature.

Absorption by atmospheric gases normally restricts thermal sensing to two specific regions: 3 to 5 μm and 8 to 14 μm. [20] In these regions, a photon has less energy than a photon of light in the visible region. Energy decreases as the wavelength increases. Thermal sensors must have larger pixel size to ensure that enough energy reaches the detector in order to allow a valid measurement. Therefore, the spatial resolution of thermal sensors is usually fairly coarse, relative to the spatial resolution possible in the visible and reflected infrared.

Thermal imagery can be acquired during the day or night (because the radiation is emitted rather than reflected) and is used for a variety of intelligence applications. In military reconnaissance, it is used to detect tanks, trucks, aircraft on the ground, and ships at sea—all of which, when operating or having recently operated, are hotter than their surroundings. Nuclear plant activity and many industrial processes result in thermal patterns that can be monitored for intelligence purposes. [21] Infrared imagery also has been explored by some countries as a method of remotely tracking submerged submarines. The technique depends on the tendency of water displaced by the submarine to rise to the surface, creating a wake that has a different temperature from the surrounding ocean that can be detected by infrared sensors. [22]

OVERHEAD PERSISTENT INFRARED SENSING

The most important radiometric sensing technique in intelligence is called *overhead persistent infrared* (OPIR) sensing, which uses a planar array or scanning system similar to those depicted in Figure 4-4 to detect and track intense emissions of IR energy over a large area of the earth. The purpose is to detect, locate, and characterize events of intelligence significance— primarily large explosions and missile launches. For example, using OPIR, explosions in the upper atmosphere and near space can be detected and identified as nuclear with great confidence for yields above about a kiloton. [23] This sensing technique was previously called *overhead nonimaging*

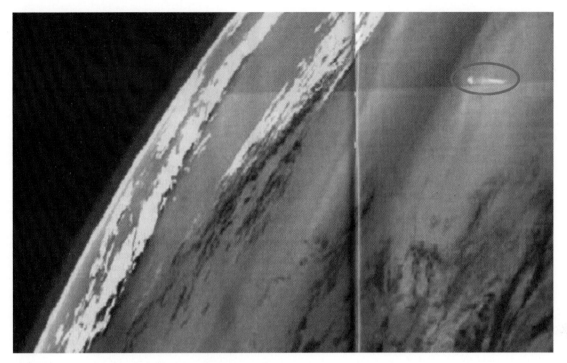

FIGURE 4-7 OPIR Collection of Delta IV Rocket Launch

infrared (ONIR), a term that did not adequately describe the result. Figure 4-7 illustrates the OPIR signature obtained from a HEO satellite of a Delta IV launch on November 4, 2006.[24] The launch vehicle itself is not visible in the picture, but the intense IR plume is clearly visible. As the figure shows, the product of OPIR is an image, though not a high-resolution image.

While OPIR has replaced ONIR as a descriptive term for the sensing technique, it suffers from a similar problem: It does not provide an accurate picture of what the sensor does. Sensors such as the one discussed next can collect very short duration signals, so the term *persistent* does not fully describe what the system can do.

Since the 1960s, the U.S. military has operated its Defense Support Program (DSP) satellites to detect ballistic missile launches or atmospheric nuclear explosions using OPIR. Figure 4-8 shows an artist's conception of the DSP satellite;[25] the optical aperture is the conical tube located in the lower left of the picture. Satellites like this rely on IR to detect and report ballistic missile launches and other infrared events having intelligence significance. The DSP constellation is being replaced by the Space

FIGURE 4-8 DSP Satellite

Based Infrared System (SBIRS). SBIRS reportedly would have higher sensitivity and more accurately estimate the missile location, launch point, and impact point.[26]

In 2009, France launched its own version of the DSP satellite, called Spirale. It is a demonstration system, designed to test the concept of a future space-based operational system for providing the French with an early warning of a missile attack. Two Spirale satellites, launched into a HEO orbit, are collecting imagery in several infrared bands.[27]

BHANGMETERS

Nonimaging radiometers do not create images per se, but they provide spatial as well as intensity information. One nonimaging optical sensor that finds use in intelligence is the *bhangmeter*. This optical radiometer has very good temporal resolution and records light fluctuations with a time resolution of less than a millisecond. It has a specific purpose: detecting atmospheric nuclear explosions. The name "bhangmeter" originated with some of the early skeptics who did not believe such sensing was possible. "Bhang" is a variation of Indian hemp that is smoked for its hallucinogenic impact;

skeptics suspected that anyone who believed such an approach was feasible must have been smoking bhang.

All atmospheric nuclear explosions produce a unique, readily detectable, signature: an extremely short and intense flash, followed by a second much longer and less intense burst of light. The initial flash typically lasts 1 millisecond. The following light burst takes up to several seconds to develop, depending on the size of the explosion, and lasts a comparable period of time.

The U.S. Vela satellites dating from the 1960s carried bhangmeters and other sensors designed to detect nuclear explosions. Controversy about a possible Israeli or South African nuclear test brought notoriety to the program. On September 22, 1979, the bhangmeter on a Vela satellite detected the characteristic double flash of an atmospheric nuclear explosion, apparently over the Indian Ocean or South Atlantic. The onboard bhangmeters were not imaging sensors and could not perform geolocation. The test event was later localized by hydroacoustic data to the Indian Ocean, in the vicinity of South Africa's Prince Edward Island. The characteristics of the bhangmeter signature indicated that it was a low kiloton explosion (approximately 3 kt).[28]

The detection raised the possibility that some nation—particularly South Africa or Israel, or the two in collaboration—had conducted a covert test. A U.S. presidentially appointed panel in 1980 examined the evidence and concluded that the signature did not result from a nuclear test. Many U.S. government officials and scientists have disagreed with the findings of the presidential panel,[29] and the controversy remains unresolved to this day.

Polarimetry

Radiometry is usually thought of as measuring the intensity of electromagnetic energy emitted by an object (or received within one pixel), but it can also involve measuring the polarization of the received signal. In the optical band, such measurements are usually called *polarimetry;* in the RF band, the term *polarimetric radiometry* is commonly used.

Polarimetric imaging measures the polarization of energy in each pixel of an image. This measurement allows an imagery analyst to distinguish between different materials in the image more effectively than simply measuring the intensities.

Natural light, such as light from the sun, has random polarization (as discussed in chapter 1) and is called *unpolarized light*. When such light is scattered from a rough surface—and most natural surfaces are rough—the

light may be weakly and unpredictably polarized. In contrast, when the light is reflected from a relatively smooth surface—and man-made objects often have smooth parts—the light acquires a strong polarization, as Figure 4-9 illustrates. A polarized wave can be linearly polarized, circularly polarized, or some polarization in between (called elliptical polarization). In polarimetric imaging, two linear polarizations—horizontal and vertical—are usually measured.

Polarimetric imaging is useful for penetrating shadows and for detecting weak signature or camouflaged targets, which can be important in intelligence. The U.S. Naval Research Laboratory has demonstrated the effectiveness of polarimetric imaging for these purposes in tactical reconnaissance.[30] Contrast enhancement techniques, discussed earlier, can improve contrast in shadowed regions. Polarimetric imagery is an improved form of contrast enhancement because it provides four distinct images, each containing different contrast information from the others.[31] The four images can be exploited together to obtain more details about shadowed or camouflaged objects.

Polarimetry can also be used with microwave radiometers. Polarimetric radiometry has been developed over the last two decades as a means of measuring wind direction by observing the polarization of microwave emissions from the ocean surface. In January 2003 the Coriolis spacecraft was launched carrying WindSat, the first spaceborne radiometer to be fully polarimetric at

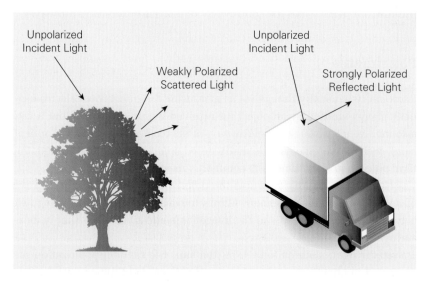

FIGURE 4-9 Polarization Effects of Man-made and Natural Features

18.7, 23.8, and 37 gigahertz (GHz). The WindSat instrument was built for the U.S. Navy, the U.S. National Polar-orbiting Operational Environmental Satellite System, and the U.S. Air Force Space Test Program. The WindSat mission demonstrated the value of passive polarimetry for measuring ocean surface wind direction.[32]

Commercial Imagery

The assumption in this chapter has been that government-owned systems are used to collect imagery for intelligence purposes. The bulk of imagery intelligence is, in fact, derived from such systems. Increasingly, though, imagery from commercial satellites such as GeoEye is being used by intelligence agencies.[33] The quality of such imagery has improved to the point that it can be used by nongovernmental organizations or private citizens to produce useful intelligence, as the following example illustrates.

On September 25, 2008, Somali pirates captured the Ukrainian cargo ship MV *Faina*, which was carrying rocket-propelled grenades, antiaircraft guns, and T-72 tanks, ostensibly for the Kenyan military. The pirates subsequently released the ship after being paid a ransom.

Some observers suspected that Kenya was a transit point, not the final destination for the weaponry. *Jane's Defence Weekly* assigned an imagery analyst to track the movement of the recovered weapons using commercial imagery. The analyst identified the T-72 tanks in DigitalGlobe imagery at the Kahawa Barracks northeast of Nairobi. A subsequent search in imagery of southern Sudan found vehicles parked under camouflage in a Sudan People's Liberation Army compound. The signatures, including tracked-vehicle ground scars, established that the vehicles were tanks—most likely from the Kenyan shipment.[34]

Summary

Optical imaging systems are usually called electro-optical imagers because the incoming optical signal hits a detector array, where it is converted to an electrical signal for transmission and storage. Electro-optical imagers are attractive because they can cover large areas of the earth's surface, with spatial resolutions that are sufficient for obtaining useful signatures and doing imagery interpretation.

Optical sensors are, for all practical purposes, telescopes with cameras attached. The optics focus the incoming energy at a point called the focal

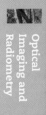

Optical
Imaging and
Radiometry

point. Two dimensions of a telescope (or of any optical system) define its performance: the size of the aperture and the focal length. In order to resolve separate targets, it is necessary to make the ratio of focal length to aperture diameter (the f number) as large as possible. The tradeoff is that increasing the f number both narrows the sensor's field of view and decreases its sensitivity.

An electro-optical imager uses an array of sensitive detectors located in the focal plane that detects incoming light from the entire field of view. The goal is to make the detectors as small as possible (to improve resolution) and as sensitive as possible (to detect weak signals). Each detector collects light energy from a specific resolution cell in the target area, and that light creates one pixel in the resulting image.

Three types of EO imagers are widely used. Simplest is the cross-track scanner, which uses a scanning mirror to focus the light energy from each resolution cell onto a single detector and scans through all the resolution cells in the field of view. Because it spends little time staring at any part of the target area, its sensitivity is poor. A pushbroom imager uses a linear array of detectors to "sweep" the target area as the platform moves, giving it better sensitivity than a cross-track scanner. Most complex and most common is the framing camera, which uses a detector array to provide the best sensitivity of the three.

In order to get an image that is useful for intelligence, at least two processing functions have to be carried out. The first is preprocessing: Radiometric corrections are made to eliminate noise and accurately represent the intensity of features in the image, and geometric corrections remove image distortions. The second is image enhancement, which improves the appearance of the imagery to assist in visual interpretation and analysis by enhancing contrast and enhancing specific spatial patterns such as edges. Processing also can involve using false color in order to display image features that are not in the visible spectrum.

Image exploitation and analysis relies on identifying a unique signature in the image. One example is cratology, the discipline of identifying the contents of a crate by its physical measurements. Exploitation is helped by the use of stereo imagery, which is created by imaging a target area from two different angles to obtain a 3-D image.

Radiometers are used in both the microwave and infrared parts of the spectrum to create images that rely on heat-generated emissions from the target. Infrared radiometers have better resolution, but microwave radiometers can see through clouds and fog. Space-based infrared radiometers are used to detect ballistic missile launches and atmospheric nuclear detonations. Radiometers can measure the polarization as well as the intensity of a signal, and this measurement frequently has intelligence value: Light reflected from a smooth surface such as a vehicle or aircraft runway will be strongly polarized, but light from natural features is randomly polarized.

NOTES

1. National Reconnaissance Office, "Corona Fact Sheet," www.nro.gov/corona/facts.html.
2. Ibid.
3. Ibid.
4. Ibid.
5. Both SPOT and Ofeq are acknowledged to be intelligence collectors by the French (www.spotimage.fr/web/en/1803-defence-intelligence-security.php) and the Israelis (www.haaretz.com/hasen/spages/869771.html), respectively.
6. Jean-Luc Lamard, Catherine Gaudin-Delrieu, David Valentini, Christophe Renard, Thierry Tournier, and Jean-Marc Laherrere, "Design of the High Resolution Optical Instrument for the Pleiades HR Earth Observation Satellites," *Proceedings of the 5th International Conference on Space Optics,* Toulouse, France, March 30–April 2, 2004, 149–156, http://articles.adsabs.harvard.edu//full/2004ESASP.554.149L/0000149.000.html.
7. Airforce-technology.com, "RQ-4A/B Global Hawk High-Altitude, Long-Endurance, Unmanned Reconnaissance Aircraft, USA," www.airforce-technology.com/projects/global/.
8. Helen Anderson, "Edge Detection for Object Recognition in Aerial Photographs," University of Pennsylvania Department of Computer and Information Science Technical Report No. MS-CIS-87-14, 1987, http://repository.upenn.edu/cgi/viewcontent.cgi?article=1634&context=cis_reports.
9. NASA Image of the Day, posted November 8, 2007, http://earthobservatory.nasa.gov/IOTD/view.php?id=8196.
10. Irvine, John M., "National Imagery Interpretability Rating Scale (NIIRS): Overview and Methodology," in Wallace G. Fishell, ed., *Proceedings of SPIE,* 3128 (*Airborne Reconnaissance XXI*), November 21, 1997, 93–103.
11. Northrup Grumman, "Global Hawk Brochure," www.is.northropgrumman.com/systems/system_pdfs/GH_Brochure.pdf.
12. Melissa Kelly, John E. Estes, and Kevin A. Knight, "Image Interpretation Keys for Validation of Global Land-Cover Data Sets," *Journal of the American Society for Photogrammetry and Remote Sensing,* 65, no. 9 (September 1999): 1041–1050.
13. Thaxter L. Goodell, "Cratology Pays Off," *Studies in Intelligence* 8, no. 4 (Fall 1964): 1–10.
14. Ibid.
15. John Diamond, "Trained Eye Can See Right Through Box of Weapons," *USA Today,* August 17, 2006, www.usatoday.com/news/world/2006-08-17-missiles-iran_x.htm.
16. Katie Walter, "Surveillance on the Fly," *Science and Technology Review,* October 2006, Lawrence Livermore National Laboratory, www.llnl.gov/str/Oct06/Pennington.html.

17. Pablo O. Arambel, Jeffrey Silver, and Matthew Antone, "Signature-Aided Air-to-Ground Video Tracking," *Conference Proceedings of the 9th International Conference on Information Fusion*, Florence, Italy, July 10–13, 2006.

18. Walter, "Surveillance on the Fly."

19. M. R. Fetterman, J. Grata, G. Jubic, W. L. Kiser Jr., and A. Visnansky, "Simulation, acquisition and analysis of passive millimeter-wave images in remote sensing applications," *Opt. Express* 16, 20503-20515 (2008), www.opticsinfobase.org/abstract.cfm?URI=oe-16-25-20503.

20. Nicholas M. Short Jr., "The Warm Earth: Thermal Remote Sensing," in NASA Remote Sensing Tutorial, rst.gsfc.nasa.gov/Sect9/Sect9_1.html.

21. Alfred J. Garrett, Robert J. Kurzeja, B. Lance O'Steen, Matthew J. Parker, Malcolm M. Pendergast, and Eliel Villa-Aleman, "Post-Launch Validation of Multispectral Thermal Imager (MTI) Data and Algorithms," U.S. Department of Energy Report #WSRC-MS-99-00423, 1999.

22. Guo Yan, Wang Jiangan, and He Yingzhou, "Detecting the Thermal Track of Submarines by Infrared Imagery," *Wuhan Haijun Gongcheng Xueyuan Xuebao*, June 1, 2002, 89.

23. National Academy of Sciences, *Technical Issues Related to the Comprehensive Nuclear Test Ban Treaty* (Washington, D.C.: National Academy Press, 2002).

24. USAF Briefing, "Infrared Space Systems Wing: Contributions to Transforming Space," November 6, 2007, www.californiaspaceauthority.org/conference2007/images/presentations/071106-1000b-McMurry.pdf.

25. Public domain image from official USAF Web site "Air Force Link," www.af.mil/factsheets/factsheet.asp?id=96.

26. Ibid.

27. "France Accepts Spirale Early Warning System Demonstrator," *Defense Technology News*, May 20, 2009, www.defencetalk.com/france-spirale-space-early-warning-system-19033/.

28. Carey Sublette, "Report on the 1979 Vela Incident," September 1, 2001, http://nuclearweaponarchive.org/Safrica/Vela.html.

29. The National Security Archive, "The Vela Incident: Nuclear Test or Meteoroid?" May 5, 2006, www.gwu.edu/~nsarchiv/NSAEBB/NSAEBB190/index.htm.

30. Rulon Mayer, Richard Priest, Christopher Stellman, Geoffrey Hazel, Alan Schaum, Jonathon Schuler, and Michael Hess, "Detection of Camouflaged Targets in Cluttered Backgrounds Using Fusion of Near Simultaneous Spectral and Polarimetric Imaging," Naval Research Laboratory Report, August 8, 2000.

31. Michael J. Duggin, "Factors Controlling the Manual and Automated Extraction of Image Information Using Imaging Polarimetry," *Proceedings of SPIE*, 382, no. 85, www.personal.umich.edu/~jvalenz/Literature/factors_controlling_manual_and_automated_info_extraction_from_PI.pdf.

32. Karen St. Germain, Peter Gaiser, and Mustafa Bahrain, "Polarimetric Radiometry and Ocean Surface Wind Vector: From Windsat to CMIS," www.ursi.org/Proceedings/ProcGA05/pdf/F10.2(01469).pdf.

33. Richard A. Best Jr., "Imagery Intelligence: Issues for Congress," *CRS Report for Congress: 20*, April 12, 2002.

34. Nathan Hodge, "Sat Marks the Spot, Uncovers Pirate Weapons Haul," *Wired*, July 2009, www.wired.com/dangerroom/2009/07/satellite-uncovers-pirate-weapons-haul/.

5. Spectral Sensing and Imaging

Chapter 4 concentrated on imaging in a single spectral band that creates the simplest type of optical image: a panchromatic image. Black and white film records wavelengths extending over the visible portion of the electromagnetic spectrum, but it conveys no spectral information. The various wavelengths of the visible spectrum are not individually distinguished. Instead, the overall reflectance in the entire visible portion is recorded. The same thing is true for single-frequency radiometric imaging in the infrared and microwave bands. The image records variations in intensity but not variations in intensity across the spectrum. To do that, spectral imaging must be used to provide a rich set of signatures.

The simplest type of spectral image is provided by color film, which conveys some spectral information but does not measure it. Color film is sensitive to the reflected energy over the visible portion of the spectrum, containing more information than panchromatic film. In technical terms, it has higher spectral resolution. For intelligence purposes, it is necessary to look beyond the visible range and examine features in the infrared part of the spectrum. Furthermore, to get a complete signature the intensity of the received energy in various parts of the optical spectrum needs to be measured.

The Optical Spectrum

An introductory overview of the EM spectrum was presented in chapter 2. This chapter will revisit the spectrum in detail in order to clarify how spectral imaging works.

Starting in the millimeter wave band and moving up in frequency toward the optical spectrum, increasingly the atmosphere affects the propagation of EM waves. Figure 5-1 illustrates the absorption that occurs across the EM spectrum. Above the green shaded area in the figure, the atmosphere effectively blocks the passage of EM energy. Below the shaded area, the energy passes through with little loss. In the shaded region, the losses may or may not allow a detector to obtain a readable signal.

At any time a given sensor will only observe a small part of the overall spectrum shown in Figure 5-1. The sensor is designed only to collect radiation within a specific bandwidth or set of narrow bands for a specific purpose. Chapters 1 and 4 discussed the division of the optical spectrum into two major regions—reflective and emissive. Solids and liquids are usually examined in the reflective spectral region from about 0.5 μm to about 2.5 μm. A source of radiant energy—typically the sun—is necessary to produce spectra in this reflective spectral region. The emissive region, which is found at longer wavelengths, is more typically used to examine gases.

The infrared part of the spectrum is subdivided into smaller sections, as discussed in chapter 1. Again, there are no standard divisions. Following are some of the commonly used ways to define divisions:

- Some band definitions characterize the type of signature obtained; an example is the division into emissive versus reflective signatures, as previously discussed. Finer distinctions are sometimes made among types of target signatures—characterizing fires and hot missile exhausts, for example, versus characterizing thermal radiation from a tank engine.
- Some definitions separate the infrared spectrum by the presence of *atmospheric windows*—the regions where the atmosphere is transparent, as indicated in Figure 5-1.
- Some definitions are based on the sensitivity of IR detectors. Different detectors work well in different parts of the band. For example, silicon detectors are sensitive in the visible band and in the IR band to about 1 micron, while indium gallium arsenide detector sensitivity starts around 1 micron and ends between 1.7 and 2.6 microns.

While there is no widely accepted way to define the infrared bands, a frequently used scheme is outlined below and used throughout this book.

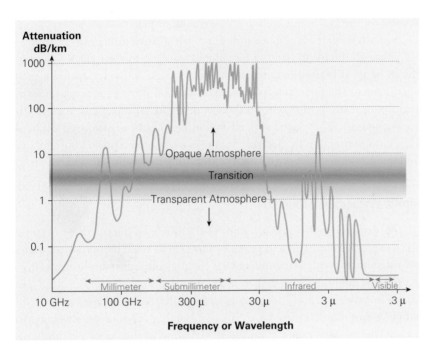

FIGURE 5-1 Atmospheric Attenuation of EM Waves

NEAR-INFRARED BAND

The NIR band is closest to visible light and extends from 0.75 µm to 1.5 µm in wavelength. Night vision devices work in this band. The longer wavelengths in the NIR band reflect uniquely from minerals, crops and vegetation, and moist surfaces; for example, different tree types can be distinguished. The 0.76–0.9 µm part of the band is useful for shoreline mapping. The band is used in imaging to counter the effectiveness of camouflage; poorly designed camouflage reflects differently than the surrounding vegetation. Image intensifiers are commonly used in this part of the spectrum up to about 1 micron; an image intensifier amplifies the weak incoming NIR signal to provide a viewable image in low-light conditions.

SHORT WAVELENGTH INFRARED BAND

The short wavelength infrared band extends from 1.5 µm to 3 µm. Sensors in this band are used to detect the presence of water and for vegetation analysis; oil on water can be recognized and the moisture content of soil and

vegetation can be determined. SWIR signals can penetrate clouds to a limited extent. Detectors are made of indium gallium arsenide or lead sulfide.

Although the SWIR band is considered as being in the reflective part of the IR band, it is used to detect a class of emissions that have intelligence significance. The hot exhausts of ballistic missiles during the boost phase of flight emit a strong signature in this band; explosions also create an SWIR band signature. The overhead persistent infrared sensors discussed in chapter 4 tend to function in this band for characterizing missiles in boost phase and to determine the type of munitions causing an explosion.

MID-WAVELENGTH INFRARED

The mid-wavelength infrared band, also known as *intermediate infrared* (IIR), extends from 3 μm to 8 μm. It is a transition band that produces emissive signatures, with a few reflective signatures of importance. Solar reflectance from bright objects (such as metal roof buildings) is significant in this band. In guided missile technology this is the "heat seeking" region, in which the sensors carried by passive IR homing missiles are designed to work. The missiles home in on the IR signature of the target aircraft, typically the jet engine exhaust plume. This region is also used to characterize the temperature of objects on the earth's surface. For intelligence purposes, it is used to characterize some gaseous effluents.[1] An atmospheric window exists in this band between 3–5 μm, and the detectors indium antimonide and mercury cadmium telluride work in this band.

LONG WAVELENGTH INFRARED

The long wavelength infrared band is a major atmospheric window extending from 8 μm to 15 μm. The region near 10 microns is often called the *thermal imaging region* because objects near room temperature emit more strongly in this region. LWIR sensors use this signature to obtain a completely passive image of the earth based on thermal emissions only, and they require no external light or thermal source such as the sun. This is the primary band used to characterize gaseous effluents for intelligence purposes. *Forward-looking infrared* (FLIR) systems that are mounted on vehicles and aircraft also use this area of the spectrum to view the surrounding region during darkness. Detectors such as mercury cadmium telluride function in this band, but they generally must be cooled to obtain acceptable sensitivity. This band is sometimes also called the *far infrared*, but many definitions treat this as a separate band, as discussed next.

FAR INFRARED

Sometimes called the *very long wavelength infrared* (VLWIR) band, the far infrared band extends above 15 µm to the millimeter wave range. For overhead imaging purposes, the cutoff is around 30 µm, since the atmosphere is opaque at longer wavelengths. Doped silicon detectors are used in this band.

Spectral Imaging

Spectral imaging involves simultaneously acquiring images at different electromagnetic wavelengths in the optical spectrum. Imaging an object at different wavelengths allows intelligence analysts to identify unique spectral "signatures" of targets. The more wavelength bands that are separately acquired and processed in separate images, the more information that can be obtained about targets in the images. As Figure 5-2 indicates, increasing the number of spectral bands allows a progression from detecting a target, to classifying it, and then to identifying a specific object or gas. How this is done is discussed in the following section.

Three classes of spectral images are currently used for intelligence and earth resources sensing; the division is based on the number of distinct spectral bands that can be collected. Most commonly used today are *multispectral images* (MSI), which range from 2 to 100 bands. *Hyperspectral* images

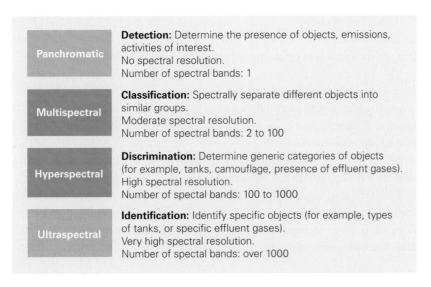

Panchromatic

Detection: Determine the presence of objects, emissions, activities of interest.
No spectral resolution.
Number of spectral bands: 1

Multispectral

Classification: Spectrally separate different objects into similar groups.
Moderate spectral resolution.
Number of spectral bands: 2 to 100

Hyperspectral

Discrimination: Determine generic categories of objects (for example, tanks, camouflage, presence of effluent gases).
High spectral resolution.
Number of spectal bands: 100 to 1000

Ultraspectral

Identification: Identify specific objects (for example, types of tanks, or specific effluent gases).
Very high spectral resolution.
Number of spectal bands: over 1000

FIGURE 5-2 Spectral Imaging Resolution and Levels of Information Obtained

Spectral
Sensing and
Imaging

(HSI) contain between 100 and 1,000 bands, and *ultraspectral* images (USI) contain over 1,000 bands. HSI and USI images contain far more spectral information than MSI images, making them much more information-rich but also more difficult to process and analyze. They have the potential to provide details about an intelligence target that simply cannot be achieved with conventional or MSI imagery. However, processing and analyzing HSI and USI data is a difficult and time-consuming process, often requiring custom software and very expensive expert labor.

HSI and USI signatures are collected by complex sensors that detect hundreds or thousands of very narrow spectral bands throughout the visible, near infrared, and mid-infrared portions of the electromagnetic spectrum. Their very high spectral resolution allows us to discriminate between different targets based on their spectral response in each of these narrow bands. The following section discusses how these sensors work.

HOW SPECTRAL IMAGERS WORK

A spectral image can be thought of as many images combined. To illustrate how the images are created and used to create signatures, consider the simplest type of image—a panchromatic (black and white) image—and select two of the pixels that comprise the image for comparison. The Landsat 7 satellite is the imager in this example, since it has a panchromatic sensor having 15 meters resolution (so that 1 pixel represents approximately a 15 square meter area of the earth). Figure 5-3 shows a Landsat 7 image of the Rocky Mountain National Park in northern Colorado taken on October 5, 1999.[2] Two pixels from an image—one pixel covering an area forested with green fir trees and a pixel that covers a region of light gray-colored clay*—are to be compared.

The two pixels, plotted on a chart of wavelength versus intensity of return, would look like Figure 5-4. In a panchromatic photograph of this scene, the film would record the clay pixel as brighter than the tree pixel; the Landsat 7 panchromatic imager measures this difference in brightness as part of the process of creating the image, but otherwise it does not tell us anything that a photograph could not tell. The vertical scale in the figure measures reflectivity in the reflective band (up to about 2.5 microns).

Landsat 7 also has an imaging spectrometer that provides additional information from the same scene. The incoming reflected or emitted radiation from each pixel is separated into several spectral components that are detected independently. The imaging spectrometer is a pushbroom imager

---

*The box sizes in the image actually contain many 15 × 15 meter pixels, but a larger size box has been used for clarity.

(see Figure 4-4) containing several linear detector arrays. (Figure 4-4 shows an example with a single array.) Each detector array is sensitive to a specific range of wavelengths. It detects and measures the intensity of energy in a specific spectral band, converts the energy to an electrical signal, and then records the received intensity as digital data for subsequent computer processing. Landsat 7 has seven such detectors for each pixel—six covering the visible, near IR, and short wave IR bands with 28.5 meters resolution, and one operating in the LWIR band with 60 meters resolution.

If the Landsat 7 imaging spectrometer is used to measure the returned signal from the two pixels, the result is additional information about the content of the pixels, as illustrated in Figure 5-5.

Three of the detectors shown in the figure cover the panchromatic band that was shown in Figure 5-4. These three detectors cover the following:

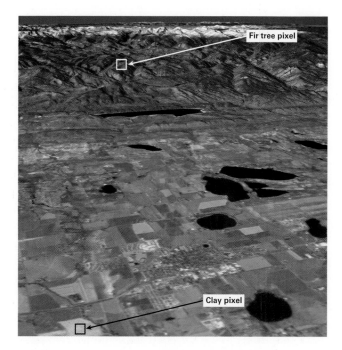

FIGURE 5-3 Two Landsat 7 Pixels in Northern Colorado

- The blue band (.42–.52 microns), which is useful for such things as soil, vegetation, and coastal water mapping. Objects in shadows tend to show up more strongly in this band than in the other visible bands. The blue band also offers the best penetration of clear water.
- The green band (.52–.60 microns), which most effectively depicts the green reflectance of vegetation. This band also can penetrate clear water and provides good contrast between clear and turbid water.
- The red band (.63–.69 microns), which is used for such things as differentiating vegetation based on chlorophyll absorption.

As the figure indicates, the fir tree pixel shows a stronger green signal, with weaker blue and red signals—not an astonishing result from a green tree. The clay surface shows nearly equal returns from all three detectors, which, when combined, give the clay the light gray color that we perceive with our eyes. But all three of the clay spectral components are stronger than even the strong green signal from the tree because the clay is a better reflector at all visible wavelengths.

Spectral Sensing and Imaging

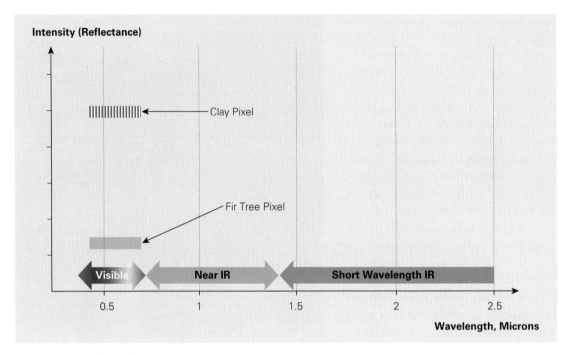

FIGURE 5-4 Comparison of Two Pixels in a Panchromatic Image

So far, no information has been obtained about the scene that a color photograph could not display. But a color photograph pixel only gives the relative strength of the red-green-blue bands. It does not provide the numerical measurements of strength that are essential in creating signatures, as discussed later.

Furthermore, the remaining Landsat 7 detectors provide additional measurements of the two pixels—providing information that is not captured in standard color photography and cannot be discerned by the human eye:

• The NIR detector (.76–.90 microns) provides more information about the reflectivity of vegetation and is useful for distinguishing normal vegetation from camouflage.

• The two SWIR detectors (1.55–1.75 and 2.08–2.35 microns) sense the reflections that are affected by vegetation moisture, by different mineral types, and by snow/cloud reflectance differences.

• The LWIR detector (10.4–12.5 microns) detects thermal emissions from warm objects.

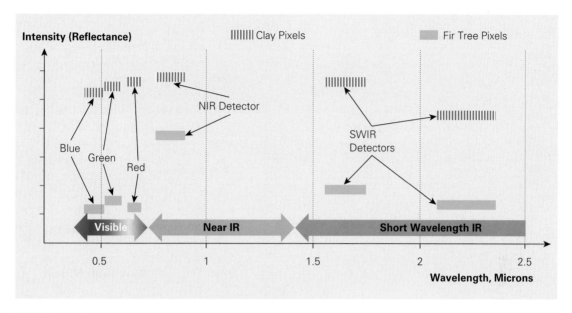

FIGURE 5-5 Comparison of Two Pixels in a Multispectral Image

As Figure 5-5 indicates, the NIR and SWIR detectors receive a stronger return from the clay pixel than from the fir tree pixel because of the higher reflectivity of the clay surface. The LWIR detector's output is not shown.

Spectral Signatures

Although spectral imaging provides an image somewhat like the ones that are commonly seen, the spectral information is what makes it valuable. The more spectral information available, the better defined is the spectral signature and the more accurate is the identification of materials.[3] Spectral signatures, as noted in chapter 2, depend upon the interactions of radiant energy and various materials (solids, liquids, and gases) through processes of scattering, absorption, reflection, and emission. Reflected or emitted radiation is affected by the absorption, reflection, and emissive properties of different materials. Understanding the various interactions allows imagery analysts to identify materials. Spectral interactions typically result in spectral signatures that are uniquely related to the materials involved.

From the different detector readings of the two pixels displayed in Figure 5-5, signatures can be developed and associated with each pixel. This

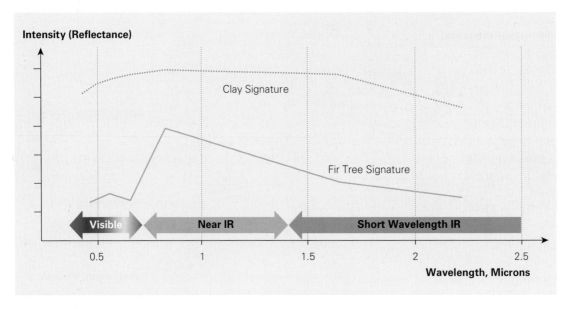

FIGURE 5-6 Spectral Signatures of Two Pixels in a Multispectral Image

is accomplished by drawing a curve (really, a series of lines) to connect each of the measurements shown in the figure. The result is the two *spectral signatures* shown in Figure 5-6. The two signatures are quite different. But the signature from another pixel that included a clay pit would look very similar to the clay pit signature in the figure; the signature from a pixel containing another tree, or even a patch of green grass, would resemble the tree signature in the figure.

The signatures shown in this figure are called *spectral response* curves in the reflective part of the band—"response" because they characterize the reflectance of features or targets over the wavelengths in this part of the band. The curves are usually referred to as *spectral emissivity* curves at wavelengths longer than 2.5 microns because they characterize the emittance of a feature or target over the longer wavelengths.

MULTISPECTRAL IMAGING

The Landsat sensor used to collect data over a variety of different wavelength ranges as shown in the previous figures was described earlier as an imaging spectrometer; it also is called a *multispectral scanner*. It is the most commonly used spectral imager. A multispectral scanner uses either the cross-track scanner or the pushbroom imager, as described in chapter 4, with one major difference: A separate detector or separate linear array of detectors is required to measure each spectral band or channel. During the scan, the energy detected by each separate detector or linear array of detectors is sampled electronically and digitally recorded. Each of these two sensor designs has advantages and disadvantages.

The rotating mirror design of the cross-track scanner is simpler to design and use, and it is easier to calibrate. But the length of time the IFOV "sees" a ground resolution cell as the rotating mirror scans (the dwell time) is quite short, and so the spectral, spatial, and radiometric resolution are relatively poor.

The pushbroom scanner with linear arrays of detectors, combined with the pushbroom motion, allows each detector in an array to measure the energy from each ground resolution cell for a longer period of time (longer dwell time) compared to the cross-track scanner. This allows more energy to be detected and improves the radiometric resolution. The increased dwell time also allows using smaller IFOVs and narrower bandwidths for each detector. The result is finer spatial and spectral resolution without losing radiometric resolution. But the detectors must be calibrated so that the measurements are consistent.

Landsat 7 is typical of the multispectral sensors in use today. It senses radiation in the thermal infrared as well as the visible and reflected infrared portions of the spectrum. Such multispectral sensors are in wide use in the military, intelligence, and commercial communities. Other examples include the Quickbird and Ikonos satellites, each having five bands (blue, green, red, near-infrared, and panchromatic); the Worldview 2 satellite, which has eight multispectral bands ranging from visible through NIR; and France's SPOT 5, which has the standard three visible bands plus an SWIR band.

Multispectral sensors have relatively poor spectral resolution. The spectra cannot be resolved in fine detail. Quickbird, for example, can only "see" in five bands and image in the red, green, blue, and near-infrared regions. It cannot image any other wavelengths. This limits material detection because many of the fine-grain features have been eliminated in the resulting image. However, although specific materials cannot be identified, it is possible to differentiate between materials. It is easy to tell that some materials are different because the spectral signatures are different—even in five bands. To obtain the higher resolution needed to identify specific materials, it is necessary to use HSI or USI.

Despite resolution limitations, multispectral imaging has many uses. It is used extensively in environmental studies, including agriculture,

geology, and bathymetry (the study of sea bottom composition and topography). In agriculture, healthy vegetation can be distinguished from stressed, or dying, vegetation. This capability is useful in intelligence support to drug eradication efforts, as healthy coca or opium poppy crops can be distinguished in multispectral imaging from crops that have been damaged by herbicides.

MSI has a number of other intelligence applications. It is useful for studying the rock structures of the earth, determining mineral composition, and assessing mining operations and underground facilities construction. Bathymetry is useful for maritime intelligence. Knowledge of the ocean depth is used to identify shipping channels and for a number of military applications. These applications generally need a large coverage area and use a commercial or civil satellite such as Landsat, Ikonos, or Quickbird.

HYPERSPECTRAL AND ULTRASPECTRAL IMAGING

Hyperspectral imaging functions much like the multispectral imaging discussed above. But multispectral imaging is characterized by a relatively coarse spectral resolution, as Figure 5-6 shows. As a result, the signatures of different objects are often similar. In the example of Figure 5-6, more specific classes (such as different clay types or different types of trees) could not be distinguished. Two similar objects cannot be differentiated unless their signatures contain many more wavelengths than in this example. This means that a sensor with higher spectral resolution is required. Spectral resolution, as noted earlier, describes the ability of a sensor to define fine wavelength intervals. The finer the spectral resolution, the narrower the range of wavelengths included in a particular channel or band.

Hyperspectral and ultraspectral imagers provide this high spectral resolution by acquiring many more images simultaneously in many narrow, contiguous spectral bands. Each pixel in a scene has an associated spectrum that is substantially more detailed. As a result, hyperspectral and ultraspectral data offer a more detailed examination of a scene than multispectral data, which are collected in broad, widely separated bands.

Figure 5-7 illustrates the difference between the spectral signatures from the two pixels (the fir tree and the clay surface) in the image. Because this is the reflective band, the vertical axis has been labeled as both intensity and the amount of reflectance of the target.

In this hyperspectral image two pixels have been added: a pixel from a limestone deposit located near the clay pit and a pixel from a nearby stand of juniper trees. The clay and limestone pixels have clearly distinct hyperspectral signatures; the same pixels using multispectral signatures would differ only in brightness. A multispectral imager could not distinguish between the two. The case is even more dramatic for the two trees, which look very similar to the human eye. The hyperspectral signatures of the two trees differ very little, and a multispectral imager would detect no difference at all.

For intelligence purposes, the major advantage of hyperspectral imaging occurs in the emissive (MWIR and LWIR) region, especially in detecting, characterizing, and identifying effluent gases. Gases in the emissive region tend to have very narrow, sharply defined spectral features. In contrast to the relatively smooth curves for solid matter shown in Figure 5-7, gas signatures in these bands are jagged, with many sharp peaks and valleys.

High spectral resolution is necessary for the detection, location, identification, and characterization of gases in the LWIR. The designers of a hyperspectral sensor face another tradeoff problem. They want the bandwidth of each detector to be as narrow as possible to obtain a useful signature. If the bandwidth is too broad, the sharp features that make a signature unique shrink and eventually are lost altogether. If the bandwidth is too narrow,

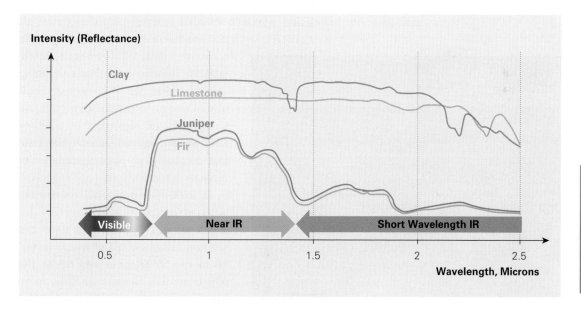

FIGURE 5-7 Spectral Signatures of the Pixels in a Hyperspectral Image

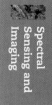

there will not be enough energy (enough photons) for a detectable signal in the band.

A number of hyperspectral sensors have been deployed on aircraft. Most are designed to provide coverage in the visible, NIR, and SWIR bands for earth resources sensing. Typical is the NASA/JPL Airborne Visible/Infrared Imaging System sensor, which collects 224 contiguous spectral bands between 0.4 and 2.5 microns from aircraft platforms.[4]

Airborne hyperspectral imagers operating in the MWIR and LWIR bands have also been developed. These sensors are specifically designed to detect gaseous effluents or objects of intelligence significance. One is the Airborne Hyperspectral Imager, an LWIR hyperspectral imager that collects narrow-band images from 7.5 to 11.5 microns in 256 spectral bands. This sensor was originally designed to detect the presence of buried land mines, relying on the change in infrared absorption features of disturbed soil. This sensor also has been used to detect gas releases and to classify mineral types.[5]

A few hyperspectral sensors have been carried on satellites. In 2000, NASA launched the Earth Observing-1 (EO-1) Advanced Land Imager satellite carrying the Hyperion sensor. Hyperion is a high-resolution hyperspectral imager capable of collecting 220 spectral bands (from 0.4 to 2.5 μm) with a 30-meter spatial resolution. The instrument images a 7.5 km by 100 km land area per image and provides detailed spectral mapping across all 220 channels with high radiometric accuracy.[6] Figure 5-8 is a true color image taken by Hyperion that shows a farming area in Argentina.[7] The spectral signature of one pixel is shown in the figure along with the signatures of a fallow field, vegetation, and water to illustrate that the pixel likely has a combination of these three terrain types.

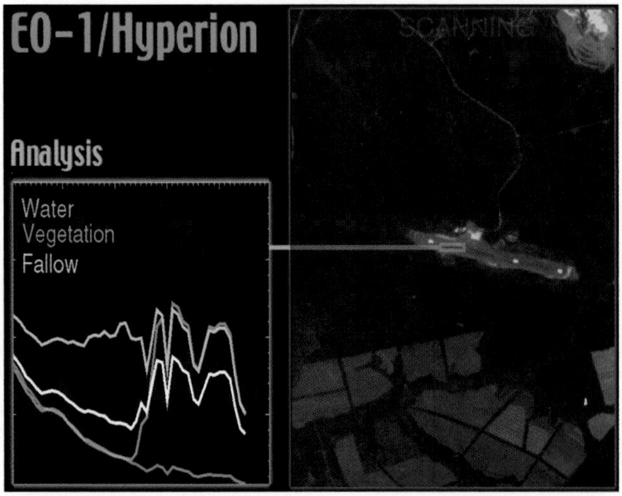

In 2009, Germany was developing a hyperspectral imaging satellite for intelligence use that would have 218 spectral channels, 122 of which would be in the SWIR band and 96 in the NIR band. The German satellite, to be launched in 2012, would have a spatial resolution of 30 meters within a 30 km wide swath.[8]

FIGURE 5-8 Hyperspectral Imagery Collected by the Hyperion Sensor

Ultraspectral sensing is characterized by even higher spectral resolution and narrower bandwidths than HSI. Ultraspectral sensors are still being developed and tested.

Processing, Exploitation, and Analysis of Spectral Signatures

After it has been collected, spectral imagery has to go through the three phases of processing, exploitation, and analysis so that users can make sense of the signatures that have been collected. After processing, the imagery is exploited and analyzed. In these phases, the different classes of features and details in an image are distinguished by comparing their spectral signatures over different wavelength ranges. Exploitation is a complex process, but it is well suited to automated processing techniques. Multispectral, hyperspectral, and ultraspectral images are processed in much the same way, but the signatures produced and the information that can be extracted are different.

PROCESSING

The processing discussed in chapter 4 for imagery has to be done before the spectral processing begins. For example, geometric corrections are used to accurately fit the image to a map of the target area. Then comes a number of processing steps that are unique to spectral imaging. The raw data have to be adjusted using radiometric (intensity) and spectral calibrations prior to exploitation. In order to be useful, the spectral signatures also must be corrected for the effects of the atmosphere on the reflected or emitted radiant energy as it travels between the ground target and the collector.

The importance of this calibration step can be illustrated by an example from the commercial world: People would not want to purchase a digital camera if they could not be assured that the colors in the scene would be faithfully reproduced in the image, and they would generally be displeased if the image were much brighter or darker than expected. Calibration is necessary to ensure faithful reproduction of image intensity and spectral characteristics.

The next step involves a series of image transformations—operations similar in concept to those for image enhancement that were discussed in chapter 4. But the processing is considerably more complex for spectral signatures. Unlike image enhancement operations, which are normally applied only to a single channel of data at a time, spectral image transformations

involve combined processing of data from multiple spectral bands. The images have to be manipulated to combine and transform the original bands into new images that better display or highlight certain features in the scene.

EXPLOITATION AND ANALYSIS

After processing, the raw spectral data have to go through a sophisticated exploitation process in order to translate the narrow-band pixels into a form useful to an analyst. Exploitation depends heavily on computer algorithms that examine spectral information in each pixel to identify and, in some cases, quantify materials—including gases—present in the scene. The spectra are then compared to available signatures in a spectral library (discussed in the next section) for identification.

A standard exploitation technique in searching large geographical areas is called *anomaly detection*. Anomaly detection is commonly used when nothing is known about the scene under surveillance, but collectors are looking for anything that might be out of place (for example, a vehicle partially concealed in a forest or an oil or chemical spill in an otherwise uncontaminated area). Anomaly detection algorithms flag any suspicious areas in a scene and pass those cues to an imagery analyst, a spectral analysis system, or to another sensor for a more detailed look.[9]

Target identification is, in a sense, the opposite of anomaly detection. This technique is used when the analyst is looking for the spectral signature of a specific material of intelligence interest. For example, imagery analysts look for specific chemical effluents in a gas plume when investigating possible WMD production or performing environmental monitoring. The targets, and the processes used for target identification, are different depending on whether an MSI, HSI, or USI sensor is being used. The following sections discuss these targets and processes.

TARGET IDENTIFICATION FOR MULTISPECTRAL SIGNATURES

Different classes of materials such as water and vegetation can usually be separated using very broad wavelength ranges in the visible and near-infrared regions. Multispectral imaging is quite capable of doing this. In addition, MSI from the infrared regions can discriminate features invisible to the naked eye. Specific land features become obvious to the trained analyst. For example, oil-bearing rock appears different from rock having no oil content. Underground structures appear different from the naturally occurring ground surface. Heat generation facilities stand out prominently, as do other mechanical heat producers, such as aircraft and tank engines. Natural substances such as vegetation produce their own unique signatures, as well.[10]

Healthy vegetation appears green in the visible spectrum because it contains chlorophyll, which absorbs blue and red light waves. Stressed vegetation (for example, vegetation with inadequate water or recently cut brush for camouflage) has less chlorophyll and therefore absorbs less of the blue and red light waves, so it appears different when viewed with multispectral sensors. Many countries apply this process to determine healthy crop rotations, assess deforestation around the globe, and obtain information for archeology and urban analysis.[11] Military and law enforcement organizations use multispectral imagery to reveal marijuana crops cultivated under forested canopies because marijuana leaves reflect a different color of green than the surrounding vegetation. Even commercially available visible imagery has been used successfully to identify marijuana fields, and MSI can do such identification more readily than visible imagery.[12]

TARGET IDENTIFICATION FOR HYPERSPECTRAL AND ULTRASPECTRAL SIGNATURES

Hyperspectral and ultraspectral signatures are more challenging to analyze than the MSI signatures described above, as far more detail is contained in the signature. Ultimately, it would be useful to identify the materials in every pixel in a scene; however, doing so would require access to representative spectral signatures for every known material. A database holding all these spectra could conceivably contain millions of spectral signatures.

A more manageable technique for target identification is to filter the data against a target spectrum of interest. All pixels whose spectra match the target spectrum (to a specified level of confidence) are marked as potential targets. The underlying assumption with this approach is that the pixels containing the target are "pure"—that is, the target material fills the entire pixel and is not mixed with any background material.

However, a hyperspectral or ultraspectral image pixel will typically have more than one material present in it. The result will be a composite spectrum for that pixel—that is, a combination of the spectra of each individual material present. The composite spectrum has to be resolved into its individual components, assuming that the spectrum of each pure component is present in the spectral library. For example, a gas plume may be transparent, so any pixel containing the plume will be a mixture of the plume and the ground beneath it. The pixel spectra in this case will not resemble the target spectrum unless the background material can somehow be suppressed.[13]

The objective of target identification is to determine the materials present in the target scene. For example, an analyst tasked with assessing the

Spectral
Sensing and
Imaging

chemical warfare (CW) potential of a production facility within a target country would need to address the following questions about the facility:

- What does the facility produce?
- What process is being used?
- What is the production capacity and rate?
- What is the current facility status?

Detailed hyperspectral signatures can resolve the first question, provided a sufficient number of materials can be identified from the spectral data set to allow identification of the process taking place. In order to identify the process, the analyst needs access to a library of signatures associated with the different processes for the production of the CW agents.

Determining the production capacity and rate usually requires repeated collection from the target facility. The production processes are usually not continuous, as plants typically produce chemicals in batches. As a result, effluents may not be expelled continuously. There may be periods of apparent inactivity for maintenance or other purposes. Establishing the current facility status may require multiple collection passes for the same reasons.

For the proliferation or the arms control analyst, the final step in exploiting a hyperspectral data set is to determine what all this means. Answering the four questions outlined above requires more than simply exploiting hyperspectral data. The analyst must often pull in information from other sources and disciplines. Plant modeling and process simulation may be required in difficult cases.

Signature Libraries

To identify a material in the analysis phase as discussed above, an analyst has to have access to a spectral library. Exploitation and analysis of spectral signatures are not possible without a library of signatures. Such a library has to include each of the signatures shown in Figure 5-7, for example. A library that is useful for intelligence analysis would include a large number of minerals, organic and volatile compounds, vegetation, and man-made materials.

Many spectral libraries are openly available, and they can be useful for assessing vegetation, geology, and common materials. The spectra for camouflage, military metals, and other materials of intelligence significance are typically kept in classified libraries.

But these signatures alone are not sufficient. Analysts might need to distinguish kaolin clay from illite clay, for example, or to distinguish different types of fir trees. Even this level of detail does not solve the problem. Kaolin clay will have different spectral signatures at different temperatures. A healthy fir will have a different signature than a diseased fir or a moisture-starved fir. As a result, to adequately exploit hyperspectral data, the libraries have to be constantly expanded. The existing multispectral libraries are not useful for hyperspectral exploitation.

Getting good hyperspectral signatures is a slow process. Furthermore, getting good signatures on materials of importance for intelligence can be especially challenging. For example, special facilities are needed to get signature data for toxic substances such as nerve agents.

The creation of a spectral library follows the process illustrated in Figure 5-9. For each pixel, an intensity measurement is made at each wavelength (each spectral channel). The result is a set of intensity measurements

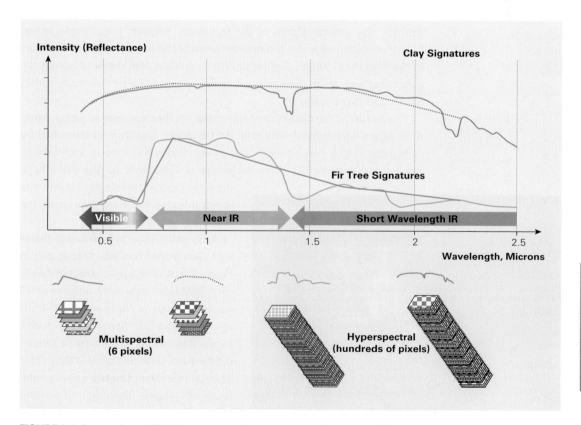

FIGURE 5-9 Comparison of Multispectral and Hyperspectral Signatures of Two Pixels

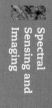

(six for each of the multispectral pixels in the figure, hundreds for the hyperspectral pixels). These are tagged, in this case as clay and fir tree signatures, and retained in the library.

A library of such pixels has to be at the proper spectral resolution, but the proper resolution varies across the spectral band. Signatures behave quite differently in the reflective and emissive bands. Material signatures in the reflective region, as noted earlier, tend to exhibit broad features that generally change very slowly with wavelength. In contrast, the signature can vary rapidly with wavelength in the emissive region, and this complex structure has to be captured for the library. The trick is to get enough spectral resolution in each part of the band—but not too much; greater spectral resolution than needed adds to the size of the spectral data set but does not add to the information content.

Spectral signatures have to be characterized in some way so that they can be searched when placed in a library. One method is to use a three-step characterization. First, a technique called *wavelet analysis* is used to describe the general shape of the signature. Second, a technique called *binary encoding* provides a coarse measure of the major features embedded in the signature. Third, *feature analysis* captures fine detail about all the significant features in the signature, such as position in the spectrum, width, depth, and asymmetry.

The results of the signature characterization then are used to group signatures into a hierarchical structure. An unknown spectrum is identified by comparing it to a very general class of signatures and then to increasingly smaller and more tightly clustered groups of signatures. In this way a large database can be traversed to identify the spectral signature most similar to the unknown spectrum.[14]

Each pixel in a hyperspectral image will have a spectrum like that shown in Figure 5-9. A very large amount of data is contained in a single pixel, and a massive amount of data is contained in a hyperspectral image. A hyperspectral image can be represented in the form of a three-dimensional data set called a *data cube*. The top of a data cube is a conventional image of a region. The depth dimension represents wavelength. An example of a data cube is illustrated in Figure 5-10.[15]

Galileo Group, Inc.

FIGURE 5-10 A Hyperspectral Data Cube

The radiometric intensity of any given pixel at any given wavelength is represented by a color code. The top level image appears as it would to the eye. The layers behind it indicate intensities at increasingly long wavelengths in the infrared bands. The white pavement at the top of the figure, for example, remains bright as one goes through the layers of the cube; the black (water) area to the left of it remains dark in many of the infrared layers.

Summary

Imaging in a single spectral band creates the simplest type of optical image: a panchromatic image. But it conveys no spectral information. The various wavelengths of the visible spectrum are not individually distinguished, and only the overall reflectance in the entire visible portion is recorded. The same thing is true for radiometric imaging in the IR and microwave bands. The image records variations in intensity but not variations in intensity across the spectrum. Spectral imaging, in contrast, records intensity variations and therefore can provide a rich set of signatures.

Spectral imaging is done in the visible and the infrared parts of the spectrum. The IR part is subdivided into bands, but there are no standard divisions for the bands. At any time only a small part is usually of interest because a given sensor is designed only to collect radiation within a specific bandwidth for a specific purpose.

- The NIR band is closest to visible light and extends from 0.75 µm to 1.5 µm in wavelength. Night vision devices work in this band. The longer wavelengths in the NIR band reflect uniquely from minerals, crops and vegetation, and moist surfaces.
- The SWIR band extends from 1.5 µm to 3 µm. The region is used to detect the presence of water and for vegetation analysis based on reflective signatures.
- The MWIR band, extending from 3 µm to 8 µm, is a transition band that produces both emissive and reflective signatures. Solar reflectance from bright objects such as metal roof buildings is significant in this band. This is the "heat seeking" region in which the sensors carried by passive IR homing missiles are designed to work.
- The LWIR band is a major atmospheric window extending from 8 µm to 15 µm. The region near 10 µm is often called the "thermal imaging" region because objects near room temperature emit more strongly in this region. LWIR sensors use this signature to obtain a completely passive image of the

earth based on thermal emissions only. This is the primary band used to characterize gaseous effluents for intelligence purposes.

Spectral imaging involves simultaneously acquiring a number of images at different electromagnetic wavelengths within these bands. Imaging an object at different wavelengths allows intelligence analysts to identify unique spectral "signatures" of targets. The more wavelength bands that are separately acquired and processed in separate images, the more information can be obtained about targets in the images. Increasing the number of spectral bands allows one to progress from detecting a target, to classifying it, and then to identifying a specific object or gas. Most commonly used today are multispectral images, which are available from aircraft and from satellites. Hyperspectral and ultraspectral images, on the other hand, contain far more spectral information than does MSI, making them much more information-rich but also more difficult to process and analyze.

The first step in processing spectral information is to calibrate the raw data from the sensor. Other corrections, such as radiometric and spectral calibrations, must also be applied to the data set. The raw data must be georectified—that is, accurately fit to a map of the target area. In order to be useful, collected spectral signatures also must be corrected for the effects of the atmosphere on the reflected or emitted radiant energy as it travels between the ground target and the collector. The next processing step is image transformation, which takes nonvisible bands and translates them to the visible, usually through the use of false color. Image transformation also highlights features of intelligence interest.

In the exploitation phase, the different classes of features and details in an image are distinguished by comparing their responses over distinct wavelength ranges. To do this, an analyst has to have access to a spectral library. Exploitation and analysis of spectral signatures is not possible without a library of such signatures. A library that is useful for intelligence analysis would include a large number of minerals, organic and volatile compounds, vegetation, and man-made materials. The spectra for camouflage, military metals, and other materials of intelligence significance are typically kept in classified libraries.

NOTES

1. Alfred J. Garrett, Robert J. Kurzeja, B. Lance O'Steen, Matthew J. Parker, Malcolm M. Pendergast, and Eliel Villa-Aleman, "Post-Launch Validation of Multispectral Thermal Imager (MTI) Data and Algorithms," U.S. Department of Energy Report #WSRC-MS-99-00423, 1999.

2. NASA image posted on April 4, 2001, at http://earthobservatory.nasa.gov/IOTD/view.php?id=1311.

3. "Abacus: Hyperspectral Image Processing," www.saic.com/abacus/.

4. Jet Propulsion Laboratory, "AVIRIS Airborne Visible/Infrared Imaging Spectrometer," http://aviris.jpl.nasa.gov/.

5. Paul G. Lucey, Tim J. Williams, Michael E. Winter, and Edwin M. Winter, "Two Years of Operations of AHI: A LWIR Hyperspectral Imager," *Proceedings of SPIE,* 4030, no. 31–40, www.higp.hawaii.edu/~winter/pubs/Two%20years%20of%20operations%20of%20AHI%20a%20LWIR%20hyperspectral%20imager.pdf.

6. USGS: "Earth Observing 1 (EO-1) Sensors—Hyperion," http://eo1.usgs.gov/hyperion.php; *Space Daily,* "EO-1 Offers First Hyperspectral Imager," January 17, 2001, www.spacedaily.com/news/eo-sats-01b.html.

7. NASA imagery, http://earthobservatory.nasa.gov/IOTD/view.php?id=1420.

8. "Germany Contracts for Hyperspectral Satellite," *Aviation Week & Space Technology,* November 17, 2008, 17.

9. Edward Ashton, Brian Fianagan, and Sherry Olson, "Analyzing Hyperspectral Data," The Edge (MITRE Corporation publication), September 1999, vol. 3, no. 3, p. 1, www.mitre.org/news/the_edge/september_99/first.html.

10. W. F. Belokon, M.A. Emmons, W. H. Fowler, B. A. Gilson, G. Hernandez, A. J. Johnson, M. D. Keister, J. W. McMillan, M. A. Noderer, E. J. Tullos, and K. E. White, *Multispectral Imagery Reference Guide* (Fairfax, Va.: Logicon Geodynamics, Inc., 1997), 2–8.

11. Belokon et al., 2–5, 6.

12. Associated Press, "Swiss Police Spy Marijuana Field with Google Earth," January 29, 2009, www.breitbart.com/article.php?id=D960T7180&show_article=1.

13. Ashton, Fianagan, and Olson, "Analyzing Hyperspectral Data."

14. Ibid.

15. Galileo Group, "Applied Spectral Imaging Sample Gallery," March 2007, www.galileo-gp.com/home.html.

Spectral
Sensing and
Imaging

6. Active Sensing: Radar

The term *active sensing* usually means radar. In contrast to the passive sensors discussed in the previous chapters, radars produce their own illumination energy. This feature gives radars some advantages in technical collection. For example, they operate day or night, not needing the sun to reflect energy off an object. Radars that operate in the microwave band can function in all forms of weather, except for severe weather conditions, such as heavy rain squalls. While cloud cover mostly blocks IR and visible sensors, it does not affect microwave radar views of a target.

Radars have a wide range of civil and military applications. Most radars are used to geolocate a target and track its movement. Examples include commercial air traffic radars, naval ship surface and air search radars, and air defense radars. Surface-based radars are used to search the sky (or the surface, at relatively short ranges) and track targets such as ships, aircraft, or satellites. Most airborne and spaceborne radars are used to map the earth's surface, detecting and tracking targets of interest on the surface. Airborne radars also search the sky for weather or other aircraft.

Radar therefore is used for a number of purposes, most of which have nothing to do with intelligence. If radar data are used for immediate operational purposes and then discarded, then it is considered operational information, not intelligence. As examples, air traffic control radars and ship and aircraft navigational radars fall in this category; the information has little value later. If the radar data are collected and retained for its value beyond the moment, then it can be either for intelligence or scientific research. Most aircraft and satellite imagery, for example, is used for either intelligence or research.

The distinction between operational military use and intelligence use can be difficult to draw, and the two uses often overlap. For example, radar tracks of a hostile aircraft or ship usually have little value after the mission is over. However, if the aircraft or ship is a new version, not previously seen, then the radar tracking data are likely to contain valuable intelligence information about the performance of the ship or aircraft, and the intensity of the radar return might tell something about the use of antiradar (stealth) technology. Some general rules of thumb concerning radar use are as follows:

- Searching for and tracking aircraft or ships is mostly operations but can also be intelligence.
- Searching for and tracking ballistic missile reentry vehicles (R/Vs) that are being used in conflict is operations, but the same tracking of R/Vs that another country is testing is intelligence.
- Searching for and tracking another country's satellites is intelligence when the information is used to determine the satellite's mission; the same information, when used to avoid satellite collisions, is operations.
- Imaging the earth's surface can be intelligence, scientific research, or operations, depending on how the data are used.

As an example of the last rule of thumb, the JSTARS aircraft carries an imaging radar that provides details about targets moving in the scene. The movement information could be used for targeting moving vehicles such as tanks and trucks in combat situations, and so would be considered operations. However, information about such movements could also be used to get a general picture of enemy intentions, and so would have intelligence value. Clearly, there is overlap between the two: The same radar can be used for both operations and intelligence collection simultaneously.

How Radar Works

A radar transmitter generates EM waves that radiate from an antenna that "illuminates" the air or space with radio waves. A target that enters this space, such as an aircraft, scatters a small portion of this radio energy back to a receiving antenna. This returned signal is amplified by an electronic amplifier, processed, and displayed for a radar operator. Once detected, the object's position, distance (range), and bearing can be measured. As radio waves travel at a known constant velocity (the speed of light—300,000 km/sec or 186,000 mi/sec), the range may be found by measuring the time it takes for a radio wave to travel from the transmitter to the object and back to the receiver. For example, if the range were 186 miles, the time for the round trip would be $(2 \times 186) / 186,000$ = two-thousandths of a second, or 2,000 microseconds. Most radars are pulsed, meaning that the radiation is not continuous but is emitted as a succession of short bursts, each lasting a few microseconds. An electronic timer measures the time delay between pulse transmission and the returned signal and calculates the target range.

Radars also provide moving-target indication by observing the Doppler shift in frequency when RF energy is reflected from a moving target. The Doppler shift is an important part of the target signature. It is used in many ways in technical collection and is essential to the functioning of imaging radar, to be explained in chapter 7.

RADAR FUNCTIONS

Most radars are optimized for one of the functions discussed below.

Search radars transmit a beam that is scanned across a volume of space to detect targets. The beam "blankets" the volume with radar energy. Airport surveillance radars are of this type: the beam from the radar is rotated so it scans 360 degrees in azimuth to monitor air traffic in the immediate area. The Giraffe surveillance radar shown in Figure 3-13 is an example of a search radar designed to monitor air activity over a battlefield.

Tracking radars keep the beam on a target (usually a target detected by a search radar) to follow or track the target throughout the radar's volume of coverage. The radar transmits a single beam of radar energy out toward the target. The energy is reflected off the target and returned to the radar receiver for measurement of both range and angle to the target. The transmitter then sends out another beam of radar energy, and the cycle repeats itself as the radar follows the target throughout its coverage. The radar provides the precise location of the target and, based on target movement between pulses, predicts the future position of the target. Surface-to-air missile systems have specific radars designed to track aircraft targets and to guide missiles to the target.

Imaging radars create a picture of the target. Some aircraft radars create an electronic map of the earth's surface that is used for navigation. Some imaging radars are specifically designed to create high-resolution images. These radars, known as synthetic aperture radars (SARs), are discussed in detail in chapter 7.

Target measurement radars serve a variety of purposes. Some, such as radar altimeters, are used by aircraft to measure the aircraft's altitude above the earth. Some obtain signatures by measuring the physical characteristics of an airborne or spaceborne target in order to identify the target. These target identification radars are discussed in chapter 9.

Some radars can perform two or more of the roles discussed above and are known as *multifunction radars*. Fighter aircraft radars, for example, are multifunction radars; they can track an aircraft while simultaneously searching for other aircraft in the area. The Cobra Dane radar, previously discussed and shown in Figure 3-12, is another example of a multifunction radar. It can search for targets, track them, and obtain target measurements by changing its mode of operation.

RADAR DESIGN

The basic radar consists of a transmitter, antenna, receiver, signal processor, and display. Most radars use the same antenna for transmission and reception of signals. A few radars, called *bistatic radars,* have the transmitter and receiver widely separated in order to obtain a different target signature or to defeat jamming.

Early radar designs were simple by today's standards. The transmitter produced a single pulse; the antenna transmitted the pulse in a single beam; and the receiver, which had the same basic design as a communications receiver, received the echo from the target and displayed the target's range on a cathode ray tube. The process was repeated, again and again, as the antenna moved to search a volume of space. Today's radar designs differ in all these components, but the biggest difference is in the receiver and signal processor.

Modern radar receivers digitize the returned signal, transforming it into a series of bits that can be processed in several different ways to extract more information about the target signature than was possible with previous generation radars. These digital receivers allow the detection of weak target returns and the determination of target position, movement, and configuration. The receivers allow the radar to operate in different modes; depending on the nature of information desired about the target, the radar can change its pulse shape and modulation, transmitting the pulses in different directions and at different pulse repetition rates. The digital receiver processes all the received data and automatically extracts the desired information.

To handle all this information, antennas have evolved into new configurations. Most radars continue to use some variant of the familiar parabolic antenna, which shapes the RF energy into a beam. However, the disadvantage of the parabolic antenna is that it must be mechanically moved to detect or track a target.

Increasingly, radars use phased array antennas instead of parabolic antennas. Rather than move the antenna mechanically, the phased array steers radar energy electronically. In a phased array there are many thousands of small antenna elements placed on a flat structure. If the signals from the separate elements are released at the same time and in phase, they form a radar beam where the beam direction is perpendicular to the array face. To detect objects that do not lie directly in front of the array face, devices that shift the phase of the signal reaching the antenna elements are used. These phase shifters change the direction in which waves leave or enter the antenna and thereby control the direction of the main beam.

Since phased array radars have several thousand antenna elements, multiple beams can be formed in rapid sequence or even at the same time. Thus, a phased array radar is capable of simultaneously tracking several hundred targets, since a computer calculates the proper target measurements for each of these beams. Phased array radars have several advantages. They are inherently multifunction. They can both search for and track many different objects at the same time. However, phased arrays have two major disadvantages: the high cost of building them and the high maintenance costs.

Radar Frequency Bands

Radars operate in designated blocks of frequency bands. The International Telecommunications Union (ITU) has assigned specific frequency blocks for radar throughout the very high frequency (VHF), ultra high frequency (UHF), and microwave bands. The U.S. military and the Institute for Electrical and Electronics Engineers (IEEE) have assigned much broader frequency bands to the same designators, as Table 6-1 illustrates. However, the ITU bands more precisely describe where radars actually operate throughout most of the world. U.S. radars normally operate within the ITU designated frequencies. A few countries, such as Russia, operate radars outside the ITU bands, so the broader band IEEE and military designators have some utility.

The V band designation in Table 6-1 is notable because radars in this band cannot detect targets at any distance in the earth's atmosphere. As Figure 5-1 showed earlier, this frequency band is characterized by strong attenuation created by the presence of molecular oxygen; more than nine-tenths of the energy transmitted by the radar is absorbed by oxygen in a distance of

TABLE 6-1 Radar Frequency Bands

Radar Band Designation	International Telecommunications Union Frequency Bands	IEEE and Military Frequency Bands
HF	—	3–30 MHz
VHF	138–144 MHz; 216–225 MHz	30–300 MHz
UHF	420–450 MHz; 890–942 MHz	300–1000 MHz
L	1215–1400 MHz	1–2 GHz
S	2.3–2.5 GHz; 2.7–3.7 GHz	2–4 GHz
C	5.250–5.925 GHz	4–8 GHz
X	8.50–10.68 GHz	8–12 GHz
K_u	13.4–14.0 GHz; 15.7–17.7 GHz	12–18 GHz
K	24.05–24.25 GHz; 24.65–24.75 GHz	18–27 GHz
K_a	33.4–36.0 GHz	27–40 GHz
V	59.0–64.0 GHz	40–75 GHz
W	76.0–81.0 GHz; 92.0–100.0 GHz	75–110 GHz

one kilometer. The V band might be useful, however, for a very short-range radar because the radar could not be detected by ELINT receivers at any distance. V band is also useful for spaceborne radars because such radars cannot be detected from the earth.

Following is a discussion of some radars that have been used for intelligence purposes in the various frequency bands. The radars divide into two general classes: *over-the-horizon* (OTH) radars that can see targets beyond line-of-sight and radars that are limited to line-of-sight operation.

OVER-THE-HORIZON RADAR

OTH radar operates in or near the high frequency (HF) band, where radio waves are reflected from the ionosphere—the phenomenon that allows international radio broadcasts to be received from stations thousands of miles away. Conventional radars operate at line of sight, meaning that they cannot see targets close to the earth's surface at long distances. In contrast, OTH radars bounce signals off the ionosphere to see around the earth's curvature, making it possible to conduct radar surveillance of otherwise inaccessible regions. For intelligence purposes, OTH radars have the advantage of monitoring targets that are moving at substantial distances inside a country and providing almost continuous surveillance at very long ranges. They also can monitor ship movements, and a single radar can monitor a very large area of the earth. But such radars are expensive to build and tricky to operate. They depend on the ionosphere, which is a continuously changing reflector. The operating band is very noisy; the band has many interfering signals, and an HF radar has no reserved frequencies (as Table 6-1 indicates). The radar gets intense clutter from the backscattered ground return, from which the desired signal has to be separated. These problems require the design of a radar with a very large antenna, very high power, and sophisticated signal processing. Two such radars that the United States has used for intelligence are Cobra Mist and the Air Force's FPS-118 (OTH-B).

The FPS-95 OTH radar, code-named Cobra Mist, was built on the English North Sea Coast in the late 1960s to monitor air and missile activity in Eastern Europe and the western areas of the USSR. The FPS-95 was expected to detect and track aircraft in flight over the western part of the Soviet Union and the Warsaw Pact countries, as well as missile launches from the USSR's Northern Fleet Missile Test Center at Plesetsk. The radar operated in the frequency range from 6 to 40 MHz.

The FPS-95 was one of the largest, most powerful, and most sophisticated OTH radars of its time, and the OTH radar community expected it to set new standards for performance and capability. It was designed to detect and track aircraft movements and missile launches at ranges of 500 to 2,000 nautical miles, corresponding to one bounce off the ionosphere. A searchlight mode was provided for high-priority targets whose approximate locations were known *a priori*. These targets could include single aircraft, compact formations of aircraft, or missile launches.

The key to this radar's performance, as with any OTH radar, was to separate target returns from the strong ground clutter. However, the detection performance of the radar was spoiled from the beginning by noise that appeared at all ranges where ground clutter* was present. The sophisticated signal processors were unable to separate targets from what became known as "clutter-related noise."

---

*Any radar that observes the earth's surface must deal with "clutter"—unwanted signals returned from the ground or water surface. The clutter return often is strong enough to conceal the targets of interest. Radars also encounter clutter from weather phenomena, such as rain.

Experiments performed at the site failed to uncover the source of the noise. The noise appeared to be associated with imaging of land areas and not of sea surfaces. The possibility of electronic countermeasures was considered and not ruled out. After many attempts to locate the source of the noise and correct the problem, the radar program was terminated in June 1973 and the equipment removed from the site or allowed to deteriorate. The cause of the noise is still unknown.[1]

OTH-B, the U.S. Air Force's over-the-horizon-backscatter air defense radar system, was the largest radar system in the world in terms of earth coverage. Six OTH-B radars were built over a 25-year period starting in 1970 and deployed to monitor aircraft traffic approaching the United States. Three radars located in Maine monitored traffic over the north and south Atlantic Ocean and the Caribbean Sea. Three radars located in Oregon and California monitored traffic over the North and South Pacific Ocean.

The OTH-B program suffered from an accident of timing. The Cold War ended shortly after the radars were deployed. The three OTH radars on the West Coast were mothballed. The three radars in Maine were redirected to counternarcotics surveillance—specifically, to detect aircraft approaching the United States across the Gulf of Mexico. The OTH-B tracking data were transmitted directly to Department of Defense (DoD) and civilian law enforcement agencies that were responsible for counternarcotics operations. The East Coast radars formally ceased operations in October 1997.[2]

Figure 6-1 illustrates the breadth of area coverage that OTH-B provided. The very large area that an OTH radar can surveil is one of this radar's major advantages. The disadvantage is that the target must move in order to be distinguished from clutter—but most targets of intelligence interest, over water at least, move.

At closer ranges, but still beyond the visible horizon, radars also can be designed to operate as *surface-wave radars.* Customarily, such radars are used to detect and track oceangoing ships or low-flying aircraft at ranges up to a few hundred kilometers. Though they are called OTH radars, these radars do not bounce their signals off the ionosphere. Instead, the radar signal travels along the sea surface, is reflected from obstacles such as ships, and returns to the receiver antenna. Australia has deployed one such radar, called the Surface-wave Extended Coastal Area Radar (SECAR), in Northern Australia. SECAR makes use of separate transmission and reception sites and is designed to provide coastal surveillance, economic asset protection, smuggling deterrence, weather/storm monitoring, illegal immigration monitoring, and seaborne traffic control.[3]

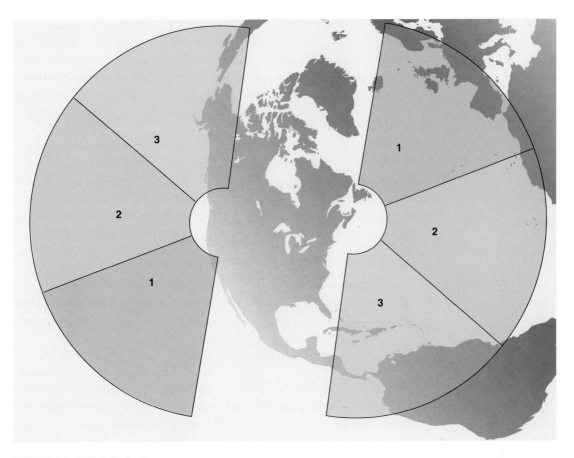

FIGURE 6-1 OTH-B Radar Coverage

LINE-OF-SIGHT RADARS

Most radars operate at frequencies higher than HF and, because they cannot see targets below the horizon, are called *line-of-sight radars*. Following is a discussion of the main line-of-sight radar operating bands, with some examples of radars used for intelligence that operate in the VHF and higher frequency bands. This is an illustrative list of such radars and does not include all radars used for technical intelligence.

VHF. Radars operating in the two standard VHF bands (138–144 and 216–225 MHz) are usually designed for long-range search. Formerly these bands were used for airspace search, but now the most common application of

VHF radars—at least in intelligence—is for ballistic missile and satellite detection and tracking. These radars typically use large antennas (although smaller than those used in the HF band). A major disadvantage is that, like the HF band, the VHF band is quite crowded with other signals and generally very noisy.

The French Graves is an example of a VHF radar used in intelligence. It was specifically designed for space surveillance. It has a novel design: a bistatic radar, meaning that the transmitter and receiver are spatially separated. The Graves transmitter is located near the Dijon Air Base in eastern France. The receiver is located on the Albion Plateau in southern France, some 400 kilometers away. The transmitter electronically scans a volume of space continuously using a VHF signal. The receiver scans the same volume of space, detecting satellites and estimating the satellite velocity and direction from the Doppler shifted return. The radar reportedly can detect objects in orbit at an altitude of between 400 and 1,000 km.

The Graves radar became operational in November 2005. Since then, it has been keeping a database of some 2,000 satellites up to date. According to the French, Graves has tracked a few dozen "sensitive" satellites for which the United States does not publish orbital elements.[4]

UHF. The UHF radar bands (420–450 and 890–942 MHz) are used to operate radars similar in design and purpose to those in the VHF band. The UHF band, though, encounters less noise and interference. The UHF band is defined as extending from 300 to 3,000 MHz, which includes the radar L and S bands that are discussed below, but by convention the term "UHF radar" only is used to denote a radar operating in these two lower bands.

Figure 6-2 is a picture of the FPS-85 radar, located in Florida.[5] It is an example of a radar dedicated to perform space surveillance, which includes searching for, detecting, tracking, and reporting objects in space. The FPS-85 operates at 442 MHz.

This radar was built in 1961. It was developed as a scientific experiment because it was the first phased array radar of such size and power. Destroyed

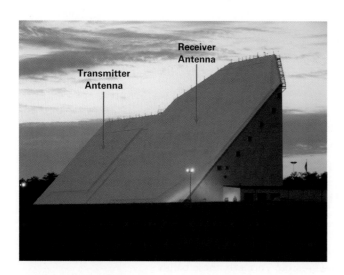

FIGURE 6-2 FPS-85 Radar

by fire in 1965, the facility was brought back on line in 1969 and has operated continuously day and night since then.

The radar has a database of more than 7,000 satellites and space debris,
and it tracks these objects as they enter the radar's coverage area. It makes
about 20,000 observations each day and relays the time, elevation, azimuth,
range, and range rate data on each object to the NORAD facility at Cheyenne
Mountain, Colorado. It can observe deep space objects out to the range of
geosynchronous orbiting satellites—up to 37,500 kilometers—and can track
200 near-earth targets simultaneously.

The FPS-85 is well-suited for space surveillance. Its location and its main
beam boresight at 180 degrees in azimuth (due south) and 45 degrees elevation angle above the horizon allow it to achieve excellent coverage of space.[6]
In chapter 3, it was noted that the Cobra Dane radar, located and aimed to
accomplish a specific intelligence mission, could not collect intelligence
about satellites that have some orbits. The FPS-85, in contrast, is optimized
to obtain orbital information about satellites in all orbits.

Note that the FPS-85 has two antennas, one for transmitting and one for
receiving. This does not make it a bistatic radar, as is the Graves radar discussed previously. A bistatic radar has its antennas separated by a distance
comparable to the distance from the radar to its targets, usually on the order
of several hundred kilometers. The use of two antennas in the FPS-85 sim-
plifies the RF hardware design and allows the radar to both search and track
more efficiently.

L Band. The 1215–1400 MHz band is heavily used worldwide for air surveillance, but it also finds intelligence uses for ballistic missile and satellite
detection and tracking. It is a good compromise band: high enough in frequency to avoid the noise and interference effects of lower frequencies but
low enough that high power search radars can be built at a reasonable cost.

Cobra Dane was described briefly in chapter 3. It is a phased array radar,
officially designated the FPS-108. The radar was built in 1977 on the island
of Shemya, Alaska. Cobra Dane operates in the 1215–1400 MHz band. It uses
a narrow bandwidth signal for target acquisition and tracking, and uses a
wide bandwidth (200 MHz) signal for signature analysis of ballistic missile
reentry vehicles and satellites.[7]

The FPS-108 has the primary mission of technical intelligence collection. It is used to track and collect precise radar signature data on Russian
ICBM and SLBM test launches directed toward the Kamchatka impact
area and the North Pacific. It detects, tracks, and catalogs satellites at
ranges up to 40,000 km. Cobra Dane also has an operational mission; it

provides early-warning and attack assessment for missiles that would impact the continental United States.[8]

S Band. The two S bands (2.3–2.5 and 2.7–3.7 GHz) are used both for air search radars and target-tracking radars. These radars tend to have smaller antennas than L band radars, so they are often mobile. Both mobile ground-based and shipboard radars make use of the band.

An example of an S band radar used in intelligence is the Cobra Judy radar, which was described briefly in chapter 3 (see Figure 3-9). This radar uses a phased array antenna mounted on one face of a nearly cubical rotating turret that houses the transmitter and microwave circuitry. The radar's primary mission is to collect precise data against strategic ballistic missiles to verify compliance with arms control treaties. A secondary mission is to collect data for U.S. missile development and theater missile defense systems testing. The S band radar detects and tracks targets using a narrow bandwidth transmission, and it classifies or identifies targets using a wide bandwidth transmission. It uses a wide repertoire of signal waveforms to aid in target discrimination and analysis.[9]

C Band. Radars in the 5.25–5.925 MHz band typically are tracking radars designed to provide very precise tracking. Radars in this band also are commonly used for fire control (that is, to track ship or aircraft targets for missile batteries).

ALCOR, a satellite and ballistic missile tracking radar, is one of three space surveillance radars located at Kwajalein Island in the South Pacific. The other two radars are the ARPA Long-range Tracking and Identification Radar (ALTAIR) and the TRADEX (Target Resolution and Discrimination Experiment). ALCOR is a high-power, narrow-beam tracking radar. It uses a narrowband (6 MHz bandwidth) pulse for tracking targets and a wideband (512 MHz bandwidth) pulse for obtaining images of targets. The wideband waveform provides a range resolution of approximately 0.5 meters. These high-resolution data, coupled with advanced radar signal processing, support the rapid generation of the satellite images. The images are used to identify and characterize space objects and to assess spacecraft health and mission status.[10]

X Band. The 8.5–10.68 GHz band has traditionally been used for precision tracking radars; it was not considered a good band to do long-range searches because the typical radar antenna is rather small (on the order of 1 meter to a few meters in size) and getting the high power needed for long-range search was not easy. Newer radar designs in this band, such as the X-band radar shown in Figure 6-3, have obviated this traditional perception; to get the high power, the X-band radar uses a phased array containing 22,000 modules, each having its own transmitter.

The sea-based X-band radar is a floating, self-propelled, mobile radar station designed to operate in high winds and heavy seas. It is part of the U.S. government's ballistic missile defense system. The radar can detect and track ballistic missiles and satellites at long ranges. Its operation at X band, around 10 GHz, allows it to transmit a wide bandwidth signal, obtain high resolution of tracked objects, and consequently obtain very detailed signatures. The signatures enable the radar to discriminate an R/V from decoys, the rocket body, and debris.[11]

FIGURE 6-3 The X-Band Radar at Sea

The X-band radar was designed to be mobile to allow mission flexibility. As noted earlier in the examples of the Cobra Dane and FPS-85, these two radars have a fixed location and antenna orientation that is advantageous for their design missions, but their spatial coverage is also fixed. Cobra Dane, for example, can cover Russian missile tests but is not well positioned to cover North Korean missile tests.

Laser Radars

Laser radars operate much like microwave radars. The radar transmits pulses of laser light and detects energy reflected from the target. As with microwave radars, the time required for the energy to reach the target and return to the sensor determines the distance between the two. Unlike microwave radars, laser radars cannot penetrate clouds. But the laser radar's big advantage is that its beam is very narrow, so it can illuminate an extremely small surface (on the order of 1 cm diameter at short ranges, less than 1 meter at aircraft-to-ground distances).

Another major advantage of laser radars is that they can transmit very short pulses and measure distance to a high degree of precision. For this reason, laser radar finds use in measuring the height of features (such as forest canopy height relative to the ground surface). It is also used in atmospheric studies to examine the particle content of various layers of the earth's atmosphere, acquire air density readings, and monitor air currents.

An important intelligence application of laser radar is in exploiting the phenomenon of fluorescence. Some targets fluoresce, or emit energy, upon receiving incident light energy. This is not a simple reflection of the incident radiation. In practice, a laser illuminates the target with a specific wavelength of radiation. A sensor carried with the laser is capable of detecting multiple wavelengths of fluoresced radiation. When the target is irradiated, it absorbs the laser energy; its molecules, atoms, or ions are excited and emit energy at longer wavelengths. The emission of longer wavelength radiation is then measured by the sensor, and the wavelength of the emitted radiation provides a characteristic signature of the target material. The technique relies on much the same spectral sensing process that was discussed in chapter 5.

Many chemical and biological agents, and spoil from excavations, have characteristic fluorescence spectra when exposed to ultraviolet and visible light, so UV or visible lasers are used for fluorescence sensing. For intelligence usage, UV light has an obvious advantage in such roles: It is not visible to the human eye, so UV illuminators are less likely to be detected. Rare earth elements and some heavy atom elements such as uranium can fluoresce efficiently. In daytime, the fluorescence is difficult to detect because of the strong reflection of normal sunlight, but special filters can be used to block out the visible sunlight and pass the fluorescence. Sensors have demonstrated the ability to detect pollutants such as oil slicks on the ocean using laser-induced fluorescence.[12]

Laser radars also can produce images. The use of lasers for radar imaging is discussed in the next chapter.

Vibrometry

Vibrometry is a radar technique for remotely sensing vibrations from a target. A coherent radar (one having a measurable phase pulse-to-pulse) is used to illuminate the target area; the radar receiver extracts the Doppler shift backscattered from the target to obtain a signature. Use of vibrometry for COMINT purposes is well known, as discussed below. But a vibrometer also can sense vibrations from the surface of a building or the ground above an underground facility to identify processes going on in the facility or machines that are operating in the facility. The acoustic signatures generated by machinery often uniquely identify the machine, and both the machine identity and its pattern of operation over time can provide valuable intelligence insights.

MICROWAVE VIBROMETRY

Microwave vibrometers have been in use for decades. One intelligence use of the vibrometer that has been publicly disclosed was in Moscow. In the 1940s, the Soviets presented U.S. representatives with a carved wooden replica of the Great Seal of the United States. The ambassador hung the seal in his office in Spaso House (the ambassador's residence), where it hung prominently for years. During George F. Kennan's ambassadorship in 1952, a routine security check discovered that the seal contained a microphone and a resonant cavity that could be stimulated from an outside radio signal. The Soviets would illuminate the Great Seal with a coherent UHF signal from a nearby location, and a receiver would receive the returned signal, modulated by any sound that was present in the ambassador's office.[13]

LASER RADAR VIBROMETRY

Lasers have been used for years to exploit audio vibrations from windows or similar fixtures within a building for COMINT purposes. The technique also works for identifying the unique signature created by moving parts of a target. The technology to use such devices is now widely available.[14]

Figure 6-4 shows a simplified diagram of how the process works. A laser beam is aimed at the target, and energy is backscattered from the target, via a beam splitter, to a detector. The backscattered energy is a sine wave, modulated by Doppler shift due to the vibrations or other movement of the target. The detector captures the signal modulation. The technique has been used to recover audio from inside rooms, but it can also be used to obtain signatures, for example, of machine noise or of a helicopter blade's rotation rate. For example, it was used to identify a helicopter at 5 km range in the 1980s.[15]

The sensor's performance is limited by the frequency stability of the laser, by atmospheric distortion or turbulence, and by mechanical vibrations of the laser platform. For monitoring vibrations from a building or the earth's surface, corner reflectors can be positioned on the ground or the building to increase the backscattered energy and eliminate target speckle; such corner reflectors can be as small as centimeter size and therefore can readily be concealed.

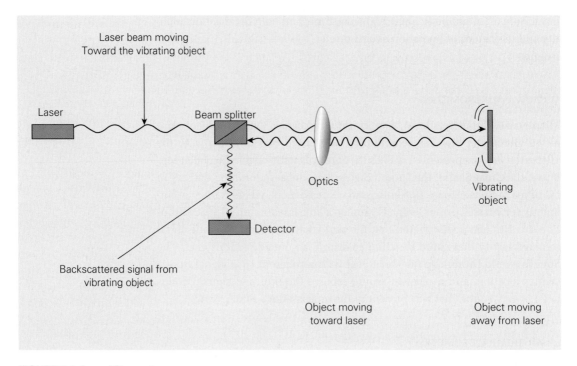

FIGURE 6-4 Laser Vibrometry

Summary

Radars have a wide range of civil and military applications. Most radars are used to geolocate a target and track its movement. Airborne and spaceborne radars also are used to map the earth's surface, detecting and tracking targets of interest on the surface; airborne radars also search the sky for weather or for other aircraft. Radar therefore is used for a number of purposes, most of which have nothing to do with intelligence. The general rule is that if the radar data has enduring value beyond the immediate demands of the mission, it is either intelligence or research data. If it has no such enduring value, it is usually operational data.

Radars usually are optimized to perform one of four functions. Search radars transmit a beam that is scanned across a volume of space to detect targets. Tracking radars keep the beam on a target (usually a target detected by a search radar) to follow or track the target throughout the radar's volume of coverage. Imaging radars create a picture of the target. Some imaging radars are specifically designed to create high-resolution images and are discussed in chapter 7. Target measurement radars measure the physical characteristics of an airborne or spaceborne target in order to obtain intelligence details about the target. Multifunction radars perform two or more of these functions.

Most radars operate in designated blocks of frequency bands, and technical intelligence radars use these operating bands for specific purposes:

- OTH radars operate in or near the HF band; they bounce signals off the ionosphere to see around the earth's curvature, making it possible to conduct radar surveillance of otherwise inaccessible regions. They have the advantage of monitoring targets that are moving at substantial distances inside a country and providing almost continuous surveillance at ranges on the order of thousands of kilometers.
- VHF and UHF radars are used for space surveillance.
- L band radars find wide use for monitoring air activity and also are used to monitor ballistic missile testing.
- S and C band radars provide precise tracking of aircraft, missiles, and satellites. In addition to a tracking role, C and X band radars also are used to obtain imagery of these targets.
- Laser radars have the advantage of using a much narrower beam and more precise range measurement capability than microwave radars.

Both microwave and laser radars are capable of acquiring vibrometry signatures. In vibrometry, a coherent radar illuminates the target area; the Doppler shift backscattered from the target provides a signature that has intelligence value.

NOTES

1. E. N. Fowle, E. L. Key, R. I. Millar, and R. H. Sear, "The Enigma of the FPS-95 OTH Radar," www.cufon.org/cufon/cobramst.htm.
2. USAF Fact Sheet: "Over the Horizon Backscatter Radar: East and West," www.acc.af.mil/library/factsheets/factsheet_print.asp?fsID=3863&page=1.
3. Jane's Defence Review, "Surface Extended Coastal Area Radar (SECAR) (Australia)," www.janes.com/extracts/extract/jrew/jrew2202.html.
4. ONERA, "Graves: The French Space Surveillance System," www.onera.fr/dprs-en/graves-space-surveillance-system/index.php.
5. Photo courtesy of the U.S. Air Force, peterson.af.mil/photos/mediagallery.
6. J. Mark Major, "Upgrading the Nation's Largest Space Surveillance Radar," www.swri.edu/3PUBS/BROCHURE/D10/survrad/survrad.HTM.

7. USAF, "Aerospace Control," www.maxwell.af.mil/au/awc/awcgate/au-18/au 18004c.htm.

8. National Security Space Road Map, "Cobra Dane," 1998, www.wslfweb.org/docs/roadmap/irm/internet/surwarn/init/html/cobradan.htm.

9. William W. Camp, Joseph T. Mayhan, and Robert M. O'Donnell, "Wideband Radar for Ballistic Missile Defense and Range-Doppler Imaging of Satellites," *Lincoln Laboratory Journal,* 12, no. 2 (2000): 267–280, www.ll.mit.edu/news/journal/pdf/vol12_no2/12_2widebandradar.pdf.

10. "The ARPA Lincoln C-Band Observables Radar (ALCOR)," www.smdc.army.mil/KWAJ/RangeInst/ALCOR.html.

11. GlobalSecurity.org, "Sea-Based X-band (SBX) Radar," www.globalsecurity.org/space/systems/sbx.htm. Photo, U.S. Army Space and Missile Defense Command.

12. T. Sato, Y. Suzuki, H. Kashiwagi, M. Nanjo, and Y. Kakui, "A Method for Remote Detection of Oil Spills Using Laser-Excited Raman Backscattering and Backscattered Fluorescence," *IEEE Journal of Oceanic Engineering*, 3, no. 1 (January 1978): 1–4.

13. "The Great Seal Bug Story," www.spybusters.com/Great_Seal_Bug.html.

14. "Laser Microphone," December 22, 2007, www.bobjunior.com/project/laser-microphone/.

15. *U.S. Army Communications–Electronics Command Annual Historical Review*, October 1, 1985–September 30, 1986, 200.

7. Imaging Radar

Chapters 4 and 5 discussed passive imaging that relies on the sun as an illuminator or on emissions from the target. In contrast, radar imagery is active and for that reason has some substantial advantages, as discussed below.

A conventional microwave band radar can create an image as it scans the earth's surface, as noted in the previous chapter. Airborne and ship-borne search radars routinely provide an image of the surrounding area that is useful for navigation. Laser radars are becoming valuable because of their ability to produce imagery that is useful for intelligence purposes. But when "imaging radar" in intelligence is discussed, the reference is to the synthetic aperture radar (SAR), which is definitely not a conventional radar.

Conventional microwave band radars cannot produce imagery with much detail. The image has poor resolution because the pixels are quite large (on the order of hundreds of meters, depending on the radar's pulse width and on distance from the radar). The pixel becomes larger with increasing distance from the radar. Such is not the case with SAR. The pixel size in SAR imagery can remain constant as distance from the radar increases, for reasons explained in this chapter.

Introduction to SAR

A SAR is one of the most important remote sensors used in intelligence. SARs have a number of advantages:

- SARs operate at microwave frequencies and can function under most weather and cloud conditions.
- SARs can penetrate numerous materials or surfaces that would normally hide equipment or facilities (for example, canvas tents and most wooden sheds become transparent to radar).
- SARs acquire their images by observing sideways from the SAR platform; this means they can look into openings in buildings, sheds, and tunnels.
- SAR imagery is capable of characterizing the ground texture, vegetation, sea surface, snow, and ice. It can even note slight changes.
- SAR imagery can be combined with visible, IR, and hyperspectral imagery to produce unique insights about a target that are not possible with any one imagery type alone.

FIGURE 7-1 Airborne SAR Image of the Pentagon

Synthetic aperture radar creates a high-resolution image of the target area based on the microwave energy backscattered from a target area. A SAR image is a map of the intensity of this energy that is backscattered from points in the scene. Brighter image pixels correspond to points of higher backscatter return. Figure 7-1 illustrates the effect, in a radar image of the Pentagon taken from an airborne SAR.[1] A number of points on the building, especially the building edges, are very strong radar reflectors and show up as bright returns.

How a SAR Operates

A SAR differs from a conventional radar in that it electronically creates (synthesizes) a long antenna using a sequence of pulses. Longer antennas produce better resolution images, as discussed below. A SAR does this by transmitting, receiving, and processing what is effectively a short pulse by using a very wide bandwidth signal. Transmitting a short pulse is important for range resolution, as will be explained below.

Synthetic aperture radar imaging is a two-step process of coherent data acquisition and subsequent coherent processing of a series of radar range echoes to recover a fine resolution image of a scene. A SAR works by transmitting a series of *coherent* pulses at a target area; coherent means that the pulses all have the same phase, as though they had been transmitted as a continuous sine wave that is shut on and off to generate pulses—Figure 7-2 illustrates a coherent pulse train. For a SAR to work, it is essential that all the pulses that will be used to form an image are transmitted coherently and that the radar retains a memory of the exact frequency and phase of the transmitted signal.

When a backscattered signal returns, the radar measures the intensity of the return and compares the backscattered signal frequency and phase to that of the transmitted signal. Slight differences in frequency, or phase differences, are noted, and these signal intensity and phase differences are recorded. This record, collected over many pulses, is called *phase history data* (PHD). This intensity and spectral information, collected over time, is used to create a target image.

The resolution of the focused SAR imagery is an important parameter in determining the interpretability of the imagery and the quality of the information that may be extracted. The goal is for the SAR to obtain the highest possible resolution, for the same reason that high-resolution optical imagery is desired: High-resolution imagery has greater intelligence value because the imagery analyst can tell more from more detailed signatures. Trucks can be distinguished from tanks and bombers from transport aircraft, given sufficient resolution. In general, the SAR's performance in target detection and classification depends on good image resolution. For applications such as

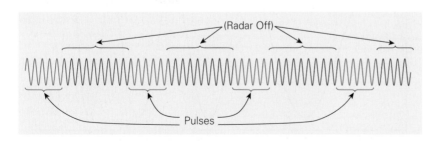

FIGURE 7-2 Coherent Pulse Train

change detection that are covered later in this chapter, good image resolution is critical.

A SAR has to have good resolution in both range (in the direction of the SAR beam) and azimuth (perpendicular to the radar beam) in order to form a high-resolution image. Getting good range resolution requires a completely different technique than getting good azimuth resolution.

Range resolution is relatively straightforward. For any radar, range resolution depends on the duration of the transmitted pulse (called pulse width). A one nanosecond pulse (one-billionth of a second) has a range resolution of approximately one foot, which provides very good range resolution. But a one nanosecond pulse has very little energy in it, so the backscattered signal will be difficult for the radar receiver to detect. A longer pulse, say one microsecond, would provide 1,000 times as much energy, which gives a more detectable backscattered signal. But a one microsecond pulse has a range resolution of about 1,000 feet, which is totally unacceptable for intelligence applications. The challenge is to illuminate the target with a one microsecond (or longer) pulse, but to obtain the range resolution of a one nanosecond pulse.

The solution for most SAR applications is to use a long pulse that is frequency modulated (FM), called a *chirped pulse:* its frequency smoothly changes over the duration of the pulse, as shown in Figure 7-3. A pulse like that shown contains many frequencies and thus has a wide frequency bandwidth. Consequently, it can be processed to give the range resolution of a much shorter pulse having the same bandwidth. The energy of a long pulse combined with the resolution of a short pulse is obtained using a technique called *pulse compression*. Using this technique, airborne radars have demonstrated 1.8 GHz transmit bandwidths with corresponding range resolutions of 0.1 meter.

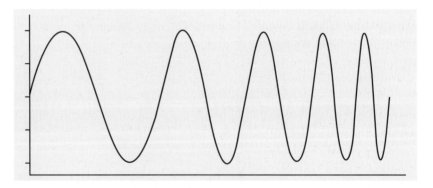

FIGURE 7-3 Frequency Change in a Chirped Pulse

It is highly desirable to get as much energy on the target as possible. Transmitting a long pulse helps. An additional way to do this is to transmit more pulses. Instead of waiting for the backscattered energy to return to the radar before transmitting another pulse, most SARs transmit a rapid stream of pulses. The time between transmitted pulses is much shorter than the pulse-to-target round-trip time. There are typically 5–20 pulses in-flight at any moment for a SAR, so the next pulse received is not the same pulse that was just transmitted. After a pulse is transmitted, the next pulse received was actually sent 5–20 pulses earlier.

Azimuth resolution is much harder to obtain than range resolution. It requires a completely different approach. The problem is that a conventional radar has its azimuth resolution determined by its beamwidth and its range to the target. Beamwidth is determined by antenna size and frequency—the higher the frequency and the larger the antenna, the narrower the beam and the better the resolution.

To illustrate: A 1 degree wide radar beam has an azimuth resolution of about 1 kilometer at a distance of 60 kilometers, which is completely unacceptable. Azimuth resolution should be about the same as range resolution, so that the result is a square pixel in the image. Using the 0.1 meter range resolution mentioned above as a goal, assuming 1,000 km range from the radar to the target, getting an azimuth resolution of 0.1 meters at X band (10 GHz) would require an antenna about 150 km long. An antenna this long is, of course, impractical.

The solution, and the critical feature that makes a SAR so valuable for technical intelligence, is to use a physically small antenna but to use signal processing to make it act like a very long antenna. That is, the radar system *synthesizes* the long aperture by collecting and storing coherent pulse returns, as discussed earlier. The returns are then processed so that, in effect, the result is as if the pulses had all been transmitted simultaneously from an antenna tens or hundreds of kilometers in length. During the collection period, the SAR moves through some angular extent as seen by an observer on the ground patch. Figure 7-4 illustrates the collection geometry.

The physical size of a SAR antenna therefore only governs scene size, or field of view; a larger antenna provides a smaller field of view. It also affects sensitivity because a larger antenna is more sensitive. However, its size does *not* affect azimuth resolution because of the way signals are processed.

To help understand how the SAR can precisely locate a small target within the large ground footprint shown in Figure 7-4, it helps to understand how Doppler shift works. If you were sitting on the SAR and looking exactly broadside to the flight direction (called zero squint), the ground targets will

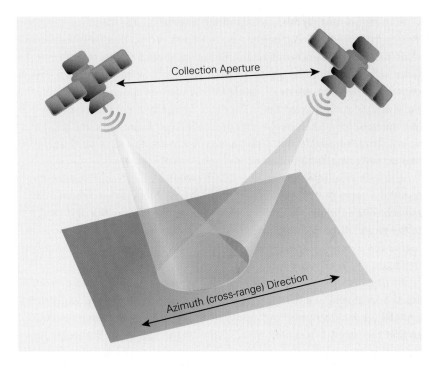

FIGURE 7-4 Geometry of Synthetic Aperture Creation

appear to be stationary. Looking slightly forward in the direction of SAR flight (positive squint), you would see the ground targets moving toward you slowly. The radar pulse that returns from these targets will be shifted upward in frequency (positive Doppler shift). Looking further forward toward the direction of flight, you would see the targets moving toward you much more quickly—giving the returns a larger positive Doppler shift. Similarly, when looking backward away from the direction of flight (negative squint), targets will appear to recede from you and the target returns will be shifted downward in frequency (negative Doppler shift). This perception of relative speed is used to place targets in the azimuth or cross-range direction. The greater the perceived relative speed, the further in cross-range the target will be placed away from scene center. The SAR system captures all these returns and their associated Doppler shifts, and subsequent processing of the phase history data provides the desired high azimuth resolution on each target in the scene. Because of this reliance on the Doppler shift, a SAR cannot image well from directly overhead.

Most of us have experienced the Doppler shift, or Doppler effect, in sound waves. The sound heard from a rapidly moving vehicle such as an airplane, or the horn on a passing train, drops to a lower key as the vehicle passes by. The Doppler effect works the same way in both sound and electromagnetic waves and, in fact, can be used for imaging in both cases. Ultrasound imaging for medical diagnosis relies on the Doppler effect both to image inside the body and to measure blood flow in the image.

Forming a SAR Image

SAR imaging can be done by *spotlight* or by *strip map*. Either of these two modes can be used, depending on the tradeoff that is made between the level of resolution needed and the desired area of coverage.

In spotlight mode, the entire spacecraft is rotated into the direction of the target to increase the integration time and therefore the in-track resolution. To get the best resolution, a SAR is usually operated in spotlight mode, where data are collected from a single patch of terrain. As the SAR platform moves past the scene the radar beam is continuously adjusted so that it always points to the same area of the ground. The SAR image resolution improves (that is, the distance between distinct pixels becomes smaller) as the total collection time on the patch of ground increases. Thus, the longer the collection time, the better the resolution because the movement of the spacecraft in effect creates a longer antenna.

Figure 7-4 shows an example of the spotlight SAR imaging geometry. As the radar moves past the scene the antenna is steered so as to continually illuminate the same ground patch. High azimuth resolution is achieved by using an antenna of modest size and coherently processing a series of range echoes obtained as the radar moves past the scene. The coherent processing combines the information from the series of range echoes to, in effect, create a synthetic array that is as long as the flight path while the SAR is "spotlighting" the ground patch.

Strip map imaging involves an antenna pointing into a fixed direction (normally perpendicular to the direction of aircraft or satellite movement). In Figure 7-4, if the radar were operated in strip map mode, the effective length of the synthetic aperture would be the same as the size of the area illuminated on the ground; this still provides good azimuth resolution, but it is considerably worse than the resolution provided in spotlight mode. The advantage of strip map imaging is that it covers a much larger area.

One trades resolution for area coverage. As with any remote sensor, the goal is to get large area coverage with high resolution, but improving one of these generally makes the other worse.

As an illustration of the tradeoff between strip map and spotlight mode, the German radar satellite TerraSAR-X can obtain 1 meter resolution in spotlight mode, but it is limited to covering an area of 5 km × 10 km. In strip map mode, the area of coverage grows to 30 km × 50 km, but resolution drops to 3 meters.[2]

Airborne versus Spaceborne SARs

Like other remote sensing systems, an imaging radar sensor may be carried on either an airborne or spaceborne platform. Depending on the tactical situation and the intended use of the imagery, there are tradeoffs between the two types of platforms. Regardless of the platform used, a significant advantage of using a SAR is that the spatial resolution is not heavily dependent on range to the target. Thus, fine resolution can be achieved from both airborne and spaceborne platforms.

Although spatial resolution is not determined by altitude, viewing geometry and swath coverage can be greatly affected by changes in altitude. At aircraft operating altitudes, an airborne radar must image over a wide range of incidence angles, perhaps as much as 60 or 70 degrees, in order to achieve relatively wide swaths (on the order of 60 km). But as discussed in the following sections, incidence angle (or look angle) has a significant effect on the backscatter from surface features and on their appearance on an image. Image characteristics such as layover and shadowing (discussed below) will be subject to wide variations if the incidence angle varies greatly. Spaceborne radars are able to avoid some of these imaging geometry problems since they operate at much higher altitudes than airborne radars. At altitudes of several hundred kilometers, spaceborne radars can image the same swath widths as airborne radars but over a much narrower range of incidence angles, typically ranging from 5 to 15 degrees, as illustrated in Figure 7-5. This provides for more uniform illumination and reduces undesirable imaging variations across the swath due to viewing geometry.

Aircraft have some advantages because they can get the SAR closer to a target and generally can transmit more power than spaceborne radars. Airborne SARs can therefore detect smaller targets, enabling them to generate more detailed (finer grain) imagery.

FIGURE 7-5 Swath Width and Incidence Angle in Airborne and Spaceborne SARs

SAR Image Processing and Exploitation

Image processing is required to transform the stored pulse returns from each pixel (the phase history data) into a recognizable image. The chain of processing is:

> **Phase history data** are collected and processed to form a **complex image**, which is then further processed to form a **detected image.**

The task of the image processor is to combine all of the returns received from a given area to recover a focused image. The SAR processing algorithms are very complex because they must account for a steadily changing scene as the radar moves; individual targets scatter energy differently at different aspect angles between the target and radar.

SAR data are collected by rapid pulsing over a period of several seconds. During this period the angle between the SAR antenna and the ground is changing. The initial processing of phase history data is done using the assumption that the intensity of return from each point in the scene is the same for each pulse. The following processing assumptions are made:

- flat terrain
- stationary targets
- constant radar cross-section (RCS) throughout the collection time frame
- quiet microwave environment (no interference)

Both natural and artificial features in the scene typically violate one or more of the above assumptions. Each of these artifacts will be discussed in turn.

THE NONFLAT TERRAIN

The assumption that the terrain is flat is violated most of the time. Very few land areas are completely flat. Mountains and vertical structures create two artifacts in a SAR image: *shadowing* and *layover*. More complex structures can create apparent targets downrange from the complex structure, as discussed below.

Shadowing is fairly easy to understand because it is much like the shadows created by the sun. Shadowing occurs in the down-range direction from targets elevated above the surrounding terrain, such as mountains and buildings. The shadowed region appears as a black area in the SAR image because no signal was returned from that region of the scene. Figure 7-6 illustrates how shadowing works; the area behind the building is in shadow and objects located in that area cannot be observed.

Elevated targets also produce layover toward the SAR flight track, also illustrated in Figure 7-6. The effect of layover is to position the tops of tall targets closer in imagery toward the SAR than their base. Layover occurs because a SAR puts all scene points that are at the same range into the same range cell in the image. In Figure 7-6, the radar pulse hits the building top first, because it is closer to the radar. Because of the flat earth assumption, when the imagery is processed the return from the top of the building is placed closer to the radar, while the return from the bottom of the building is placed at its correct flat earth position. Tall structures thus appearing to "lay over" on top of the ground return on the near-range side of the target.

Both the shadowing and layover effects show up in the SAR image of the Pentagon in Figure 7-1. The airborne SAR was located south of the building, looking north; the shadowing effect is clearly displayed on the northeast and north sides, and a layover effect may be seen in a bright line offset from the building parallel to the southwest side.

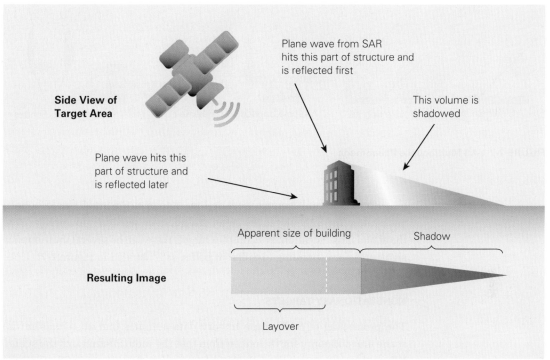

FIGURE 7-6 Layover and Shadowing in SAR Imagery

The extent of layover depends on grazing angle and the height of the elevated target. In Figure 7-6, if the SAR is at a lower elevation angle (lower grazing angle), then the difference in time between the pulse hitting the top of the building and the bottom will be less, and the layover will be smaller.

Image interpretation is complicated in layover regions due to the overlap of the elevated structure with features on the near-range side of the structure. Layover will also cause a distortion of any topographic variations in the scene.

Multibounce creates the opposite effect from layover. When a SAR looks at an urban area or a complex structure or cavity, the backscattered signal does not necessarily return directly to the radar. Multibounce signatures can appear in SAR imagery for complex targets, where the microwaves reflect off more than one point before returning to the sensor. Multibounce scattering can be simple double bounce or more complicated multiple-bounce scattering.

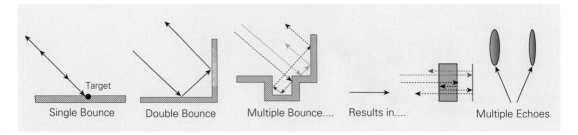

FIGURE 7-7 SAR Multibounce Phenomena

Because the multibounce path is longer than the normal single bounce backscatter, the SAR places the target multibounce signature downrange from the actual target location. For complex targets there can be several multibounce signatures corresponding to different paths, as illustrated in Figure 7-7.

NONSTATIONARY TARGETS

The processing of SAR phase history data assumes that all targets in the scene are stationary for the entire time that the radar illuminates the scene. When this is not the case, such as for moving targets, an artifact is produced in the SAR image. As the target moves across the scene, it creates an artifact due to improper focusing. The phenomenon is much the same as when a camera with slow shutter speed takes a picture of a fast-moving object. The object will be blurred in the picture because while the shutter is open, the object occupies several different locations in the image frame. It is the same with a SAR and a moving target: While the SAR is transmitting its pulses to form an image, the target is moving through several pixels in the image frame.

The artifact resulting from target movement depends on the nature of the movement; some of the most common are target displacement, smearing, and target distortions. Which artifact occurs is determined by the geometry between the SAR platform and the target and their motion with respect to each other. Following is a description of the most common artifacts.

Target Displacement. Figure 7-8 shows the displacement effect due to target movement toward or away from the SAR. If the target (in the figure, a ship) is moving toward the SAR platform, then the target image shift is in the direction of the SAR platform movement. If the target is moving away from the SAR, the shift is in the opposite direction, away from SAR platform movement.

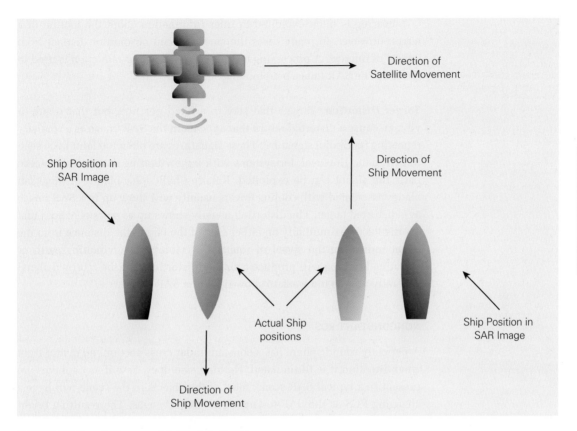

FIGURE 7-8 Target Movement Artifacts in SAR Imagery

Smearing. Suppose the ships in Figure 7-8 were not moving at a constant velocity but instead were accelerating or decelerating toward or away from the SAR. This acceleration or deceleration causes a constantly changing displacement when the image is formed. Instead of a simple displaced image as shown in the figure, the result is a smeared image of the target along the direction of SAR movement (called the azimuth direction). The changing target speed causes the shift to vary during the collection interval. This variation generates the azimuth smear. The shape of the smear depends on grazing angle and squint, as well as the target motion.

Azimuth motion also causes smearing in the azimuth direction. If the target is moving at a constant velocity in the azimuth direction, the smear will be linear. In contrast, if the target is accelerating or decelerating, the smear will have a curved shape.

Smearing is often exploited to infer information about the motion of a target; however, in many cases the smearing can obscure or distract from targets of interest. A processing technique called *smear reduction* is used to clean up the SAR image by removing smearing.

Target Distortion. Targets that stay in a fixed position, but that rotate or vibrate, cause a distorted return that appears in the SAR image as a spatially repeating (periodic) signature. These signatures are often too faint to be seen in SAR data. However, for systems with large vibrating or rotating metallic parts the signal can be exploited. Rotating helicopter blades or large fan blades associated with cooling towers usually will show up in a SAR image as a distorted target. The distortion usually shows up as pairs of echoes that are displaced azimuthally on either side of the target, the distance from the target indicating the speed of rotation or vibration. A vibrating earth or vibrating building will produce a similar distortion, but the returned signal generally will be too weak to show up in the SAR image.[3]

NONCONSTANT RCS

A perfectly round sphere has a constant radar cross-section, no matter from what direction it is illuminated. Nothing else does. Few if any spheres are present in a typical SAR scene; most of the objects in the scene will have a changing RCS as the SAR-to-target geometry changes. The resulting bright spots in the SAR image (where the RCS of objects becomes suddenly very large) are called *glint*. For example, edges that are perpendicular to the SAR beam will return a higher signal leading to bright image pixels, or glint. Some curved surfaces can create bright streaks along the curved edge. This effect is especially noticeable from power lines or telephone wires.

Flat surfaces can vary greatly in RCS. A common example is a flat metallic rooftop that becomes very bright when the SAR beam is perpendicular to it at some point in the collection period. If this is strong enough it can lead to receiver saturation. The target seems expanded on the image, a phenomenon called image "blooming." As with smear reduction, glint reduction techniques are used to clean up a SAR image by removing this artifact.

THE UNQUIET MICROWAVE ENVIRONMENT

The imaging capability of a SAR can be seriously limited or denied by an interference signal in the SAR operating frequency band. Such interference can be deliberate (jamming) or due to radio frequency interference occurring in the SAR frequency band. The way an interfering signal looks in the SAR imagery depends on the type of interference; it typically is a streak in range, in azimuth, or in both, sometimes resulting in a bright cross centered on the interfering transmitter.[4]

The SAR-Lupe

An example of the current state of the art in SAR for reconnaissance applications is Germany's SAR-Lupe satellite, an artist's conception of which is shown in Figure 7-9.[5] The first of five SAR-Lupe satellites was launched in December 2006, and the fifth was launched in June 2008. The five satellites operate in three 500-kilometer orbits in planes roughly 60 degrees apart. The radar operates in X-band at a center frequency of 9.65 GHz. The SAR-Lupe's average power consumption is about 250 watts, and its expected life is ten years.

The SAR-Lupe has performance characteristics that make it an excellent technical collection sensor. Its three-meter diameter dish antenna, the back of which is shown in the figure, reportedly provides a resolution of about 0.5 meter over a frame size of 5.5 km on a side in the spotlight mode where, as previously noted, the satellite rotates to keep the dish pointed at a single target. Resolution is about 1 meter over a frame size of 8 km × 60 km in the strip map mode, where the satellite maintains a fixed orientation over the earth and the radar image is formed simply by the satellite's motion along its orbit. The radar is able to image a given area of earth once every ten hours or less.[6]

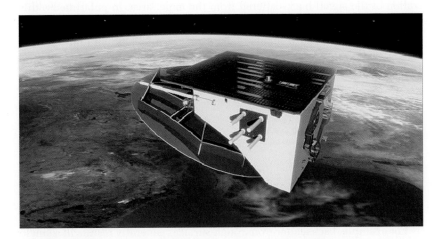

FIGURE 7-9 Artist's Concept of Germany's SAR-Lupe Spacecraft

Synthetic aperture radars are highly flexible; they can collect or process data in a number of ways that have intelligence value. The following sections discuss a few of these.

Polarimetric SAR

Chapter 4 introduced polarimetry and described its uses in optical imaging. SARs can also use polarimetry to obtain signatures that have intelligence value.

SAR images are generated by sending and receiving microwave pulses. The microwaves are generally transmitted as either horizontally or vertically polarized electromagnetic waves. In older SAR designs, the radar could only receive the same polarization that it transmitted. Most current SARs transmit and receive multiple polarizations, for reasons explained below.

When a polarized pulse strikes a target and is reflected back toward the radar, the polarization is changed by the reflecting surface. Typically, the reflected signal contains a combination of horizontal and vertical polarizations, which is described as elliptically polarized. The relative amount of horizontal and vertical polarization in the return depends on the structure, reflectivity, shape, orientation, and roughness of the reflecting surface. Therefore, measuring the returned polarization from an object can provide additional information about the object. This measurement is the basis of the process of polarimetry.

SAR polarimetry involves acquiring, processing. and analyzing the polarization of the signal backscattered from the target area. In polarimetry, this backscattered signal is processed to determine scattering mechanisms, or the "fingerprint," of the surface materials. A radar can operate in four different ways to obtain this polarization information. The backscattered signal from a given target will be different for each of these scenarios:

- transmitting and receiving the same polarization—the conventional approach
- transmitting one polarization and receiving the opposite (known as cross-polarization)
- transmitting one polarization and receiving both
- transmitting and receiving both polarizations (a SAR that does this is called *fully-polarimetric*)

For example, backscatter from rough surfaces generally results in a single polarization coming back to the receiving antenna. In contrast, backscatter from trees is diffuse and contains a mix of polarizations because the radar wave interacts with the trunks, branches, and leaves of the canopy. These properties of such a complex surface can be determined by a fully polarimetric SAR.

Polarimetric SAR is of value for nonintelligence topics such as monitoring crops, soil moisture, forests, snow cover, sea ice, and sea conditions. It is used for geological mapping. Some of these applications also are relevant in intelligence. Intelligence uses include ship, aircraft, and military vehicle detection and classification.[7] As discussed later, low frequency polarimetric SARs have an additional advantage. Because lower frequency microwave radars can penetrate foliage and earth, they can detect and classify objects located under jungle canopy or buried objects, such as land mines.[8]

An early example of a polarimetric SAR is the SIR-C radar that was carried on the space shuttle *Endeavor* in April and October, 1994. The SIR-C was actually three radars, one operating at L-band, the second at C-band, and the third at X-band. The L-band and C-band antennas could measure both horizontal and vertical polarizations.

SIR-C was a fully polarimetric radar, providing data on the relative phase difference among all four of the modes of operation described above. The polarimetric data from the two shuttle flights provided detailed information about the surface geometric structure, vegetation cover, and subsurface features.[9] Subsequent processing of the data showed that the SIR-C radar had the ability to obtain very high-resolution images of ships at sea, sufficient for identifying specific ships.[10] Germany's TerraSAR-X and Israel's TECSAR are two examples of currently operational satellites that carry a fully polarimetric SAR.

Change Detection

One of the major advantages of SAR is its ability to detect changes in a scene over time. Change detection is an application to which SAR is particularly well suited. Examples of surface changes that have been observed include vehicle tracks, crops growing or being harvested, and soil excavation. Changes in the terrain surface due to underground construction can also be observed by change detection. The underground excavation results in both vertical settlement and a horizontal straining that is detectable.[11]

Three techniques are used for change detection: incoherent change detection, coherent change detection, and SAR interferometry. The first two techniques require repeat passes, separated in time by hours, days, weeks, or

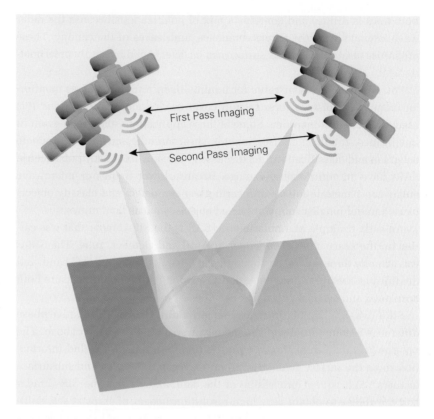

FIGURE 7-10 Geometry for Repeat Pass Imaging

even years, wherein the SAR looks at the same target area at approximately the same azimuth and elevation. Figure 7-10 illustrates the repeat pass case. The third technique, SAR interferometry, can be done in a single pass but requires two separate receive antennas located on the same platform.

Incoherent change detection identifies changes in a scene by comparing the intensity of energy backscattered from individual pixels between successive passes. Significant changes in local regions (for example, due to a truck, ship, or tank being present in one image but not in the next) will show up as significant changes in the backscattered energy intensity. The technique can also be used to detect changes in soil or vegetation moisture content or surface roughness.

Coherent change detection (CCD) requires a more sophisticated level of signal processing but can detect very subtle scene changes.[12] These change images provide valuable intelligence by revealing information such as traffic patterns, type of traffic, and terrain maps of critical areas where tunnels may be in use, as in Afghanistan.[13] CCD can provide signatures indicating not only that traffic has occurred in the area, but that a certain type of traffic has occurred.[14] Germany's TerraSAR-X and SAR-Lupe are two examples of operational radars that can perform coherent change detection.

Coherent change detection relies on, in effect, overlaying two radar images to produce a picture of what changed in the time between the two images. It does this by measuring and storing both the intensity and phase (phase history data) of each image pixel—in contrast to incoherent change detection, where only intensity is measured. On a subsequent pass, intensity and phase are again measured. Very slight changes in the surface—fractions of an inch—are detected as phase changes in the phase history data. Of course, the return from vegetation will usually change between the passes due to growth or to wind, and the ground may change due to natural causes such as rain. These changes also show up in CCD imagery.

CCD is affected by what is called *image decorrelation* or *baseline decorrelation*. If there is a significant difference in the imaging geometry between the primary and repeat pass collection, the two images will not correlate (that is, coherence will be lost). To avoid decorrelation, the collector tries to use exactly the same flight paths in the two passes. When the paths are identical or nearly so, any intensity or phase differences between the image pair can be attributed to changes in the scene. In practice, however, it is very difficult to fly the same flight track due to inaccuracies in the platform navigation information. This is particularly true in airborne systems where the effects of wind and turbulence may result in significant flight track offsets. The resulting decorrelation has to be dealt with in processing.[15]

SAR interferometry, also known as interferometric SAR, requires acquiring images using two independent receive antennas located on the same moving platform. The two images are then processed to identify and exploit differences in the intensity and phase of the image pair. Depending on how the two receive antennas are deployed on the platform and how they are operated, two different types of intelligence information may be obtained.[16]

One approach is to use SAR interferometry to detect moving targets in the scene. To do this, the two receive antennas are located side-by-side on the platform. As the platform moves, the front antenna receives the backscattered return from a target area. A few milliseconds later, the rear antenna is in the exact position that the front antenna had occupied, and at that exact time it receives the backscattered return *from the next pulse* of the same target area. Because the target geometry is identical for the two received

Imaging
Radar

pulses, any change in the return intensity or phase must be caused by movement in the target area. All the unchanged backscatter return can be eliminated, and only slow-moving targets in the scene will remain.[17] The technique may also be used for mapping ocean currents.

The other approach is to use SAR interferometry for terrain mapping. For this use, the two receive antennas may be located side by side or one above the other. The difference is that both antennas receive and process the same backscattered pulse simultaneously. Because the two antennas view the scene with slightly different imaging geometries, changes in terrain features may be measured precisely. This approach can potentially provide highly accurate measurements of terrain elevation.[18] SAR interferometry is used to generate topographic maps, map surface deformation, monitor landslides, measure the velocity of objects, determine the structure and composition of vegetation, and, as noted above, detect change.

Two-color multiview (or multicolor multiview, where more than two images are compared) is the best technique for observing small changes in SAR imagery between images taken days, weeks, or even years apart. The technique shows in one color objects that appeared in the first image but have left the scene in the second image. Objects that have appeared in the scene since the first image are shown in a second color. Changes in position of vehicles, fences, coastlines, or buildings under construction are easily identified using two-color multiview from image pairs collected weeks to years apart.[19]

Foliage Penetration SAR

An application of SAR that has obvious intelligence uses is foliage penetration SAR. Most SARs operate in the microwave bands—L, S, C, and X bands. Radars in these frequency bands do not penetrate foliage well, and their penetration capabilities get worse as frequency increases. At lower frequencies, however, a radar can penetrate even dense foliage to detect objects located underneath the forest canopy. SARs operating in the UHF or, better still, the VHF bands can effectively image objects concealed in foliage.[20] SARs in these lower frequency bands can also penetrate into dry earth for short distances, allowing the radar to detect buried objects.[21] Newer SARs in the VHF/UHF range using very wide bandwidths are capable of detecting moving targets concealed in foliage and of precisely determining both the position and velocity of moving targets.[22] The use of SARs for moving-target detection is discussed in more detail in a later section.

SAR Imaging over Water

Over water, SAR sensors observe only the ocean's surface; unlike ground returns, there is almost no water penetration. A completely smooth water surface or biological and man-made slicks (such as oil slicks) return very little energy to the radar and appear to be black in the resulting image. The sea surface, however, is seldom smooth, and backscatter from a rough sea surface produces a return that can be measured and analyzed. Steep incidence angles (greater than 20° for airborne SAR systems, greater than about 40° for spaceborne SARs) are usually needed to get an adequate return.

Wind speeds from 2 to 15 knots provide optimal imaging conditions. Greater wind speeds produce a high clutter return, hiding subtle wave or slick signatures that might have intelligence value. Lesser wind speeds do not provide enough contrast to detect these signatures.

Polarimetric SAR has some special advantages in SAR imaging over water. When a vertically polarized signal is transmitted, the return is generally weaker for the backscattered horizontally polarized signal and stronger for the vertically polarized backscatter. But spherical point targets (such as mines) give similar signals for both polarizations. As a result, the horizontally polarized backscatter often will show small, point-like targets, such as mines floating in the water.

Even though radar energy does not significantly penetrate into sea water, SAR measurements can indirectly provide information about water depth—often a critical piece of intelligence for naval operations. As swell or long waves move toward shore, they are affected by the seabed, which acts to shorten their wavelength and decrease their apparent speed. The water depth can be determined by measuring these changes. The wavelength can be determined from the image either through direct measurement or by spectral analysis. By collecting the SAR phase history data over several seconds, it is also possible to track the propagation of the wave as a function of time and thereby determine its apparent speed.

Figure 7-11 illustrates some of the features that can be obtained by imaging the open ocean. This is a SAR image taken by the Spaceborne Imaging Radar on the space shuttle *Endeavor* in 1994. It demonstrates some of the richness of SAR capabilities because it includes multiple frequencies and multiple polarizations. The image is actually a combination of three different radar images, and three colors are used to distinguish them. Red colors are from the L-band transmissions that are horizontally polarized on transmission and reception. Green colors are from the C band radar, again

Imaging Radar

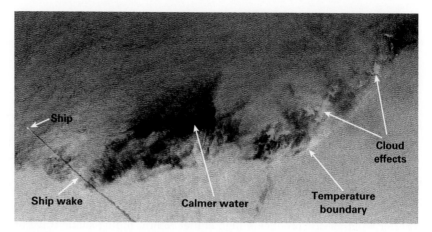

FIGURE 7-11 SAR Image of the North Atlantic

horizontally transmitted and received. Blue colors are from the vertically transmitted and received L band radar. The line in the lower left shows the stern wake of a ship; it is about 28 km long. The length of the wake indicates that the ship is probably discharging oil, which makes the wake last longer and causes it to stand out in the image. A fairly sharp temperature boundary, probably a front, extends across the image and separates two water masses having different temperatures. The different water temperatures cause two different wind patterns that are creating two different wave patterns. The light green area in the lower part of the image is rougher water with more wind. The purple area is calmer water with less wind. The dark patches are smooth areas of low wind, probably caused by clouds along the front, and the bright green patches are likely due to ice crystals in the clouds that scatter the radar waves.[23]

Moving Target Indicator

As discussed earlier, moving objects create distortions and artifacts in a SAR image. But moving targets clearly can be of high intelligence interest, so instead of eliminating the blurs and displacements created by moving targets, there is information to be gained by singling out those movements for detailed analysis.

SARs, it turns out, can be operated in a mode designed to enhance the detectability of target motion. This mode is commonly called *moving target indicator* (MTI) or *ground moving target indicator* (GMTI) mode. The term *MTI* is more often used because it is a more accurate description. MTI can be used to detect aircraft, helicopter, or ship movements, as well as ground vehicular movement. SAR interferometry, discussed in a preceding section, is one way to do MTI.[24]

The MTI mode has been demonstrated in a number of SARs and used both for combat operations support and for intelligence. An example is the AN/APY-3 radar carried by the Joint Surveillance and Target Attack Radar System (JSTARS) aircraft, a modified Boeing 707. JSTARS has the capability to obtain images of moving targets and can tell the difference between wheeled and tracked vehicles. JSTARS can even tell whether a potential target moving down a road is a tank or a jeep—a capability that proved critical during the Gulf War of 1990–1991.[25]

MTI radars rely on the Doppler shift in order to detect and track moving targets at long ranges. The JSTARS radar is an example of the genre. The antenna can be tilted to either side of the aircraft, where it can develop a 120 degree field of view covering nearly 50,000 square kilometers. It is capable of simultaneously tracking 600 targets within a 250 km range. The radar can track any moving objects of vehicle size. The MTI mode cannot pick up stationary objects; the radar can alternate between MTI mode to detect moving objects and SAR mode to produce images of stationary objects. In addition to being able to detect, locate, and track large numbers of ground vehicles, the radar has a limited capability to detect helicopters, rotating antennas, and slow-moving fixed-wing aircraft.

Figure 7-12 illustrates the type of display that a JSTARS-class radar can produce.[26] The bright objects in the figure are moving targets that have been superimposed on a separately generated map of the target area.

The figure illustrates another important capability that GMTI can offer for intelligence. It allows the imagery analyst to extract road map information and to assess traffic flows. Once the roads have been mapped and normal traffic flows have been established, the analyst is well positioned to identify priority targets and to identify changes in traffic that have intelligence significance

FIGURE 7-12 JSTARS MTI Image

(for example, the traffic increase that would presage a major military operation).[27]

Another example of a SAR having MTI capability is the Global Hawk. In addition to its electro-optical and infrared sensors (discussed in chapter 4), the Global Hawk carries a synthetic aperture radar that can image an area the size of Illinois (40,000 nautical square miles) in just 24 hours. Through satellite and ground systems, the imagery can be relayed in near real-time to battlefield commanders. The radar operates at X-band with a 600 MHz bandwidth and 3.5 kilowatt peak power. Like JSTARS, it can operate in SAR imaging mode or MTI mode. Unlike JSTARS, it also can operate in both modes simultaneously:

- the wide-area MTI mode can detect moving targets within a radius of 100 kilometers
- the combined SAR-MTI strip mode provides 1 meter resolution over a swath 37 kilometers wide at ranges from 20 to 110 kilometers
- the SAR spot mode can provide 0.3 meter resolution over 10 square kilometers, as well as provide a sea-surveillance function.[28]

Laser Radar Imaging

Laser radars can also use SAR techniques to create an image of the earth's surface.[29] While still in the prototype stage, laser SARs have the potential to provide substantially improved images at longer ranges than conventional optical systems can provide.

Laser radars also can develop three-dimensional images without using SAR techniques, and such radars have a capability that is of special intelligence interest: Like the foliage penetration SAR, discussed previously, they can locate and identify objects under foliage or camouflage. They do it differently, though, by taking many measurements of the same target area, so the laser in effect finds "holes" in the covering material. The laser is therefore able to penetrate through the camouflage mesh to obtain a return from the object inside. Using this technique, laser radars have demonstrated a capability to provide three-dimensional imagery of military vehicles concealed under foliage or camouflage. The images are of sufficient quality for analysts to perform object classification and identification.[30] Figure 7-13 illustrates an example of the visible image of a camouflaged tank (on the left) and a laser image of the same tank (on the right).[31]

 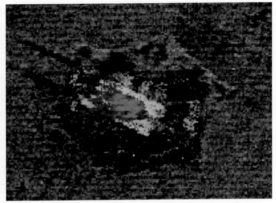

FIGURE 7-13 Visible Image and Laser Radar Image of a Tank

Summary

A conventional radar can create an image as it scans the earth's surface. Air-borne search radars do this routinely, but the image has poor resolution because the pixels are quite large and become larger with increasing distance from the radar. Such is not the case with a synthetic aperture radar.

A SAR creates a high-resolution image of the target area based on the microwave energy backscattered from a target area. A SAR image is a map of the intensity of this energy that is backscattered from points in the scene. Brighter image pixels correspond to points of higher backscatter return.

A SAR differs from a conventional radar in that it "synthesizes" a long antenna using a sequence of pulses. Longer antennas produce better resolution images in the azimuth direction. To form what is effectively a long antenna, the radar transmits pulses coherently and retains a memory of the exact frequency and phase of the transmitted signal. When a backscattered signal returns, the radar measures the intensity of the return and compares the backscattered signal frequency to that of the transmitted signal. Slight differences in frequency, or phase differences, are noted, and these signal intensity and phase differences are recorded. This record, collected over many pulses, is called phase history data and is used to create the long synthetic antenna.

To get good range resolution, a SAR transmits what is effectively a very short pulse by using a very wide bandwidth signal. Most SARs use a long pulse that is frequency modulated, called a *chirped pulse*; its frequency smoothly increases or decreases over the duration of the pulse. It thus has a wide frequency bandwidth, and in processing it can give the range resolution of a much shorter pulse having the same bandwidth.

The initial processing of phase history data is done using the assumption that the intensity of return from each point in the scene is the same for each pulse. This requires four processing assumptions to be made: the terrain is flat, the targets are stationary and have a constant radar cross-section, and the radiofrequency environment is quiet. Both natural and artificial features in the scene typically violate one or more of the above assumptions, so additional interpretation and analysis have to be done to correct for the resulting artifacts in the image:

- because the terrain is not flat, shadowing hides the region behind mountains and buildings, and layover causes the top of a structure to appear closer to the radar than it should be
- target movement causes the target to be smeared or displaced, or both, in the resulting image
- unless the target is a perfect sphere, its radar cross section will change during the imaging process, causing streaks and image distortion
- unintentional radiofrequency interference or deliberate jamming will usually create streaks in the resulting image.

SARs can also use polarimetry to obtain signatures that have intelligence value. They do this by transmitting at least one polarization and receiving two polarizations. A SAR that both transmits and receives two polarizations (forming four possible combinations of transmit and receive polarization) is called fully polarimetric. When the polarized pulse strikes a target and is reflected back toward the radar, the polarization is changed by the reflecting surface. The relative amount of horizontal and vertical polarization in the return depends on the structure, reflectivity, shape, orientation, and roughness of the reflecting surface, so measuring the returned polarization from an object can provide additional information about the object.

One of the major advantages of SAR is its ability to detect changes in a scene over time by making successive passes and imaging the same scene from the same SAR location. Change detection can identify objects that have entered or left the scene between imaging passes and can also observe new vehicle tracks, crops growing or being harvested, soil excavation, and changes in the terrain surface due to underground construction.

SARs operating in the VHF or low UHF bands can image objects concealed in foliage. These SARs can also penetrate into dry earth for short distances.

SARs can also be operated in a special mode called moving target indicator or ground moving target indicator that is designed to enhance the detectability of target motion. MTI mode can be used to monitor aircraft, helicopter, or ship movements, as well as for tracking ground vehicular movement.

NOTES

1. Sandia National Laboratory, www.thespacereview.com/article/790/1.
2. S. Buckreuss, R. Werninghaus, W. Pitz, "The German Satellite Mission Terra-SAR-X," *IEEE Radar Conference 2008*, May 26–30, 2008, INSPEC Accession #10425846, 306.
3. Merrill Skolnik, ed., *Radar Handbook*, 3rd ed. (New York: McGraw-Hill, 2008), 17.25–17.27.
4. Skolnik, *Radar Handbook*, 24.49–24.51.
5. OHB System, "Technology for Space," www.ohb-system.de/gb/Satellites/Missions/sarlupe.html.
6. OHB System, "Technology for Space."
7. Dai Dahai, Wang Xuesong, Xiao Shunping, Wu Xiaofang, and Chen Siwei, "Development Trends of PolSAR System and Technology," *Heifei Leida Kexue Yu Jishu* (February 1, 2008): 15.
8. L. Carin, R. Kapoor, and C. E. Baum, "Polarimetric SAR Imaging of Buried Landmines," *IEEE Transactions on Geoscience and Remote Sensing*, 36, no. 6 (November 1998): 1985–1988.
9. Jet Propulsion Laboratory, "JPL Imaging Radar," http://southport.jpl.nasa.gov/.
10. D. Pastina, P. Lombardo, A. Farina, and P. Daddi, "Super-Resolution of Polarimetric SAR Imaging," *Signal Processing*, 83, no. 8 (August 2003).
11. "Characterization of Underground Facilities," JASON Report JSR-97-155, April 1999.
12. Mark Preiss and Nicholas J. S. Stacy, "Coherent Change Detection: Theoretical Description and Experimental Results," Australian Department of Defense, DSTO-TR-1851, August 2006, http://dspace.dsto.defence.gov.au/dspace/handle/1947/4410.
13. John L. Morris, "The Nature and Applications of Measurement and Signature Intelligence," *American Intelligence Journal,* 19, nos. 3 & 4 (1999–2000): 81–84.
14. Preiss and Stacy "Coherent Change Detection."
15. Ibid.
16. Sun Xilong, Yu Anxi, and Liang Diannong, "Analysis of Error Propagation in Inteferometric SAR," *Heifei Leida Kexue Yu Jishu* (February 1, 2008): 35.
17. Ibid.
18. Skolnik, *Radar Handbook*, 17.30–17.33.
19. John W. Ives, "Army Vision 2010: Integrating Measurement and Signature Intelligence," April 9, 2002, www.iwar.org.uk/sigint/resources/masint/Ives_J_W_02.pdf.
20. Skolnik, *Radar Handbook,* 17.33–17.34.
21. D. J. Daniels, *Ground Penetrating Radar*, IEE Radar, Sonar, and Navigation Series, 2004.

22. Zhou Hong, Huang Xiaotao, Chang Yulin, and Zhou Zhimin, "Ground Moving Target Detection in Single-Channel UWB SAR Using Change Detection Based on Sub-Aperture Images," *Heifei Leida Kexue Yu Jishu* (February 1, 2008): 23.

23. NASA, "North Atlantic Ocean," http://southport.jpl.nasa.gov/pio/srl1/sirc/naocn .html.

24. Zhou Hong, Huang Xiaotao, Chang Yulin, and Zhou Zhimin, "Ground Moving Target Detection," 23.

25. USAF Factsheet, "E-8C Joint Stars," www.af.mil/factsheets/factsheet.asp?fsID=100.

26. Photograph from the U.S. Air Force.

27. M. Ulmke and W. Koch, "Road Map Extraction Using GMTI Tracking," *Conference Proceedings of the 9th International Conference on Information Fusion*, Florence, Italy, July 10–13, 2006.

28. Airforce-technology.com, "RQ-4A/B Global Hawk High-Altitude, Long-Endurance, Unmanned Reconnaissance Aircraft, USA," www.airforce-technology.com/projects/ global/.

29. "NG Demonstrates Synthetic Aperture Laser Radar for Tactical Imagery," *Space Mart*, August 13, 2006, www.spacemart.com/reports/NG_Demonstrates_ Synthetic_Aperture_Laser_Radar_for_Tactical_Imagery_999.html.

30. Richard M. Marino and William R. Davis Jr., "Jigsaw: A Foliage-Penetrating 3D Imaging Laser Radar System," *Lincoln Laboratory Journal*, 15, no. 1 (2005): 23.

31. Photo from Alfred B. Gschwendtner and William E. Keicher, "Development of Coherent Laser Radar at Lincoln Laboratory," *Lincoln Laboratory Journal*, 12, no. 2 (2000): 393. Used with permission.

8. Passive RF Collection

A great deal of the technical collection for intelligence uses passive radio-frequency sensors, usually called signals intelligence (SIGINT) systems—although the term *SIGINT* also includes communications intelligence (COMINT), which is covered only briefly in this chapter. Radar signals, collected as electronic intelligence (ELINT), and telemetry signals, collected as foreign instrumentation systems intelligence (FISINT), are two important technical intelligence sources. One set of intentional and unintentional emissions has intelligence value but does not fall into any of these source categories; it is often referred to as RF MASINT. Following a discussion of these, this chapter will briefly cover the sensors used for passive RF collection and then finish with a discussion of one of the most important applications of RF sensors in intelligence—that of geolocation.

ELINT Collection and Analysis

Electronic intelligence refers to the information extracted through the collection, processing, exploitation, and analysis of signals transmitted by radars, beacons, jammers, missile guidance systems, and altimeters. Because most ELINT is conducted against radars, the following discussion assumes that the target is a radar. Communications transmitters are not included as ELINT targets; they are considered a target of COMINT.

The acronym *ELINT* may be unfamiliar to some, but it is widely used around the world. The radar detector that some motorists use to detect police radar is an ELINT sensor. The proliferation of radars worldwide has made ELINT collection and analysis an essential part of planning for any military operation and increasingly important in law enforcement. Airborne, spaceborne, seaborne, and ground-based radars must be identified and located continuously to support such operations. For a country such as the United States that has worldwide interests, this is a massive undertaking.

ELINT to support these operations divides broadly into two types: operational and technical, as illustrated in Figure 8-1 and discussed in the following sections. Both types have a common end goal—support to countermeasures against the radar—but they use different techniques to get there, and they have different time frames.

TECHNICAL ELINT

Technical ELINT is used to assess a radar's capabilities and performance, to determine the level of technology used in building the radar, and to find weaknesses in the radar to help electronic warfare designers defeat it. This category of ELINT was originally called *precision parameter measurements*. It involves either the measurement of radar signal characteristics to a very high order of accuracy or measurements to determine something about a radar's operation that will reveal its detection and tracking capabilities. Technical ELINT has strategic goals of assessing a country's level of technology and preventing technological surprise. The primary objective is to obtain technical parameters that will allow assessment of the radar's mission, targets, performance, and vulnerabilities. Of particular importance are measurements that will reveal a radar's vulnerability to electronic countermeasures, as Figure 8-1 suggests.

Technical ELINT collection and processing typically concentrates on signals that already have been identified and on evolutionary modifications to these signals. However, the highest priority signals for ELINT collection are always new and unidentified signals because they presumably represent the most advanced capability. Newly developed radars tend to radiate only for short periods in tests and only during times when it is believed that hostile intercept potential is at a minimum. Therefore, short duration intercepts are the best that can be expected for such radars. Close behind in importance is

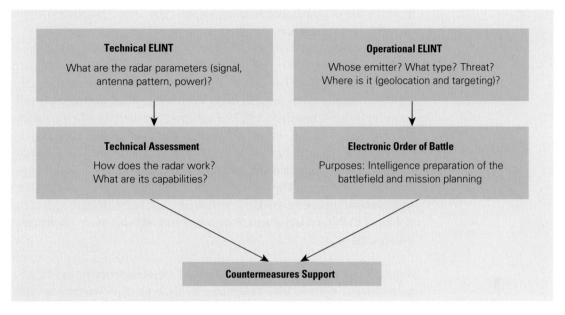

FIGURE 8-1 Operational and Technical ELINT

identifying new and unusual modes of operating existing radars. Some radars, for example, have what is called *wartime reserve modes* that are supposed to be concealed until needed in wartime—so that the radar will be less susceptible to countermeasures. These wartime modes must be identified if countermeasures against them are to be planned.

Technical ELINT is a two-step process: First, ELINT collectors must obtain a detailed signature of the radar; second, ELINT analysts must conduct a detailed assessment of that signature to obtain performance information. The typical signature comprises three distinct elements: signal parameters, antenna pattern, and power. These three together permit analysts to estimate detection performance.

Signal Parameter Measurements. The traditional radar signal parameter measurements used in ELINT are the radar's frequency, pulse duration, pulse repetition frequency (PRF) or pulse repetition interval (PRI), main beam scan pattern, and bandwidth. Frequency and pulse duration help establish the radar's detection range. The PRF or PRI determines the radar's maximum unambiguous range. The radar's main beam scan pattern helps to identify the purpose and modes of radar operation as the radar goes through its functions of search and tracking targets. The radar's bandwidth determines its range resolution.

Radars, when first developed, transmitted a simple unmodulated pulse. Modern radars can be very complex, so they have other parameters that need to be measured. They have become much more sophisticated over time. They now modulate the pulse in many ways, either to improve radar performance or to defeat hostile ELINT. The radars may be modulated in frequency, a technique known as *linear frequency modulation* (LFM). They may be modulated by changing phase, a modulation that is called *phase coding*. Each pulse may jump randomly to a different frequency, a technique known as *frequency hopping*. The radar signal may look like a burst of noise due to *spread spectrum coding*. All these techniques, and more, make the job of the technical ELINT collector and the analyst considerably more challenging than it used to be.

Antenna Pattern Measurements. The total radiofrequency power fed to a radar antenna is essentially determined by the type of power tube or solid-state device used in the transmitter, the characteristics of the pulses, and the losses by attenuation in the system. The function of the antenna is to concentrate this power in the desired direction, and its ability to do so is called *antenna gain*. The relative distribution of the energy in all directions is called the *antenna radiation pattern*. This antenna pattern and the level of power radiated are critical parameters in establishing the performance of the radar. These parameters need to be accurately measured for intelligence and electronics countermeasures (ECM) purposes.

The accurate and comprehensive measurement of a radar antenna pattern is a tedious process, even for the radar's designer. It is a tougher problem for the ELINT analyst because ELINT collection is not usually done under favorable conditions. On a radar test range, the range engineers control the test environment, and they usually strive to make that environment unfavorable for ELINT collectors. Moreover, the patterns seen on the test ranges are not always the ones observed in operational use because environmental and ground effects at the site can make significant changes in the pattern.

Power Measurements. The objectives of ELINT power-pattern measurements are to obtain precise data on the maximum beam power, total radiated power, antenna gain, and variation in gain (side and back lobe distribution) around the antenna. This requires the use of an airborne or spaceborne measuring platform. In theory, the ELINT approach is the same as that used on the antenna test range; the power density is measured and then converted to radiated power on the basis of the known geometry between the radar antenna and the collection system. In practice, the ELINT operation has all the problems encountered on the test range plus additional ones intrinsic to intelligence collection; the target radars are not cooperative; they may not radiate when the ELINT system is searching for them, and they may not radiate in the direction of the ELINT receiver. These handicaps increase the number of potential sources of error that must be eliminated, minimized, or calibrated.

OPERATIONAL ELINT

Most of electronic intelligence is devoted to the intercept and analysis of radar signals in order to locate radars, identify them, determine their operational status, and track their movements. This type of ELINT is generally referred to as *operational ELINT.*

The product of operational ELINT is called the *radar order of battle.* Military forces determine an opponent's radar order of battle in order to deny information to those radars or destroy them in conflict. Operational ELINT proved to be of great value in recent Mideast conflicts, where the U.S. Air Force and Navy both conducted large-scale operational ELINT in support of combat missions.

Operational ELINT is primarily of interest to military field commanders and increasingly to law enforcement officers for tactical intelligence. A ship, aircraft, or surface-to-air missile unit can often be tracked best by continuously pinpointing the location of a radar that it carries. Operational ELINT is used extensively in modern warfare to pinpoint targets for air attack and to locate threat radars so that attacking aircraft can avoid the defenses that the radars control. Highly accurate geolocation of these emitters is critical for targeting highly accurate munitions.

Operational ELINT in a Dense Signal Environment. Spaceborne ELINT systems typically observe a large portion of the earth's surface. Airborne ELINT systems cover a smaller portion of the surface, but the coverage still is in the thousands of square kilometers. In either case, the result is that the ELINT receiver sees a dense signal environment; many pulses are coming into the ELINT receiver continuously. The environment becomes even denser if the ELINT receiver has a wide bandwidth. But in order to function, the ELINT system (which includes the ELINT receiver and the signal processing components) must assign each incoming pulse to a specific radar.[1] Then, in most cases, the ELINT system must geolocate the radar; geolocation techniques are discussed later in this chapter. Finally, the system must identify the radars that are of special interest, specifically threat radars in a battlefield environment.

The first step, assigning incoming pulses to a specific radar, requires classifying and sorting the radar pulses according to signal parameters such as radiofrequency, pulse width, and pulse repetition frequency. Signal separation using RF as a sorting parameter has been used quite successfully; however, many different emitters are likely to use the same RF band. For most ELINT environments, the second most useful sorting parameter is the PRF.[2] To sort these signals, ELINT processors rely on a technique called *pulse train deinterleaving*. Pulse train deinterleaving relies on the fact that for radars having a fixed PRF, the pulses will arrive at a constant rate, and a constant rate sequence is easy to identify.[3] Radar designers are aware of this technique, of course, and modern radars often make this signal sorting process more difficult by constantly changing their PRF.

Operational ELINT can do more than just identify a radar by type. It can also use fine-grain signatures of radar signals to identify and track specific radars. This technique is called *specific emitter identification* or "fingerprinting." Just as no two fingerprints are identical, no two radars have identical signal parameters, even though they may be physically identical otherwise. The technique normally requires good technical ELINT to first obtain a very detailed target signature.

On the modern battlefield, a radar that stays in one place, transmitting a recognizable signal at high power continuously on a single frequency, is likely to quickly become a smoking pile of rubble. The development of sophisticated ELINT systems that can precisely geolocate radar signals, combined with the advent of highly precise ("smart") munitions, has changed the shape of battlefield conflict. Battlefield threat radars have become highly mobile; they are on the air for brief periods, only when necessary, and they are prone to relocate quickly after going on the air (a technique known as "shoot and scoot"). This places a premium on very fast geolocation and fast transmission of the collected intelligence to combat units.

Low Probability of Intercept. Radars continue to be developed that are hard for ELINT systems to collect. A major class of such radars is called *low probability of intercept* (LPI) radars. Such radars use any one of several techniques to make the radar harder to intercept or harder to locate if intercepted. The simplest such technique is emission control by reducing the transmitted power to the minimum possible level. Because most

ELINT systems must rely on detecting the radar sidelobes, another useful LPI technique is sidelobe suppression. Some radars transmit each pulse on a different frequency (the technique of frequency hopping that was previously discussed) to avoid interception or to defeat the ELINT system's pulse deinterleaving feature. Other LPI radars transmit noise-like signals to hide their presence from ELINT. Radars can even mimic benign signals (such as airport surveillance radars or television stations) to avoid attack.

An example of an ELINT collection satellite is shown in Figure 8-2. GRAB was a U.S. Navy ELINT satellite. Launched in June 1960 and operated until August 1962, GRAB obtained information on Soviet air defense radars. The radar locations, deep within the Soviet Union, were inaccessible to U.S. Air Force and Navy ELINT aircraft, which had to fly outside the borders of the Soviet bloc to avoid Soviet antiaircraft defenses.

FIGURE 8-2 The GRAB ELINT Satellite

Passive RF Collection

GRAB carried two electronic payloads: the classified operational ELINT package and an unclassified set of instrumentation designed to measure solar radiation. This instrument was known as the SolRad experiment. It was publicly disclosed and used as the cover story* for the missions. The SolRad experiment was actually quite useful. Its solar radiation measurements were used by the U.S. Navy to predict the effects of the ionosphere on high-frequency radio communications.[4]

A more recent example of an ELINT satellite is the French ELISA (Electronic Intelligence by Satellite), planned for launch in 2010. ELISA is the latest in a series of French SIGINT satellites (the previous ones were called Cerise, Clementine, and ESSAIM).[5] ELISA will comprise a constellation of four satellites, located a few kilometers apart in space. Each satellite will receive and record incoming radar pulses and transmit the pulse data to a ground station. The ground station then will combine the received signals to geolocate radars using one of the geolocation techniques discussed later in this chapter.[6]

---

*A "cover story" is an openly acknowledged explanation for an operation or system that has a classified objective.

Telemetry Collection and Analysis

Vehicles that are undergoing testing—missiles, aircraft, and even farm tractors and earth-moving equipment—carry instruments called *transducers* that monitor conditions on the vehicle, such as velocity, pressures, temperatures, and subsystems performance. The instrument readings are typically recorded for later laboratory analysis. In vehicles where the recorder might not survive a catastrophic failure (aircraft) or where recorder recovery is impractical (missiles and satellites), the readings are transmitted via radio back to a ground site. Such transmissions are called *telemetry.*

Because telemetry involves the deliberate transmission of information, its interception could be considered a part of COMINT. But because it is nonliteral information and because it transmits measurements, telemetry intercept logically fits as part of technical collection.

Complex and expensive systems such as missiles and satellites have a large number of instrument readings to transmit. It is impractical to devote a separate transmission link to each reading. Telemetry systems therefore combine the signals from the readings in a process called *multiplexing* for transmission using a single transmitter. Each signal occupies a "channel" in the multiplex system. At the receiver, the channels are separated (demultiplexed) and sent to separate displays or recorders.

Some telemetry systems, especially older ones, multiplex by allocating a different part of the radio frequency spectrum to each signal; this technique is known as *frequency division multiplexing.* A more complex, but increasingly popular, approach is *time division multiplexing,* where each signal periodically gets to use the entire frequency bandwidth of the transmitter for a short time interval.

Interpretation of intercepted telemetry is difficult, in part because of what is called the *scaling problem.* The engineers running the instrumentation know the scales for the readings they receive and which channels of telemetry come from which instrument. The intercepting party must often infer both the nature of the instrument and the scale of the readings from external evidence—correlating the readings with external events such as aircraft or missile altitude or speed.

Merely to have made a few key identifications brings a considerable intelligence benefit, because the telemetry analyst can then relate a current launch to earlier ones and decide whether the launch is one of a series. Also, the comparison of telemetry with previous launches might indicate the test of a new vehicle or a new model of a known missile. Given a fair sample of powered-flight telemetry, an analyst can usually say whether a launch vehicle is liquid- or solid-fueled, whether it has a single burning stage or multiple stages, and what ratio of payload to total weight it probably has. The analyst can do this by looking for characteristic signatures in the different telemetry channels. For example, the velocity profile of a ballistic missile has a characteristic signature: Velocity increases steadily with time as the missile accelerates, then flattens when the motor cuts off. A multiple-stage missile then again increases its velocity when the second stage motor kicks in. These acceleration patterns create a unique signature in the telemetry.

Telemetry can be denied to an opponent by encryption, and digital telemetry that is typically sent by time division multiplexing is particularly amenable to encryption. Encryption denies the collector information on what are called *telemetry internals* (that is, the values of the readings themselves). Encryption therefore forces the collector to rely on what are called *telemetry externals* (that is, changes in the signal due to the flight profile of the vehicle), which provide information about aspects of the vehicle's performance.[7] Using externals, the flight profile can be measured using the multipath technique described later in this chapter.

COMINT Signatures

As noted in the preface, COMINT is primarily concerned with analysis of literal information and therefore is beyond the scope of this book. However, a very important part of COMINT is concerned with signatures. No two communications systems are exactly identical, and the knowledge of what communications system is being used by a particular person or organization often has intelligence value.

In addition, the identity of the communications equipment operator can sometimes be ascertained using the biometrics techniques, such as voiceprints (discussed later in this book). The technique is quite old; in the Middle Ages, when "COMINT" usually meant intercepting and reading letters, handwriting analysis was sometimes used to identify the author. When Morse code telegraphy was in wide use from the late 1800s through World War II, a code operator could recognize another operator by his characteristic pattern of keying the code, known as his "fist."

Modern communications technologies have made the identification process even easier. Two identical brands of cell phone will differ slightly in the signals they transmit—perhaps in frequency, signal stability, or the emissions of spurious signals.[8] Two optical fibers will have fine-grained differences in the signals they transmit. If these differences can be measured, then a unique signature can be established for each piece of communications equipment.

Furthermore, consumer electronics are providing more unique signatures that can be associated with an individual. As these devices infiltrate our personal and professional lives—Wi-Fi, Bluetooth, BlackBerrys, iPods, smart watches, and GPS devices—we are increasing the number of possible RF signatures that together can create a unique pattern. By passively monitoring the signatures generated by a person's devices, a statistical correlation can be drawn to not only infer the identity of the person but also to track the person.[9]

Other RF Emissions

Several categories of RF emissions are of intelligence value but their collection is not called SIGINT, even though they often are collected by SIGINT systems. The difference is that these emissions are not intended to transmit a signal. As noted earlier, they customarily are referred to as RF MASINT.

Some of these RF emissions are deliberate, some are not. A variety of events can cause unintentional emissions of radio frequency energy. Some equipment also radiates RF: internal combustion engines, electrical generators, and switches. These emissions are typically weak, but sensitive equipment can detect the signals and locate the emitter or use the characteristic "signature" of the emission to identify the target. In addition to highly sensitive receiving equipment, analysts need highly sophisticated signal processing equipment to deal with unintentional radiation signals and derive useful intelligence from them.

ELECTROMAGNETIC PULSE

The electromagnetic pulse (EMP) effect was first observed during the early testing of high-altitude airburst nuclear weapons. The effect is characterized by the production of a very short (hundreds of nanoseconds) but intense electromagnetic pulse, which propagates in all directions from its source. The electromagnetic pulse is, in effect, an electromagnetic shock wave. The field can be strong enough to produce short-lived, transient voltages of thousands of volts on exposed electrical conductors, such as wires or exposed parts of printed circuit boards. The potential for widespread damage from EMP was demonstrated during the Starfish high altitude nuclear detonation in July 1962. The detonation at 400 km altitude created an EMP effect that blacked out street lights and caused radios and TVs to malfunction in Hawaii, almost 1500 km away.

This transient voltage aspect of the EMP effect is of military significance because it can result in irreversible damage to a wide range of electrical and electronic equipment, particularly computers and radio or radar receivers. The amount of damage depends on how well the electronics are protected against EMP and the intensity of the field produced by the weapon. The damage that is inflicted is similar to the damage that can be caused to consumer electronics by nearby lightning strikes. Computers used in data processing systems, communications systems, displays, industrial control applications (including road and rail signaling), and those embedded in military equipment, such as signal processors, electronic flight controls, and digital engine control systems are all potentially vulnerable to the EMP effect.[10]

Technical intelligence collection is used for detecting EMP because of its value in monitoring nuclear weapons tests. During the suspected South African or Israeli nuclear test incident described in chapter 4, the EMP sensor carried on the Vela satellite was not operational. As a result no independent confirming EMP signature could be obtained, helping to cast doubt on whether a nuclear test had actually occurred.[11]

HIGH-POWER MICROWAVE AND NON-NUCLEAR EMP WEAPONS

The discovery that a nuclear detonation-caused EMP could disrupt or destroy electronic equipment led to the creation of a class of weapons to create a similar effect and accomplish the same result over shorter ranges without the need to detonate a nuclear device. As a class, they have different names, but RF *radiation weapons* and RF *damage weapons* are two common names. These weapons generate a very short, intense energy pulse producing a transient surge of thousands of volts that kills or disrupts semiconductor devices. They can disable unshielded electronic devices, including practically any modern electronic device within the effective range of the weapon. Their targets typically are electronic systems, such as aircraft or guided missile sensors, tactical computers, and artillery fuses. There are two distinct types of such weapons.

The first type, called a *non-nuclear EMP device*, generates a single very powerful short pulse much like that produced by a nuclear detonation. The second type is usually referred to as a *high-power microwave* (HPM) weapon. It transmits a beam of microwave radiation, similar to a radar beam, in short bursts to affect its target. As discussed below, HPM weaponry has the potential to be a nonlethal antipersonnel weapon. It can do this by heating the

water in the body, much as a microwave oven heats food, to create an unpleasant sensation in the victims. At high power levels, HPM is an extremely effective weapon against electronics; a pulse only a few milliseconds in length can destroy or cripple sensitive electronics in computers, communications networks, and power plants.

The following are some weapons that the United States reportedly has developed that rely either on HPM or that mimic EMP effects without the necessity of a nuclear explosion.

- One device is an antimissile defense system, mounted on aircraft to defend against man-portable air defense systems (MANPADS).[12]
- HPM weaponry can be incorporated into unmanned aerial vehicles, bombs, and cruise missiles. Targeted microwaves with sufficient power can disable or destroy electronic systems found in much of today's military gear. The U.S. military is already using HPM technology as a nonlethal antipersonnel weapon. The weapon works by emitting a directed beam of millimeter wave energy toward people, causing an extremely painful burning sensation without physical injury.[13]
- Another class of weapon is the E-bomb, a bomb or cruise missile warhead that uses explosive energy to produce a single, instantaneous, broadband pulse of power resembling EMP. According to several sources, E-bomb warheads have been designed for the USAF's air launched cruise missile, the U.S. Navy's Tomahawk cruise missile, and the newer Joint Air-to-Surface Standoff Missile.[14] The E-bomb has two advantages compared to a conventional warhead: It is less likely to kill people, and its lethal radius (against equipment) can be greater than that of a conventional warhead.
- Versions of HPM weaponry have been developed that can be carried on an automobile and can be aimed at another vehicle. A roof-mounted antenna beams high-power pulses of microwave energy toward an opposing vehicle; the energy penetrates through a part of the car, such as the windshield, window, grill, or spacing between the hood and main body that is not made of metal. The radiated microwave energy will upset or damage the vehicle's electronic systems, particularly the microprocessors that control important engine functions, such as the ignition control, the fuel injector, and the fuel-pump control.[15]
- EMP generators can be built that fit into a suitcase. They can be placed near an important but vulnerable installation such as a computer center and go off to either disrupt or destroy the facility's electronics.

Intelligence has a role in detecting the testing of EMP and HPM devices so suitable countermeasures can be taken (primarily shielding sensitive electronics to protect them from damaging pulse power levels). But collection of testing poses challenges. EMP-like weapons have a low frequency pulse that has very wide bandwidth. HPM weapons usually operate with comparatively narrow bandwidths, in the microwave region above 4 GHz. Tests of such weapons are not conducted frequently and usually would be timed to avoid the known presence of opposing ELINT collection. The consequence is that collection against RF damage device tests is unlikely unless one is able to conduct continuous broadband surveillance of likely test ranges, preferably from a location close to the suspected test range.

UNINTENDED EMISSIONS

Most electronic equipment emits some form of electromagnetic energy. Some of the radiation is intended to transmit information, but much of it is not and is merely incidental to whatever work the electronic device is performing. These unintended emissions are often referred to by the term *electromagnetic radiation* (EMR).

Specific pieces of equipment can often be identified by their EMR signatures. The functions being performed within a factory building and the rates of production, for example, can sometimes be determined by monitoring the radio frequency emission patterns.

One source of unintended emissions having military significance is the electromagnetic rail gun, a type of gun that uses an intense burst of EM energy to accelerate a projectile instead of using explosive propellant. The rail gun thereby generates a unique EM signature that could be collected and recognized by intelligence collectors;[16] however, the collecting organization encounters the same problem as in collection against RF damage weaponry. That is, rail gun tests are not likely to occur very often, and the collection system would therefore need to conduct surveillance at close range to be sure of monitoring the test.

Electronic equipment can radiate EM energy both through the air and through power lines or other conducting paths. Such emissions are formed when components or cables act as antennas to transmit the EMR. Sources of EMR include cables, ground loops, printed circuit boards, internal wires, the power supply to power line coupling, the cable-to-cable coupling, switching transistors, and high-power amplifiers.[17] A similar effect may occur with metal pipes, such as those used for domestic water supplies. If a grounding system is not installed correctly such that there is a path in the circuit with a very high resistance (for example where paint prevents electrical conduction), then the whole grounding system could well act in a similar fashion to an antenna.

This information can be intercepted, interpreted, and analyzed. Sensors placed nearby often can recover information of intelligence value from the equipment—sometimes literal, sometimes nonliteral. As an example, it is possible to reconstruct the display of older designs of computer video monitors (which employed cathode ray tubes, using electron beams to create characters on the screen) from sensors located at distances on the order of 100 meters. The newer display types (for example, plasma displays) have substantially less EMR. Reconstructing the contents of a computer's memory or the contents of its mass storage devices is more complicated and must be performed closer to the computer. U.S. government concern for protection against the collection of such emanations resulted in the development of TEMPEST technology, which uses shielding and other electronic design techniques to reduce the EMR.[18]

STIMULATED EM EMISSIONS

An alternative to the passive collection of EMR is to stimulate such emissions. Strictly speaking, this is not passive collection because the collector must transmit a signal in order to receive a usable signal. In that respect, collecting stimulated EM emissions is more like operating a radar. However, the concept is closely related to the collection method discussed in the previous section.

The concept is to transmit a strong RF signal, usually a coherent signal, at a nearby target (on the order of a few hundred meters away). The target then re-radiates an RF signal that is modulated by the slight vibrations (usually acoustic vibrations) that it experiences. The re-radiated signal is then recovered by a receiver antenna and demodulated to recover the acoustic signal. The technique, sometimes referred to as radio frequency flooding, has been used for COMINT but can be used to recover nonliteral information about the target area or activity in the area. The section on vibrometry in chapter 6 provides details.

Since at least the 1960s, radio frequency flooding of installations has been used for intelligence data collection. The flooding signals are used to collect data remotely, much as a radar senses its target. The flooding was directed at devices such as typewriters. Signals directed at the typewriters were modulated by the keystrokes and the modulated signal received by other antennas, thereby compromising the information typed. Innocuous signals such as those emanating from a television or radio station can be used successfully to flood an installation.[19]

Intentional radiation from a source near the target also can be used to obtain target signatures. Usually, this occurs because moving parts on the target modulate a nearby radio frequency signal. A radar or radio mounted on an aircraft, for example, will have its signal modulated by the aircraft propellers or jet turbine blades. The modulation, though weak, can provide both the aircraft type and identification of the specific aircraft. The concept is similar to the use of microwaves or lasers to illuminate an object and to pick up conversations as audio vibrations that modulate the signal.

Passive RF Sensors

Passive RF sensors used in intelligence generally include a combination of an antenna, receiver, and signal processor. Some RF sensors have human operators working directly with the sensor, and so may have display and storage systems. Remotely operated sensors, such as those on satellites, usually transmit collected signal information to a ground site. But an antenna and a receiver are the minimum requirements for all such sensors. The sensor's performance is determined almost solely by the design and performance of the antenna and the receiver.

ANTENNAS

The design of a SIGINT antenna depends on its intended usage. Two general types of antennas are used in intelligence. For close-in work, where a clandestinely emplaced sensor is located near the target signal, the antenna has to be small and easily concealed. Such antennas can be not much more than a short wire or a patch antenna, such as those used in cell phones; some examples of small, easily concealable antennas are shown in Figure 8-3.[20] In contrast, long-range monitoring requires antennas that are very large in order to obtain high gain and capture weak signals. This often means using a parabolic dish antenna, though phased arrays are increasingly used.

SIGINT systems can use antennas such as the ones shown in the upper part of Figure 8-3; the antenna on the left is called a horn antenna, and the antenna on the right is called a loop antenna. When the sensor must collect signals in a narrow frequency band, then the antenna can be fairly simple—the horn and loop are examples of narrowband antennas. But ELINT antennas usually must cover a very broad frequency band; although specific radar bands are identified in Table 6-1, radar signals can appear anywhere in the microwave spectrum. Some antennas are called *frequency-independent* antennas because of their wide bandwidth. They come in a variety of shapes—flat spirals, conical spirals, and log-periodic antennas, which look vaguely like the traditional rooftop-mounted home TV antennas. Two examples are shown in the lower half of Figure 8-3. On the left is a log-periodic antenna; on the right is a conical spiral.

Antennas used for FISINT can be much narrower in bandwidth, since the collection frequency is usually known. The design of the antenna also is affected by the operating band. VHF and UHF antennas often use a helical

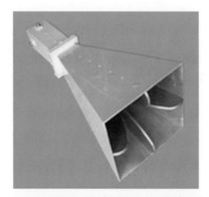

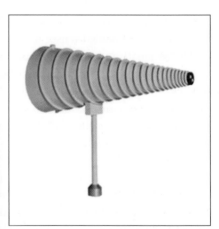

A-Info, www.ainfoinc.com

FIGURE 8-3 Types of SIGINT Antennas

antenna. For signals at frequencies above 1 GHz, a parabolic dish or similar type of antenna is more common.

The tradeoffs in the design of SIGINT receiver antennas are size, gain, beamwidth, and tracking requirements. For high gain, which is desirable since it allows the SIGINT system to detect weaker signals, the antenna size is large and the beamwidth is narrow. However, high-gain antennas have reduced angular coverage; the performance advantages of the narrow beam (selectivity and sensitivity) must be balanced against the need to cover large areas. A wide-band SIGINT receiver needs to use a highly directional antenna in a dense signal environment to identify and classify complex signals. To cover larger areas it is necessary to mechanically scan the antenna, use multiple antennas, or use a single antenna such as a phased array that generates multiple beams.

Ground-based antennas can be quite large because they rest on a very stable platform. In contrast, an antenna system on board ship is limited in its size by pointing and tracking requirements because it must dynamically correct for heading changes, pitch, and roll. This limits the shipboard SIGINT dish antenna diameter to the 5–6 meter range. Larger shipboard antennas are possible, but they are difficult to build and operate. Shipboard phased arrays can use electronic steering to compensate for the ship's yaw, pitch, and roll.

Passive RF Collection

RECEIVERS

SIGINT receivers are designed differently from the ones used in communications and radar. A radar or communications receiver is designed to receive and process a specific signal at a specific frequency. SIGINT receivers do not have this luxury; they must receive and process a wide range of signal types over a wide frequency band. Furthermore, they must be able to measure a number of signal parameters. These requirements dictate that any SIGINT receiver will be a compromise design that depends on the intended use of the receiver. Different RF receiver designs address the different problems posed by trying to collect everything that is needed from the target signal while maintaining the necessary time, frequency, and spatial coverage. The same three issues discussed in chapter 2—coverage, resolution, and accuracy—also apply here. Receiver tradeoffs must be made among the following:

- total bandwidth range (spectral coverage)[21]
- instantaneous frequency bandwidth—how wide a frequency band can be intercepted at one time (spectral coverage)
- frequency and time measurement accuracy

- time and frequency resolution—over how small a band of time or frequency can different signals be distinguished without loss of information
- sensitivity—what is the smallest signal energy that can be detected (intensity coverage)
- dynamic range—what is the range of signal energies that can be detected simultaneously (intensity coverage)

The nature of the expected target signals determines which of these characteristics is emphasized in receiver selection and design. Different receiver designs have been optimized to perform well for specific purposes. For weak signals such as telemetry signals, sensitivity is most important. In contrast, target radars have strong signals but increasingly use very wide bandwidths (up to 1 GHz or higher), so wide instantaneous bandwidth is more important for ELINT receivers. Table 8-1 summarizes some of the important types of RF receivers used in intelligence.

Following is a brief summary of the strengths, weaknesses, and SIGINT uses of each of these major types of receivers.

Crystal Video. These receivers are primarily attractive because they have wide instantaneous RF bandwidth. They have no simultaneous signal capability or

TABLE 8-1 Summary of Microwave RF Receivers

Receiver	RF Range (GHz)	Instantaneous Bandwidth	Frequency Accuracy	Frequency Resolution	Sensitivity	Dynamic Range
Wide-band crystal video	0.5–40	very wide	poor	very poor	poor	fair
Instantaneous frequency measurement	0.5–40	very wide	fair	good	fair	good
Narrow band superhet	0.01–40	narrow	good	very good	very good	very good
Wide band superhet	0.5–18	moderate	fair	poor	fair	fair
Channelized	0.5–60	wide	good	fair	good	good
Microscan	0.5–18	wide	very good	good	very good	fair
Acousto-optic	0.5–18	moderate	good	good	good	poor

frequency measurement ability. They are useful in SIGINT for finding new signals, especially at short ranges.

Instantaneous Frequency Measurement. The instantaneous frequency measurement (IFM) receiver works well against a signal that jumps around in frequency (a frequency hopper), so it is useful for detecting signals that are attempting to evade SIGINT. IFM receivers have wide bandwidth and dynamic range and moderate sensitivity. They have no simultaneous signal capability, so they can measure the frequency of a single signal only.

Superheterodyne. The superheterodyne (typically called a *superhet*) can search a wide bandwidth over time, but this receiver has a low probability of signal intercept because its instantaneous bandwidth is narrow. Its high sensitivity allows it to detect weak signals, however. The superhet is preferred for FISINT collection, since most telemetry signals are transmitted at well-established frequencies.

Channelized. A channelized receiver has good sensitivity and frequency measurement capability, and can handle simultaneous signals. Like the IFM receiver, it is useful against frequency hoppers.

Microscan. This receiver is in effect a rapidly scanning superheterodyne to improve detection probability over a wide bandwidth. It has problems against signals with very wide instantaneous bandwidths. Its dynamic range is limited. Its ability to handle many simultaneous signals and weak signals makes it useful for ELINT.

Acousto-optical. Using a device called a *Bragg Cell* (which uses the incoming electrical signal to modulate a light wave traveling through glass) and working much like a channelized receiver, this receiver's primary advantage is that it can have many more parallel channels (typically one thousand or more), allowing both good frequency resolution and wide frequency coverage. The acousto-optical receiver works very well against a frequency hopper and is one of the preferred receivers for ELINT.

Receiver Combinations. It is apparent from this list that no one type of receiver can handle all the requirements of an ideal SIGINT receiver. The solution, in general, is to use a system of receivers and signal processors of different types working together. One receiver, for example, may be designed to search for and acquire new signals; a microscan receiver could do this. Another receiver, such as a superheterodyne, might be used to closely

examine signals of interest that are detected by the search receiver. A special processor might then be accessed to measure the signal parameters, such as pulse width and PRF.[22] The technique is another example of using sensor suites. Using a combination of complementary sensors, when a single sensor did not meet the mission requirements, was discussed in the radar and optical collection sections in chapter 2.

RADIOMETERS

The radiometer is not listed in Table 8-1 because it traditionally is considered to be an energy detector rather than a signal receiver. Radiometers were discussed in chapter 4 for their use in imaging, but they also find use in SIGINT. Their primary value is in searching the RF spectrum for new, not previously identified, sources of RF energy. They are particularly useful for detecting low probability of intercept signals, such as spread spectrum signals. A radiometer simply measures the total energy within a bandwidth. Although a radiometer can detect the presence of a signal, it cannot measure signal parameters, and its temporal and frequency resolution are generally poor. It must rely on one of the receivers listed in Table 8-1 to obtain signal parameters.

SIGNAL PROCESSORS

The signal processor must perform a number of functions that vary depending on the type of intelligence being collected. The first processing step is normally to sort the incoming signals, by frequency and by the pulse deinterleaving technique described previously. After the signals have been sorted, they must be identified as coming from a specific type of emitter, assuming that the emitter has previously been collected and analyzed. If the emitter is of a new type, then technical ELINT processing is used to analyze the signal parameters. If the emitter has an electronic signature that is recognized (for example, in an existing signals catalog), then operational ELINT processing techniques are usually employed (for example, to geolocate the emitter and to uniquely identify it for future reference).

A wide range of signal processing techniques are used in ELINT, again, depending on the functions to be performed. For technical ELINT, the emphasis usually is on precise measurements of frequency and modulation characteristics. For operational ELINT, the emphasis is more on the identification and geolocation of specific emitters. Most of these processing techniques in modern ELINT systems start by digitizing the incoming signals; once digitized, the signals can be processed in many different ways, depending on what information is desired about the signal. The desired information then can be displayed—also in different ways—depending again on how it is to be used. Operational ELINT displays often are spatial—that is, a map display with specific signals named and located on the map. Technical ELINT tends to make use of some type of spectrum analyzer, which typically shows a plot of signal strength versus frequency. The analyzer provides a visual signature that describes the signal bandwidth and modulation, power, and other signal parameters.

Geolocation

Pinpointing the location of a target is called *geolocation* in the technical collection business. Geolocation is often thought of as locating the target on the surface of the earth or ocean; the definition of the term *geolocation* implies that the target is located on the globe. Most geolocation does, in fact, involve locating surface targets, but in intelligence a broader meaning is applied that includes locating targets under the earth or ocean, in the air, or out in space. For moving targets, such as vehicles, ships, aircraft, missiles, and satellites, geolocation may have to be done repeatedly in order to track the target's movement. Conventional search radars routinely perform geolocation and tracking of aircraft, ships, and satellites. Military forces geolocate opposing units using a number of techniques, some of which are intelligence techniques.

In addition to the collection of signals, COMINT, ELINT, and FISINT operations all attempt to precisely locate the source of a signal. The key performance parameter here is geolocation accuracy. Geolocation using optical and radar imaging was discussed in chapters 4 and 7. Both optical and radar imagery allow very accurate geolocation, either by geometric computations based on the sensor's known location and pointing angles or by reference to an already geolocated object in the image. This section focuses on geolocation of targets for intelligence purposes using passive RF sensing, which can approach but cannot match the geolocation accuracy of optical and radar imaging.

A number of different techniques may be used to obtain the location data on the emitter. The three most widely used are angle of arrival, time difference of arrival, and frequency difference of arrival.

ANGLE OF ARRIVAL

The oldest passive RF geolocation technique is to determine the direction of signal arrival. Because electromagnetic waves from a transmitter travel in a straight line, the direction of arrival of the signal is the direction in which the transmitter lies.

These traditional *direction-finding* (DF) systems use a pair of sensors working together. Each direction-finding sensor in the system produces a direction-of-arrival estimate for an intercepted signal. An estimated emitter position can be calculated from the intersection of the individual directions of arrival, as illustrated in Figure 8-4. The figure assumes that the transmitter is located on the earth's surface. If the transmitter is airborne or spaceborne, a third DF system would be needed to determine the transmitter location.

Figure 8-4 indicates the accuracy problem for angle-of-arrival geolocation. DF antennas have a definite beamwidth that causes the intersection of the beams to be an area of the earth's surface, not a point. The problem of geolocation accuracy for angle of arrival becomes more severe in an urban

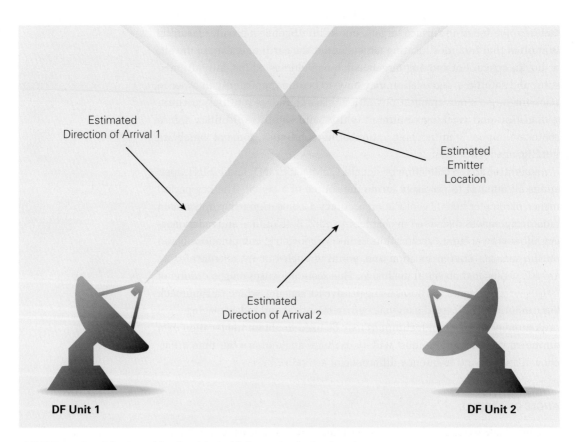

FIGURE 8-4 Combination of Angle-of-Arrival Information in Geolocation

environment because the signal may bounce off multiple buildings before arriving at the DF unit—a phenomenon called *multipath propagation.* The effect of multipath propagation is that the DF unit tends to estimate the signal as coming from the building that it last bounced off.

The oldest and still widely used direction-finding technique is to move the antenna and look for the point of maximum received signal. A very narrow-beam antenna must be used for an accurate measurement. With a broad-beam antenna, the signal variation is slight as the antenna is rotated off boresight. Therefore, it is sometimes necessary to estimate the point of maximum signal. The directional antenna technique has the advantage of relatively high gain because the DF is taken on the peak of the antenna beam.

A somewhat more accurate DF method than that above is to use an antenna with one or two nulls* in its radiation pattern. The antenna is rotated to determine the minimum signal received between two stronger signals. This technique is more accurate because the signal variation around the null is more rapid than the signal variation around the beam maximum of most antennas. The disadvantage of this technique is that DF is done at a point of very low gain in the antenna pattern. If the signal is weak, it may be lost around the null, eliminating accurate DF.

Probably the best DF technique is lobe comparison. Two antennas are placed near one another and pointed at slightly different angles so that their patterns overlap. When two antennas receive equal signal strength, the target is located midway between the two pointing directions.

Three techniques are often used to determine angle of arrival: spinners, phased arrays, and interferometers.

Spinners. A spinner is a single small antenna that is used for direction finding by moving the antenna rapidly (usually spinning it to provide 360 degrees azimuth coverage) and noting the direction the antenna is pointing when the signal is strongest.

Phased Arrays. Phased arrays were introduced in chapter 6. Some arrays are specifically designed for geolocating targets in SIGINT because they allow instantaneous coverage of a spatial sector. One widely used array in SIGINT is the circularly disposed antenna array (CDAA), known commonly as the Wullenweber.

---

*A null, in antenna parlance, is the point in space of minimum antenna gain between two regions of higher gain; despite its name, the null is not usually a point of zero gain.

The Wullenweber is a large circular antenna array used by the military to triangulate high frequency (3–30 MHz) radio signals for radio navigation, intelligence gathering, and search and rescue. Because of its immense size and huge circular reflecting screen, the antenna is colloquially known as the "elephant cage." The CDAA was originally developed by the Germans during World War II to receive high frequency (HF) transmissions from German submarines in the North Atlantic and to determine the general locations of the submarines. The name "Wullenweber" was the cover term they used to identify their CDAA research and development program.[23] Two CDAAs, such as the one shown in Figure 8-5,[24] located sufficiently far apart can geolocate an HF emitter at ranges of thousands of kilometers, using the fact that HF signals reflect off the earth's ionosphere. The geolocation is not very accurate. It depends on the state of the ionosphere and on the accuracy of angular measurement; accuracies are in the tens of kilometers.

Interferometers. Interferometers are sensors that receive EM energy over two or more different paths and deduce information from the coherent interference between the received signals. They determine the direction of arrival

FIGURE 8-5 AN/FLR-9 CDAA Located Near Augsburg, Germany

by measuring the phase difference of arrival of an RF signal at two or more antenna elements. These antenna elements are physically separated in space by some portion of a wavelength, and the phase difference recorded at the individual elements determines the direction of arrival. Therefore, an interferometer is just a phased array with wider spacing. The simplest interferometer consists of a pair of directional antennas that are tuned to receive radio emissions from a source in a desired RF band. The signal phases from the two receivers are then compared to determine the direction of arrival of the wave front from the signal. The direction of arrival of the wave front determines the precise direction to the target radio emitter.

TIME DIFFERENCE OF ARRIVAL

Another technique for geolocating a signal depends on the fact that signals travel at a defined velocity—acoustic signals at the speed of sound, electromagnetic signals (including optical signals) at the speed of light. This speed can be used to geolocate the source of a signal. The speed of travel differs in different media, which can be a problem for acoustic signals, but for all practical purposes, the speed of radio waves is the speed of light. Radars, as noted in chapter 6, determine the distance to a target by measuring the time delay for the round trip of a pulse. SIGINT systems do not transmit, but they can use a similar technique for geolocating a target, as discussed below.

Multilateration, also known as *hyperbolic positioning,* is the process of locating an object by computing the *time difference of arrival* (TDOA) of a signal at different locations. Multilateration is commonly used in civil and military surveillance applications to accurately locate an aircraft, vehicle, or stationary emitter by measuring TDOA of a signal from the emitter at three or more receiver sites. It is widely used in SIGINT.[25] The technique also works with acoustic signals, to be discussed in chapter 10.

A pulse from an emitter will arrive at slightly different times at two spatially separated receiver sites, the TDOA being due to the different distances of each receiver from the platform. In fact, for given locations of the two receivers, a large series of emitter locations would give the same measurement of TDOA. For two receivers at known locations, the TDOA geolocates an emitter on a curved surface called a *hyperboloid* (which is why the name hyperbolic positioning is used). Note that the receivers do not need to know the absolute time at which the pulse was transmitted; only the time difference is needed.[26]

Suppose now that the SIGINT collection system has a third receiver at a different location, and it also can intercept the signal. This makes a second and third TDOA measurement available, as Figure 8-6 indicates. A comparison of the three time differences of signal arrival at the three sensors defines a curve in space; the emitter must be somewhere on this curve. If the emitter is on the earth's surface, the geolocation problem is easily solved: The emitter is located where the curve touches the earth's surface. If the emitter is known to be somewhere above the earth, a fourth sensor would be needed to precisely locate it on the curve.[27]

Multilateration can be far more accurate for locating an object than techniques such as angle of arrival. It is easier to measure time accurately than it is to form a very narrow beam. The accuracy of multilateration is a function of several variables, including:

- the geometry of the receiver(s) and transmitter(s)
- the timing accuracy of the receiver system
- the accuracy of the synchronization of the receiving sites (this can be degraded by unknown propagation effects)
- the bandwidth of the emitted pulse(s)
- uncertainties in the locations of the receivers[28]

Time difference of arrival has been the technology of choice for high accuracy location systems since the advent of radar. The global positioning system is TDOA based, as are most of the systems proposed for locating emitters. TDOA systems operate by placing location receivers at multiple sites geographically dispersed in a wide area; each of the sites has an accurate timing source. When a signal is transmitted from a mobile device, its signal reception is timestamped at all antenna sites. The differences in time stamps are then combined to produce the intersecting hyperbolic lines previously discussed.[29] Note in the figure that the emitter location estimate is not shown as a point; instead, it is shown as an ellipse, called an *error ellipse* in the geolocation trade. The error ellipse indicates the geographical region in which the emitter most likely is located.[30]

TDOA systems are subject to many of the same urban multipath problems as angle of arrival systems. As with angle of arrival systems, a major source of error in a TDOA system comes from signals arriving on paths other than the direct path from emitter to receiver. This multipath reception distorts the shape of the signal and the time delay, causing the TDOA system difficulty in accurately determining the point in the signal to be measured by all receivers.[31]

Multipath has been generally found to be the single largest contribution to error in a TDOA system. The first signal received at an antenna arrives

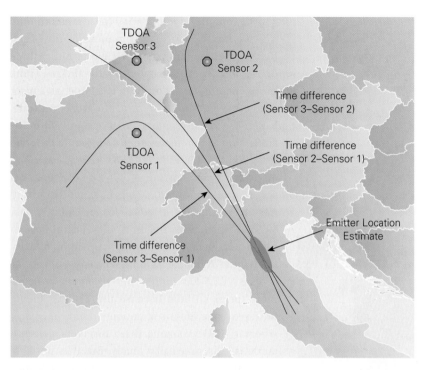

FIGURE 8-6 TDOA Geolocation

from the most direct path from the transmitter to the receiving antenna. Typically, especially in an urban environment, additional copies of the signal are received from hundreds of nanoseconds to tens of microseconds later, overlapping the first signal. These copies are arriving from reflections occurring off natural or man-made reflective surfaces in the area, such as hills, buildings, bridges, cars, or even dense woods.[32] The signal processor has to correct for these additional spurious signals.

TDOA ELINT receivers can be located on the ground to locate and track aircraft or satellites. Shipborne TDOA receivers locate and track aircraft, satellites, antiship missiles, or other ships. But these receivers are most effective for locating and tracking surface targets when they are located above the earth—on aircraft, satellites, or UAVs.[33] Airborne and spaceborne platforms offer a better coverage of the earth's surface than ground sites or ships. The disadvantage of airborne and spaceborne sensors is that their TDOA accuracy can be no better than their knowledge of their location when collecting the signals.

FIGURE 8-7 VERA-E TDOA System

An example of a modern TDOA system is the VERA-E, an ELINT system produced by the Czech Republic, shown in Figure 8-7. It uses either three or four receivers, separated by 10–25 km. Three receivers provide the location of a target on a map; four receivers can also provide target altitude. VERA-E can only detect and track pulsed emissions, due to the requirement to measure the time of arrival of pulses for TDOA. The receivers operate in the frequency range of 1–18 GHz. Position accuracy is stated as 20 meters in azimuth and 200 meters in range at a target distance of 150 km. VERA-E also uses fingerprinting techniques to identify targets. The system can automatically track up to 200 targets simultaneously.[34]

The VERA-E requires four receivers to determine target altitude because the TDOAs among four receivers define a unique point in space, whereas TDOAs among three receivers define a curve, as discussed previously. But it is possible for a single receiver to determine a target's altitude, as discussed next.

USING MULTIPATH TDOA TO DETERMINE TARGET ALTITUDE

As noted previously, multipath reception occurs when a signal arrives directly at the receiver antenna and indirectly due to bouncing off some object—usually the earth's surface. It can be a problem in receiving a signal because it causes interference with the desired signal. As noted earlier, it is an especially serious problem in urban environments because the signal can bounce off buildings several times before arriving at the receiver antenna.

Multipath reception can also be used to determine the height of an emitter. The difference between time of arrival of a direct signal and a signal reflected from the earth's surface can be used, with some knowledge of the geometry involved, to estimate the height of the emitter, as Figure 8-8 illustrates. The technique can be quite accurate if the reflective surface is smooth (for example, over water), so *specular* (mirror-like) reflection is received. It becomes less accurate as the reflection surface becomes rougher; the reflection becomes smeared by a rough surface, so diffuse reflection occurs.

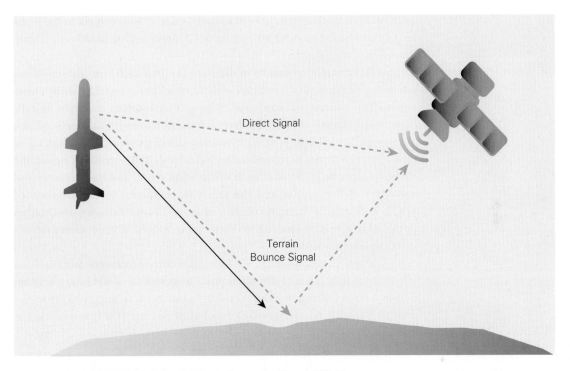

FIGURE 8-8 Use of Multipath Reception to Determine Target Altitude

The result is that the signal at the receiver is smeared in time, and it becomes harder to pick out the exact arrival time of the reflected signal.[35]

In tracking an aircraft or a missile using multipath, the TDOA from multipath gives target altitude; the Doppler profile indicates the target movement speed over time. The combination, possibly with the inclusion of angle of arrival information, enables intelligence analysts to establish the target's flight profile.[36]

FREQUENCY DIFFERENCE OF ARRIVAL

The third technique for geolocation, *frequency difference of arrival* (FDOA), depends on the fact that signals emitted or received by moving targets have an associated Doppler shift that can be used to determine target location or speed of movement. FDOA is a technique similar to TDOA in that an estimate is made for the location of a radio emitter based on observations from other points. It differs from TDOA in that the FDOA observation points must be in relative motion with respect to each other or with respect to the emitter. (It can also be used for estimating one's own position based on observations of multiple emitters.[37])

This relative motion results in different Doppler shift observations of the emitter at each location. The relative motion can be achieved by using observations from aircraft or spacecraft. The emitter location can then be estimated with knowledge of the receiver locations and velocities and the observed relative Doppler shifts between pairs of receivers. The accuracy of the location estimate is related to the bandwidth of the emitter's signal, the signal-to-noise ratio (SNR) at each observation point, and the geometry and velocities of the emitter and the receiver locations.[38] A disadvantage of FDOA is that large amounts of data must be moved between observation points or to a central location to do the processing that is necessary to estimate the Doppler shift.

Figure 8-9 illustrates how FDOA works. Three receivers moving from left to right in the figure are attempting to geolocate a stationary emitter. Sensor 1 observes negative Doppler shift because it is moving away from the emitter. Sensor 2 observes zero Doppler shift because it is broadside to the

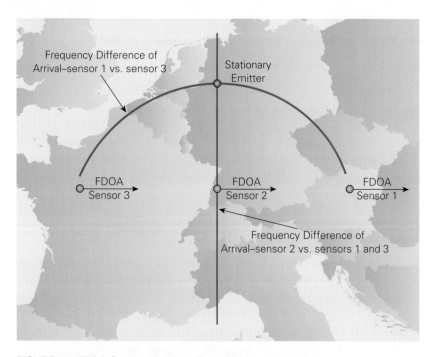

FIGURE 8-9 FDOA Geolocation from Three Moving Receivers

emitter (no relative movement between the two). Sensor 3 observes positive Doppler shift because it is moving toward the emitter. By comparing the frequencies observed by sensors 1 and 3, a SIGINT processor can determine that the emitter lies somewhere on the curve shown. Comparing the frequency observed at sensor 2 with the other two frequencies, the processor can determine that the emitter is located on the line broadside to sensor 2. The intersection of these three lines determines the location of the emitter. Note that there is an inherent ambiguity in this geolocation; an emitter located on the opposite side of sensor 2 at the same distance would give the same FDOA measurements.

Figure 8-9 suggests another problem with FDOA by noting that the emitter must be stationary. Of course, many emitters of intelligence interest are not stationary; a moving emitter will result in an invalid location unless the ELINT processing system applies some sort of correction. This is the same phenomenon that was discussed in the previous chapter: a moving target causes geolocation error for both SARs and ELINT systems by changing the Doppler shift. However, either by adding additional FDOA sensors or by watching the change in FDOA over time, the ELINT system can make the necessary correction.

IMPROVING GEOLOCATION ACCURACY

As noted earlier, the accuracy of geolocation is very important in intelligence support to military and law enforcement operations, and considerable effort goes into improving this accuracy.

A fairly straightforward technique for improving geolocation accuracy is to simply use more geolocation assets against a target. For example, to reduce errors in the measurement of the time of arrival of pulses for TDOA, the collector can add more receivers at dispersed locations. Four receivers will provide six hyperboloids, five receivers will provide ten hyperboloids, and so forth. With perfect measurements, all the hyperboloids would intersect at a single point. In practice, the surfaces rarely intersect because of various errors—which is why the result always is an error ellipse. But the TDOA of multiple transmitted pulses from the emitter can be averaged to improve accuracy.[39]

Another method for improving accuracy is to combine some of the techniques discussed above. More accurate geolocation results when geolocation techniques are combined. TDOA and FDOA are sometimes used together to improve location accuracy, and the resulting estimates are somewhat independent.[40] Angle of arrival can be combined with either to help resolve ambiguities in the target location.[41] For example, if in Figure 8-6 only receivers 1 and 2 were operating, then any emitter could only be geolocated to the curve on the earth that is shown in the figure and labeled "Time difference (Sensor 2—Sensor 1). But if either receiver also could obtain an angle of arrival, the location of the emitter on the curve could be established.

A completely different technique for improving accuracy is to get some help from an emitter in the target area that has a precisely known location. TDOA and FDOA accuracy can be greatly improved by using a reference signal transmitter, known as a *reference emitter* or *reference beacon*. The reference emitter can be, for example, a radar in the target area, the position of which is already known, or a GPS-equipped beacon that has been emplaced in the target area to act as a reference emitter. When a new signal in the target area must be geolocated, the geolocation system receives both the reference emitter signal and the new signal and uses some comparison techniques in its signal processors to reduce the geolocation error.[42]

RF TAGGING AND TRACKING

RF tagging and tracking are widely used in intelligence and law enforcement. A well-known example is the use of RF tags to track stolen automobiles. These tags, which typically include a GPS receiver that tracks the automobile's position, are concealed in the automobile to discourage theft. If a tagged auto is stolen, police can pinpoint its location by receiving the tag's RF signal.

The widest use of RF tagging, however, is in the commercial sector. The simplest and most commonly used type of RF tag is the radiofrequency identification (RFID) tag. These tags are extensively used in the retail business and supply chains to track the movement of goods. An RFID tag is a microchip combined with an antenna in a compact package; the packaging is structured to allow the RFID tag to be attached to an object to be tracked. A computer chip is attached to an antenna, and they are often referred to together as an RFID tag. Data stored on the chip transmits wirelessly through the antenna to an RFID reader or scanning device that operates on the same frequency as the antenna. The tag's antenna picks up signals from an RFID reader or scanner and then returns the signal, usually with some additional data (such as a unique serial number or other customized information).

RFID devices can be active or passive:

- Passive RFID tags get their power from the RFID reader. When an RFID reader is directed at a passive RFID tag that is tuned to the reader frequency, the reader sends an EM signal to the tag. The energy received by the tag effectively is used to power its response to the reader. Passive

RFID usually requires a reader to be within a foot of the chip, but depending on the frequency, it can be read from up to 20 feet away.

- Active RFID tags have a battery that provides power to transmit data on the chip, and it can transmit data very long distances. Some active tags contain replaceable batteries for years of use; others are sealed units, designed essentially as throwaways. Some active tags are connected to an external power source.[43]

RFID tags can be very small. Passive tags can be the size of a large grain of rice. Active devices are typically larger—the size of a small paperback book. For intelligence uses, the tags have even been placed in personal objects, such as a walking stick that was provided to Osman Ato, a Somali arms importer. The tag allowed a U.S. Delta Force team to capture Ato in Mogadishu.[44]

Cell phones are, in effect, RFID tags and can be tracked by several techniques. The phones do not have to be in use. They simply have to be turned on. One technique compares the strength of the signal received by nearby cell phone towers to obtain an approximate position of the phone. Much higher accuracy is possible for phones equipped with GPS. Cell phones using the popular standard global system for mobile communications (GSM) that are GPS equipped can be located to within 10 meters in Europe and the United Kingdom and to within 25 meters in the United States, South America, and Canada.[45]

The Department of Homeland Security's Marine Asset Tag Tracking System (MATTS) is an example of an active tag that has intelligence applications. It consists of a miniature sensor, data logging computer, radio transceiver, and GPS tracking system integrated into a compact and inexpensive box, about the size of a deck of cards. Affixed to a shipping container, the tag reportedly can transmit through shipboard communications systems, even if the container is placed deep below deck. The tag's signal "jumps" from container to container until it finds a path it can use. The MATTS box stores its location history and reports it back when in range (up to 1 km) of an Internet-equipped ship, container terminal, or a cell phone tower. At any point in a container's journey, the container's location history can be examined, and if anything has gone amiss, authorities are alerted to inspect that particular container.[46]

Summary

Passive RF sensors used in intelligence usually are called SIGINT collectors, and they are used to produce COMINT, ELINT, and FISINT. Passive sensors also are used to collect RF MASINT.

Passive RF Collection

ELINT includes information extracted through the collection, processing, exploitation, and analysis of signals transmitted by radars, beacons, jammers, missile guidance systems, and altimeters. Most ELINT is conducted against radars and divides broadly into two types: operational and technical.

Technical ELINT is used to assess a radar's capabilities and performance, to determine the level of technology used in building the radar, and to find weaknesses in the radar to help electronic warfare designers defeat it. It involves either the measurement of radar signal characteristics to a very high order of accuracy or measurements to determine something about a radar's operation that will reveal its detection and tracking capabilities. The highest priority signals for ELINT collection are always new and unidentified signals.

Operational ELINT involves the intercept and analysis of radar signals in order to locate radars, identify them, and determine their operational status. The product of operational ELINT is called *radar order of battle* and is used mostly for planning and executing military operations.

FISINT includes the interception and interpretation of telemetry that is transmitted during missile and aircraft testing. Telemetry can be encrypted to deny the collector information on what are called *telemetry internals*—the values of the telemetry readings. Encryption forces the collector to rely on what are called *telemetry externals*—changes in the telemetry signal due to changes in the target's flight profile.

RF MASINT captures and exploits unintentional emissions of radio frequency energy from internal combustion engines, electrical generators, and switches. These emissions are typically weak, but sensitive RF receivers can detect the signals and locate the emitter or use the characteristic signature of the emission to identify the target. RF MASINT also includes collection that is targeted on electromagnetic pulse and RF damage devices.

The two critical components of a SIGINT system are the antennas and receivers. Both involve tradeoffs. Antennas would ideally have high gain and cover a large spatial volume with wide frequency bandwidth. Improving any one of these three tends to degrade performance in another. Receivers must trade off among sensitivity, bandwidth, ability to collect many signals simultaneously, dynamic range, resolution, and measurement accuracy. A number of receiver designs exist to optimize one or more of these qualities. As a result, SIGINT systems often use a mix of different antennas and receivers, each designed to collect a specific class of signals.

One of the most valuable contributions of SIGINT sensors is in geolocating and tracking emitters of intelligence interest.

The oldest passive RF geolocation technique is direction finding, which determines the angle of signal arrival. Because electromagnetic waves from a transmitter travel in a straight line, the direction of arrival of the signal is the direction in which the transmitter lies. Spinner antennas, phased arrays, and interferometers can determine the angle of arrival. Two such antennas, well separated, can locate a target on the earth. Three can locate a target in the air or in space.

Another technique for geolocating a radar signal depends on the fact that EM signals travel at the speed of light. This speed can be used to geolocate the source of a signal by measuring the time difference of arrival at widely separated receivers. It is critical to be able to identify specific pulses from the radar for TDOA to work.

A third technique for geolocation depends on the fact that signals emitted or received by moving targets have an associated Doppler shift that can be used to determine target location or speed of movement. Frequency difference of arrival is a technique similar to TDOA in that one estimates the location of a radio emitter based on observations from widely separated points. It differs from TDOA in that the FDOA observation points must be in relative motion with respect to each other or with respect to the emitter.

A fourth geolocation technique requires the presence of an RF tag on the target. These tags are often concealed to prevent removal. They typically include a GPS receiver that determines the target's location and transmits the information to a remote receiver.

Because geolocation accuracy is of high importance, a number of techniques are used to improve it. Geolocation errors can be reduced by using additional SIGINT collectors above the minimum necessary to geolocate the target signal. Another method for improving accuracy is to combine several geolocation techniques; TDOA and FDOA are sometimes used together to improve location accuracy. Angle of arrival information can be combined with either to help resolve ambiguities in the target location.

Passive RF
Collection

NOTES

1. David Adamy, *EW 101: A First Course in Electronic Warfare* (Boston: Artech House, 2001), 112–120.
2. Richard G. Wiley, *ELINT: The Interception and Analysis of Radar Signals* (Boston: Artech House, 2006), ch. 13.
3. Adamy, *EW 101*, 82.
4. Mark F. Moynihan, "The Scientific Community and Intelligence Collection," *Physics Today*, 53, no. 12 (December 2000): 51. Photo of satellite courtesy of the Naval Research Laboratory.
5. Arianespace press release, "Arianespace to launch ELISA satellites," September 11, 2007, www.arianespace.com/news-press-release/2007/09-11-07-Arianespace-to-launch-ELISA-satellites.asp.

6. CNES report, "Mapping Radar Stations from Space," www.cnes.fr/web/CNES-en/5940-elisa.php.

7. Angelo Codevilla, *Informing Statecraft* (New York: The Free Press, 1992), 122.

8. U.S. Federal Highway Administration, "Assessment of Automated Data Collection Technologies for Calculation of Commercial Motor Vehicle Border Crossing Travel Time Delay" April 2002, http://ops.fhwa.dot.gov/freight/freight_analysis/auto_tech/sect_2a.htm.

9. George Spafford, SearchSecurity.com, "Underlying Patterns Can Reveal Information Security Targets," http://searchsecurity.techtarget.com/news/article/0,289142,sid14_gci1193714,00.html.

10. www.globalsecurity.org/military/library/report/1996/apjemp.htm.

11. Carey Sublette, "Report on the 1979 Vela Incident," September 1, 2001, http://nuclearweaponarchive.org/Safrica/Vela.html.

12. Jane's Defence Review, "High-Power Microwave Weapons—Full Power Ahead?" August 25, 2006, www.janes.com/defence/news/jdw/jdw060825_1_n.shtml.

13. Sebastian Springer, "Air Force Shops for High-Power Microwave Technologies," October 2, 2007, www.fcw.com/online/news/150339-1.html?topic=defense.

14. Jane's Defence Review, "High-Power Microwave Weapons—Full Power Ahead?"

15. Brittany Sauser, "Stopping Cars with Radiation," November 13, 2007, www.technologyreview.com/computing/19699/.

16. "U.S. Navy Demonstrates World's Most Powerful EMRG at 10 Megajoules," Sensiac (Military Sensing Information Analysis Center), *Sensing Horizons*, March 2008, p. 6.

17. D. White and M. Mardiguian, *EMI Control Methodology and Procedures*, 10.1 (Gainsville, Va.: Interference Control Technologies, 1985).

18. Ryan Singel, "Declassified NSA Document Reveals the Secret History of TEMPEST," *Wired,* April 29, 2008, http://blog.wired.com/27bstroke6/2008/04/nsa-releases-se.html.

19. Ibid.

20. Photos courtesy of A-Info, www.ainfoinc.com.

21. P. Hyberg, "Spread Spectrum Radar Principles and Ways of Jamming It," [Swedish] Defense Research Institute, December 1980.

22. Adamy, EW 101, 59.

23. Michael R. Morris, "Wullenweber Antenna Arrays," www.navycthistory.com/WullenweberArticle.txt.

24. Photo provided courtesy of the Naval Research Laboratory.

25. Li Tao, Jiang Wenli, and Zhou Yiyu, "TDOA Location with High PRF Signals Based on Three Satellites," *Chengdu Dianzi Xinxi Duikang Jishu* (July 1, 2004): 7.

26. Ibid.

27. Pan Qinge, Yan Meng and Liao Guisheng, "Joint Location by Time Difference of Arrival and Frequency Difference of Arrival at Multiple Stations," *Heifei Leida Kexue Yu Jishu* (December 1, 2005).

28. Huai-Jing Du and Jim P. Y. Lee, "Simulation of Multi-Platform Geolocation Using a Hybrid TDOA/AOA Method," Technical memo, Defence R&D Canada TM 2004-256, December 2004, http://pubs.drdc.gc.ca/PDFS/unc33/p523132.pdf.

29. Louis A. Stilp, "Time Difference of Arrival Technology for Locating Narrowband Cellular Signals," *Proceedings of SPIE*, 2602, no. 134–144 (1996).

30. Li Tao, Jiang Wenli, and Zhou Yiyu, "TDOA Location with High PRF Signals Based on Three Satellites," 7.
31. Ibid.
32. Ibid.
33. Nickens Okello, "Emitter Geolocation with Multiple UAVs," *Proceedings of the 9th International Conference on Information Fusion*, Florence, Italy, July 10–13, 2006.
34. OMNIPOL a.s. marketing brochure, www.omnipol.cz/OMNI2224/OMPO-Vera-E.pdf. Photograph courtesy of Miroslav Gyurosi via Air Power Australia.
35. Yang Shihai, Hu Weidong, Wan Jianwei, and Zhou Liangzhu, "Radar Detection of Low Altitude Target in Multipath," *Beijing Dianzi yu Xinxi Xuebao*, April 1, 2002, 492.
36. Ibid.
37. Pan Qinge, Yan Meng, and Liao Guisheng, "Joint Location by Time Difference of Arrival and Frequency Difference of Arrival at Multiple Stations."
38. K.C. Ho and Y.T. Chan, "Geolocation of a known altitude object from TDOA and FDOA measurements," *IEEE Transactions on Aerospace and Electronic Systems*, 33, no. 3 (July 1997): 770–783.
39. Huai-Jing Du and Jim P. Y. Lee, "Simulation of Multi-Platform Geolocation Using a Hybrid TDOA/AOA Method."
40. Pan Qinge, Yan Meng and Liao Guisheng, "Joint Location by Time Difference of Arrival and Frequency Difference of Arrival at Multiple Stations."
41. Huai-Jing Du and Jim P. Y. Lee, "Simulation of Multi-Platform Geolocation Using a Hybrid TDOA/AOA Method."
42. Layne D. Lommen, David O. Edewaard, and Henry E. Halladay, "Reference Beacon Methods and Apparatus for TDOA/FDOA Geolocation," USPTO Application # 20070236389, October 10, 2007.
43. Technovelgy.com, "RFID Tags," www.technovelgy.com/ct/Technology-Article.asp?ArtNum=50.
44. Jeffrey T. Richelson, *The U.S. Intelligence Community*, 5th ed. (Boulder, Colo.: Westview Press, 2008), 25.
45. "Mobile Phone GPS Tracking Technology," SunSat Satellite Solutions Co., www.themobiletracker.com/english/index.html.
46. "DHS Puts MATTS in Play" *Telematics Journal,* September 6, 2007, www.telematicsjournal.com/content/topstories/2158.html.

9. Missile and Space Intelligence

The preceding chapters have discussed the characteristics of radar optical and SIGINT sensors that are used in technical collection. This chapter focuses on what has become one of the most important strategic intelligence applications for those sensors: missile and space surveillance. Its purpose is to illustrate how different technical collectors can work together to obtain a more complete picture of a target.

As more nations orbit satellites, it is increasingly important to know the locations and missions of these satellites. An increasing number of them have military or intelligence uses. Also, more countries are developing and testing ballistic missile and antimissile systems. Monitoring foreign tests to determine missile and antimissile performance is an intelligence mission.

The sensors used in carrying out the intelligence mission have a number of functions. They must search for, track, and identify space and missile targets. They must support performance assessments of foreign missiles that are undergoing testing and assess the performance of satellites. Three sensor types—radar, optical, and SIGINT—have been used in carrying out these missions against aircraft since World War II (and optical techniques have been applied since World War I). Most such surveillance has been done for operational purposes, not for intelligence. The transition from surveillance and identifying aircraft to doing the same for missiles and satellites is straightforward, but modern sensors have to work at longer ranges and under more difficult constraints, especially time constraints. Missiles and satellites move much faster than aircraft.

This chapter is concerned only with ballistic missiles that are in the test phase. A missile that is launched in anger is the responsibility of ballistic missile defense (BMD); it is an operational, not an intelligence, problem.

Radar

Radar systems provide a high-volume, all-weather means of finding and tracking missiles and space objects. They are commonly used to provide highly accurate tracking information on all ballistic missiles and on spacecraft in low earth orbit, typically at an altitude of less than 3,000 km. They are seldom used to track geosynchronous satellites because of the difficulty of radar detection at such great ranges.

These radars are designed to perform one or more of three functions: search for ballistic missiles, including reentry vehicles, or space objects (satellites or space debris); precisely track such objects; and identify them. Each function requires a somewhat different radar design, though radars can be built to perform all three functions by compromising functionality.

SEARCH RADAR

Search radars usually require large phased array antennas and high power, and they tend to operate in the lower radar frequency bands (VHF and lower UHF bands). The U.S. PAVE PAWS radar; the FPS-85 radar at Eglin AFB, Florida, which was described in chapter 6; and the Russian Dnepr and Dar'yal radars are examples of search radars. Their purpose is to detect previously unknown targets so the targets can be tracked and identified.

TRACKING RADAR

Tracking radars are used to establish where a target is and where it is going; for a satellite, this is known as establishing the satellite's orbital elements. Tracking radars can use either phased array or dish antennas and usually operate at higher frequencies (L, S, and X bands or higher). Phased arrays are useful for both search and track, and one of their advantages is that they can simultaneously track many targets—a particularly important advantage in BMD. Parabolic dish antennas are less expensive and can maintain precise tracking, but only on one target at a time. For both antenna types, the accuracy of tracking is limited by the antenna beamwidth; narrow beamwidths are better.

For highly precise tracking, interferometric radars are sometimes used. In an interferometer design, several comparatively small antennas are deployed in the pattern of an "L" or "X" on the ground; one or more of the antennas transmits a signal at the target, and the return signal from the target is received by all the antennas. By comparing the phase differences in the return signal among the antennas, the radar can accurately determine the azimuth and elevation to the satellite or reentry vehicle and provide more accurate trajectory or orbital parameters.

The tracking information provides a type of signature.

- For ballistic missiles, the signature is the reentry vehicle's (R/V) trajectory. The trajectory allows the radar to identify the R/V target. Also, the radar can identify R/V maneuvers during reentry (such maneuvers usually are designed to avoid antimissile defenses or to improve warhead accuracy).
- For satellites, the signature is the satellite's orbital parameters. The orbital parameters help to determine the satellite's mission. An historical record of an object's orbital behavior can be used to determine what is "normal" versus unusual behavior. A satellite will sometimes maneuver in order to correct for drift or drag, and these maneuvers provide additional intelligence about the satellite's mission and operational status.

OBJECT IDENTIFICATION RADAR

Object identification radars obtain a unique signature from a target such as a satellite, aircraft, ship, or vehicle. The signature then is used to identify the target's mission or purpose. In the case of satellites, the signature is usually a combination of the satellite's orbit, its shape, and its reflectivity characteristics. Object identification can be done by radars or optical systems, but a combination of the two usually gives better identification.

The use of radar to identify objects constitutes a subfield of MASINT called *radar intelligence* (RADINT). RADINT targets include satellites, missiles, ships, aircraft, and battlefield vehicles. An object identification radar can do many things, depending on its design. It can image the target, determine its radar cross-section, identify and discriminate among targets, precisely measure components, determine the motion of the target or its components, and measure the target's radar reflectance and absorption characteristics. Radar returns can be used, for example, to reconstruct the trajectories of missiles and convey the details and configuration of the missile reentry vehicle itself.[1]

A specific type of object identification radar called *space object identification* (SOI) radar uses a combination of techniques to obtain information

about satellites, reentry vehicles, and space debris. Such radars rely on three techniques for object identification:

- target movement (trajectory or orbital parameters) and changes in movement
- radar cross-section (RCS) and variations in RCS with time
- radar imaging

Target Movement. As noted in the above section on tracking, target movement is a relatively easy way for a tracking radar to provide some identification of the target. It is particularly important in collecting information about ballistic missile tests. A ballistic missile R/V has a ballistic coefficient, or *beta.* Beta is a number based on the weight, drag, and cross-section. Vehicles with a high beta are usually slender, smooth, and have little drag; they zip through the upper atmosphere without decelerating much and slow down only when reaching the thick lower atmosphere. They get very hot for brief periods of time. Vehicles with a low beta do most of their slowing down in the upper atmosphere. They take longer to slow down and generate less heat, and they experience this heat over a longer period of time. Radar decoys that may accompany an R/V are typically lighter than reentry vehicles, and so they are more affected by the atmosphere. Finally, some reentry vehicles can maneuver, either to improve accuracy or to avoid BMD defenses, and intelligence customers want to know whether an R/V is capable of maneuvering.

For satellites, target movement also can tell a great deal, for much the same reasons. A heavy satellite in near-earth orbit is slowed less by atmospheric drag than a light item of debris. The movement of a satellite out of its predicted orbit can indicate its operational status and its intentions. Satellites can be moved by thrusters, for example, to avoid attack or to escape surveillance.

RCS Variations. A tracking radar can measure the RCS of a satellite or R/V, and the RCS will vary over time. A periodic variation in RCS may indicate that the target is tumbling. Some variations can indicate that the target is changing its orientation—for example, that an onboard antenna is being moved.

Imaging Radar. Conventional search and tracking radars lack the resolution needed to provide useful radar imagery. SOI radars have the necessary resolution and use it to identify radar returns from different parts of a satellite or R/V, creating a signature. Each target reflects radar energy in a unique radiation pattern or radar cross-section (signature) that is a function of the shape and material properties of the target and the radar-to-target geometry. Different types of objects produce different but definable patterns or signatures that can be measured to determine shape and size and used to identify and classify targets of interest.

By recording the range and magnitude of the energy reflected from all parts of a target as it passes by, a two-dimensional image of the surface can be produced. Figure 9-1 shows the radar image of a cone-shaped reentry vehicle, as compared with the actual shape of the vehicle.[2]

High-resolution microwave radars have been used by the United States and other countries for remote identification of targets for several decades. Such radars have particular advantages in object identification, as compared to the optical imaging devices, which also are used for SOI. Microwave radars are able to operate through long atmospheric paths and in cloud or weather conditions that would render an optical system ineffective. Also, they offer a rich variety of waveforms and associated processing techniques that can be used both to create images of, and to observe operations of, satellites and aircraft.

A satellite is comprised of several interconnected objects, each of which scatters radar energy back toward the radar. At certain orientations of the satellite relative to the radar, the arms that interconnect these centers also strongly reflect radar energy back toward the radar. Furthermore, each major

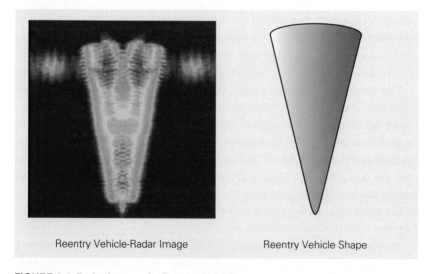

Reentry Vehicle-Radar Image   Reentry Vehicle Shape

FIGURE 9-1 Radar Image of a Reentry Vehicle

scattering center is comprised of several smaller scattering centers, which can be separated (resolved) by a high-resolution radar.

Imaging radar techniques attempt to resolve these scattering centers with the highest possible resolution, so that the scattering centers form a detailed image of the satellite. Some SOI techniques also attempt to observe motion of the centers (for example, the reorientation movement of antennas or solar panels). The combination of imagery and observation of component movements can reveal a great deal about the mission and operations of the satellite.

Conventional long-range search radars cannot provide images. They have a wide beamwidth (on the order of hundreds of meters) at satellite ranges, so that the scattering centers cannot be resolved in azimuth; normal radar pulse widths are on the order of tens to hundreds of meters, so that the scattering centers cannot be resolved in range. The satellite appears to such radars as a single large scattering center.

In contrast, an object identification radar uses very wide bandwidth, giving a pulse that can effectively separate scattering centers that are less than 1 meter apart in range. A technique called *range-Doppler processing* can then be used to obtain good azimuth resolution. In particular, a technique called *inverse synthetic aperture radar* (ISAR) can be used to create an array that is effectively thousands of meters long in the direction of travel of the satellite; such an array has a very narrow beamwidth along the direction of travel, so that scattering centers can be resolved in azimuth. The technique follows the same principle used by the airborne and spaceborne SARs discussed in chapter 7, except that the radar is stationary and the target moves, instead of the reverse (which is why it is called *inverse* SAR). The U.S. Haystack radar in Massachusetts and the German tracking and imaging radar (TIRA) are examples of SOI radars that have an ISAR capability.

The combination of high range resolution and high azimuth resolution can be used to generate a radar image that resolves the scattering centers.[3] Figure 9-2 shows a radar image of a U.S. space shuttle in flight. As the figure suggests, radar imaging is not as easily understood as optical imaging. The image requires interpretation and an understanding of how satellites or aircraft are designed. The objects at the top and bottom of the image are the wings, and the shuttle nose is at the left. The image is created in the plane of the satellite velocity vector and the range vector from the radar to the satellite.

The Cobra Judy system described in chapter 6 collects high precision metric and signature data on targets of interest. Its data collection system is comprised of two radars—an S band phased array radar and an X band dish

FIGURE 9-2 Radar Image of the Space Shuttle

radar. The S band radar uses a mission profile to perform surveillance (target detection and acquisition), tracking, and object classification. The X band radar uses its wider bandwidth and higher resolution to create images of objects designated by the S band radar.[4]

Optical Sensing: Ground-Based

Ground-based optical sensors are primarily used in intelligence to detect and track satellites. Reentry vehicles also can be tracked optically during missile tests by using infrared sensors to track the hot R/V body.

Unlike radars, most optical sensing systems do not have their own dedicated transmitters. Instead, they generally use the sun as their transmitter. This is perhaps the single most significant difference between optical and radar operations against satellites. Using the sun as the transmitter allows optical systems to operate at shorter wavelengths, but it also makes them dependent on favorable lighting and weather conditions. Two conditions must be satisfied to optically detect or track a satellite from a ground site using the sun as an illuminator:

- The site must normally be in darkness while the sun illuminates the target (a situation called the *terminator condition*). But LEO satellites may have almost half their orbit in earth's shadow, making optical tracking possible only during several hours before sunrise and after sunset, when the terminator condition is satisfied. A LEO satellite may overfly an optical site many times each day, but opportunities for optical tracking may only occur

many days apart. For certain satellites, such as sun synchronous satellites, favorable lighting conditions may not occur for several months at a time. HEO and GEO satellites present fewer problems since they remain illuminated during much of the night.

- The site must have favorable atmospheric conditions. The inability to operate during adverse weather is a severe limitation for optical sensors. Clouds, fog, and haze severely reduce an optical system's ability to function, while the same conditions have little effect on radars. The best locations for clear, dark skies are typically at higher elevations. Geographic locations less subject to adverse atmospheric effects and light pollution also are desirable.

Though the terminator condition is optimal for optical tracking, passive daytime sensing is possible. LEO satellites have been tracked during daylight hours using visible light filters and narrow field of view optics. The filters pass only specific light wavelengths and reject all others, significantly reducing light from sources other than the satellite. The infrared signature of a satellite viewed against the cold background of space has also been used to track satellites during the day.

While optical systems have disadvantages when compared to radars, they have some advantages for intelligence collection. Whereas a satellite can detect that it is being tracked by radar, it cannot detect that it is being tracked by a passive optical system. Since the sun is being used as an illuminator, the optical site does not give away its location in performing its observations.

SENSOR PERFORMANCE

Optical sensor performance is determined primarily by the size of the optics. In general, larger apertures provide better performance. Performance is measured by the *visual magnitude* that the sensor can detect. The maximum detectable visual magnitude of an optical system is a function of many variables, including the aperture of the optical system, the efficiency of the receiver, and the exposure time.

Visual magnitude (m_v) is a measure of the relative brightness of an object. The higher the m_v, the dimmer the object. The brightest stars have a visual magnitude near 1. The dimmest stars that can be seen by the unaided eye have magnitude 6. Satellites have a highly variable m_v; their reflectivity changes depending on how much of the satellite is visible (the aspect ratio) and the material of the visible portion. A typical geostationary satellite has a visual magnitude of between 11 and 13—about the magnitude of the moons of Mars. GEO satellites can be detected and tracked with telescope apertures on the order of 0.5 to 1 meter diameter.

Passive optical systems cannot directly measure the range to a target like radars can. Radar systems measure the round-trip transmission time to a target to determine the range. But an optical system using the sun as its illuminator has no reference starting time from which to determine range. A network of optical systems can obtain range, though, by using the angle of arrival technique discussed for RF systms in chapter 8. If several sites simultaneously track an object, triangulation on the object will yield its range.

Alternatively, an active optical system can be used to obtain range. A laser can function as both an illuminator and radar transmitter. Laser rangefinders use light in the same way radars use radio waves to measure the round-trip transmission time to an object to determine its range. Using a laser rangefinder for reliable satellite ranging normally requires the satellite to carry a *retroreflector* to reflect the laser light pulse back to its source.

Passive optical systems are used in searching for, tracking, and identifying satellites. The following three sections discuss how they do this from ground sites.

SEARCH

Occasionally, optical systems must conduct full- or partial-sky searches to detect new or lost satellites. Optical search for satellites is done by using a telescope drive. The drive moves the telescope across the sky at the same rate that the stars appear to move. This keeps the distant stars in the same positions in the field of view (FOV). As the telescope slowly moves, its camera takes very rapid electronic snapshots of the field of view. Star images, which remain fixed, are electronically erased. Satellites, however, do not remain fixed and their movements show up as tiny streaks that can be viewed on a console screen. Computers measure these streaks and use the data to determine the position and calculate the orbit of a satellite.[5]

Searches for satellites in GEO, or near the apogee of HEO, require a different approach since satellites in these orbits exhibit motion relative to the earth only over a prolonged period of time. A process of elimination is typically used. Star catalogs are used to account for the stars in the field of view, while space object catalogs are used to account for known satellites, thus leaving only new or moved satellites. Another approach that is used to detect GEO satellites is to turn off the telescope drive. A GEO satellite or debris then appears as a point, with the stars appearing as streaks.

Using a telescope with a wide field of view makes it easier to search for and acquire the target. However, a telescope's tracking accuracy suffers when it has a wide FOV. Several solutions to this problem exist. Attaching a small, wide FOV "finder" telescope to a larger, narrow FOV tracking telescope is one method. Another solution uses a separate acquisition telescope.

TRACKING

One way to optically track satellites is to measure the distance between the satellite and reference stars at various points along the satellite's track. Since the reference stars' positions are known, the position of the satellite and its orbit can be calculated. The process is much the same as for search: the telescope moves to keep the stars apparently stationary, and times and positions of the satellite are compared with known stars and the position of the satellite is determined. Alternatively, it is possible to track very dim objects by moving the telescope to follow the tracked object, so that the object's image remains stationary on the detector. Long exposure times, allowing the detector to collect additional light, are then possible. The problem is that the trajectory of the target satellite must be known in advance in order to move the telescope with the satellite's trajectory.

Optical tracking systems are rarely used to track LEO spacecraft because the high orbital velocity of the object limits the observation period by the optical sensor. They are, however, used to track space objects in GEO or HEO orbits; these orbits permit long observation periods during favorable lighting conditions.

The main advantage of optical tracking systems is their relative cost effectiveness in tracking satellites that are in HEO and GEO orbits. While it is possible to use radar to track satellites at GEO altitudes, such radars are extremely expensive because of the necessary specialized high-power equipment and their overall power consumption. Optical tracking systems, on the other hand, cost less on a per-unit basis. The low cost and ease of use of optical equipment makes them attractive to third world countries wishing to develop a space surveillance capability.

For a number of years, the primary U.S. ground-based optical sensor for obtaining tracks on space objects was the Baker-Nunn camera, shown in Figure 9-3.[6] The camera had a 0.5-meter aperture and weighed approximately 3.5 tons. The Baker-Nunn was originally a film camera, but many of these cameras were modified to use CCD sensors on the focal plane.

Baker-Nunn cameras have been replaced by the ground-based electro-optical deep space surveillance (GEODSS) system. The GEODSS sensor is an electronically enhanced telescope that uses low-light television cameras and a computer instead of film. Sensor data can be stored for analysis locally or transmitted in near real time to the Space Surveillance Center for analysis, if required. The GEODSS sensors are more sensitive than were the Baker-Nunn cameras; they can detect and track smaller and dimmer objects. They provide tracking that is accurate enough to maintain a space object catalog, including satellites in GEO orbits. The sensors operate only at night.

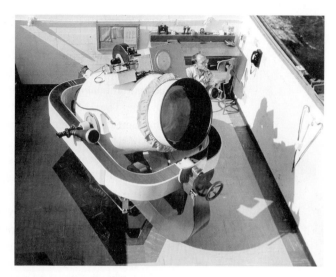

FIGURE 9-3 Baker-Nunn Camera

Each GEODSS site has three telescopes, each facing a different section of the sky. As the satellites cross the sky, the telescopes apply the techniques described earlier; they take rapid electronic snapshots, showing up on the operator's console as tiny streaks. Computers then measure these streaks and use the data to figure the current position of a satellite in its orbit. Star images, which remain fixed, are used as a reference or calibration points for each of the three telescopes. There are three GEODSS sites, located at Socorro, New Mexico; Diego Garcia, in the Indian Ocean; and Maui, Hawaii.[7] The Maui GEODSS site is part of the Maui Space Surveillance System that was discussed briefly in chapter 3.

OBJECT IDENTIFICATION

Optical SOI systems may be either passive or active. Passive optical SOI systems use the sun's illumination to provide optical signature information. Active optical SOI systems, as previously noted, rely on a laser to illuminate the target. A laser illuminator has several advantages when compared to using only the sun. First, the laser may be used for both day and night operations. Second, it can obtain the object's spin rate from the Doppler signature. Third, it can provide better imaging than is possible using only passive illumination.

Three passive optical techniques are used for object identification. Two of these—spectral sensing and photometry—can provide identifying details without imaging, though both can also be used with the third technique, which is imaging.

Spectral Sensing. It is highly desirable in space object identification to be able to determine the materials that the satellite is made of, detect degradation of the surface, identify hidden payloads, resolve satellite anomalies, and classify and identify the satellite. Spectral imaging, and in particular hyperspectral imaging, shows considerable promise of being able to assist in doing this. The U.S. Advanced Electro Optical System (AEOS) Spectral Imaging Sensor has demonstrated the capability to do such hyperspectral imaging of satellites.[8]

A sensor that can observe a satellite or reentry vehicle in the emissive band, especially in long wavelength infrared, can measure the hot spots on the satellite and determine some indications about the object's mission and operational status. Spectral analysis of reentry vehicles also allows analysts to identify the materials in the reentry vehicle.[9] LWIR sensing is best done at night, when the sky background causes less noise to enter the sensor. Figure 9-4 shows an infrared image of the U.S. space shuttle made during shuttle mission STS-96, taken in the MWIR band. The nose and forward parts of the wings show the intense heat experienced by the shuttle during reentry.[10]

Photometry. Some passive optical SOI systems use photometers to measure the intensity of light being emitted or reflected from an object. The variations of intensity at one or more wavelengths constitute an optical signature. Multicolor photometry, gathering optical signatures at different spectral wavelengths, can be a powerful tool when performing SOI. For example, multicolor photometry allows one to discriminate between satellite types; each type of satellite has a characteristic optical signature. Satellites of the same type or with similar configurations will yield similar signatures. In addition, photometry can help determine the status of a satellite. Inactive objects tumble, resulting in an erratic variation in its optical signature.[11]

Optical Imaging. Perhaps the most useful optical technique for space object identification is to obtain an optical image of the object. The Air Force Maui Optical Station, described in chapter 3, has an imaging capability: the AEOS described above. With its 3.67-meter aperture, AEOS is the largest U.S. optical

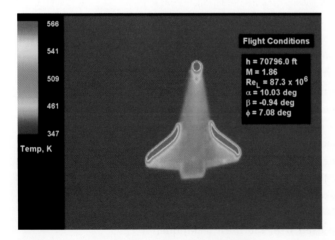

FIGURE 9-4 Infrared Image of the Space Shuttle

telescope designed for tracking satellites. The 75-ton telescope points and tracks very accurately for deep space tracking, yet is fast enough to track both low-earth satellites and missiles. Its sophisticated sensors include an adaptive optics system, radiometer, spectrograph, and long-wave infrared imager, providing a variety of signatures that help in object identification.[12]

The earth's atmosphere makes it difficult to obtain high quality optical imagery. Air turbulence distorts the light passing through the atmosphere. Following are some of the main techniques used to deal with turbulence and obtain improved imagery resolution.

- *Uncompensated imaging.* This technique involves the imaging of satellites with optics that do not correct for atmospheric turbulence. If atmospheric effects and mirror quality are momentarily disregarded, image resolution is a function of aperture diameter and the wavelength of light. In theory, a telescope with a mirror could image a satellite at 400 km with 26 cm resolution. In reality, atmospheric turbulence and mirror imperfections cause the average resolution using a mirror to be worse than 2.4 m at 400 km. It is possible to process these uncompensated images, though, to obtain some details about the satellite's configuration—for example, to identify solar panels, antennas, and telescope bodies.[13]

- *Compensated imaging.* This technique uses adaptive optics, which can greatly reduce image degradations caused by atmospheric turbulence. Adaptive optics attempt to cancel turbulence-induced distortions of an object's image. Adaptive optics use moveable mirror segments or deformable continuous mirrors to compensate for image degradation. The mirror segments are moved or the mirror surface is deformed until an acceptable image is created.

- *Video imaging.* The availability of sensitive, fast framing video cameras has led to the use of video imaging. To do this, a satellite is tracked while video is being taken of it. Over a period of time several thousand frames are taken of the satellite. Occasionally, the atmospheric turbulence cancels itself out and a near turbulence-free image is taken. Those images are then integrated to form a picture.

- *Multiple mirrors/segmented mirrors.* Once atmospheric effects are reduced, either through adaptive optics or some form of processing, then increasing the size of the optics would improve resolution. However, large mirrors are expensive, heavy, and difficult to make. The solution is to use a number of mirrors and integrate the images, eliminating the need to construct a single large mirror. The diameter of the array of smaller mirrors determines the effective aperture, not the diameter of the individual mirrors.

Missile and Space Intelligence

Recent advances in mirror manufacturing have made it possible to build large honeycomb mirrors of approximately 8 meters in diameter; several telescope projects in planning will use such mirrors or even separate telescopes cooperatively to form a larger effective aperture. One example of a segmented mirror telescope is the Keck telescope, which consists of a 10 meter diameter, 36 segment mirror; it is housed at the W. M. Keck Observatory at the summit of Mauna Kea, Hawaii. The separate telescope approach is exemplified by the Very Large Telescope located at the European Southern Observatory in Chile. It uses four 8.2 meter telescopes to form an equivalent aperture of 16 meters.

Optical Sensing: Space-Based

While most optical sensing is done from ground-based sites, there are substantial advantages to operating the sensors from space platforms. The atmosphere no longer is a factor, images can be obtained at closer ranges to provide more detail, and more opportunities exist for getting acceptable sun illumination of the target. Furthermore, more opportunities exist for sensing outside the visible band. Both satellites and reentry vehicles can be tracked and imaged from space. The USAF Space Based Visible Sensor, for example, was designed to track both types of vehicles. Its sensor suite includes a visible sensor in the 300–900 micron band and sensors that function in the long wave infrared and ultraviolet bands.[14]

On occasion, an imaging satellite will fly close enough to another satellite to obtain a high-resolution picture of it. This technique is called *satellite-to-satellite* imaging or *sat-squared* imaging.[15] In May 1998, the French SPOT 4 imaging satellite took a spectacular picture of the European ERS-1 radar observation satellite. The antennas on the ERS-1 satellite, bearing dimensions of only 3.6 × .25 meters, were clearly visible in the image.[16]

The use of spaceborne infrared (IR) sensors to detect ballistic missiles and space launch vehicles was illustrated in chapter 4. Similar IR techniques can be used to detect and track reentry vehicles from space.[17]

SIGINT

In order to carry out their missions, satellites must communicate with ground stations. Missiles in their test phase must communicate telemetry to ground stations. As a result, SIGINT sensors can be used to identify signals that provide valuable intelligence. They can confirm an object's type, determine mission status, or aid in determining orbital position.

Intelligence collection against satellites and reentry vehicles uses both ELINT and FISINT. Any country with a satellite communications capability can derive tracking information from the intercepted beacon or downlink signal emanating from the communications satellites. Such passive tracking systems are commonly available on the open market.

In addition to the collection of signals, SIGINT for space surveillance and ballistic missile test monitoring attempts to precisely locate the source of a signal and track it over time to obtain orbital or trajectory information. Any emission source on the satellite or the ballistic missile—communications, radar, or beacons—can be used as a source of tracking information, and the target's position can then be determined using one of the geolocation techniques discussed in chapter 7.

Ground-based SIGINT systems are used to track and provide position data on satellites. They typically use collection antennas on mounts capable of tracking azimuth and elevation. While such tracking systems are generally not as accurate as their optical and radar counterparts, they can provide an all-weather, 24-hour, passive tracking system that can support space catalog maintenance. The accuracy of such SIGINT tracking can be greatly improved by using interferometers.

During the course of SIGINT collection, a considerable amount of information may be gleaned that would help to identify vulnerabilities in satellites. Such things as command system back-doors, actual satellite commands, signal characteristics and power levels, or channel spacing can be exploited and used later for antisatellite operations.

When encountering a new signal, collection and processing is required to understand the function and characteristics of the signal. While encryption systems can dramatically increase the difficulty of assessing a signal, a basic level of ELINT/FISINT operations is possible without requiring the capability to demodulate and demultiplex any signals.

ELINT

ELINT collection against satellites usually is directed against the satellite's beacon (assuming that it has one) and is used for tracking and orbital determination. If the satellite carries a radar, as is the case for SARs, then technical ELINT against the radar is used to determine the radar's parameters and performance.

Ballistic missile reentry vehicles do not normally carry radar, so they are not ELINT targets. Cruise missiles typically carry at least a radar altimeter and many of them—especially antiship cruise missiles—also carry a target

acquisition and homing radar to guide the missile into the target. Typical of this class is the French Exocet, an antiship cruise missile equipped with an X band acquisition and homing radar.[18] Technical ELINT on cruise missile radars is of critical importance in developing countermeasures, especially those needed for ship defensive systems.

FISINT

Almost all satellites must carry a means for receiving communications from the ground (command signals or command uplink) and a means for transmitting information about the satellite status to the ground (telemetry or telemetry downlink). The combination of the two is called *telemetry, tracking, and commanding* (TT&C). Both the command uplink and the telemetry downlink may be intercepted and analyzed to obtain information about the satellite's location and status. Ballistic and cruise missiles also carry telemetry systems during their test phase (operational missiles do not carry telemetry). The following discussion uses ballistic missile test telemetry to illustrate how FISINT works in general.

As a ballistic missile goes through its launch sequence, almost the last event before liftoff is the disconnection of the umbilical cable linking the missile to the launch pad. From that moment on, the missile's designers must rely on telemetry for their observation of the missile's performance.[19]

While the missile is in flight, it transmits telemetry signals to ground stations along its flight path. These signals are relayed back to the control center, where the measurements are simultaneously recorded and displayed on a video screen. The intended recipients of telemetry in the ground station have a telemetry channel assignment key that identifies which trace is recording which kind of measurement, a list of calibrations, and conversion factors for translating a given telemetry value into units of pressure, temperature, flow rate, or some other variable.

Of course, the intelligence analyst does not have the channel assignment key. The analyst therefore must identify the channels before making use of the measurements, but certain basic measurements are required on any flight. The propulsion system will always have a measurement of acceleration and one of thrust chamber pressure. If the engine is liquid-fueled, with gas-driven turbopumps feeding in the propellants, then there will be pairs of measurements of the pressures at the inlet and outlet of the pumps for both fuel and oxidizer, as well as readings of gas generator pressure, turbine speed, and fuel and oxidizer flow rates. Knowing what the readings look like for one's own ballistic missile telemetry allows an analyst to search the intercepted telemetry for similar readings.

Once a tentative identification is made, various tests can be applied, based on the laws of physics and on reasonable design practice, to check its validity. A trace suspected of being an acceleration measurement, for example, can be checked against the theoretical plot of acceleration against time for a constant-thrust missile. After identifying the acceleration, the analyst can make use of the fact that the force producing the acceleration (the rocket thrust) is proportional to the pressure in the thrust chamber. Minor changes in the acceleration record will be mirrored in the thrust chamber pressure and can be used to identify the thrust chamber pressure channel.

If a good sample of telemetry is available, then it is possible to identify all the major measurements. The sample must include a major flight transition period, such as engine shutdown. In a liquid-fueled turbopump-fed engine, for example, the pressures in the propellant feed system drop to zero at shutoff in considerably less than a second, while the turbine, rotating at high speed with a great deal of inertia, takes 4 to 8 seconds to coast to a stop; this type of data is useful for identification purposes.

The single most important measurement and the one most useful in the analysis is the acceleration of the missile. If the telemetry is intercepted before first-stage burnout, the trace looks like the example shown in Figure 9-5. From this record it is apparent that the missile had two main burning stages, and the first shut down at 100 seconds. The missile then

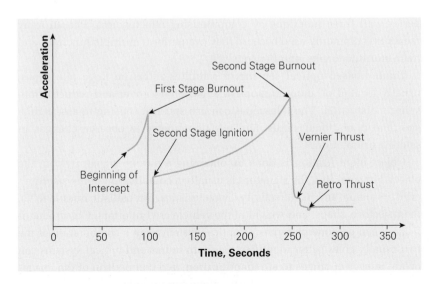

FIGURE 9-5 Typical Missile Acceleration History

coasted for 5 seconds until the second stage ignited, and this burned for an additional 145 seconds to shutdown. The low plateau in the record after second-stage shutdown indicates that small auxiliary rocket engines used for fine regulation of burnout velocity (vernier engines) operated for 10 seconds after main-engine cutoff, and the ratio of this acceleration to that at main-engine cutoff would be the ratio of vernier engine thrust to total thrust. The short negative displacement at 270 seconds signals the firing of retrorockets to separate the rocket body from the payload.[20]

Summary

Missile and space surveillance rely heavily on technical collection sensors to provide strategic intelligence. It is an area where different types of technical collectors are used together to obtain a more complete picture of a target. Radar, optical, ELINT, and FISINT sensors all are used to collect intelligence on ballistic missile testing and on satellite operations. These sensors search for, track, and identify space and missile targets. They support performance assessments of missiles that are undergoing testing and assess the performance of satellites.

Radars are designed to perform one or more of three functions: search for ballistic missiles, including reentry vehicles or space objects (satellites or space debris); precisely track such objects; and identify them. Each function requires a somewhat different radar design, although radars can be built to perform all three functions by compromising effectiveness. Phased array radars are commonly used because they can perform multiple functions and track multiple targets simultaneously.

Ground-based optical sensing of satellites relies on large telescopes, usually located on mountaintops to avoid cloud cover and reduce atmospheric distortion. The telescopes can use spectral sensing to assess mission and operational status, and use photometry to observe changes in satellite orientation.

Object identification is done by obtaining a unique signature from the object. For satellites, the signature is usually a combination of the satellite's orbit, its shape, and its reflectivity characteristics. For ballistic missile R/Vs, the trajectory, shape, and weight of the vehicle are important. Object identification can be done by radars or optical systems, but a combination of the two usually gives better identification. Both radars and optical systems can obtain images of targets to aid identification, and comparison of the images yields information that neither image alone can provide.

Space-based optical sensors can obtain high-resolution images of satellites to aid identification because the atmosphere is not a factor and the image can be obtained at closer ranges than with ground-based imaging.

Satellites and missiles that transmit RF signals can be tracked using SIGINT systems. In addition to geolocating the target, the SIGINT system can also obtain valuable intelligence by analyzing the received signals. ELINT is used to obtain information about radars carried on satellites and cruise missiles. Telemetry collection (FISINT) is used to assess the performance of ballistic missiles during testing and to assess satellite status and mission.

NOTES

1. Robert M. Clark, *Intelligence Analysis: A Target-Centric Approach*, 3rd ed. (Washington, D.C.: CQ Press, 2009), ch. 6.

2. Daniel R. Martenow, "Reentry Vehicle Analysis" CIA, *Studies In Intelligence*, Summer 1968; figure taken from Kevin M. Cuomo, Jean E. Piou, and Joseph T. Mayhan, "Ultra-Wideband Coherent Processing," *Lincoln Laboratory Journal*, 10, no. 2 (1997): 203.

3. Nicholas L. Johnson, "U.S. Space Surveillance," paper presented at World Space Congress, Washington, D.C., September 1, 1992.

4. M. Gaudreau, J. Casey, P. Brown, T. Hawkey, J. Mulvaney, M. Kempkes, "Solid-State Upgrade for the Cobra Judy S-Band Phased Array Radar," report presented at the 2006 IEEE Radar Conference.

5. Federation of American Scientists (FAS) Space Policy Project, Military Space Program, www.fas.org/spp/military/program/track/geodss.htm.

6. Smithsonian Institution Archives, Smithsonian Astrophysical Observatory, Photographic print, Negative no. 2002-32252.

7. "Ground-Based Electro-Optical Deep Space Surveillance," USAF Fact Sheet, www.af.mil/factsheets/factsheet.asp?id=170.

8. Robert Plemmons, Wake Forest University, "Tensor Methods for Space Object Identification using Hyperspectral Data," Slides 30–36, www.wfu.edu/~plemmons/talks/Maui07.pdf.

9. John A. Adam, "Peacekeeping by Technical Means," *IEEE Spectrum,* July 1986, 42–80.

10. Daniel W. Banks, Robert C. Blanchard, and Geoffrey M. Miller, "Mobile Aerial Tracking and Imaging System (MATrIS) for Aeronautical Research," NASA/TM-2004-212852, August 2004.

11. T. Schildknecht, R. Musci, C. Fruh, M. Ploner, "Color Photometry and Light Curve Observations of Space Debris in GEO," *International Astronautics Congress Proceedings,* IAC-08, paper IAC-08-A6.1.04, September 29, 2008.

12. USAF, "Air Force Maui Optical and Supercomputing Site," www.maui.afmc.af.mil/.

13. Yulia Zhulina, Vympel Corporation, Moscow, "Extracting Useful Information from Distorted Images with Multiframe Blind Deconvolution," *SPIE Newsroom,* April 5, 2007, http://spie.org/x14617.xml.

Missile and Space Intelligence

14. Jayant Sharma, Grant H. Stokes, Curt von Braun, George Zollinger, and Andrew J. Wiseman, "Toward Operational Space-Based Space Surveillance," *Lincoln Laboratory Journal*, 13, no. 2 (2002): 309–334.

15. FAS Space Policy Project, www.fas.org/spp/military/program/track/index.html.

16. ERS-1 Seen by SPOT4, http://spot4.cnes.fr/spot4_gb/im-ers-0.htm.

17. Statement of Lt. Gen. Ronald T. Kadish before the House Armed Services Committee, Subcommittee on Military Research and Development, June 14, 2001, www.mda.mil/mdaLink/html/kadish14jun01.html.

18. Federation of American Scientists, "Exocet AM39/mm.40," www.fas.org/man/dod-101/sys/missile/row/exocet.htm.

19. David S. Brandwein, "Telemetry Analysis," www.cia.gov/library/center-for-the-study-of-intelligence/kent-csi/docs/v08i4a03p_0001.htm.

20. Ibid.

10. Non-EM Signatures

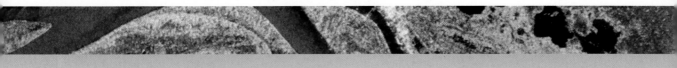

The previous chapters have focused on EM sensing, which was defined to include RF sensing in frequencies up through the millimeter wave band and optical sensing in wavelengths from infrared through ultraviolet. But technical collection also makes use of devices that sense chemical or physical changes in the environment immediately surrounding the sensor. These *in situ* sensors measure phenomena within an object or at short ranges and typically detect sound, temperature, contaminants, nuclear radiation, or electric or magnetic fields. Air sampling equipment, carried aloft by reconnaissance aircraft to detect the debris from atmospheric nuclear tests, is an example of an in situ sensor. Satellite-borne in situ sensors measure the intensity of the earth's radiation belts as the satellite passes through the belts.

Most non-EM sensors do not have the broad-area search capabilities of the EM sensors discussed in the preceding chapters. Compared to EM sensors mounted on air and space vehicles, non-EM sensors have either relatively slow search rates or relatively short ranges, or both. Consequently, most are limited to covering much smaller areas. A significant exception is that class of sensors that detect low frequency sound (infrasound) in the earth and undersea; depending on the strength of the source, such sound may be detected at distances of thousands of kilometers. These infrasound sensors are, in fact, remote sensors, but because they do not fit within the definition of remote sensing given previously (operating in the electromagnetic spectrum), they are covered in this chapter.[1]

Magnetic and Electric Fields

Magnetic and electric field sensing is not the same as EM sensing. EM waves propagate and can be detected at great distances. Electric and magnetic fields do not propagate; they typically can only be sensed at very short ranges. The field produced by a magnet, for example, can be noticed only at distances from a few inches up to a few feet unless special sensing equipment is used.

Magnetic field sensing can detect the presence or motion of vehicles, ships, or submarines by the weak changes they create in the earth's magnetic field. Magnetic sensing only works against materials that react to magnets (known as *ferromagnetic materials*). Such sensors can, at close ranges, detect ferromagnetic objects such as weapons and improvised explosive devices (IEDs).

The device for sensing weak changes in the earth's magnetic field is called a *magnetometer*. Magnetometers work by detecting the changes in certain types of atoms when the atoms are subjected to an external magnetic field. A *magnetic anomaly detector* (MAD) is a specific type of magnetometer. In geology, a MAD is used to search for minerals by observing the disturbance of the earth's normal magnetic field. A MAD also can locate underground tunnels or structures because the empty space where rock would normally be creates a slight change in the earth's magnetic field. MAD operation is similar in principle to the metal detector used by a treasure hunter or the devices used by utility companies to find underground pipes.

One of the most common military uses of MAD devices is in locating submerged submarines from aircraft. The aircraft must be almost overhead or very near the submarine's position to detect the change or anomaly. The detection range is normally related to the distance between the MAD and the submarine, and it is on the order of a few hundred meters. The size of the submarine and its hull material composition normally determine the strength of the anomaly. The close proximity required for magnetic anomaly detection makes the MAD system an excellent sensor for pinpointing a submarine's position prior to an air-launched torpedo attack.

The detection range of the MAD is greatly affected by the operation of the aircraft that carries it. The direction traveled by both the aircraft and the submarine relative to the earth's magnetic field is also a factor in detectability. Rapid changes in aircraft direction or the operation of certain electronic equipment and electric motors can produce so much aircraft RF noise that the detection of a submarine's magnetic signature is almost impossible. MAD aircraft carry special electronic circuitry to compensate for and null out this aircraft noise. Also, the MAD is placed as far as possible from the interfering sources. The result is that a MAD aircraft has a distinct tail extension, called the *MAD boom.* Figure 10-1 shows a P-3C Orion aircraft with its MAD boom.

Ships and submarines also produce an electric field in seawater because of electric currents flowing between the vessel's hull and its propellers. This field can be detected up to a few kilometers from the target, depending on the water depth and sea conditions.[2]

Mark Wagner

FIGURE 10-1 P-3 Orion Aircraft with MAD Boom

Nuclear Radiation

All nuclear reactions result in the emission of particles and waves—neutrons, electrons, ions, gamma rays, or X-rays. The radiation is strongest from a surface or atmospheric nuclear detonation, but nuclear power reactors also emit. The strength and type of radiation allows one to characterize the emitter. A number of nuclear radiation detectors have been developed; one of the oldest is the Geiger counter, which operates by sensing the ionization effect caused by the presence of radiation. Modern solid-state radiation sensors are more sensitive and are capable of detecting concealed nuclear devices at close ranges. Some are quite small, the size of a shirt button.

In the case of nuclear weapons, the primary fissionable isotopes of interest are uranium-233, uranium-235, and plutonium-239. In most cases, nuclear radiation detectors are effective only if they are relatively close to the source. For example, the signature from a plutonium weapon's spontaneous decay processes will be gamma rays and neutrons, but the threshold for detection of neutrons is about 15 meters from a nuclear weapon. Beyond that range, background noise (that is, the background of naturally occurring neutrons) overrides the weapon signature. Nuclear materials detectors therefore have

relatively short detection ranges and are best suited for choke points and monitoring portals or where one has good *a priori* intelligence about the presence of the nuclear material.

X-rays and gamma rays are a form of nuclear radiation; they fall into the EM spectrum (being at shorter wavelengths than UV radiation). But because they must be detected at short ranges and fit best in a discussion of the other types of nuclear radiation, they are included here.

X-ray and gamma ray detectors are being developed to address a threat of increasing intelligence concern: Dirty bombs, using conventional explosives that spread radioactive materials such as cesium 137, can be developed by terrorist groups. Worldwide, there exist substantial supplies of radioactive material that could be made into dirty bombs. Such weapons can be detected at choke points by a combination of gamma ray detectors and X-ray scanners. If the radiation source is unshielded, the gamma ray detector can sense it. If it is shielded (for example, by lead), then an X-ray scanner will observe a large opaque blob that can be further investigated. Any technique used to conceal radioactive material tends to make it more vulnerable to detection.[3]

Nuclear radiation sensors must deal with a tradeoff that is common to many types of sensors: The device can be made to be extremely sensitive, but the number of false alarms then rises dramatically. This has been a recurring problem in radiation monitors installed at ports and border checkpoints, where items that naturally emit radioactivity (such as cat litter, ceramic tile, and porcelain) have repeatedly triggered false alarms.[4]

Sound and Infrasound

Unintentional emission or modulation of sound waves (acoustic energy) can provide the same types of intelligence information as those for radio frequency energy. This specialized area of unintentional emissions intelligence is often called either *ACINT* (for underwater sound) or *ACOUSTINT* (sound in air). Sound and infrasound sensing, sometimes called *geophysical intelligence*, involves the collection, processing, and exploitation of environmental disturbances transmitted through or over the earth at audible (above 20 Hz) or infrasound (below 20 Hz) frequencies.

Such collection works best under conditions where sound carries well over large distances, as sound does underwater and infrasound does in the earth under certain conditions. For example, the use of passive sonar to obtain the signatures of submarines and to locate them is well known. The submarine's turbines, propellers, and other on-board machinery generate

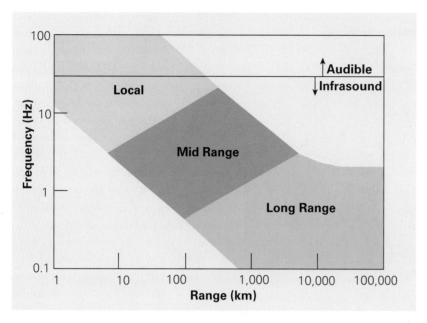

FIGURE 10-2 Sound and Infrasound Monitoring Regimes

acoustic noise that can be detected and used for identification at ranges of many kilometers in water.

But sensing often is done at very short ranges for intelligence purposes. Figure 10-2 illustrates the general ranges at which sound and infrasound sensing are carried out at different sound and infrasound frequencies.

The importance of obtaining good signature libraries for EM spectral sensing was discussed in chapter 5. Acoustic signature exploitation for intelligence also depends on having good signature libraries. Following is a discussion of some of the types of signatures that are encountered and how they are used.

ATMOSPHERIC ACOUSTIC SENSING

Battlefield intelligence increasingly makes use of short-range sound or infrasound collection. Land and air vehicles such as trucks, tanks, helicopters, and UAVs typically have a continuous acoustic power spectrum that extends across the audible range. Many such vehicles also show distinct narrowband acoustic signatures (for example, at harmonics of a gasoline or diesel engine's cylinder cycle rate, at tire-slap intervals, or at tread-slap intervals).

Non-EM
Signatures

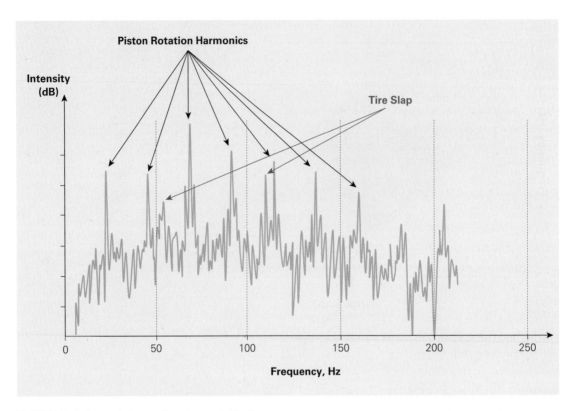

FIGURE 10-3 Acoustic Power Spectrum of a Truck

Figure 10-3 shows the acoustic signature of a large truck.[5] It contains significant power in the acoustic spectrum from above 200 Hz down to about 25 Hz. There are distinct narrowband features at harmonic frequencies representing the rotary motion of the engine's cylinders and the periodic slap of slightly asymmetric tires as they roll along the ground. Narrowband features such as these can be used in signal-processing algorithms to enhance detectability and allow identification of the vehicle type.

In the case of moving vehicles with the sharp acoustic "spikes" such as those shown in Figure 10-3, one can use the Doppler shift of one or more of these features to obtain a radial velocity measurement. With multiple sonic detectors at different locations, the vehicle's direction of travel and range can be estimated. Furthermore, the amount of detail present in the signature could permit intelligence analysts to identify specific vehicles and track their movements. A number of such identification techniques are being developed

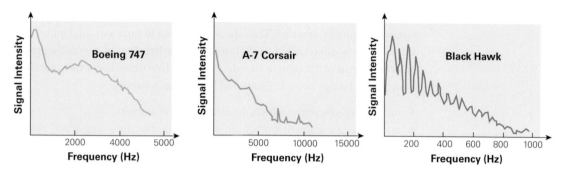

FIGURE 10-4 Comparison of Aircraft and Helicopter Acoustic Signatures

to support what is sometimes called *battlefield acoustics*, emphasizing frequencies of more than 10 Hz. Many of these same techniques can be used for short-range intelligence collection throughout the acoustic spectrum between a fraction of a Hz and a few hundred Hz.[6]

Figure 10-4 shows a comparison of acoustic signatures for a Boeing 747, an A-7 Corsair Fighter, and a Black Hawk Helicopter. In general, each type of jet engine has a unique acoustic signature; however, the same jet engine, in a different aircraft, will have a slightly different signature due to differences in the aircraft structure or in engine maintenance, allowing an intelligence analyst to identify specific aircraft. Helicopters are even easier to identify. Note in the figure the characteristic spiked signature associated with the helicopter rotor blades.[7]

Most of these acoustic signatures are only detectable at short ranges, on the order of a few kilometers or less, but the launches of large ballistic missiles can be detected by acoustic or infrasound detection at greater distances. The acoustic signature from a Scud missile launch was successfully measured at a range of 27 km in the frequency band between 1 Hz and 25 Hz.[8]

Under favorable atmospheric conditions, sound will propagate in air for relatively long distances. Usually, this is when a temperature inversion exists near the ground (that is, when temperature increases with altitude, instead of the normal decrease). Sound also will propagate farther over water or downwind.

UNDERWATER ACOUSTICS

Surface ships and submarines emit high levels of underwater noise that can be detected and tracked by a passive device called a *hydrophone* (essentially

Non-EM
Signatures

a microphone that is designed to operate most effectively underwater) at ranges of many kilometers. This specialized area of unintentional emissions intelligence is often called ACINT, as noted earlier. Sound generally propagates farther in water than in the air and about five times faster in water than in air. Underwater noise is generated by several sources:

- machinery vibration, which dominates at low speed
- water flow over the vessel's hull, which becomes more important at vessel speeds above about 10 knots
- propeller rotation, which generates a signal at the blade turning rate
- propeller cavitation, which occurs when a high propeller speed creates bubbles in the water
- crew activity

Ship identification relies on the monitoring and analysis of the sound produced when a ship is under way, especially the vibration produced by its main and auxiliary engines and the sound produced by the propeller revolving. The combination of these noises constitutes the ship's acoustic signature. Each ship theoretically has its own unique acoustic signature, a sort of sonic fingerprint similar to those discussed earlier for aircraft and vehicles. These sonic signatures can be used for identification purposes. The identification is made by comparing the signal, recorded by means of hydrophones, with a prerecorded specimen signature. Once a library of such signatures has been developed, subsequent collection and analysis of a signature can provide valuable information regarding vessel classification, identification, activities, and capability.

Ships of identical design, built by the same shipyard, may have almost identical characteristics and thus very similar acoustic signatures, but by using fine-grain measurements of the signatures, an intelligence analyst can differentiate the two ships. The problem is that a ship's acoustic signature changes over time and under different conditions. When a ship's load changes, so does its draft; this alters the acoustic signature. The ship's signature changes as a result of age, damage, and modifications made to it. Some experts believe that the acoustic signature should be measured and recorded every six months to make reliable identification possible.[9]

The spectrogram in Figure 10-5 shows the acoustic signature of the large National Oceanic and Atmospheric Administration (NOAA) ship *Ronald H. Brown,* as it approached a hydrophone site in the equatorial Pacific Ocean. The horizontal, continuous, yellow "lines," or bands of noise, are created by the rotation of the propeller blades. In the figure, strong lines occur at 21, 35, and 42 Hz. The military routinely uses the characteristics of these "blade lines" to identify ship characteristics, class, and often individual vessels.[10]

The U.S. Navy reportedly uses specially configured attack submarines to obtain the acoustic signatures of foreign submarines. The program reportedly began in 1959, targeted on obtaining a signature library of Soviet submarines. Recent reports indicate that the program has expanded to include obtaining the acoustic signatures of and tracking Russian, Chinese, and Iranian submarines.[11]

The operational challenge in underwater acoustics is to detect the signature of a ship or submarine in a very difficult environ-

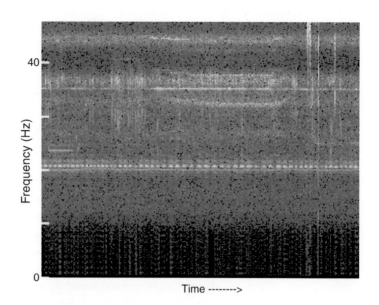

FIGURE 10-5 Spectrogram of a Surface Ship

ment. Underneath the surface, the sea is a noisy environment. This background noise can make it difficult to receive an acoustic signal. For example, the signal can be disrupted or even blocked by changes in water temperature as the signal travels. Other factors, including variations in depth, salinity, and the nature of the seabed, also affect the propagation of sound under water. In relatively shallow water such as that of the Baltic and North Seas, acoustic propagation is a very complex process, and signatures are often very difficult to obtain. But because underwater sound can propagate in so many different modes, it is possible to collect sonic signatures at both short and long ranges using a combination of sensors. The following two sections discuss how.

Short-Range Sensing—Sonar and Sonobuoys. Sonar (sound navigation and ranging) is a well-known technology; it has been used by sea creatures for communication and object detection for millions of years. During World War I, the need to detect submarines resulted in major advances in both active and passive sonar technology. Hydrophones subsequently were mounted on ships and submarines. Sonobuoys, first developed by the British in 1944, could be dropped by an aircraft to remotely identify and track submarines. A sonobuoy is simply a hydrophone attached to a flotation device (buoy); the buoy carries a radio transmitter that transmits a received sonic signature to the aircraft.

Non-EM
Signatures

Long-Range Sensing—Hydrophone Arrays. The signature shown in Figure 10-5 was collected at a relatively short range, as many acoustic signatures are. But acoustic signals also travel to great distances in oceans within a waveguide, sometimes called a *sound channel*. The sound channel is a layer in the oceans, about 1 km deep, that is somewhat isolated from the ocean layers above and below. Once in the channel, sound tends to stay in it and travel long distances without significant amounts getting to the surface. Sound created at the surface (from ships and waves) does not easily get into the sound channel. But low-frequency sound generated by submarines readily enters the sound channel and can be detected at long ranges.

In the mid-1950s, the U.S. Navy took advantage of this phenomenon by installing an underwater surveillance system to track submarines. The *sound surveillance system* (SOSUS) is a multibillion-dollar network of hydrophone arrays mounted on the seafloor throughout the Atlantic and Pacific oceans. SOSUS takes advantage of the sound channel that exists in the ocean, which allows low-frequency sound to travel great distances. These hydrophone arrays listen to the oceans, record sounds, and transmit the data via undersea cables back to shore stations for analysis. A hydrophone array obtains high sensitivity in the same way that a radiofrequency phased array does. It adds the signals from the desired direction while subtracting signals from other directions. The array is steered electronically by adding the signals received from each hydrophone in a specific time sequence.

A hydrophone array can also be towed behind a ship or submarine instead of being fixed to the ocean bottom. Most commonly, such an array of hydrophones is towed in a line behind a vessel, but two or three dimensional arrays are also used. The *integrated undersea surveillance system* (IUSS), which incorporates SOSUS, also includes mobile acoustic arrays that cue operations of tactical antisubmarine warfare forces. IUSS provides the U.S. Navy with its primary means of detecting and identifying foreign submarines.[12]

Figure 10-6 illustrates how a hydrophone array works.[13] The sound from a submarine arrives at each hydrophone at different times, depending on the direction from the array to the submarine. Processing the signals allows the direction to be determined. As the figure suggests, acoustic processing involves dealing with seconds (or fractions thereof) in the time scale; this contrasts to radar and ELINT signal processing, where time differences are measured to nanoseconds.

SEISMIC SENSING

Closely related to underwater acoustic sensing is *seismic sensing*, the detection and measurement of seismic waves that travel through the earth. A

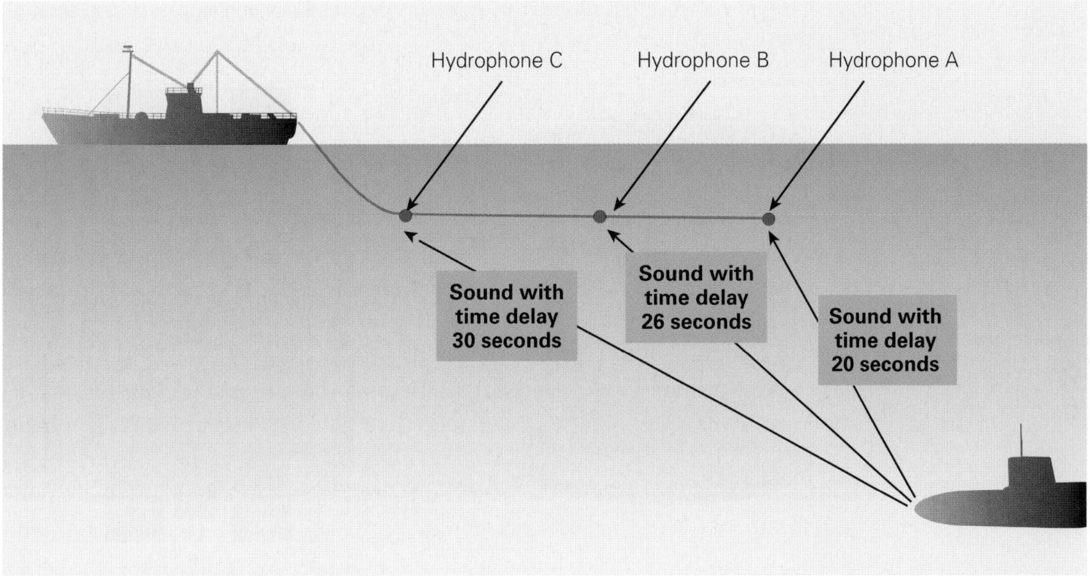

FIGURE 10-6 Towed Hydrophone Array

seismic signal or wave is created by earth vibration. Both man-made and natural activity can cause earth vibration; the vibration may be slight (a person walking on the earth or sound impact on the earth from an aircraft flying overhead) or very strong (an earthquake or large underground explosion). Most seismic sensing uses a device called the *geophone*—a type of microphone. Figure 10-7 illustrates the design. Sound and infrasound waves striking the cylinder cause it to move with respect to the magnet that it surrounds. The movement induces an electric current in the wire coil on the cylinder.

Geophones are simple but highly sensitive devices for detecting ground motion; they have been used by seismologists and geophysicists for decades. They find wide use in the oil and gas exploration industry; however, a geophone is typically only used for higher frequency (4Hz–400Hz) seismic sensing, generally at relatively short ranges. Its performance is poor at the low frequencies (below 1 Hz) that characterize the long-range teleseismic signals discussed later.

Acoustic Monitoring of Foot and Vehicle Traffic. At short ranges, seismic sensors can detect and often identify specific types of foot or vehicle traffic. Seismic collectors were used for battlefield intelligence in the 1960s during

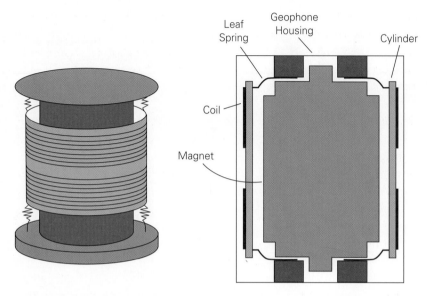

FIGURE 10-7 Geophone Design

the Vietnam War. Aircraft and special operations forces emplaced geophones along the Ho Chi Minh Trail to detect the vibrations created by personnel and equipment traversing the trail. The geophones relayed data and information to a command center, where analysts converted data into targeting information for use by combat units.[14]

Acoustic Monitoring of Buildings and Underground Facilities. Geophones can be employed to monitor activity in buildings or underground facilities. The greatest intelligence value from this specialized microphone occurs when the geophone can be placed directly in the building structure—in a wall, structural beam, electrical conduit, or air duct. The geophone picks up mechanical vibrations directly from the building structure and transmits them out of the facility via wire or secure wireless communication. The technique depends on the ability of structural objects in a room to pick up sound (such as voice and machine noise) and mechanically vibrate. Geophones therefore can be used to obtain acoustic signatures that have intelligence value, as well as to obtain COMINT from speech that occurs in the building.

If it is not possible to emplace a geophone within a building or underground facility, an array of widely spaced geophones in the vicinity of the building can be used to both locate the source of a sound and to identify the device producing the sound. It is well known that all mechanical devices, such as motors and gears, emit acoustic signals. It is possible to identify an acoustic source based on its signal spectrum. The spectral range of many building and underground activities and of machinery is in the range of 10–250 Hz.[15]

Geolocating Sound. Determining the location of a sound source depends on accurate measurement of the time of arrival of the sound at widely spaced geophones. The time delays measured by such a sensor array allow one to "triangulate" on the source and pinpoint the location of the noise. The technique is very similar to the TDOA method discussed in chapter 8, with one very important difference. As noted earlier, the speed of EM signals can be assumed to be the speed of light; it is not as simple with sound waves.

The problem is that the velocity of underground sound propagation varies greatly. In soil, it typically is 500 meters per second; in solid rock it is 5,000 meters per second. Identifying the location based on time of arrival can be a challenge. Furthermore, it is difficult to determine the depth of a sound source using a geophone array that is located near the surface. To obtain a source depth, a geophone array must be run down a vertical borehole.

At a higher level of sophistication, it may be possible to image underground facilities based on the passive monitoring of acoustic emissions from both stationary and moving equipment within such facilities. Such imaging already is done in exploration seismology, where explosions or vibrating machines at the earth's surface create waves that reflect or refract off deep structures. A geophone array collects the reflected signals so that an image of geological formations can be created. Such active sensing is obvious to those in the area, so this is unlikely to be useful for intelligence purposes. If it is possible to characterize the geology in an area, the same techniques can be applied with passive sensing. An array of passive sensors would coherently sum the data received over an array of sensors to obtain an image of the source that is similar to the image formation process used in seismic exploration.[16]

TELESEISMIC AND REGIONAL WAVE SENSING

A *teleseismic* signal is the term used to describe a seismic movement that is initiated by a strong disturbance and recorded far from its source. The term *regional wave* or *mid-range* seismic signal is used to describe seismic disturbances that are recorded at intermediate ranges, though both are often simply referred to as seismic signals.

For detecting the lower infrasonic frequencies of teleseismic and regional wave signals, a *seismometer* is used.[17] Like the geophone, the seismometer is a type of accelerometer; it measures the movement of a mass due to infrasound waves striking the seismometer housing. Three such masses are used to measure motion in three directions (up/down, North/South, and East/West). The seismometer should operate over a broad bandwidth (for example, .01–50 Hz) and have a high dynamic range (that is, be sensitive to a wide range of signal intensities).

Sensing Underground Explosions. Two types of events generally can be detected at very long ranges: earthquakes and underground explosions. The primary intelligence concern is the detection and analysis of underground explosions, especially those related to nuclear weapons testing.

Underground explosions can be reliably detected and can be identified at yields of 0.1 kiloton (100 tons of TNT equivalent) in hard rock, if conducted anywhere in Europe, Asia, North Africa, and North America. In some locations of interest, such as Novaya Zemlya in Russia (see below), detection of a 0.01 kiloton (10 tons) explosion is possible. Depending on the medium in which the explosion occurs, the signature could vary by a factor of 100; water-saturated soil gives a strong signature, while loose dry soil gives a very weak signature. Underwater explosions provide the strongest signatures; they can be reliably detected and identified at yields down to 0.001 kiloton (1 ton) or even lower.[18]

The two basic approaches to sensing underground (or underwater) explosions are to sense mid-range seismic waves or long-range seismic waves, as Figure 10-8 indicates. The difference in range is due to differences in the way that the waves propagate through the earth. Seismic signals are traditionally grouped into teleseismic waves and regional waves, depending on the distance at which they are observed. Seismic waves propagate either as teleseismic waves through the earth's deep interior, emerging at distances greater than about 1,500 km, or as regional waves (which are similar to the ripples on the surface of a pond). Because teleseismic waves do not greatly diminish with distance in the range from about 2,000 to 9,000 km, they are suited to monitoring a large country from stations deployed outside that country's borders. Teleseismic waves were the basis of most U.S. monitoring of foreign nuclear tests prior to 1987.[19]

Long-Range Teleseismic Sensing. Over the decade following the August 1949 Soviet nuclear test, the United States established a system for infrasound detection and deployed a network of seismic stations to monitor

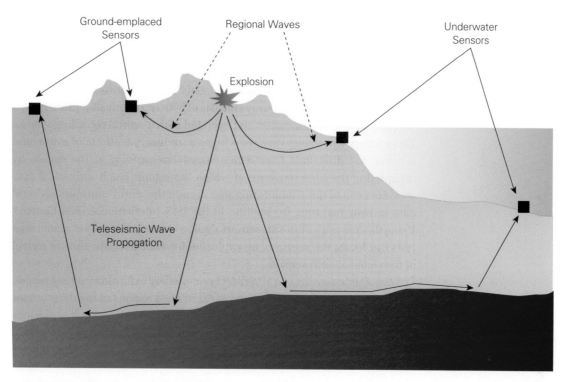

FIGURE 10-8 Seismic Wave Sensing Paths

anticipated underground testing. Over the years, the USSR conducted a number of tests at known testing areas, and these were relatively easy to identify.

The first Soviet underground test was detected in 1961, in an area some 40 nautical miles south of the atmospheric nuclear test site located at Semipalatinsk, in Kazakhstan. Prior to this event the area in question was not a known test site; however, the area in which the event occurred was not an earthquake zone, was located close to a known test area, and contained sizable mountains suitable for underground testing. The intelligence community therefore concluded that this was indeed a probable underground test site.[20]

A seismic event anywhere in the vicinity of Semipalatinsk was and still is presumed to be a nuclear test unless shown otherwise. The same is true of Novaya Zemlya, where the Soviets are known to have conducted five underground nuclear tests, the first in 1964. Seismic events detected at Novaya Zemlya always received close intelligence scrutiny because of the site's past history of atmospheric testing, the relative lack of seismic activity in the area, and the presence of sizable mountain peaks suitable for underground testing.

The Soviets confirmed the site's use as a test area by detonating there, in the fall of 1966, their largest underground nuclear test of about 1 megaton.[21]

As a requirement of the Comprehensive Nuclear Test Ban Treaty in 1966, the International Monitoring System (IMS) was set up to incorporate a network of infrasound, hydrophone, and radionuclide sensors worldwide. A typical IMS seismographic array consists of between 5 and 30 sensors spaced over several square kilometers and operated with a central recording system. These arrays can detect very weak signals, reduce the effects of noise, and estimate the directions from which signals are arriving at the station by interpreting the time sequence at which the signals reach individual sensors. Some 50 of these monitoring sites around the world continuously send data in near real time by satellite to the IMS International Data Center.[22] Using this network of in situ sensors deployed around the globe, signal analysts can locate the source of an explosion by comparing the time of arrival of the signal at each sensor.

Teleseismic sensing can also detect non-nuclear explosions at long ranges. Explosions of only a few kilograms yield in most regions of the deep oceans are readily detected at distances of thousands of kilometers. Such explosions can be identified by detecting the presence of a characteristic bubble pulse in the recorded signal, caused by gases expanding and contracting around the explosion. Because acoustic waves also transform efficiently into seismic waves at the ocean bottom, the underwater medium can be effectively monitored by a combination of underwater acoustic and seismic networks. Monitoring sound waves in the oceans is a well-advanced discipline, primarily as a result of investments in acoustic systems to detect submarines.[23]

Mid-Range Seismic Signals. Regional waves are of several types, all propagating only at shallow depths (less than 100 km). These waves typically do not propagate to teleseismic distances. They are dependent on local properties of the earth's crust and uppermost mantle, which can vary strongly from one region to another. Regional wave intensities recorded up to about 1,200 km from a shallow source are typically larger than teleseismic wave intensities recorded at distances greater than 1,800 km, but regional waves are complex and harder to interpret than teleseismic waves. Teleseismic signals from sub-kiloton explosions are often too weak to be detected, but regional signals from such explosions are detectable.[24]

The utility of regional waves is demonstrated by experience with monitoring the 340 underground nuclear tests now known to have been conducted at the Semipalatinsk test site during the period from 1961 to 1989. These explosions were mostly documented at the time by Western seismologists using teleseismic signals. But when archives of regional signals from Central Asia became openly available following the break-up of the Soviet Union, it became possible to detect and locate 26 additional nuclear explosions at this test site, most of them sub-kiloton, which had not been recognized or documented with teleseismic signals.[25]

Processing and Exploitation of Teleseismic and Regional Wave Signals. Because seismic sensors have very low detection thresholds, a large number of seismic events are detected and therefore require some analysis. Each year, somewhat more than 7,000 earthquakes occur worldwide with magnitude greater than or equal to 4, and about 60,000 with magnitude greater than or equal to 3. While chemical explosions having magnitude greater than or equal to 4 are rare (a few per year, if any), there are probably on the order of a few hundred per year worldwide with magnitude greater than or equal to 3, and many thousands per year at smaller magnitudes that are detectable by stations close enough to detect the regional waves.[26]

The problem then arises of sorting through the tens of thousands of signals each day that will be detected and collecting together all the signals that are associated with the same seismic source. The directional sensing capabilities of the IMS stations help in this process of sorting out false alarms.

The regional waves, as noted earlier, are of different types. The main two types are called *P waves* and *S waves*. P (for pressure) waves are compressional waves, similar to sound waves in the air. S (for shear) waves are transverse waves; that is, they move from side to side or up and down, like waves on the sea surface. Because underground explosions compress the surrounding earth, they radiate seismic P waves efficiently. In contrast, earthquakes result from sliding or rupture along a buried fault surface and therefore create the transverse motions of S waves. Explosions will create strong P waves and weak S waves, while earthquakes will create weak P waves and strong S waves. P waves can be identified because they travel faster and are therefore the first to arrive at the monitoring stations.

Figure 10-9 illustrates how significant the difference can be. At the top of the figure is the seismic signature taken from India's nuclear test of May 11, 1998. The signature was recorded at a monitoring station at Nilore, Pakistan. At the bottom is an earthquake measured at the same station. The differences in the P and S waves from the two events are clearly seen.[27]

Signature Libraries. Once the detections from a seismic event have been associated and an accurate location estimate has been obtained, the next step in monitoring is that of event identification.[28] This requires close analysis of the event signature and comparison with the signatures in a signature library.

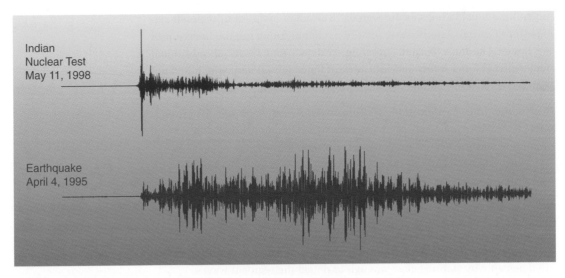

FIGURE 10-9 Comparison of Indian Nuclear Test and Earthquake Seismograms

Because there are so many seismic events, and because the main objective of seismic intelligence is to detect nuclear testing, the first step is to use the signature information to screen the events (that is, to confirm that the event either is particularly suspicious or appears not to have features associated with a nuclear explosion).

• Events are initially screened based on their location. Earthquakes are very rare or totally unknown in most regions of the world—for example, across most of Russia. Any seismic signal from such a region will attract attention and require careful scrutiny.

• Events are then screened based on their depth. For example, an event may have its depth estimated with high confidence as 50 km below the surface. It is highly unlikely that a nuclear detonation would occur below 10 km depth, so such an event would be screened out.[29]

• If the event appears to occur at a shallow depth in a region not known for earthquakes, the next step is to closely examine the signature. This requires a signature library based on past events. In an area where earthquakes are common (such as in much of China), an archive of the earthquake signatures is gradually being built up by monitoring stations.[30] As a result, there exists a large population of previous earthquake signatures against which to compare the signals of a new event.

Signature analysis relies on a comparison of the intensity ratio between different types of seismic waves, as noted above in the case of using P waves and S waves to distinguish between earthquakes and explosions.[31]

One signature problem that is not easily solved is that of distinguishing chemical from nuclear explosions. The two have identical seismic signatures, so seismic sensing alone cannot distinguish between chemical and nuclear explosions. Explosive detonations (sometimes with yields as high as several kilotons) may occur as part of canal and dam construction. If the yields are large enough (tens of kilotons or more), there is no question of their nuclear nature, but for low yield explosions, some collateral evidence has to be brought to bear to sort out the ambiguity.[32]

Summary

Technical collection makes use of non-EM sensors that sense chemical or physical changes in the environment immediately surrounding the sensor. These sensors measure phenomena within an object or at short ranges and typically detect sound, temperature, contaminants, nuclear radiation, or electric or magnetic fields. Most of them have either relatively slow search rates or relatively short ranges, or both.

A common example of short-range sensing is the magnetic anomaly detector used by many countries to locate submerged submarines from aircraft. The aircraft must be within a few hundred meters of the submarine's position to detect the change that the submarine causes in the earth's magnetic field.

All nuclear reactions result in the emission of particles and waves—gamma rays, x-rays, neutrons, electrons, or ions. The radiation is strongest from a surface or atmospheric nuclear detonation, but nuclear power reactors also emit. The strength and type of radiation allows one to characterize the emitter. Nuclear explosive devices can be identified by the presence of the fissionable isotopes uranium-233, uranium-235, and plutonium-239.

In most cases, nuclear radiation detectors are effective only if they are relatively close to the source. They encounter a problem that is common to many types of sensors: The sensor can be made extremely sensitive to allow detection at longer ranges, but the number of false alarms then rises dramatically.

Sensors that detect low frequency sound (infrasound) are an exception to the rule that non-EM sensors have short detection ranges. Depending on the strength of the source, such sound can be detected at distances of thousands of kilometers. Sound and infrasound sensing, called geophysical

intelligence, involves the collection, processing, and exploitation of environmental disturbances transmitted through or over the earth at audible (above 20 Hz) or infrasound (below 20 Hz) frequencies. Such collection works best under conditions where sound carries well over large distances, as sound does underwater and infrasound does in the earth under certain conditions.

But acoustic sensing often is done at very short ranges for intelligence purposes. Battlefield intelligence increasingly makes use of short-range sound or infrasound collection. Land and air vehicles such as trucks, tanks, helicopters, and UAVs typically have a continuous acoustic power spectrum that extends from a few hundred Hz down to a few tens of Hz. Many such vehicles also have distinct narrowband acoustic signatures that allow vehicle identification.

Surface ships and submarines emit high levels of underwater noise that can be detected and tracked by hydrophones at ranges of many kilometers. This specialized area of unintentional emissions intelligence is often called ACINT. The operational challenge in underwater acoustics is to detect the signature of a ship or submarine in the noisy ocean environment. For long-range sensing up to thousands of kilometers, long arrays of hydrophones are used.

Closely related to underwater acoustic sensing is *seismic* sensing, the detection and measurement of seismic waves that travel through the earth. A seismic signal or wave is created by earth vibration. Both man-made and natural activity can cause earth vibration; the vibration may be slight (a person walking on the earth or sound impact on the earth from an aircraft flying overhead) or very strong (an earthquake or large underground explosion).

A *teleseismic* signal is a seismic movement, usually initiated by a strong disturbance in the earth that is recorded far from its source. Explosions and earthquakes cause such disturbances. Explosions create a different teleseismic signature than earthquakes, so the two can be distinguished. But teleseismic means alone cannot distinguish between chemical and nuclear explosions unless the explosion yield is too large to be chemical; the signatures are otherwise identical. At intermediate ranges between teleseismic sensing and short-range seismic sensing, mid-range or regional waves can be sensed to detect and characterize explosions.

NOTES

1. Robert M. Clark, *Intelligence Analysis: A Target-Centric Approach*, 3rd ed. (Washington, D.C.: CQ Press, 2009), ch. 6.
2. E. Dalberg, A. Lauberts, R. K. Lennartsson, M. J. Levonen, and L. Persson, "Underwater Target Tracking by Means of Acoustic and Electromagnetic Data Fusion,"

Conference Proceedings of the 9th International Conference on Information Fusion, Florence, Italy, July 10–13, 2006.

3. Steven Johnson, "Stopping Loose Nukes," *Wired,* 2004, www.wired.com/wired/archive/10.11/nukes_pr.html.

4. Eric Lipton, "U.S. Security Devices at Ports to Be Replaced," *International Herald Tribune,* Monday, May 9, 2005, www.iht.com/articles/2005/05/08/news/secure.php.

5. From S. Tenney, Army Research Laboratory; quoted in Christopher Stubbs, "Tactical Infrasound," JASON Report JSR-03-520, The MITRE Corporation, May 9, 2005.

6. Ibid.

7. Gregory Crawford, "Netted Sensor Fence for Homeland Defense," www.mitre.org/news/events/tech04/briefings/1406.pdf.

8. Christopher Stubbs, "Tactical Infrasound," JASON Report JSR-03-520, The MITRE Corporation, May 9, 2005.

9. Daniel Frei, "International Humanitarian Law and Arms Control," *International Review of the Red Cross,* November–December 1988, 491–504, www.loc.gov/rr/frd/Military_Law/pdf/RC_Nov-Dec-1988.pdf.

10. Andra M. Bobbitt and Sharon Nieukirk, "A Collection of Sounds from the Sea," NOAA Pacific Marine Environmental Laboratory, www.oceanexplorer.noaa.gov/explorations/sound01/background/seasounds/seasounds.html.

11. Jeffrey T. Richelson, *The U.S. Intelligence Community*, 5th ed. (Boulder, Colo.: Westview Press, 2008), 233–234.

12. U.S. Navy, "History of IUSS," www.cus.navy.mil/timeline.htm.

13. Graphic from University of Rhode Island, "Discovery of Sound in the Sea," www.dosits.org/gallery/tech/bt/ha1.htm.

14. "The Conflict in Southeast Asia (SEA)," June 1996, www.wpafb.af.mil/museum/history/vietnam/sea1968.htm.

15. Preston Johnson and Shahzad Sarwar, "Recent Technology Trends in Machine Monitoring," www.averna.com/en/news_events_data/2004-10-15-averna-vibration-monitoring-oct15_2004.pdf.

16. Steve Norton, I. J. Won, Alan Witten, Alex Oren, and Frank Funak (Geophex, Ltd.), "Time-Exposure Acoustics for Imaging Underground Structures," Final Report, September 30, 2003, http://handle.dtic.mil/100.2/ADA417769.

17. Gurlap Systems, "Broadband Seismometer," http://ida.ucsd.edu/pdf/cmg-3t.pdf.

18. National Academy of Sciences, "Technical Issues Related to the Comprehensive Nuclear Test Ban Treaty" (Washington, D.C.: National Academy Press, 2002), 57.

19. Ibid, 39.

20. James R. Shea, "Winnowing Wheat from Chaff," *Studies in Intelligence*, 13, no. 3 (Fall 1969): 20, https://www.cia.gov/library/center-for-the-study-of-intelligence/kent-csi/vol13no4/pdf/v13i4a03p.pdf.

21. Ibid, 21.

22. National Radiation Laboratory of New Zealand, "CTBT International Monitoring," www.nrl.moh.govt.nz/about/ctbtinternationalmonitoringsystem.pdf.

23. National Academy of Sciences, "Technical Issues Related to the Comprehensive Nuclear Test Ban Treaty," 51.

24. Ibid, 39.

25. Ibid.

Non-EM Signatures

26. Ibid, 42.

27. Lawrence Livermore National Laboratory, "Seismic Monitoring Techniques Put to a Test," *S&T Review* (April 1999): 18. Image used by permission.

28. National Academy of Sciences, "Technical Issues Related to the Comprehensive Nuclear Test Ban Treaty," 43.

29. Ibid.

30. Ibid.

31. Ibid, 44.

32. James R. Shea, "Winnowing Wheat from Chaff," 20.

11. Materiel and Materials Collection and Exploitation

This chapter discusses some specialized fields of technical collection that do not fit cleanly into any of the previous chapters but that contribute significantly in the areas of treaty monitoring, military operations, and law enforcement. The first two fields are the following:

- materials sampling—acquiring small quantities or traces of a material and using forensic processes to determine its nature
- materiel acquisition—acquiring hardware (such as computers, airplanes, missiles or ships), usually for exploitation to determine the design and performance characteristics of the hardware

In either case, the collection or acquisition usually involves some type of HUMINT operation—and the collection may turn out to be the easiest part. Exploitation may be the most difficult. Exploitation may require extensive testing in laboratories for materials sampling or extensive field exercises to test acquired materiel.

The third field, biometric and behavioral sensing, is widely used in law enforcement but finds application in intelligence, especially in support of HUMINT operations.

Materials Sampling

Materials sampling includes the collection and analysis of trace elements, particulates, effluents, and debris. Such materials are released into the atmosphere, water, or earth by a wide range of industrial processes and military activities. Materials collection can also include sampling for environmental monitoring, which increasingly is an intelligence concern because some governments and industrial enterprises attempt to conceal their pollution activities.

Materials sampling is important in analysis for many areas of intelligence interest. Four of these areas are covered in this chapter: support to military planning and operations, nuclear testing and nuclear materials, chemical warfare production, and disease outbreaks. Economic intelligence uses materials sampling to assess factory production and environmental problems. Materials sampling has long been practiced in law enforcement, and one of its premier practitioners is fictional: Sherlock Holmes, who, as he modestly admitted, could "distinguish at a glance the ash of any known brand either of cigar or of tobacco."[1]

SUPPORT TO MILITARY PLANNING AND OPERATIONS

Military planning and operations make extensive use of intelligence collected from materials sampling. Soil and debris sampling, in particular, are done by a number of the more advanced intelligence services worldwide to support planning, as the following examples illustrate

- A controversial U.S. cruise missile attack on a Sudanese pharmaceutical factory in 1998 resulted from soil sampling and subsequent analysis. A soil sample was obtained by clandestine means near the Shifa pharmaceutical plant in Khartoum. Analysis of the sample indicated that it contained a chemical ingredient known as EMPTA. EMPTA, according to a U.S. intelligence official, has no commercial use except in the production of nerve gas.[2]
- The Soviet KGB was as adept as U.S. intelligence in material sampling. During a Cold War visit to a U.S. aircraft factory, a Soviet guest applied adhesive to his shoes to obtain metal samples for subsequent analysis to determine the metal alloys used for new U.S. fighter planes.[3]
- Material samples provided the first firm evidence that the Soviets were using titanium for the hulls of their submarines. Titanium construction represented a major advance in submarine design because it enabled submarines to operate at greater depths. The first clues came from ground

level and satellite photographs of hull sections at a Leningrad shipyard: The hull sections were too highly reflective to be steel, and they showed no signs of oxidation, as would steel. Prompted by the clues, an assistant U.S. Navy attaché was able in 1969 to obtain a sample of metal from the shipyard that proved to be a scrap of titanium, providing confirmation of the Soviet development.[4]

As an example of operational use, sensors can use sampling to track ships or submarines. As these vessels move through the water, they leave behind trace chemicals. An example of the resulting track was shown earlier in chapter 7, in Figure 7-11. Metals are continuously deposited into the water by the corrosion and erosion of the hull. Lubricants, waste flushed from sanitary tanks, and hydrogen gas discharged from a submarine's life support system are all deposited in a ship's wake. Neutron radiation from a nuclear power generator can cause detectable changes in seawater. All these contaminants leave a "track" in the ocean that can be followed by the appropriate sensors located on a trailing ship or submarine. Such tracking is, of course, real-time and has more of a flavor of operational information than of intelligence. But tracking ships or submarines over time helps to establish operational patterns and to predict future ship or submarine movements—therefore, it has use in intelligence.[5]

The potential also exists to "sample" these traces remotely. Chapter 6 discussed the use of fluorescence to detect trace materials. Contaminants released by a ship or submarine may be detectable if one illuminates the ocean surface with a laser and detects the trace elements that fluoresce when the laser energy strikes them.

Another passive sampling technique for tracking ships and submarines relies on the presence of microorganisms in seawater that will give off light when disturbed. The ship's movement and the propellers disturb the microorganisms, which then give off light—a phenomenon called *bioluminescence*. The resulting luminous trail in seawater may persist for a time after the ship or submarine has passed. The trail can be followed by either close-in or remote optical sensors. The chief problem is that bioluminescence is not a reliable phenomenon for detection; it depends on the microorganisms being present.[6]

NUCLEAR MATERIAL FORENSICS

Any handling of nuclear material nearly always leaves a trace in the environment, even if the material has been removed and the facility cleaned up.

Every nuclear explosion, even an underground explosion, leaves traces in the environment. This trace nuclear material can provide clues to its age, origin, intended use, and the way it was produced and handled. Such traces and clues can often be detected and analyzed with techniques provided by *nuclear forensics,* which functions much like medical forensics.

Loosely defined, nuclear forensics is the collection and analysis of a sample containing nuclear or radioactive material to determine the history or production process of the material. Nuclear forensics is most often used for combating nuclear smuggling, but it also helps with verification of arms control and disarmament frameworks, such as the Comprehensive Nuclear Test Ban Treaty and the Fissile Material Cut-off Treaty.[7]

Nuclear forensics for intelligence currently uses two types of collection. The first is aimed at detecting nuclear weapons testing and assessing weapons performance and relies on aircraft or ground sites to collect air samples. The second is aimed at detecting the production or movement of nuclear weapons material and relies primarily on collecting material samples in or near a suspect facility. A third type of collection is possible but fortunately has yet to be employed: obtaining debris samples after a nuclear attack for the purpose of identifying the origin of the device used.

Air Sampling. In the late 1940s, the United States began to monitor atmospheric nuclear tests by air sampling. Air samples taken over the Pacific Ocean were used to detect the first Soviet nuclear test in late August 1949. Air sampling became even more important after the Limited Test Ban Treaty of 1963. The treaty banned its signatories from nuclear testing underwater, in the atmosphere, and in space. It did not incorporate an independent international monitoring system, however; it instead depended on the major powers' satellite collection assets, which were euphemistically referred to as *national technical means* (NTM). NTM assets were directed at keeping track of each government's nuclear programs and possible testing by new entrants into the nuclear weapons club.[8] These overhead assets may provide a warning, but they can miss carefully concealed test preparations (as they did in the Indian nuclear tests of 1998). Satellite sensors may even miss the test itself or give an ambiguous signature, as in the suspect South African or Israeli nuclear test discussed in chapter 4. Therefore, air sampling, combined with underground acoustic monitoring, is important as a cross-check on the effectiveness of NTM.

Above-ground testing produces an abundant amount of radioactive isotopes (called *radionuclides*) that can be detected. But underground testing also releases radioactive substances into the atmosphere. It is very difficult to contain the gases released in a nuclear explosion. If a nuclear test occurred, radioactive particles and gases might have been vented at the time of the test, or radioactive gases might subsequently have seeped out through the cracks in the rocks above the explosion. Past experience at the test sites show that even the most skillfully conducted underground explosions may vent these gases unpredictably. All the Soviet underground tests at Novaya Zemlya and about half of the underground tests at the Semipalatinsk test site in Kazakhstan resulted in the release of radioactivity, according to Russian reporting;[9] more likely, all the tests did.

The noble gases—argon, xenon, and krypton—are the primary targets for collection and analysis to detect underground nuclear testing. These gases, like the noble gas helium, do not react chemically with other elements. Therefore, they will seep through rock cracks without being absorbed by the rock, and they will not be scrubbed out of the atmosphere by rain. Furthermore, they have different half-lives, which makes collection challenging but helps in exploitation and analysis. The challenge is to collect the samples before they decay—as all radioactive elements do. Argon-37 has a half-life of 35 days. Xenon-133 has a half-life of 5 days, and Xenon-135 has a half-life of 9 hours. An intelligence collector has to be very quick to make a successful detection. But once the collection is made, the differing amounts of each isotope remaining helps establish the length of time since the detonation.[10] For example, the ratio of the production of Xenon-135 and Xenon-133 in plutonium fission is known. Because Xenon-135 decays much more rapidly than Xenon-133, the ratio of their concentrations in the plume provides a rough measure of the number of Xenon-135 half-lives and therefore the time since the test.[11] The relative ratios also help determine the device's yield and whether the device used plutonium or uranium.

Radioactivity releases from tests can be detected in two ways: by specially equipped aircraft (as noted above) or by ground stations operated by the International Monitoring System.[12] The role of the IMS in seismic and acoustic sensing was discussed in chapter 10. The IMS also has a radionuclide monitoring network that is primarily directed at monitoring atmospheric nuclear explosions.

As previously noted, analysis of air samples confirmed that the Soviet Union had conducted its first atomic bomb test. Later analysis of fallout from the first Soviet hydrogen bomb test also revealed many details about that weapon's design. With the current moratorium on nuclear testing, intelligence collection has shifted away from air sampling and moved to on-site sampling, aimed at verifying the safety of nuclear warheads, detecting signs of nuclear proliferation, and thwarting illicit trafficking of nuclear materials.[13]

On-Site Sampling. The collection of samples for nuclear forensics commonly uses a technique referred to as "wipe and swipe"—wiping suspicious areas with specially prepared cotton weave that is designed to collect dust particles. Inspectors from the International Atomic Energy Agency use specially prepared sample kits to collect a large number of such samples each year at nuclear power plants around the world. The samples are then processed using any one of a number of techniques, including electron microscopy, X-ray diffraction, and mass spectrometry.

A primary tool for screening material samples is the spectrometer. Samples can be screened for radioactive isotopes using a technique called *gamma spectrometry.* Gamma spectrometry relies on the fact that most radioactive substances emit gamma rays, and the energy and count rate of gamma rays emitted provide information on a substance's isotopic contents. For example, the radiation emitted by nuclear material can reveal its age (that is, the time since it was first processed). As radioactive elements decay, they produce radioactive isotopes that in turn produce other isotopes. A spectroscope can determine the ratios of all the isotopes in this mix and then use these ratios to establish how much time the original material has spent decaying.

Spectrometry is capable of detecting as little as one microgram of uranium and often can estimate its level of enrichment.[14] A number of other spectrometry methods also are used to obtain details about radioactive isotopes.

As in other fields of technical intelligence, a detailed signature library is a critical part of the forensic process. The goal is to compare a sample's signature against known signatures from uranium mines and fabrication plants. This depends on having a library of nuclear materials of known origin from around the world. U.S. scientists have assembled such a library using samples provided from domestic suppliers of nuclear materials (uranium hexafluoride and uranium oxide reactor fuel).[15]

Nuclear Attack Debris Sampling. A nuclear attack delivered by missiles or aircraft would in most cases be traceable back to the country from which the attack originated. It would be more difficult to trace the origin of a terrorist nuclear attack, since such an attack is likely to result from a clandestinely emplaced device. There are two likely types of terrorist devices:

- a conventional nuclear bomb acquired from some country's nuclear stockpile or fabricated from stolen weapons-grade material
- a so-called dirty bomb comprising conventional explosives in a blast that spreads radioactive material over a wide area

In the first type of attack, forensics may be able to identify the nation that originated the fissile material or weapon and determine whether terrorists had fabricated the weapon on their own or obtained it from a nation's stockpile.[16] In a dirty-bomb attack, forensics probably could identify the source of the radioactive material used. Nuclear forensics can do this because of the widespread practice of "fingerprinting" nuclear and radiological material to prevent the illegal smuggling and trafficking of materials that have potential for application in nuclear terrorism. In all cases, it is important to conduct prompt sampling of the debris from the attack and to process and exploit the samples quickly.

Processing and exploitation of the radioactive debris can provide a number of insights that would help to identify the perpetrators of an attack. In the case of a nuclear bomb detonation, the first question would be whether the weapon was based on highly enriched uranium or plutonium. That question can be answered fairly quickly. Within hours to weeks, the investigators would determine key details about the original nuclear material and then estimate the size, weight, and complexity of the bomb, as follows

- If the device used highly enriched uranium, then scientists could determine the enrichment or share of the uranium-235 that it contained.
- If the weapon used plutonium, then scientists could determine how much time the fuel had spent in a nuclear reactor to create the appropriate plutonium isotopes, establish the length of time since an isotope was separated from spent nuclear fuel, and identify the isotopic signatures that might provide other indications of the production and separation processes.
- Another important issue is the sophistication, or lack thereof, of the weapon. Scientists could make this judgment based on the efficiency of the plutonium or uranium fission and whether fusion reactions might have been employed to enhance the yield.

If the isotopic data obtained from the debris could be compared with similar data from plutonium or highly enriched uranium stockpiles or weapons, it might be possible to conclude whether some of the fissile material came from a specific arsenal. It might even be possible, given enough time and access to actual weapons designs, to conclude whether a particular type of weapon had been employed.[17]

CHEMICAL SAMPLING

Chemical sampling using special purpose sensors has come into prominence as a result of the growing worldwide threat of chemical terrorism. But chemical sampling has been used to provide technical intelligence for years. Many industrial processes generate and release telltale chemical signatures that can provide information about the activities taking place within a facility. The ability to detect the chemicals released into the environment from a facility can provide a powerful means for monitoring treaty compliance or detecting weapons production activities. In situ sensors can be clandestinely emplaced near a factory, and the results can be communicated to a remote location for analysis. The possibility also exists that these chemicals can be detected using laser-induced fluorescence.

With the increasing importance of tracing explosives (especially those used in improvised explosive devices), chemical sampling and analysis has become an even more valuable tool for intelligence organizations, the military, and law enforcement.

To deal with the threat of terrorist chemical attacks, the challenge is to produce a sensor that can quickly and reliably detect chemical traces. A number of sensors already exist, and this is a rapidly changing field. One current example uses an integrated optics sensor to detect the presence of chemical agents in seconds. The sensor consists of a laser light source, a planar waveguide (essentially a small flat piece of glass through which the light travels), and a detector for monitoring light output. Chemicals react with the glass waveguide surface and thereby alter the speed of light through the waveguide. Signal processing software interprets the sensor's results and delivers information on the agents' identity and quantity.[18]

As with other areas of technical collection, a detailed chemical signature library is essential if sampling is to be effective. A chemical signature library needs to include location-specific signatures for chemicals, such as explosives, so that an analyst can identify the laboratory or plant that produced the chemical.

Chemical agents are identified through various techniques in a laboratory; mass spectroscopy is one of the most common methods. In mass spectroscopy, a sample is bombarded with an electron beam that has sufficient energy to break apart the sample into molecules. The positive molecules produced by this process are accelerated in a vacuum through a magnetic field, which separates them based on the ratio of their mass to their electric charge.

BIOLOGICAL AND MEDICAL SAMPLING

As with chemical sensors, biosensors have become of more importance as a result of the growing worldwide threat of biological terrorism. Biosensors can identify specific pathogens, such as anthrax or smallpox. When biological agents are detected, the goal is to quickly and accurately trace their origin in order to determine if they are endemic to a particular region and who may have intentionally introduced them.

Biological agents are more difficult to detect than chemical agents, although the same sensor can sometimes be used to detect attacks for both. The integrated optics sensor described above can be used to detect biological as well as chemical agents. To sense biological agents, the device measures the reaction of the agent with chemicals on the waveguide surface.

Biological agent strains also need to be recorded in a signature library. The signature of biological agents has to include their natural geographic distribution, so that intelligence can better track biological incidents and outbreaks. The 2001 anthrax attack described in chapter 1 could be narrowed to a specific source because detailed analysis of that anthrax signature had been obtained.

Medical sampling is closely related to biological sampling, but the focus is somewhat different. Diagnostic sampling is performed in medical and veterinary facilities worldwide. Samples taken from humans, animals, and plants are used routinely to identify diseases. Extensive medical sampling is undertaken, for example, by the United Nation's World Health Organization and the U.S. Centers for Disease Control and Prevention.

Medical sampling for intelligence purposes is performed in the United States by the National Center for Medical Intelligence (NCMI) located at Fort Detrick, Maryland. NCMI, formerly the Armed Forces Medical Intelligence Center (AFMIC), has a long history of assessing the threats from outbreaks of diseases, such as the H5N1 avian influenza. Intelligence collection and analysis in this field is necessary because some countries fail to report infectious diseases or even provide false information about them. China in particular has a history of hiding information about disease outbreaks. The Chinese government took great care to conceal information about the outbreak of Severe Acute Respiratory Syndrome (SARS) in 2003.[19] Medical intelligence collection continues to be important because of the risk that government concealment of disease information could lead to a pandemic.

Sampling can be intrusive, as characterized by a detailed physical examination of disease victims. On the other hand, it can also be very simple and broadly applied. Some of the simplest sampling for SARS involved a biometric technique (described later in more detail), specifically, taking people's temperatures. During the 2003 outbreak, Japan installed infrared thermometers at Tokyo International Airport to monitor passengers and identify possible SARS victims.[20]

→ **Case Study:** Yellow Rain. One of the more extensive sampling efforts, the Yellow Rain investigation in Southeast Asia, involved both biological and medical sampling. Starting in 1976 in Laos, 1978 in Cambodia (Kampuchea), and 1979 in Afghanistan, intelligence analysts began receiving reports of chemical or toxin weapons being used against the Hmong, the Khmer, and the Afghans. The alleged attacks were often described as a helicopter or plane flying over a village and releasing a colored cloud that would fall in a manner that looked, felt, and sounded like rain. The most commonly reported color was yellow. Thus, the reported attacks in the three countries became known as "Yellow Rain."

The similarities in the descriptions of attacks and subsequent symptoms among victims in the three countries raised suspicions that the same agent was being used. All three locations were linked in some manner to the Soviet Union. In Afghanistan, the Soviets were directly involved in a war; in Laos and Cambodia, they supported the Pathet Lao and North Vietnamese forces.

Beginning in 1979, the United Nations, the United States, and other nations began investigating these allegations of chemical/toxin weapons use. In 1981, the U.S. secretary of state announced that physical evidence had been found that showed mycotoxins (poisonous substances produced by fungi) supplied by the Soviet Union were being used as a weapon against civilians and insurgents in Southeast Asia and Afghanistan.

The U.S. determination that toxin weapons were being used was based on an investigation by U.S. government employees, who, with the assistance of volunteers and refugees from the affected countries, collected biomedical and environmental samples for laboratory analysis, acquired medical data on alleged victims, administered questionnaires regarding alleged attacks, and searched for other information that could confirm or refute aspects of the refugee reports. The United States continued its investigation through the mid-1980s, collecting and analyzing pertinent information on the alleged attacks.

Not everyone concurred with the finding that Yellow Rain was a chemical/biologicalweapons (CBW) attack involving mycotoxins. Some nations were unsuccessful in finding mycotoxins in their sample analysis. The United Nations found the evidence to be inconclusive, and an alternative hypothesis emerged, suggesting that the "yellow rain" was actually just a naturally occurring phenomenon of a swarm of Asian honeybees defecating in flight.[21]

Materiel Acquisition and Exploitation

Materiel acquisition refers to something quite different from materials sampling. It specifically refers to acquiring a piece of equipment or a component, such as

an integrated circuit chip, a vehicle, a missile, or a radar. The acquisition is usually for one of two purposes, and these purposes drive the exploitation phase that follows.

The first purpose is to reverse engineer a component or a piece of equipment (that is, disassemble it and analyze its structure, function, and processes) so that your own organization or country can reproduce it. Some materiel acquisition for business intelligence and most technology theft have this motivation, but many countries acquire products from the more technologically advanced countries for reverse engineering.

The second purpose is for performance analysis, to determine the strengths and weaknesses of the equipment. Countries often acquire military hardware in order to develop countermeasures to it (for example, to determine the type of weapon needed to penetrate a tank's armor). Business firms acquire competitors' products for evaluation in order to improve their own products or to support marketing and sales efforts.

ACQUISITION

Acquisition of military equipment is often a result of a successful HUMINT operation, as the acquisition is usually a clandestine effort. Clandestine acquisition is the preferred technique because the acquirer usually does not want the opponent to be aware of the effort's success.

In their heyday, the Soviets were very good at clandestine materiel acquisition. On one occasion, they managed to acquire a new IBM computer before it was officially on the market; however, the result must have been less than satisfactory for the Soviets because none of the IBM sales or maintenance people they subsequently contacted knew how to make it work.[22]

Materiel acquisition has long been practiced in commercial intelligence. Throughout recorded history, manufacturers have acquired samples of a competitor's product for evaluation, as part of planning sales tactics, to copy good ideas or for reverse engineering. The Hittites of Asia Minor in about 2000 B.C.E. may have been the first targets of materiel acquisition efforts, as their iron weaponry was acquired and reverse engineered by the bronze-using Egyptians,[23] and they were far from the last. Today, most materiel acquisition by governmental intelligence agencies is by purchase, usually through middlemen to conceal the intended destination. Materiel acquisition in the business world is typically done openly; when a new product reaches the market, a competitor can (and usually will) purchase samples for evaluation. Automobile manufacturers routinely acquire new models of their competitors to conduct thorough performance and quality evaluations.

Materiel acquisition can also be as a result of combat or by special operations, as the following case illustrates.

→ **Case Study:** The Bruneval Raid. One of the best known materiel acquisition efforts is known as the "Bruneval Raid" of World War II. The full details of this real-life spy thriller are given in Alfred Price's book *Instruments of Darkness.*[24]

In the fall of 1941, Britain's scientific intelligence officer, Dr. R. V. Jones, was zeroing in on a new German antiaircraft fire control radar that was believed to transmit on a frequency of 570 MHz. One of the more daring British reconnaissance pilots brought back a picture of a new radar located near Bruneval, France. The British realized that this radar was located less than 200 yards from the coast and quickly organized a commando raid to obtain detailed information about it.

The British assembled a company of paratroopers to make an airborne assault. A naval assault was too risky because of the high cliffs around Bruneval, but a light naval force was assembled to handle the evacuation. Dr. Jones, in the meantime, had identified the German radar by name—*Würzburg*—but he still could not confirm that the radar was the source of the 570 MHz signals.

Jones specified in detail the parts he wanted his acquisition team—members of the Corps of Royal Engineers and a radar mechanic—to bring back. Of special interest were the feed antenna for the radar dish, which would establish the operating frequency of the radar, and the receiver and display equipment, which would reveal whether any antijamming circuits existed. The transmitters would establish German technology for generating 570 MHz signals. Two radar operators were to be taken prisoner, if possible, so that they could be interrogated about radar operation. Finally, if equipment could not be removed, the labels and inspection stamps were to be taken because these would provide valuable background information.

On the night of February 27, 1942, the raid, codenamed Operation BITING, took place. Despite the errors and missed assignments that are inevitable in such an adventure, the raid was an unqualified success. The Bruneval force brought back exactly what Jones asked for, except that only one radar operator was captured.[25]

The Bruneval Raid was a success because the British knew exactly what they wanted to get. The acquisition team had an expert analyst in the loop at every step. Most successes in materiel acquisition since that time have involved carefully focused teams closely tied to analytical expertise. Most failures have resulted in cases where the acquirers, compartmented from the analysts, had no real idea what they were trying to get or why.

A major drawback of a seizure that results from combat or special opera-tions, like that of the *Würzburg,* is that the opponent knows about the opera-tion's success and can take countermeasures to reduce the value of information gained. The next two examples illustrate materiel collection where a great deal of effort was expended in keeping the success a secret.

→ **Case Study:** The Glomar Explorer. The most expensive single materiel acquisition effort ever undertaken may have been the U.S. effort to bring up a sunken Soviet submarine.

In March 1968, a Soviet Golf-class submarine on patrol northwest of Hawaii was racked with explosions and sank in 17,000 feet of water, carrying all 90 men aboard down with it. Soviet salvage vessels were unable to locate the sunken craft, but the U.S. Navy subsequently pinpointed its location using more sophisticated search equipment. At this point, the CIA entered the picture, as a proposal had been made to recover the submarine. This was the beginning of the project that was reportedly codenamed Project Jennifer.

To accomplish the task, Howard Hughes's Summa Corporation built a 620-foot long deep-sea recovery vessel named the *Glomar Explorer.* The ship was equipped with huge derricks, along with a companion barge to conceal the submarine when it was recovered. The *Glomar Explorer* was built under the cover of a deep sea mining mission and was completed in 1973 at a cost of $200 million.

During July and August 1974, the *Glomar Explorer* located the submarine and began recovery operations. Cables were looped around the submarine, and winches began slowly pulling the submarine up toward the barge. About halfway up, the hull broke apart and two-thirds of the submarine fell back and was lost on the bottom. The remaining one-third of the submarine was recovered and yielded valuable intelligence, but the sought-after prizes—the code books and nuclear warheads—were reportedly lost.[26]

While Project Jennifer did not totally succeed, it illustrates a valuable aspect of collection success: innovation and doing the unexpected. A consistent asset of U.S. intelligence collection—perhaps its single biggest advantage over other collection services—is that U.S. collectors are innovative and unpredictable. In materiel acquisition, as in HUMINT generally, they try things that other services are too unimaginative or too conservative to try. Of course, U.S. col-lection services also take more risks and consequently get into more trouble.

EXPLOITATION

The previous two case studies focused on materiel acquisition, but once the materiel has been acquired, it must be exploited for its intelligence value.

The next two cases focus on the exploitation phase. The first is a classic example of HUMINT-enabled technical collection. Both cases also illustrate the point that it is not always necessary to acquire in order to exploit; "borrowing" may be sufficient.

→ **Case Study:** **The Kidnapping of the Lunik.**[27] During the 1960s, the Soviet Union conducted a traveling exhibition of their industrial and economic achievements. At one stop on the tour, an unexpected shipment arrived from Moscow: the top stage of the new Lunik space vehicle. The Lunik vehicle was unpacked and placed on a pedestal.

The appearance of the Lunik provoked a discussion among U.S. intelligence analysts. Would the Soviets risk exposing a production vehicle at a trade show or was the Lunik simply a specially made mockup? The first would have much potential intelligence value; the second would be worth very little. The decision was to gamble on the chance that the Lunik was not a mockup.

After the exhibition closed at its first stop on the tour, a team of specialists clandestinely gained access to the Lunik for some 24 hours. They found that it was, indeed, a production item from which the engine and most electrical and electronic components had been removed. They examined it thoroughly from the viewpoint of probable performance, taking measurements, determining its structural characteristics and wiring format, and estimating engine size. The team then recommended a more detailed exploitation.

As the exhibition moved from one city to another, an intercepted shipping manifest showed an item listed as "models of astronomic apparatus," whose dimensions were approximately those of the Lunik crate. This information was sent to the CIA station nearest the destination with a request to try to arrange secure access if the Lunik should appear.

The Lunik crate arrived soon afterward and was delivered to the exhibition. The specialists who were brought in for the detailed exploitation came from a "factory markings" team, whose expertise was in exploiting factory-produced items and identifying their production source. On the basis of their experience at trade fairs and other exhibitions, they preferred access to the item before the opening of an exhibition to examining it while in the exhibition hall or after it had left the grounds for another destination. The physical situation at the grounds, however, ruled out access to it prior to the show's opening. During the show the Soviets provided their own 24-hour guard for the displays, so there was no possibility of making a surreptitious night visit.

This left only one chance: to get to the Lunik at some point after it left the exhibition grounds. After the exhibition, the displays would be carried by

truck from the exhibition grounds to a railroad station and then loaded onto freight cars for their next destination.

It was arranged for the Lunik to be the last truckload of the day to leave the grounds. When it left, it was preceded by a CIA station car and followed by another; their assignment was to determine whether the Soviets were escorting it to the rail yard. When it was clear that there were no Soviets around, the truck was stopped at the last possible turnoff, a canvas was thrown over the crate, and a new driver took over. The local driver was escorted to a hotel room and kept there for the night.

Half the team then climbed into the front-nose end of the Lunik with a set of photographic equipment and a drop light. They removed one of the inspection windows in the nose section, took off their shoes so as to leave no telltale scars on the metal surface, and squeezed inside. They then photographed or hand-copied all markings and components. The other half of the team did the same in the aft engine compartment.

At 5:00 a.m., a driver came and moved the truck to a prearranged point. Here the canvas cover was removed and the original driver took over and drove to the rail yard. The Soviet who had been checking items as they arrived the previous day came to the yard at 7:00 a.m. and found the truck with the Lunik awaiting him. He showed no surprise, checked the crate in, and watched it loaded onto a flatcar.

The subsequent exploitation provided identification of the producer of the Lunik stage and the electronics producers, as well as assessments of the level of technology used in the stage.

→ **Case Study: The Foxbat Exploitation.** Some materiel exploitation results from the acts of émigrés or defectors who transport the materiel with them. The most spectacular of such incidents occur when a defector flies an aircraft out of country. Such a defection in 1976 provided U.S. intelligence with a close look at the USSR's hottest jet fighter, the MiG-25 Foxbat.

Following the decision of the U.S. Congress on July 31, 1960, to fund the development of the North American XB-70 Valkyrie, the Soviet Union realized that it lacked an interceptor capable of attacking an aircraft designed to fly at Mach 3 at 70,000–80,000 feet. The MiG-25 Foxbat was originally designed in response to this future threat, with a planned capability of Mach 3.2 at 80,000 feet. The prototype first flew in April 1965. Production of the Foxbat-A fighter began in 1969, and the aircraft eventually entered Soviet service in 1973. Early U.S. intelligence assessments concluded that the Foxbat was a technically advanced and very fast fighter, capable of performing well against comparable U.S. combat aircraft.

On September 6, 1976, Soviet lieutenant Victor Belenko defected with his Foxbat-A to Hakodate Airport in Japan. When it learned what the Japanese had unexpectedly acquired, the Pentagon wanted to bring the plane to the United States, test it, fly it, and keep it. For political reasons, this was not possible. The aircraft was Soviet property, and the Japanese would have to give it back. So the question became: How long would it take engineers and technicians to extract the most valuable intelligence by disassembling and studying the plane on the ground? U.S. experts believed that 30 days would suffice. The Japanese agreed to make the MiG-25 available for at least that long, provided that American specialists wore civilian clothes and acted as consultants working under Japanese supervision.[28]

U.S. experts knew they would have to return the plane eventually. They took it apart piece by piece. The Foxbat was disassembled and the engines, radar, computer, automatic pilot, fire control, electronic countermeasure, hydraulic, communications, and other systems were put on blocks and stands for mechanical, electronic, metallurgical, and photographic analysis.

The exploitation of the MiG-25 uncovered a series of surprises. In short, the Foxbat was substantially less than the spectacular Soviet accomplishment described in intelligence estimates. It could function well as an interceptor against bombers, but it would perform poorly against U.S. fighters. It was a fuel hog having fairly primitive avionics. The airplane had, in fact, been built for one specific mission—to intercept and shoot down the B-70 (which never went into production). Its resulting limitations included the following:

- the massive turbojets could propel the aircraft to Mach 3, but it could barely maneuver at that speed
- the pilot's visibility was severely limited; the pilots could basically see only what was directly in front of them
- the avionics used vacuum tubes, at a time when U.S. combat aircraft relied on solid-state electronics
- the construction techniques were crude by western standards (for example, rivet heads sticking out and poor-quality welding)
- advanced materials, such as titanium, were used sparingly and only where essential—aluminum was used wherever possible[29]

The materiel exploitation was supplemented by debriefings of Lieutenant Belenko. The combination of the debriefing information with the exploitation results provided a more complete picture of the aircraft's design and performance. Belenko reported the following:

- the combat radius of the aircraft was at most 300 kilometers (186 miles)—by Western standards, an incredibly short range
- in maneuvers, the aircraft could not take more than 2.2 Gs with full tanks—with more, the wings would rip off. Even with nearly empty tanks, 5 Gs was the turn limit. The Foxbat was clearly not designed to dogfight; it could not match the older U.S. F-4 Phantom in a turn
- top speed was a very fast Mach 2.8, but the pilots were forbidden to exceed Mach 2.5. At high speeds the engines tended to accelerate out of control; above Mach 2.8, the engines would overheat and burn up. Any time the aircraft was flown near Mach 2.8, the engines were ruined and had to be replaced

While the Americans and Japanese methodically took apart the MiG-25 and continued their exploitation and debriefing of Belenko, the Soviets were demanding the immediate return of the aircraft and pilot. The Japanese responded by noting that the aircraft had violated Japanese airspace; the issue, therefore, was complicated. There were precedents for returning the plane and precedents for keeping it. For the time being, the Japanese retained the aircraft as "evidence," while their investigation of the matter was ongoing.[30] Material evidence in a crime such as this plainly deserved the most careful going-over, perhaps even by experts from several countries. It was possible, after all, that the pilot was carrying contraband into the country. The aircraft would have to be searched in detail. When the Soviets demanded to be allowed to fly the plane out of Japan, the Japanese replied that this was impossible. A crime had been committed by the plane's intrusion into Japanese airspace. The Japanese government could not allow a repeat violation by permitting the plane to fly out. The Foxbat would have to be transported out by ship, in crates.

The Soviets escalated from protests and pleas to threats and actions. Soviet naval vessels began seizing Japanese fishing vessels and imprisoning their crews. These actions, along with other threats and the condescending Soviet attitude, had the opposite effect to what the Soviets intended. It infuriated the Japanese public and provoked the Japanese government into a defiant posture. In a formal note rejecting the Soviet protests and charges, the Japanese government expressed surprise that the Soviet Union had not apologized for violating Japanese airspace. As for all the Soviet demands that the MiG-25 be given back, a foreign ministry official said, "The Soviet Union should first explain what it thinks of the incident. It is no way for anyone to try to take back something he has thrown, even though inadvertently, into the yard of his neighbor."[31]

On November 12, 1976, more than two months after Belenko landed the Foxbat, the Soviets got it back—in pieces. Eight Japanese trucks delivered the crated parts to a Japanese port, where a Soviet freighter waited with a crew supplemented by technicians and KGB officers. The freighter remained in the port until the Russians inventoried all the parts.[32]

Biometrics

Biometrics is a separate discipline for obtaining and analyzing signatures of humans. It is closely related to the field of material sampling, so is included in this chapter as a matter of convenience.

Biometrics uses automated methods for recognizing an individual based on his or her physical or behavioral characteristics. Common physical characteristics that are sensed for biometrics include fingerprints, facial characteristics, iris patterns, hand geometry, voice features, and keystroke dynamics. The type of biometric sensor that works best will vary significantly from one application to another.

At its most simple level, biometric systems operate in a three-step process. First, a sensor takes an observation. The type of sensor and its observation will vary by biometric type. For face recognition, the sensor is usually a camera and the observation is a picture of an individual's face. Second, the biometric system develops a way to describe the observation mathematically—a biometric signature. The method will again vary by biometric type. Third, the computer system feeds the biometric signature into a comparison algorithm and compares it to one or more biometric signatures previously stored in its database.

The biometrics concept—using a fingerprint, a hand shape, an eye structure, a voice pattern, or another physical characteristic as an identification token—has been around for many years. Its current popularity belies its age. Digitized fingerprints and voiceprints have been used in human recognition for years, and their use is increasing.

Fingerprints have long been the leading biometric technique, since it was established that no two fingerprints are ever exactly alike. Fingerprint readers are now both inexpensive and widely available.

A voice biometric or *"voice print"* is as unique to an individual as a finger- or palm print. A voice impersonation that sounds like an exact match to the human ear will, in fact, have a significantly different voice print. A person's voice is unique because of the shape of the vocal cavities and the way the mouth is moved when speaking. To enroll in a voiceprint system, a person either says the exact words or phrases that the system requires or gives an extended speech sample so the computer can identify that person no matter which words are spoken. The signature used in a voiceprint is called a *sound spectrogram* or *sonogram*. A spectrogram is basically a graph that shows a sound's frequency on the vertical axis and time on the horizontal axis. Different speech sounds create different shapes within the graph.

A problem with using voice prints is that, although the signature is unique, it can change when a person is tired or has a cold. And the media used to transmit or record the voice may also affect the signature that is provided for exploitation.

Deoxyribonucleic acid (DNA) is the well-known double helix structure present in every human cell. A DNA sample can be analyzed to identify either a DNA fingerprint or a DNA profile. DNA is not currently useful for biometric surveillance because it is not an automated process. It takes several hours to create a DNA fingerprint. While there is only about one chance in six billion of two people having the same profile, DNA tests cannot distinguish between identical twins.

Retinal scanning analyzes the pattern of blood vessels at the back of the eye. Scanning involves using a low-intensity light source and an optical sensor, and patterns can be read at a great level of accuracy. It requires the user to remove his or her glasses, place an eye close to the device, and focus on a certain point. Retinal scan is actually one of the older biometrics ideas. An article appeared in 1935 in the *New York State Journal of Medicine* that suggested that the pattern of blood vessels on the retina could be used to identify an individual.[33]

Iris scans analyze the features that exist in the colored tissue surrounding the pupil. The iris is unique; no two irises are alike, even among identical twins, in the entire human population. In the iris alone, there are more than 400 distinguishing characteristics that can be quantified and used to identify an individual. Approximately 260 of those are currently captured and used in iris identification.

Retinal and iris scans can capture their respective signatures at a distance of up to 1 meter. This makes them useful at checkpoints but generally not usable in area surveillance.

Biometric facial recognition is probably the most rapidly growing area of biometrics. It has the substantial advantage of being done at a distance, unobtrusively. Facial recognition uses camera images, measuring distances and angles between points on the face—mouth extremities, nostrils, eye corners—to create a "faceprint" that can be recognized in scanning a crowd of people. Biometric facial recognition is currently being used to control access to facilities, as well as to computers, gaming casinos, and at border crossing points around the world.[34]

Hand geometry uses the geometric shape of the hand for authenticating a user's identity. But unlike fingerprints, the human hand is not unique until observations get down to fine detail. One can use finger length, thickness, and curvature for the purposes of verification (confirming that a person is who he says he is), but this is not suitable for identification (as one cannot reliably search for a handprint in a database; there are too many likely matches).

Keystroke dynamics relies on measuring the unique ways a person types information into a keyboard. As a biometric recognition technique, it has an antecedent that is more than a century old. As noted in chapter 8, Morse code operators have long been able to recognize other operators by their characteristic pattern of keying the code, known as their "fist."

Scent identification is based on the ability to identify a unique signature based on scent, in much the same way that dogs can distinguish the scents of specific humans and other dogs. This identification is accomplished by a technique called *chromatography*, which measures the relative proportions of chemicals in a gas. Researchers also are investigating the possible use of human scent to detect deception.[35]

Biometric recognition is becoming more popular worldwide, as successful biometric systems become less expensive and easier to use and as the need for enhanced security continues to grow. This helps intelligence and law enforcement organizations track terrorists and criminals as they move between countries, but it also poses a problem for HUMINT field operatives who must travel across borders under assumed identities.

Behavioral Signatures

The science of behavioral sensing and assessment is closely related to biometrics and is often combined with biometric sensing. This is a rapidly growing field that finds application in law enforcement and intelligence. Behavioral sensing is used not to identify a specific individual but to identify a potential perpetrator. It is more than signatures; it is the study of patterns of behavior.

Patterns of suspicious behavior are well known in law enforcement. People spend time apparently doing nothing while sitting on a park bench, and such behavior is considered normal. However, if people spend the same amount of time sitting in a parked car next to a secured facility, then their intentions are suspect.

Increasingly, behavioral signatures are being used for profiling and identifying possible terrorists. Research is aimed at developing automated systems that track faces, voices, bodies, and other biometric features against scientifically tested behavioral indicators to provide a numerical score of the likelihood that an individual may be about to commit a terrorist act. The goal is to identify the perpetrator in a security setting before he or she has the chance to carry out the attack.[36]

Terrorists are often trained to conceal emotions, but some reactions of the human body are not subject to voluntary control. Skin temperature, blood-flow patterns, perspiration, and heart and breathing rates are difficult or impossible to control, and new technologies are being developed to sense these signatures at a distance. The U.S. Department of Homeland Security (DHS) is reportedly developing an automated sensing system to detect hostile intent; the system would rely on an array of sensors to measure these signatures at a distance of approximately 2 meters.[37]

Another promising area of behavioral signatures is the field called *microexpressions*. These are fleeting facial expressions, typically lasting less than one-tenth of a second and involving a small part of the human face. Microexpressions are largely involuntary. There are about 40 known microexpressions, and some of these are believed to expose lying. Microexpressions are easily missed by human eyes, though the best professional poker players are expert at reading them. But such brief expressions may be subject to automated detection and classification. The apparent persistence of microexpressions across cultures makes them signatures of interest for both intelligence and law enforcement.[38]

Summary

Though they sound much the same, materials sampling and materiel acquisition are quite different. Materials sampling involves acquiring small quantities or traces of a material and using forensic processes to determine its nature and identify its source. Materiel acquisition, in contrast, involves acquiring hardware (such as computers, airplanes, missiles, or ships), usually for exploitation to determine the design and performance characteristics of the hardware. What the two have in common is that their collection or acquisition usually involves some type of HUMINT operation.

Materials sampling includes the collection and analysis of trace elements, particulates, effluents, and debris. Such materials are released into the atmosphere, water, or ground by a wide range of industrial processes and military activities. For example, materials sampling can be used operationally to track ships or submarines. As these vessels move through the water, they leave behind a trail of trace chemicals.

Any handling of nuclear material nearly always leaves a trace in the environment, even if the material has been removed and the facility cleaned up. Every nuclear explosion, even an underground explosion, leaves traces in the environment. This trace nuclear material can provide clues as to its age, origin, intended use, and the way it was produced and handled. Such traces and clues can often be detected and analyzed with techniques provided by *nuclear forensics,* which functions much like medical forensics, and which have three main intelligence purposes:

- detecting nuclear weapons testing and assessing the weapons performance, which relies on aircraft or ground sites to collect air samples
- detecting the production or movement of nuclear weapons material, which relies primarily on collecting material samples in or near a suspect facility
- obtaining debris samples after a nuclear attack for the purpose of identifying the origin of the device used

Two classes of materials sensors—biosensors and chemical sensors—have become much more prominent as a result of the growing worldwide threat of biological or chemical terrorism. Of the two classes, chemical sensors are easier to develop and use, and they are more widely used for intelligence collection. Biosensors can identify specific pathogens, such as anthrax and smallpox. When biological agents are detected, the goal is to quickly and accurately trace their origin in order to determine whether they are endemic to a particular region or who may have intentionally introduced them.

Medical intelligence sampling is closely related to biological sampling, but the focus is somewhat different. Diagnostic sampling is performed in medical and veterinary facilities worldwide. Samples taken from humans, animals, and plants are used routinely to identify diseases.

Materials sampling is also used to identify the processes and products of a facility. The processes generate and release telltale chemical signatures that can provide information about the activities taking place within the facility.

Materiel acquisition refers to something quite different from materials sampling. It specifically refers to acquiring a piece of equipment or a component, such as an integrated circuit chip, a vehicle, a missile, or a radar. The acquisition is usually for one of two purposes. The first purpose is to reverse engineer a component or a piece of equipment. The second purpose is for performance analysis, to determine the strengths and weaknesses of the equipment.

Acquisition of military equipment often is a result of a successful HUMINT operation, as the acquisition is usually a clandestine effort. Clandestine acquisition is the preferred technique because the acquirer usually does not want the opponent to be aware of the effort's success; however, military equipment also is acquired as a result of combat operations or from defectors. Once the materiel has been acquired, it must be exploited for its intelligence value.

Biometrics is a separate discipline for obtaining and analyzing signatures about humans. It uses automated methods for recognizing an individual based on physical or behavioral characteristics. Specialized sensors can capture a number of physical characteristics to create biometric signatures, including fingerprints, facial characteristics, iris or retinal patterns, hand geometry, voice features, and keystroke dynamics.

Behavioral sensing and assessment is closely related to biometrics and is often combined with biometric sensing. It is more than signatures; it is the study of patterns of behavior. Behavioral sensing is used not to identify a specific individual but to identify a potential perpetrator.

NOTES

1. Sir Arthur Conan Doyle, "A Study in Scarlet," *The Complete Sherlock Holmes* (New York: Doubleday, 1985), 33.

2. "U.S.: Sudan Plant Sample Contains VX Nerve Gas Precursor," *CNN.com,* August 24, 1998, www.cnn.com/WORLD/africa/9808/24/bomb.damage/.

3. Gus W. Weiss, "The Farewell Dossier," CIA Center for the Studies of Intelligence, www.cia.gov/library/center-for-the-study-of-intelligence/csi-publications/csi-studies/studies/96unclass/farewell.htm.

4. Norman Polmar and Kenneth J. Moore, *Cold War Submarines* (Dulles, Va.: Brassey's, 2004), 143.

5. Aish Technologies, "Case Studies: Cathodic Protection," www.aishtechnologies.com/case_studies/aish_casestudies4.html.

6. John A. Strand, Clarence G. Pautzke, and Gordon L. Mitchell, "The Antisubmarine Warfare (ASW) Potential of Bioluminescence Imaging," January 1, 1980, Pentagon Report A421480, www.stormingmedia.us/42/4214/A421480.html.

7. Vitaly Fedchenko, "Weapons of Mass Analysis—Advances in Nuclear Forensics," *Jane's Intelligence Review*, November 1, 2007.

8. National Academy of Sciences, "Technical Issues Related to the Comprehensive Nuclear Test Ban Treaty" (Washington, D.C.: National Academy Press, 2002), 36.

9. Ibid, 45.

10. Ibid.

11. Richard L. Garwin and Frank N. von Hippel, "A Technical Analysis: Deconstructing North Korea's October 9 Nuclear Test," *Arms Control Today* (November 2006), www.armscontrol.org/act/2006_11/tech.

12. National Radiation Laboratory of New Zealand, "CTBT International Monitoring," www.nrl.moh.govt.nz/about/ctbtinternationalmonitoringsystem.pdf.

13. Jonathan Medalia, "Nuclear Terrorism: A Brief Review of Threats and Responses," CRS Report to Congress, February 10, 2005.

14. Ibid.

15. Lawrence Livermore National Laboratory, "Identifying the Source of Stolen Nuclear Materials," *Science and Technology Review* (January/February 2007).

16. Medalia, "Nuclear Terrorism."

17. William Donlop and Harold Smith, "Who Did It? Using International Forensics to Detect and Deter Nuclear Terrorism," *Arms Control Today* (October 2006), www.armscontrol.org/act/2006_10/CVRForensics.

18. "Sensing Danger: Researchers Develop New Sensing Technologies to Improve Response to Chemical and Biological Attacks," *Research Horizons Magazine,* November 23, 2004, http://gtresearchnews.gatech.edu/newsrelease/danger.htm.

19. Ellen Bork, "China's SARS Problem, and Ours," *The Daily Standard*, April 4, 2003, www.weeklystandard.com/Content/Public/Articles/000/000/002/504jlpnl.asp.

20. NIC Assessment: *SARS: Down But Still a Threat*, ICA 2003–09, August 2003, www.fas.org/irp/nic/sars.pdf.

21. U.S. Department of State, "Case Study: Yellow Rain," www.state.gov/t/vci/rls/prsrl/57321.htm.

22. Robert M. Clark, *Intelligence Analysis: A Target-Centric Approach*, 3rd ed. (CQ Press, 2009), 118.

23. Ralph Linton, *The Tree of Culture*, (Alfred A. Knopf, 1955), 105.

24. Alfred Price, *Instruments of Darkness: The History of Electronic Warfare, 1939–1945* (London: William Kimber, 1967) 80–87.

25. Ibid.

26. *Newsday*, April 11, 1989, 2.

27. From Sydney Wesley Finer, "The Kidnapping of the Lunik," www.cia.gov/library/center-for-the-study-of-intelligence/kent-csi/docs/v11i1a04p_0001.htm.

28. "MiG-25 Foxbat," www.spyflight.co.uk/foxb.htm.

29. Ibid.

30. John Barron, *MIG Pilot: The Final Escape of Lt. Belenko*, (New York: McGraw-Hill, 1980).

31. Ibid.

32. Ibid.

33. Tiffany L. Vogel, "Security: Biometric Style," published on the International Federation for Protection Officers Web site, April 25, 2003, www.ifpo.org/articlebank/biometrics.html.

34. John D. Woodward Jr., "Super Bowl Surveillance: Facing Up to Biometrics," in *Intelligencer: Journal of U.S. Intelligence Studies* (Summer 2001): 37.

35. Shaun Waterman, "DHS Wants to Use Human Body Odor as Biometric Identifier, Clue to Deception," UPI.com, March 9, 2009, www.upi.com/Emerging_Threats/2009/03/09/DHS_wants_to_use_human_body_odor_as_biometric_identifier_clue_to_deception/UPI-20121236627329/.

36. "Technology Would Help Detect Terrorists Before They Strike," *Science Daily,* October 10, 2007, www.sciencedaily.com/releases/2007/10/071005185129.htm.

37. "If Looks Could Kill," *Economist.com,* October 23, 2008, www.economist.com/science/displayStory.cfm?source=hptextfeature&story_id=12465303.

38. Ibid.

12. Managing Technical Collection

This chapter discusses some approaches to managing technical collection. The U.S. intelligence community probably has the most expensive and most effective set of technical collection assets in the world. While the chapter focuses on managing technical collection, most of it applies to all of the subcategories of intelligence collection.

Many of the management challenges of technical collection are common to all "INTs." Some are unique to technical collection or to specific subdisciplines. Even with technical collection, the management structures and processes can be quite different. Overhead imagery or ELINT collection, for example, functions much like a high-volume automated production line that must respond quickly to changing customer needs. In contrast, materiel collection and exploitation is more like a boutique business, providing specialized service and one-of-a-kind products.

But first, a caution about this chapter. A famous quote attributed to German Chancellor Otto von Bismarck, among others, is that "laws are like sausages; it is better not to see them being made." The same can be said for the management of intelligence collection, and especially of technical collection. This chapter nevertheless attempts to explain how technical collection is managed. It is not an easy topic to explain, and it is becoming harder as the management structure becomes steadily more complex. The various overlapping and competing attempts in the U.S. intelligence community to implement collaborative systems are particularly confounding. Furthermore, given the continuing changes in this field and the constant renaming of existing projects, any explanation is likely to rather quickly become outdated.[1]

To help clarify things, the discussion will begin by defining an ideal technical collection management system (in terms of both process and output).

The Ideal in Technical Collection Management

An ideal collection management system would at all times have a current understanding of customers' needs for information and the gaps in knowledge. From this understanding, it would develop coordinated requirements and allocate collection assets against the appropriate targets to maximize the value of intelligence collected. All collectors would know what the other collectors are doing so that they could anticipate collection opportunities. The system would function effectively across many different classification levels. Collection assets would be used synergistically, so that the whole is greater than the sum of its parts. The processing, exploitation, and analysis of the product would be done quickly and accurately. And the product would reach customers in time to be of use.

In large intelligence communities such as in the United States, there are many hurdles that have to be overcome in order to approach an ideal management structure. Technical collection systems have developed independently within the Department of Defense, the military services, CIA, and the FBI, among others, often to support specific customers of those organizations. The resulting compartmentation, organizational boundaries, and the desire to protect existing budgets make improvement difficult. Too often there is duplicative collection, missed collection opportunities, material that is collected but never processed or analyzed, or collection products that arrive too late to be of use to the customer.

Technical collection has great promise for dealing with a wide range of intelligence issues. It offers many ways to attack an intelligence target. But the technical collection system functions at a fraction of its potential because the tasking, operations, and processing are mostly done independently instead of interdependently. The U.S. community has made remarkable progress in the last decade, but the ideal of a truly integrated collection system remains some distance away. Getting closer to the ideal requires dealing with the challenges that are discussed in this chapter:

- matching priorities to requirements and transitioning them into collection strategies
- objectively evaluating collection performance
- managing the entire process across organizational and national boundaries, specifically dealing with the "stovepipe problem"
- managing customer expectations, especially in dealing with timeliness pressures
- bringing new technologies and capabilities online

Managing the Front End

The *front end* is a term of art in intelligence collection, referring to the process that involves collection planning—specifically, the development of requirements, collection priorities, collection strategies, and tasking of collectors. A terminology problem occurs here. Many terms are used to describe the front-end process, and they tend to overlap, get confused, or mean the same thing. Distinguishing among priorities, requirements, and needs is a particular problem.

Priorities at the national or policymaking level tend to be expressed by customers outside the community. These customers traditionally have come from the top levels of the executive branch, but increasingly the U.S. Congress is establishing national priorities.

Requirements (or needs) tend to be defined by customers within the intelligence community, except that military customers who are intimately familiar with intelligence often define requirements as well. Requirements and needs are much the same thing, but different parts of the community prefer different terms. Collectors tend to generally prefer the term *needs*; *requirements* has more of a mandatory sound to it.

A large intelligence service such as that of the United States, with its worldwide interests, many collection assets, and many targets, faces a daunting management challenge. Management of information acquisition is a major effort in large intelligence communities. High volume collection is based on a formalized process of defining requirements, needs, priorities, and information gaps. The U.S. intelligence community has for decades attempted to create structures for the consolidated handling of the collection front end, but there remain at least 13 separate U.S. processes and systems used to manage such collection (and those are just the major systems, not including special access programs). [2]

As a result, the U.S. intelligence collection management structures have received considerable criticism, and repeated attempts to define such a structure over decades suggests that something may be fundamentally wrong either with the concept or the implementation. One critic of the process, as it has been practiced in recent years, notes:

> Analysts themselves often thought that too many people were employed and too much activity was oriented solely to generating "intelligence requirements"; a better job could probably have been done by a few experienced people, working with the available data, and therefore aware of what was missing. Instead intelligence requirements were the object of repeated studies and reorganization efforts.[3]

What are often called "requirements" in the intelligence community are actually elements of a multi-stage process of defining intelligence priorities and needs, followed by collection priorities, followed by the development of a collection strategy. This process then concludes with tasking of the collection assets. The following discussion will go through the steps in the front-end process one at a time, recognizing that there is considerable overlap among them.

INTELLIGENCE PRIORITIES

Intelligence priorities are not the same as the priorities for national security policy identified above. National interests are what matters most to a country, and policy priorities obviously must take into account the inherent importance of national interests. They also must reflect existing and anticipated threats and opportunities, as well as political, economic, and military constraints. Intelligence priorities derive from these national priorities.

Intelligence priorities are particularly important to establish when collection assets can be allocated against a very large target set, and a subset must be selected for targeting. Much of technical collection fits this definition. Almost any geographical location on earth can be targeted for visible or spectral imagery collection, but targeting all the earth would saturate overhead collection capabilities, and processing and exploitation of such worldwide collection simply could not be done. The same limitation applies to ELINT collection, with the added restriction that all available ELINT assets probably could not cover the entire RF spectrum worldwide. In both cases, the collection problem has to be bounded, and intelligence priorities help to serve this purpose.

Many attempts have been made to formalize intelligence priorities since the National Security Act of 1947. The following are some of the recent ones:

- During the early 1970s, the U.S. intelligence community developed a set of key intelligence questions (KIQs) that defined intelligence priorities.[4] The community has long since abandoned KIQs but, interestingly enough, the business intelligence (or competitive intelligence) community has embraced the concept and still uses KIQs.
- During the 1970s, the Foreign Intelligence Requirements, Categories, and Priorities (FIRCAP) system was developed and maintained until the early 1990s.[5]
- In 1992, the Director of Central Intelligence replaced FIRCAP with the national intelligence needs process, a hierarchical system for defining priorities. At the top level, these were very broadly defined, including issues such as political instability and weapons of mass destruction. At the bottom of the hierarchy, they were specific and measurable—issues such as the transparency and legitimacy of elections.[6]
- After the end of the Cold War, the United States reshaped its intelligence priorities to reflect the new realities. The initial result was Presidential Decision Directive 35 (PDD-35), which defined policy goals and intelligence needs. It separated intelligence requirements into two broad categories: so-called hard targets (such as Libya, Cuba, Iraq, Iran, and North Korea) and transnational issues (such as international crime, terrorism, and weapons proliferation). PDD-35 used a tier structure, with upper-tier countries having higher priority.[7]

The National Intelligence Priorities Framework (NIPF) is the current guidance from the Director of National Intelligence (DNI) to the intelligence community on national intelligence priorities. It is reviewed by the National Security Council and approved by the president. The NIPF guides prioritization for the operation, planning, and programming of U.S. intelligence analysis and collection. The NIPF is updated semiannually. It takes the form of a matrix of countries and nonstate actors of intelligence interest versus a set of intelligence topics. It is used to guide both collection and analysis of intelligence.[8]

The repeated changes in intelligence priorities systems might suggest, as previously noted, that there is something fundamentally wrong with either the concept or its execution. These priorities systems encounter pitfalls that are common to any organization:

- collectors and analysts tend to focus their efforts on the top priorities in any priority system and avoid doing anything about lower priorities[9]
- organizational survival dictates showing that the organization's collection or analysis efforts are addressing top priorities—after all, resources and budgets are at stake

REQUIREMENTS OR NEEDS

As the above section suggests, priorities and requirements or needs are often mixed together. But they need to be thought of differently. First, the types of requirements that are commonly used need to be clarified. A collection management system has to be flexible to be able to adapt to rapidly changing situations. So, some provision has to be made for levying time-sensitive and ad hoc requirements based on new intelligence or for explaining the special circumstances surrounding a requirement. The imagery community refers to these requirement sets by the term *requirements decks,* but similar breakouts of requirements are used in most technical collection, as follows

- *standing* requirements are defined for continuing, long-term collection— often, for repeated collection in the case of imagery or ELINT targets
- *time-sensitive* requirements need immediate collection action; depending on the collection asset, this could mean a few minutes to a few days. A pending missile or nuclear weapon test would generate time-sensitive requirements
- *ad hoc* requirements are totally new, where no standing requirement exists. They usually are short term, on the order of a few days to a few weeks. Most materiel collection is ad hoc
- *amplification* of a requirement is often needed when conditions are imposed on how collection must be done (for example, at a certain time of day or a specific collector-to-target geometry). A good example is the detailed amplification associated with the Bruneval raid described in chapter 11

Collection requirements form a hierarchy. These requirements hierarchies result from a strategies-to-task problem breakdown.[10] Lower elements in the hierarchy are more specific and, in a well-drafted requirements hierarchy, are linked to the higher elements by some measures that indicate their relative value in the overall scheme of things. The number of specific, lower-level targets will be in the dozens for a specific company, in the hundreds for a small country or a consortium, and in the thousands for an illicit network target such as international narcotics. A typical requirement at the lower levels might read: "Geolocate all armored vehicles in the battlefield area."

Formal requirements structures are necessary in dealing with high-volume satellite IMINT and ELINT and with open source material, where a large number of potential targets exist, and where a large customer suite with competing priorities wants more collection than could be accomplished with the entire national budget. This requirements structure has a problem, however, in dealing with priorities below the top level.[11]

The NIPF establishes top-level priorities, but it is difficult to carry this priority structure down the requirements hierarchy. Is a requirement to geolocate a coca field in Colombia more important than one to locate a poppy field in Afghanistan? How do those priorities compare with locating a mobile missile unit in Russia? This problem of establishing lower level priorities has led senior U.S. intelligence officials to note, more than once, that everyone tasks the system, but no one prioritizes. And intelligence officers are reluctant to tell customers that "we do not need this badly enough to spend resources on it."[12]

Furthermore, if an issue has sufficiently high priority, it is relatively easy to ask for more collection resources than needed, and the collection system must respond—sometimes by taking resources away from lower priority targets. Asking for a high resolution optical imagery search over a large region to locate an airfield is a waste. An airfield can be located much more quickly and cheaply in lower-quality NIIRS 2 imagery and then imaged with high quality to obtain the needed level of detail. But a poorly designed requirements system can (and often does) result in such suboptimum resource allocation.

Managing Technical Collection

COLLECTION PRIORITIES

Intelligence collection priorities, in turn, are not the same as either intelligence priorities or requirements. Collection priorities must be derived from both, and they in turn must reflect national interests and broad policy priorities. But collection priorities have to include some other considerations. Making the transition from NIPF (or any other system of defining intelligence priorities) to collection priorities is a challenge, for several reasons.

First, a collection gap must exist. This means that there must be a demonstrated inadequacy of alternative sources. Except in rare instances, the intelligence community should not use collection assets to obtain information that is already readily available. Specifically, if information is available from unclassified sources, intelligence collection assets should not be used to get it, except where cross-checking is essential—for example, in countering suspected deception. Increasingly, commercial sources such as commercial imaging satellites can do collection that once required national intelligence assets—and can do it more cheaply.

The key to making the transition from intelligence priorities or needs to collection priorities is identifying and sorting collection gaps from all the other gaps. The material may already have been collected, but it has not been processed or exploited. It may have been processed and exploited, but it has not been analyzed. These latter cases are processing, exploitation, or analysis gaps—not collection gaps.

Second, there must be some probability of payoff. Collection assets should be allocated only where they are likely to produce a specific benefit or result for the policymaker or consumer. Collection priorities have to reflect intelligence priorities and also involve information that the intelligence community can successfully obtain.[13] Customers who possess high intelligence priorities naturally tend to demand the use of collection assets even when the probability of successful collection is nearly zero—a misuse, if not abuse, of limited resources.

Collection priorities were a simpler problem during the Cold War. The USSR always was the preeminent target, and the first priority was collecting against its nuclear and conventional military forces.[14] Furthermore, the Soviet Union was a very predictable collection target. The locations of its military bases and test ranges were well known. The United States and the USSR had a number of common interests and mutually understood patterns of behavior that limited the effects of the occasional misjudgments.

Collection priorities have become much more difficult since then. The opponents in the war on terrorism are far less predictable. Their bases and attack capabilities are not well known and change rapidly. Furthermore, there are a sizeable number of failed states where a situation that is inimical to U.S. interests could develop at any time with little warning. Consequently, collection priorities have become much more dynamic.

When collection priorities are not carefully thought through, then the bulk of raw data that is collected is irrelevant. For example, most new overhead imagery contains information that is already known; natural terrain features and fixed structures change little, if at all, in the course of a year, though they may be imaged many times during that year.

However, all data that are collected must be processed to some extent, and the handling of this volume of irrelevant data chokes the processing and exploitation systems and often chokes the analyst as well. It is essential to make the hierarchical requirements structure efficient and responsive; this is a continuing challenge for U.S. intelligence.

COLLECTION STRATEGIES[15]

A collection strategy can be described as a systematic plan to optimize the effective and efficient tasking of all capable, available, and appropriate collection assets and/or resources against requirements, where:

- effectiveness is determined by analyzing the capability and availability of assets and resources to collect against specific targets, and
- efficiency is determined by comparing the appropriateness of all available and capable assets to collect against specific targets in a given environment.[16]

For example, an intelligence imaging satellite might provide a greater NIIRS capability than is required to collect against a specific target. In this situation, a commercial imaging satellite might be quite capable of meeting the NIIRS requirement and would therefore serve as an appropriate substitute for the more capable imager, which could be more efficiently used elsewhere. The point is that a collection strategy considers all outstanding intelligence requirements, their relative priority, and the immediate situation in allocating scarce resources.

A few collection problems are easy. A missile silo needs to be checked to ensure that it is still operational. The collection involves getting an overhead optical image of the silo so that the image can be processed and exploited. This solution requires little thought and not much coordination.

Today's targets are more complex. If the target to be checked is a mobile missile instead of a fixed silo, then the missile must first be located. The immediate question becomes: What assets should be tasked to locate the missile? There are several choices—visible and SAR imagery are two choices for obtaining imagery of the possible missile locations. Each has its advantages, depending on the possible missile locations, camouflage, and the size of area to be imaged. ELINT or communications intercepts might be used to locate the missile. HUMINT collection might be possible, or some combination of these might be necessary.

Given the range of possible collection scenarios for complex targets, it is necessary to develop a collection strategy before tasking collection assets. This means considering the utility of all possible collectors and coordinating their use across several different organizations.

Collection strategies therefore try to integrate tasking and collection of multidisciplinary assets to obtain maximum value from the collection. The idea is to leverage the unique capabilities of each asset and to manage and allocate the collection resources to provide more value than independently developed strategies can achieve. Such collaborative strategies can use one of three approaches:[17]

- *Convergent collection:* Using different technical collection assets simultaneously against a target or using them at the same time or nearly the same time as COMINT or HUMINT collection.

- *Sequential collection:* Triggering technical collection of an asset based on information obtained from another technical, COMINT, or HUMINT asset; sequential collection also could mean staggering collection timing to obtain a benefit, such as greater persistence of coverage.
- *Separate collection:* Reducing the redundant tasking of collection assets against a target, where redundant tasking provides no benefit.

These collaborative approaches result in more effective collection strategies, and they are often used. Some parts of the U.S. intelligence community currently are attempting to formalize this process with an initiative called, not surprisingly, collaborative collection strategies (CCS). CCS is basically a renaming of traditional multi-intelligence collection, intended to have collectors and analysts formally collaborate throughout the intelligence cycle to support cross-discipline collection and analysis operations—from identification of the problem through the development and execution of the specific strategy. CCS operations have started with SIGINT–IMINT collaboration, and attempts are being made to include the other intelligence community disciplines.[18] For example, HUMINT enables many technical collection efforts, and vice versa:

- Construction of a new underground facility observed in imagery can be the basis of a request for HUMINT collection. The reverse is also true—HUMINT about the construction can be used to task imagery collection—but the timeliness problem sometimes intervenes. HUMINT can take time to get through the system, and imagery of the underground facility is far less valuable after the facility has been covered with earth or the excavation spoil removed.
- HUMINT reporting of suspicious aircraft landing and taking off at an airfield only during nighttime can be used to request the emplacement of acoustic sensors near the airfield to identify the aircraft.
- A HUMINT source might use a hand-held camera to obtain a picture of a new radar antenna. Measurements of the antenna can allow analysts to estimate the operating frequency for ELINT targeting.

Such cross-cueing of collectors can be done in real time or near real time, and it has a special name in the intelligence business: it is called *tip-off.* In many cases, a technical collection target has a very fleeting lifetime. So planning for tip-off is an important part of collection strategy. The actual tip-off is done in the tasking phase, but it has to be planned for in the strategy phase. Coordinated tasking of technical collection from a variety of sensor platforms and regimes is crucial to solving tough intelligence problems.

Sometimes, collection is only wanted if certain events occur. This is one purpose served by tip-off. For example, radar detection of an unidentified aircraft can be used to tip-off ELINT collection against the aircraft's radar to help identify the aircraft.

Following are some specific examples of innovative collection strategies that are used to deal with difficult collection problems.

Swarm, Surge, or Blitz Strategy. The problem of conducting reconnaissance is that if the opponent can determine the reconnaissance pattern, then the reconnaissance can be defeated by careful timing of activities to avoid the times when collectors are present. This is a particular problem with overhead ELINT and IMINT collection. While there may not be enough assets to conduct surveillance, whatever is available can be allocated for a short time to provide intensive coverage of specific targets. The intelligence community has various names for this technique, including *blitz, surge,* or *swarm* collection.

The customer of such collection—here, the analyst—has to recognize that the collected material is the result of a surge or blitz. Failure to understand this can lead to erroneous analysis, as it did in one conclusion of the national intelligence estimate on Iraqi weapons of mass destruction. Analysts concluded that there had been an increase in activity at suspect Iraqi chemical facilities; the Weapons of Mass Destruction Commission report concluded that the apparent increase in activity may simply have been a result of increased imagery of the facilities.[19]

Probing Strategy. Against targets that practice denial and deception, provocative probing can sometimes be of benefit. In the U.S. Air Force airborne reconnaissance programs dating back to the 1950s, probing was used effectively to overcome the practice of emissions control by the USSR. In emissions control, all nonessential signals were kept off the air until the SIGINT collector had left the area. The U.S. response was to send an aircraft on a penetration course toward the Soviet border and turn away at the last minute, after the Soviets had turned on their entire air defense network to deal with the threat. Probing an opponent's system and watching the response is a useful tactic for learning more about the system. The reaction to probing may have its own set of undesirable consequences; the Soviets would occasionally chase and shoot down the reconnaissance aircraft to discourage the probing practice.

Even a large and bureaucratic collection network such as that of the United States can be responsive, but the intelligence analyst has to play a more significant role in making it so. The Weapons of Mass Destruction Commission had severe criticism of the intelligence community's effectiveness in developing collection strategies. Specifically, it noted that:

> You can't analyze intelligence that you don't have. . . . [T]he Intelligence Community has not developed the long-term, coordinated collection strategies that are necessary to penetrate today's intelligence targets.[20]

> [The intelligence community] rarely adopts integrated strategies for penetrating high-priority targets.[21]

But the WMD Commission also noted that analysts have a major role to play, noting that:

> . . . analysts must be willing to admit what they don't know in order to focus future collection efforts.[22]

The message of the Weapons of Mass Destruction Commission report is fairly clear: Analysts—the customers of collection—should have a role in formulating collection strategy. That is presumably a goal of the collaborative collection strategies project described above. Analysts can bring a unique expertise and understanding of the target to the process. Helping to focus collection can place a substantial burden on the analyst. But the payoff for the analyst can be high, and there is a way to ease the burden. Analysts, as a part of their normal jobs, have to create both a problem breakdown model and a target model.[23] By sharing these models with collectors so that the collectors can identify gaps in knowledge, the analyst better equips them to effectively fill the gaps. Tracking the status of collection requests, finding out who else is asking for the same information (and thereby is part of a community of interest), and obtaining access to others' research results all are facilitated by a common system such as proposed by the collaborative collection strategies.

In the last two decades, some intelligence organizations have defined a specialized career field called *targeting analyst* to meet this need. In this terminology, the "target" often is a person who possesses information of intelligence value, but it can also mean networks, organizations, communications systems, or facilities. The job of the targeting analyst is to translate intelligence needs into potential targets, identify gaps in knowledge, identify collection assets that can be used against the target, and develop a collection plan. In essence, one analyst handles all these steps. The targeting analyst clearly does not plan routine collection, such as imagery or ELINT collection, which is best done by automated systems. The analyst is more likely to be focused on a single target of very high intelligence value.

Any system for increased analyst involvement in collection consumes valuable analyst time, but it has a high payoff for those analysts who are willing to commit the time. A formal and elaborate requirements system tends not to be very responsive. Because of the failure to prioritize in detail, and because there are more requirements than collection assets can handle, many requirements simply are not satisfied. Analyst involvement can make all the difference; for those analysts willing to spend the time to provide background, justification, detailed guidance, and follow-up evaluations, the system can be very responsive. The collection system rewards those who take the time to cultivate collectors and to apply the personal touch.

TASKING

The last step in the front-end process is tasking of collection assets. Tasking involves providing specific guidance to a specific collector. A collection requirement might request "an image of Manila harbor at sufficient quality to identify cargo vessels in the harbor." The tasking to support this requirement might specify "U-2 mission 1037: collect NIIRS 6.5 visible imagery, 2 × 2 NM frame centered on 14° 35' N, 120° 58' E, at 0144Z hours on 27 July 2010."

FISINT tasking is more event-oriented. ELINT tasking is somewhere in between—automated, but with tasking controlled by events. One seldom knows when a signal of high importance will suddenly appear.

An example of how software handles automated imagery tasking is the Earth Phenomena Observing System developed to handle tasking of the Hyperion hyperspectral imager that is on NASA's EO-1 satellite. The software stores cloud data generated by the Air Force Weather Agency and uses it to task the Hyperion instrument on NASA's EO-1 satellite. The tool also has been used to deal with the problem of rapid, optimized scheduling of ad hoc, multi-INT collection tasking. It is designed to identify available collection resources and recommend resource allocation and timing to improve collection performance: timeliness, geolocation accuracy, and image resolution.[24]

Tasking must not only be specific, as the U-2 example above illustrates. It must often include background information to help the collector. Many requirements need amplification or explanation. A formal requirements system too often does not allow the needed level of amplification. It is difficult to provide for all the nuances and conditions that accompany a requirement. Materiel collection, as noted earlier, often requires very specific guidance;

most successful collections occur when the collectors fully understand the what, when, where, and why. Consider R.V. Jones's tasking on collection against the Würzburg radar, discussed in the case study of chapter 11. The guidance was highly specific on what parts to bring back. Sometimes, the collectors even need to be told how to collect. For example, the collection of a biological sample or factory effluent may require collection under very specific conditions, and the sample may need to be handled, stored, or transported only in a certain fashion.

COLLECTION MANAGEMENT TOOLS

The preceding sections illustrate the complexity of front-end management. In an attempt to manage this complex front-end process for large collection systems with many customers, the U.S. intelligence community has developed many automated collection management tools. Sometimes these tools also are used to manage the back-end processes discussed in the next section. Over the years, a number of efforts have been made to transition from the plethora of individual tools to a set of IC-wide collection management tools that would do integrated collection management.

In 1994, the Department of Defense (DoD) began development of the joint collection management tools (JCMT), intended to be a DoD system for all-source collection management, combining IMINT, SIGINT, MASINT, and HUMINT tasking. This software package supported the gathering, organizing, and tracking intelligence collection requirements for all these disciplines. The JCMT replaced a number of existing collection management systems, including:

- Army's Collection Management Support Tools
- Defense Intelligence Agency's Collection Requirements Management Application
- Operational Support Office's National Exercise Support Terminal
- United States Southern Command's Intelligence Support Processing Tool
- USAF National Air Intelligence Center's Collection Requirements Management System[25]

The complex human-machine interface, message parsing problems, and heavy database maintenance requirements resulted in JCMT's being terminated in 2000. It was incorporated into the intelligence community's Intelligence Community Multi-intelligence Acquisition Program (IC-MAP), subsequently renamed the Intelligence Community Analysis and Requirements System (ICARS).[26]

The ICARS program reportedly was terminated in 2009.[27] But it illustrates how an integrated system might function. The concept was to build a web-based collection requirements management environment that provides a single point of entry for analysts to shape collection. It was intended to connect all intelligence community collection requirements management systems and make it easier for analysts to submit their collection needs or describe intelligence gaps. Also, analysts would have been able to search and view existing requirements that complement their own. ICARS was intended to foster collaboration across organizational boundaries, as analysts subscribe to each other's requests and work together with collectors to formulate optimal collection strategies.[28]

Another example of a cross-agency requirements system is a joint National Geospatial-Intelligence Agency (NGA) and National Security Agency (NSA) effort called *Integrated Collection Management* (ICM). ICM is intended to synchronize these agencies' collection and exploitation efforts through all phases of the intelligence cycle—tasking, collection, production, exploitation, and dissemination—with a vision to do so across all intelligence disciplines.[29]

At the time of this writing, a number of discipline-specific requirements management systems continue to exist at the national level, and a number of parallel systems exist within DoD:

- the Requirements Management System (RMS) is used to manage and task imagery collection, exploitation, and production. It is managed by NGA[30]
- the MASINT requirements system (MRS) performs a similar function for MASINT collection[31]
- National SIGINT Requirements Process (NSRP) is a system for requesting SIGINT (including ELINT and FISINT) collection and processing. It evaluates and prioritizes requirements[32]
- the Open Source Requirements Management System (OSRMS) is handled by the Director of National Intelligence's Open Source Center (which is organizationally within CIA). This system allows users to research existing open source requirements, submit new ones, and track their status[33]

The picture one sees from all these efforts is that of possibly complementary, possibly duplicative and competing, programs having the goal of the ideal collection management system described at the beginning of this chapter. Exactly what sort of management tool will emerge from these programs, and what it will look like, remains an open issue.

Managing
Technical
Collection

Managing the Back End

A critical phase of technical collection is the processing and exploitation of the raw intelligence that has been collected. This phase has to be planned for, and resources allocated to it before a collection system becomes operational. And yet, this part of the overall collection effort often is the most difficult to know how to plan for. It is easy to build collection systems; what they can do usually is well understood in advance. But the value added of processing and exploitation is not as well understood. The processing of literal intelligence information (primarily from open source, HUMINT, and COMINT) is fairly straightforward. It usually involves translation of text. In contrast, nonliteral information can require the continuing efforts of technical experts and the development and maintenance of large software packages. Processing and exploitation of hyperspectral and SAR imagery can be very expensive. And the changing target set forces additional modifications. For example, when a country deploys new radars, the ELINT processing and exploitation system may have to be updated to accommodate these new targets—often at a substantial cost because it has to be done quickly.

Furthermore, with new types of collection, planners may not know in advance how to best design processing and exploitation. Also, new ways to use technical collection are sometimes discovered after the collection system has been in operation for awhile. These factors all tend to make the back-end development lag behind the collection system itself.

The exploitation of technical collection often requires correlating a signature with a signature database for identification purposes. As discussed throughout this book, this requires a signature library: a large database of processed, exploited, and accessible material that can be used to monitor activity and detect significant changes in signatures or patterns. So, complete and up-to-date signature libraries are critical components of the back end. The importance of signature libraries has been stressed throughout this book. A large number of such libraries is needed, including a basic IMINT library, ELINT and FISINT libraries, and hyperspectral and acoustic signature libraries.

Managing the signature libraries is a continuing challenge. The libraries must be constantly updated and made available to all potential users. The challenge is much like that of managing the FBI's fingerprint library, which also must be constantly updated and available to a large number of law enforcement agencies. Collaborative sharing and exploitation of the signatures has resulted in better intelligence wherever it has been tried. The law enforcement community recognizes the value of sharing fingerprint libraries.

In contrast, collection organizations have in the past tended to protect and compartment their libraries. This natural tendency to protect against the loss of sources limits the potential value of the libraries and the potential for better use of the intelligence they provide. [34]

Evaluating Collection

Because a large part of any intelligence service's budget is spent on collection, especially on technical collection, those services want to know that they are getting their money's worth. So collection performance must be evaluated both prospectively and retrospectively.

Prospective evaluation typically employs simulation modeling; it is often used before a collection system is developed, especially for evaluating the potential of overhead collection systems. These systems are very expensive, so the simulations are well worth the costs of development and operation. Once a collection system is in use, three methods have been used to evaluate the collection product:

- Survey the analysts, asking them to evaluate collection reports that were used in finished intelligence (which consumes valuable analyst time).
- Audit access to the collection databases. Multiple accesses by the same person in some defined time frame indicate that a report has more value. A problem with this method is that the most valuable reports often are accessed once and then printed, so you also need to know when a report is printed.
- Use citation analysis—that is, count the number of times a report is cited in finished intelligence. But the most useful reports are not necessarily cited, and highly compartmented reports are typically used as background since they cannot be used in lower classification reporting.

All these evaluation techniques depend on having some form of metrics—things that can be assigned numbers, where the numbers indicate relative value. Metrics are used wherever possible in evaluating collection. We have almost a compulsion to quantify even the things that are not quantifiable. So evaluators have to know what to measure and how to measure it. The customary metric is some type of measure of user satisfaction.

Measures of user satisfaction can be taken after collection to evaluate how well the intelligence process performed against that need or closed that gap. Expressed another way, the measurement is a quantification of how well a particular requirement or condition has been satisfied. Meaningful measures of user satisfaction could be answers to questions such as the following:

- What percent of all Iranian mobile missiles were located?
- Where are the petroleum industry's planned oil exploration regions?
- What is the expected size of the 2002 opium crop in Pakistan, Laos, Mexico, Thailand, Afghanistan, and Burma? Where are the opium processing centers in these countries and how much can they process?
- Where are the concealed weapons of mass destruction production centers in Syria?

All these questions call for analytic conclusions, but all lead to more specific definitions of measures of user satisfaction.

A poor example of a measure of user satisfaction would be: How much of the target area was searched in imagery at a given resolution? One hundred percent of the target area could be searched without turning up a single item of useful intelligence. Collectors are fond of using such quantitative measures because they provide a firm and technically computable measure. As a result, many collection organizations have become fixated on numbers—both on quality and quantity of collection—and insufficiently concerned with content. For example: [35]

- Collectors often have their performance rated by the number of reports submitted, encouraging the submission of many short reports instead of a few comprehensive ones.
- A FISINT collector probably gets credit for continuous copy of a complete missile test, even if the entire transmission was unbreakably encrypted and provides no intelligence.
- If the IMINT collectors take 100 pictures of a critical installation, they get credit for each image in their collection performance ratings, even if 99 of the pictures contain nothing new.

The first example above illustrates a flaw that is common to metrics-based systems: They can be "gamed"—that is, collection and reporting can be shaped to make the metric look good, not to provide better intelligence. The problem is especially severe where the metric is used for determining budgets. Any metric can and will be gamed if it is used for resource allocation.

In summary, formal collection metrics tend to focus more on what can be easily counted than on what is important. Content, not quantity, is the critical measure, and formal requirements structures do not handle content evaluation well. Analysts and customers have to evaluate content and place a value on collection. Done properly, such evaluation can effectively control gaming.

Managing across Boundaries

Technical collection is spread across organizational and national boundaries and security compartments. As explained earlier in the description of an ideal collection system, the goal is synergy. A need exists for real-time cross-INT collaboration between technical collection groups and their counterparts in the COMINT, HUMINT, and open source communities. But the boundaries hinder the effective allocation of requirements to assets and the collaboration needed to achieve synergy. The problem is so widespread that these barriers to collaboration have a special name in the intelligence community: *stovepipes.*

These stovepipes have adversely affected intelligence for a long time, but leadership finds this a difficult problem to fix. Persistent intelligence community stovepipes inhibit cross-INT innovation and the adoption of new approaches. Cross-INT business processes (managing the multi-INT environment) have been missing; what exists is largely ad hoc. The successes that occur have often been the result of informal contacts that occur in spite of the system, not because of it.

These intelligence community stovepipes are sometimes mistakenly thought of as collection stovepipes—that is, as being divided by collection "INT." [36] The stovepipes exist, but they should not be thought of as being HUMINT or COMINT stovepipes, for example. There are, in fact, four types of stovepipes: organizational, compartmentation, technical, and international. All four of these have valid reasons to exist. The challenge is to make the collection system function effectively, given that the stovepipes are not likely to disappear.

ORGANIZATIONAL STOVEPIPES

Organizational separation creates the dominant stovepipes within the U.S. intelligence community. The responsibilities for technical collection, in particular, are fragmented. A large number of IC organizations do technical collection. Major collection assets are owned by the CIA, DIA, NGA, NRO, NSA, and the military services. Technical collection does not have a single champion agency in the sense that traditional HUMINT and COMINT do (though parts of technical collection, such as IMINT and ELINT, have their champions). There is no national processing and exploitation center to provide visibility for technical collection, no senior authority, and no clear ownership. A number of powerful incentives exist for these organizations to maintain their separate stovepipes.

- DoD organizations and combat units all strongly prefer to have their own intelligence collection and analysis units. A long-standing principle of military commanders is summed up by the statement: "If I don't control it, I can't rely on it."
- All organizations want their intelligence successes to be recognized and strongly resent seeing another organization take even partial credit. IC managers naturally tend to highlight their successes and downplay the contributions of other IC organizations. This general unwillingness to share the fruits of successes hurts the potential for collaboration.
- A closely related incentive is provided by the competition for funding. Funding decisions depend on achieving recognition by the organization providing funds—in this case, the U.S. Congress. Groups that Congress regards as providing highly valuable intelligence tend to get funded; less visible contributors see their funding cut.

As a result, technical collection is a continuing focus for bureaucratic infighting or competition over ownership of the assets.[37] The ideal, as noted in the beginning of this chapter, would be to manage by issue across all technical collection with a collaborative focus on targets, addressing the priorities discussed in previous sections, so that the available assets can complement each other. Such a level of collaboration requires a common objective, compatible policies among agencies, and interoperable systems. Information sharing among collectors has improved in recent years, but it has a long way yet to go. Policy and cultural incentives inhibit interoperability. IC managers want to retain control and remain concerned about who will get the credit and funding for intelligence successes.

The DNI has established a National Intelligence Coordination Center (NIC-C) to oversee the use of all IC collection assets and to facilitate collaboration among collection organizations. The NIC-C has an ambitious agenda that includes front-end management, coordination, and collection evaluation. It appears to have the goal of achieving the ideal collection management system described at the beginning of this chapter. Whether it can succeed, given the tenacity of the organizational stovepipes, is an open question. Strong incentives exist to maintain these stovepipes. Until the incentives are dealt with, no organization such as NIC-C is likely to succeed. More success in collaboration is likely if people who work across these organizational boundaries respect the sensitivities of their partners and understand their cultural mores.

COMPARTMENTATION STOVEPIPES

The U.S. intelligence and defense communities have a large number of special access programs (SAPs), often called *black programs.* These programs also are referred to as compartmented programs because they are protected by special security compartments to which access is highly restricted. Compartmentation has an obvious benefit: The program's success is usually dependent on an opponent's being unaware of its existence or what it does. The steady loss of collection assets supports those who argue for more compartments, and in fact the compartments continue to proliferate. But compartmentation stovepipes have their price:

Managing Technical Collection

- Compartmentation often keeps intelligence from getting to those who need it—other collectors, analysts, and customers. The guardians of compartmented intelligence programs face a constant tradeoff between protecting their source and making the product available. They have to balance security versus effectiveness.[38]
- Compartmentation means that different security levels must somehow coexist in the overall system. The difficulty of achieving multilevel security in information networks makes collaboration difficult.[39]
- Compartmentation tends to protect the stovepipes from pressures to change, and competition for funding provides incentive to maintain the stovepipe and make it stronger. IC managers focus on protecting their special compartment. The result is that the IC is becoming even less agile.

Compartmentation has an added dimension when intelligence must support law enforcement agencies and homeland security. Few people in these organizations have any security clearances at all. So, the intelligence product requires sanitization and carries with it policy challenges, security and oversight issues that are not easily addressed.[40]

TECHNICAL STOVEPIPES

Technical stovepipes exist because specialists in one field of technical collection usually do not have in-depth knowledge of the other fields, and so do not recognize the opportunities for cooperation. The fields, require a wide variety of skill sets, and practitioners have little in common in the different subdisciplines. Also, technical collection is characterized by a wide range of cultures speaking in different tongues; communication across technical disciplines is difficult, mirroring a problem that exists in the world of basic and applied research. Furthermore, because many technical collection assets are poorly understood, and because there are so many of them, users do not take advantage of their potential. It is difficult to task and to exploit the results of tasking.

The signature libraries may be the most "stovepiped" part of a stovepiped community. Each library is designed for effective use by the subdiscipline that it supports. The result is that any effort to reach across libraries in collaborative analysis efforts is very frustrating; analytical software that can access one library generally cannot make use of any other library.

In spite of the problems created by technical stovepipes, they fill an important need. A critical mass of expertise is necessary for progress in any technology, and technical stovepipes serve this purpose.

INTERNATIONAL STOVEPIPES

An important part of technical collection management is managing collection and product sharing across national boundaries.

U.S. intelligence has done a superb job in leveraging the assets, capabilities, and territory of its international partners. Partnerships may be the single biggest U.S. collection advantage over its adversaries. Of course, the resultant sharing of intelligence benefits the partners as well. The USSR also had liaison relationships with its satellite intelligence agencies in Eastern Europe, but this was not a true partnership. The KGB tended to dominate the relationship and reap most of the benefits.[41]

Increasingly, the United States shares technical collection with its international partners and in turn depends on these partners for collection. For ELINT and FISINT, this is not new. The United States has collaborated with the British, Australians, Canadians, and New Zealanders in this area for years. Some technical sensors must be deployed on the territory of allies. Such sensors usually are deployed via cooperative operations with foreign military or intelligence services. The FPS-95, described in chapter 6, was deployed in the United Kingdom. The IUSS, discussed in chapter 10, was deployed with the assistance of Canada, the United Kingdom, and Iceland.[42] The X band radar, described in the same chapter, has been deployed to Japan.[43] And the Japanese cooperation in exploitation of the MIG-25 illustrates the beneficial results to the United States of these relationships. Such sharing of collection assets necessitates a great deal of planning and collaboration.

Furthermore, the increasing frequency of multinational operations has forced sharing with a wider range of coalition partners. Treaty monitoring agreements often require international collaboration; an example is the IMS network for monitoring nuclear testing that was discussed in chapter 10. The United States increasingly relies on a multinational network of collectors or processing and exploitation staff for load-sharing. The growing U.S. network of foreign partners has a number of benefits but also raises some concerns:

- Foreign partners can be encouraged to carry out certain missions, but they cannot be directed to do so.
- Over time, these partners learn a great deal about U.S. technical collection assets and capabilities; some partners potentially are a source of leaks that reduce the effectiveness of these collection assets.
- Sharing of intelligence with coalition foreign partners is increasingly important but appears to lack a coherent policy. Many U.S. intelligence organizations have direct liaison relationships with many countries. The closest analogue would be if each department of the U.S. government dealt directly with its foreign counterpart in other countries, independent of the State Department.

Managing Customer Expectations

After a technical collection capability has been operating for many years, it has developed a customer set that understands what it can do. The customers have integrated that capability into their own planning. They depend on the continuing existence of the capability—which is both an asset and a liability, because it leads to the "legacy system" problem. It is very difficult to drop a capability, even though it may have declined in overall value, because the customers depend on it.

New technical collection assets, though, have a quite different problem. Users do not understand how new systems work or what value the collection has, so they neither ask for nor use collection from those systems. They need to learn the capabilities and limitations of new technical collection. So the U.S. intelligence community faces the continuing challenge of educating customers about the capabilities of new collection assets. That, of course, is a primary purpose of this book.

KNOWLEDGE OF COLLECTION VALUE

Customers include both the all-source analysts who must use the technical collection product and their customers in the military, law enforcement, and national policy communities who must accept the results—and are unlikely to rely on systems that they do not understand. But much of technical collection is poorly understood. Among analysts, the understanding varies according to the analytic specialty:

- Scientific, technical, and weapons systems analysts are the most comfortable with technical collection disciplines. They depend on the collection product for assessing foreign weapons systems and weapons proliferation issues.

- Military analysts are next in line in understanding. They have relied for years on materiel exploitation, for example. And technical collection is of particular value for countering denial and deception (D&D) because a typical target has multiple signatures, and it is difficult to hide or simulate them all. The fact that some techniques are poorly understood by foreign intelligence services helps here. [44]
- Political and economic analysts, in contrast, tend to rely less on technical collection and have less understanding of its potential value for helping to answer their questions.

Even among its users, though, technical collection often is poorly understood, in part because it is highly technical, in part because it covers a broad range of intelligence disciplines having a highly diverse customer set. A large expertise gap exists between the practitioners (collectors and processors) and users of the product. The practitioners rely heavily on technical jargon. As a result, technical collection is not as persuasive as its literal counterpart. The end users of intelligence usually do not see the product of technical collection. It has to go through analysts for interpretation. Even visible imagery, which most users can understand, needs some analysis of the signatures involved.

Because technical collection is poorly understood, end users often do not recognize its value, lack confidence in the product, and are slow to accept it. It often does not get the respect that it deserves, and it does not have a strong customer base. Some end users refer to the more arcane technical intelligence products as "witchcraft" or "voodoo-INT." As the intelligence community becomes familiar with the products over time, some established technical collection capabilities gain acceptance. However, the rapidly advancing technologies in many collection areas mean that the understanding problem will continue to exist for new capabilities coming into the inventory.

Because analysts have an inadequate knowledge of many technical collection capabilities, collection managers need to reach out and continually educate these customers. The analyst–collector relationship needs to be strengthened. The knowledge problem is especially severe in the high-tech disciplines covered in this book, but it varies significantly in specific disciplines. For example, visible imagery is well understood by customers, but disciplines such as radar intelligence, as well as acoustic and material signature collection and analysis are poorly understood.

DEALING WITH TIMELINESS PRESSURES

The customers of intelligence continue to demand more timely access to intelligence, for several reasons:

- Policymakers tend to want intelligence *now*, and they often are reacting to current events—meaning that their needs are unpredictable. Today, it is Sri Lanka; tomorrow, it is Vanuatu; next week, it is the Seychelles.
- Combat operations units increasingly are customers and reliant on national collection assets for targeting. As with policymakers, these customers have a timeliness requirement, but they have more predictable needs. Intelligence as a result is becoming more closely tied to operations, even pulling the trigger in some military operations (for example, the CIA using Hellfire missile-equipped Predator UAVs to target terrorists).
- The law enforcement community is increasingly reliant on intelligence, and law enforcement operates at a fast pace. One hour of delay is often too much.

Intelligence analysts get the most pressure from these timeliness demands because they are close to the customer, but the collectors also feel it. Many of the literal intelligence sources have difficulty meeting these demands for timeliness because language translation is often required.

Technical collection, though, is able to deliver real-time or near real-time products directly to operational units and policymakers. ELINT and imagery sources routinely do so today. Some of the newer technical collection capabilities require extensive processing to obtain the signature because they rely on experimental and immature technology. The associated processes are technology intensive, dependent on specialized expertise, and therefore slow. The trend as these technologies mature, though, is to automate the processing and disseminate the product in near real time.

Bringing New Collection Capabilities Online

The exciting aspect of technical collection is that it is so reliant on new technologies. The advance of technology affects technical collection positively in two ways:

- The proliferation of new technologies worldwide means that there are more opportunities for collection; the collection targets exhibit new vulnerabilities over time. There are more signatures, as electronic systems such as radars and personal digital assistants (PDAs) proliferate. To illustrate: If the collection target was an Old Order Amish community (admittedly, a highly unlikely intelligence target), you would almost be reduced to HUMINT and open source for collection. But the typical person, object, organization, or installation today offers a rich set of potential signatures for technical collection and exploitation.

- New technologies can be applied to obtain better collection of existing signatures or to collect new signatures. RFID tags, hyperspectral and ultraspectral imaging, radar and optical polarimetry, and a number of materials sensing techniques all did not exist during most of the Cold War.

To take advantage of these opportunities, an intelligence organization must do at least three things: maintain a technological edge; shorten the research, development, testing, and evaluation (RDT&E) cycle in order to get collection, processing, and exploitation systems into the field more quickly; and effectively manage the difficult transition from R&D into operational systems.

MAINTAINING A TECHNOLOGICAL EDGE

Collection assets have a finite useful lifetime, and sometimes a very short one. Compromises tend to reduce the value of technical collection assets, especially in the United States. No other country seems to compromise its intelligence assets as quickly as the United States does, and the impact on technical collection is especially heavy. The consequence is that new technologies need to be developed and applied constantly, which requires a robust R&D effort. There are a number of challenges, though, in maintaining this technological edge.

First, a common failing of intelligence organizations is to rely on known sources, technology, and targets instead of developing new ones. It is very easy for collectors to rely on traditional sources and traditional ways of doing business. Searching for new radar signals, for example, often is not encouraged in ELINT; all assets are consumed by the existing signals, and demands for coverage of known targets makes it difficult to search for new ones. Analysts support this inclination by demanding more of the same. In summary, these legacy demands constrain new collection. Once there is an established set of customers for a set of ELINT or IMINT targets, it is difficult to stop providing that intelligence. The customers often have developed a dependency on continuing to receive the information. For example, if the military's precision targeting systems depend on the existence of multispectral imagery of the target with a certain level of accuracy, then halting the collection of such imagery kills the effectiveness of an important military capability.

Second, when new collection systems are developed, the workforce has to be trained to use them. The intelligence community faces a continuing problem of training its workforce to employ new technologies and to use the capabilities of new collection assets.

Finally, the U.S. intelligence community must deal with consequences of a long-standing not-invented-here (NIH) attitude. Many of the IC components have been reluctant to adopt either commercial technologies or those developed by other U.S. government agencies. For many decades, this worked; the IC was ahead of the commercial world in developing and applying new technologies. But today commercial entities lead in several technical collection areas. Las Vegas gambling casinos were leaders in the application of facial recognition. Microsoft and other companies took the lead in developing and applying information technology. Google Earth has raced ahead in the geospatial arena. Accustomed to being leaders, large IC segments have not adjusted easily to being followers.

ACCELERATING THE RDT&E CYCLE

Closely related to maintaining a technological edge is accelerating the RDT&E cycle. But the RDT&E cycle through which new systems must go can take a very long time. Satellites, ships, and aircraft have a development cycle measured in years. Ground sites such as the Maui space surveillance facility discussed in chapter 3 have a development cycle measured in decades. The time frame, especially for large systems, seems to be becoming longer. Part of the problem is the increasing complexity of the systems. Part is due to the increasing amount of time spent on program reviews and approvals.

It is possible to shorten the development time frame by using an accelerated process. The U.S. Air Force coined the term *quick reaction capability* (QRC) for this fast-track process back in the late 1950s, and the process is still used today, sometimes under other names. The QRC concept is to dispense with many of the formal acquisition and systems engineering processes in order to get a piece of equipment into the field quickly. For small items such as sensors, the QRC process has been demonstrated to work and even to be less costly than the normal development cycle. It does not work so well for a large and complex system, where a great deal of systems engineering needs to be done.

Accelerating the RDT&E cycle seems to be an attractive option, but it has its risks. Some of the most advanced technical sensors are little more than experimental prototypes. They are technologically immature and are not readily deployed or used in the field. This deploy-before-ready approach helps the United States maintain an R&D edge, but supporting the deployment can be very expensive.

MANAGING THE TRANSITION TO AN OPERATIONAL COLLECTION SYSTEM

Some types of technical collection systems have been around for years. ELINT and optical imagery have been developed and steadily improved since the 1940s. For systems with such a history, no great difficulty exists in moving the improvements into operational status. The entire intelligence organization is already familiar with the collection system and what it can do. Improvements are readily accepted, even demanded. Intelligence analysts, for example, want more of the same optical imagery but with better NIIRS quality, and they want it to cover a larger area more often. The resulting transition of such user-demanded improvements to operations is relatively smooth.

New types of collection systems face a different, far more difficult, process. For these new and highly technical assets, there are many barriers in getting to operational status. It is typically difficult to move sophisticated technical sensors from R&D to an operational system for several reasons:

- Customers typically do not understand what the new system can offer or how to use the product, so there is no customer demand.
- As noted earlier, there is a continuing demand for existing collection, and customers are unwilling to abandon existing programs. These legacy programs have to be funded, taking away funding for new initiatives. No matter how big the collection system budget, it eventually will be consumed by legacy programs, so no new starts occur unless they are forced.
- Processing and exploitation typically must be developed from scratch. Many of the new collection techniques require intensive processing and exploitation, along with specialized technical expertise, which is in short supply.
- Finally, new systems face an obstacle that system improvements do not have to deal with, an obstacle so prevalent that it has the ominous name of the *valley of death*.

The term *valley of death* comes to us from the commercial world. There, the road between a discovery generated from basic research to a commercial product or process is long and, according to some, rife with significant roadblocks. Innovators describe the valley as a funding gap that exists at an intermediate stage of the development process, between basic research and commercialization of a new product. In this intermediate stage of the innovation process, there is a dearth of funding for technology projects that no longer count as basic research but are not yet far enough along for the benefits to be readily recognized. As one source describes it, this valley is "where good lab discoveries go to die because they lack the funding necessary to become a commercial product."[46]

The same valley of death occurs in the intelligence community's RDT&E process. It is an inevitable consequence of the ease of funding R&D and the difficulty of getting funding to transfer a project into the acquisition phase.

Conclusion

The collection management challenges discussed in this chapter stem in part from the success that the United States has had in developing collection assets and the wide range of U.S. interests. Intelligence literature often makes a point of criticizing U.S. intelligence collection capabilities as being cumbersome and inefficient. It is true that some small government intelligence services, such as Israel's Mossad, and a number of multinational corporations can be successful within the areas where they have concentrated their intelligence expertise. They also have all the advantages that accrue to a small, tightly knit organization. Still, U.S. government technical collection capabilities remain the best in the world. The U.S. intelligence community has the most resources and does the best systems planning. It innovates constantly and attempts things few other services would try. In breadth and depth of coverage, the United States is the benchmark worldwide.

Summary

The ideal collection management system would maintain a current understanding of customers' needs for information and the gaps in knowledge. It would develop coordinated requirements and allocate collection assets to maximize the value of intelligence collected. All collectors would be aware of what the other collectors are doing so collection assets would be used synergistically. The system would function effectively across many different classification levels. The processing, exploitation, and analysis of the product would be done quickly and accurately so the results would reach customers in time to be of use.

All national intelligence services find that the ideal is difficult to achieve. Getting closer to it requires dealing with the following challenges:

- matching priorities to requirements and transitioning them into collection strategies
- objectively evaluating collection performance
- managing the entire process across organizational, compartmentation, technical, and national boundaries
- managing customer expectations, especially in dealing with timeliness pressures
- bringing new technologies and capabilities online

Collection management begins at the *front end*—that part of the process that involves collection planning. National priorities have to be translated into intelligence priorities and then into specific requirements or needs. From these, collection strategies have to be developed and specific collectors tasked to obtain the needed information.

The first step is to establish national intelligence priorities. Many attempts have been made to establish such priorities over the last several decades. The current system in use is called the National Intelligence Priorities Framework. Like its predecessors, the NIPF has to deal with a natural tendency of collectors to focus on the top priorities at the expense of the lesser ones.

The requirements that derive from national intelligence priorities form a hierarchy. Formal requirements structures are necessary in dealing with high-volume satellite IMINT and ELINT and with open source material. Requirements can take several forms. Standing requirements are long term and usually involve continuing or repeated collection; time-sensitive requirements need immediate collection action and are usually focused on a single event; ad hoc requirements are totally new (and may also be time-sensitive).

The key to making the transition from intelligence priorities or needs to collection priorities is identifying and sorting collection gaps from all the other gaps. After this is done, there must be some assessment of the probability of successful collection before proceeding to collection strategy.

A collection strategy can be described as a systematic plan to optimize the effective and efficient tasking of all capable, available, and appropriate collection assets and/or resources against requirements. Given the range of possible collection scenarios for complex targets, it is necessary to develop a collection strategy before tasking collection assets. Collection strategies therefore try to integrate tasking and collection of multidisciplinary assets to obtain maximum value from the collection. Strategies that have been successful in the past include swarm, surge, blitz, and provocative probing.

The last step in the front-end process is tasking of collection assets. Tasking involves providing specific guidance to a specific collector. Tasking must be specific, and it often must include background information to help the collector. Many requirements need amplification or explanation.

In an attempt to manage this complex front-end process for large collection systems with many customers, the U.S. intelligence community has developed many collection management tools. Sometimes these tools are also used to manage the back-end processes. Over the years, a number of efforts have been made to transition from the plethora of individual tools to a set of IC-wide collection management tools that would do integrated collection management.

The other major phase of technical collection is the *back end*, which involves the processing and exploitation of the raw intelligence that has been collected. This phase has to be planned for, and resources allocated to it, before a collection system becomes operational. This part of the overall collection effort often is not planned in advance. With new types of collection, planners may not know in advance how to best design processing and exploitation. Also, new ways to use technical collection are sometimes discovered after the collection system has been in operation for some time.

Collection systems performance must be evaluated both prospectively and retrospectively. Simulation modeling is used to predict the performance of very expensive systems. Content-based measures of user satisfaction can be used for retrospective evaluation, but they should be done by all-source analysts and customers, not by collectors.

Technical collection is spread across organizational and national boundaries and security compartments. These boundaries can hinder the effective allocation of requirements to assets and the needed collaboration. The problem is so well known that these barriers to collaboration have a special name in the intelligence community: *stovepipes*. There are, in fact, four types of stovepipes: organizational, compartmentation, technical, and international. All four of these have valid reasons to exist. The challenge is to make the collection system function effectively, given that the stovepipes are not likely to disappear.

After a technical collection capability has been operating for many years, it has developed a customer set that understands what it can do. New technical collection assets, though, have a quite different problem. Users do not understand how new systems work or what value the collection has. They need to learn the capabilities and limitations of new technical collection. The customers of intelligence continue to demand more timely access to intelligence, both for policy decisions and to support modern fast-reaction battlefield needs.

Technical collection relies heavily on new technologies. The advance of technology affects technical collection positively in providing new targets for collection in other countries and in providing new sensor types. Collection assets have a finite useful lifetime, so it is necessary to maintain a technological edge. This means keeping the RDT&E cycle short to get new equipment in the field rapidly and to find a mechanism for transitioning promising research into operational collection systems.

NOTES

1. "Report of the Commission on the Intelligence Capabilities of the United States Regarding Weapons of Mass Destruction," March 31, 2005, p. 353.
2. Robert M. Clark, *Intelligence Analysis: A Target-Centric Approach,* 3rd ed. (Washington, D.C.: CQ Press, 2009): 151.
3. John Prados, *The Soviet Estimate* (Princeton: Princeton University Press, 1987), 181.
4. Center of the Study of Intelligence, Intelligence Monograph, "Critique of the Codeword Compartment in the CIA," March 1977, www.fas.org/sgp/othergov/codeword.html.
5. Douglas Gartoff, *Directors of Central Intelligence as Leaders of the U.S. Intelligence Community,* Center for the Study of Intelligence, March 16, 2007, ch. 12, www.cia.gov/library/center-for-the-study-of-intelligence/csi-publications/books-and-monographs/directors-of-central-intelligence-as-leaders-of-the-u-s-intelligence-community/chapter_12.htm.
6. Ibid.
7. Thomas C. Bruneau and Steven C. Boraz, *Reforming Intelligence: Obstacles to Democratic Control and Effectiveness* (Austin: University of Texas Press, 2007), 41–45.
8. ISC Document #001, "Concept of Operations for the Information Sharing Environment," February 23, 2006, Appendix B—National Intelligence Priorities Framework, 34, www.ise.gov/docs/eds/edspo-conops.pdf.
9. IC21, Section III: Intelligence Requirements Process.
10. Clark, *Intelligence Analysis: A Target-Centric Approach.* See chapter 2 for a discussion of the strategies-to-task methodology.
11. Ibid, 152.
12. Roy Godson, *Intelligence Requirements for the 1990s* (Lanham, Md.: Lexington Books, 1989), 68.
13. Council on Foreign Relations, "Making Intelligence Smarter," January 1996, www.cfr.org/content/publications/attachments/Making_Intelligence_Smarter.pdf.
14. Council on Foreign Relations, "Making Intelligence Smarter."
15. This section is covered in more detail in Clark, Chapter 8: "Collection Strategies," and in IC21, Section IV: Collection Synergy.
16. DoD Joint Publication 2-01, "Joint and National Intelligence Support to Military Operations," 7 October 2004, p. III-21, www.iwar.org.uk/sigint/resources/joint-pub/JP-2-01.pdf.
17. IC21, Section IV: Collection Synergy.

18. Scott C. Poole, "Integrated Collection Management Accelerates Interagency Coop-
    eration," *NGA Pathfinder*, 6, no. 3 (May/June 2008): 8, www.nga.mil/NGASite
    Content/StaticFiles/OCR/mayjune08.pdf.

19. "Report of the Commission on the Intelligence Capabilities of the United States
    Regarding Weapons of Mass Destruction," March 31, 2005, p. 125; http://govinfo
    .library.unt.edu/wmd/about.html.

20. Ibid, 12.

21. Ibid, 17.

22. Ibid, 12.

23. Clark, *Intelligence Analysis: A Target-Centric Approach*, ch. 2.

24. Mark Abramson, David Carter, Brian Collins, Stephan Kolitz, John Miller, Peter
    Scheidler, Charles Strauss, "Operational Use of EPOS to Increase the Science
    Value of EO-1 Observation Data," http://esto.nasa.gov/conferences/ESTC2006/
    papers/a3p1.pdf.

25. "Joint Collection Management Tools," www.globalsecurity.org/intell/systems/
    jcmt.htm.

26. Ibid.

27. AFCEA Intelligence White Paper, "Congress and the Intelligence Community:
    Rebuilding Trust," May 1, 2009, www.afcea.org/signal/articles/templates/intel_
    whitepapers_template.asp?articleid=1925&zoneid=216.

28. DoD Joint Publication 2-01, "Joint and National Intelligence Support to Military
    Operations," October 7, 2004, GL-21, www.iwar.org.uk/sigint/resources/joint-
    pub/JP-2-01.pdf.

29. Poole, *"Integrated Collection Management Accelerates Interagency Cooperation,"* 8.

30. NGA Publication 1.0, "National System For Geospatial Intelligence: Geospatial
    Intelligence (GEOINT) Basic Doctrine," www.fas.org/irp/agency/nga/doctrine
    .pdf.

31. DoD Joint Publication 2-01, "Joint and National Intelligence Support to Military
    Operations."

32. U.S. Commission on National Security/21st Century, Road Map for National
    Security: Addendum on Structure and Process Analyses, vol. VI, "Intelligence
    Community," April 15, 2001, National Security Agency/Central Security Service,
    p. 12, http://govinfo.library.unt.edu/nssg/addedum/Vol_VI_Intel.pdf.

33. Bonnie Klein, "Open Source Enterprise," April 4, 2006, www.dtic.mil/dtic/
    annualconf/Tuesday/1100.ppt.

34. Mark M. Lowenthal, *Intelligence: From Secrets to Policy*, 4th ed. (Washington,
    D.C.: CQ Press, 2009): 76.

35. Clark, *Intelligence Analysis: A Target-Centric Approach*: 165.

36. Gregory F. Treverton, "Toward a Theory of Intelligence," RAND, 2006, 24, http://
    rand.org/pubs/conf_proceedings/CF219/.

37. Pamela Hess, "Intelligence Agencies in Turf War," Associated Press Report,
    May 28, 2008, http://ap.google.com/article/ALeqM5gcFEMjMTQs1VX2BzaaZr4
    tkZ9rmwD90UTK803.

38. "Report of the Commission on the Intelligence Capabilities of the United States
    Regarding weapons of Mass Destruction," March 31, 2005: 444.

39. Ibid, 439.

40. Clark, *Intelligence Analysis: A Target-Centric Approach*: 298.

Managing
Technical
Collection

41. "Intelligence and Counterintelligence," www.globalsecurity.org/intell/world/russia/kgb-su0522.htm.
42. "History of IUSS," www.cus.navy.mil/timeline.htm.
43. "Forward-Based X-Band Radar–Transportable," Missilethreat.com, www.missilethreat.com/missiledefensesystems/id.19/system_detail.asp.
44. Clark, *Intelligence Analysis: A Target-Centric Approach*: 177–179.
45. Lowenthal, *Intelligence: From Secrets to Policy*: 107.
46. J. Heller and C. Peterson, "Valley of Death" in Nanotechnology Investing, Foresight Nanotech Institute, www.foresight.org/policy/brief8.html.

Recommended Books and Reports

A number of books and reports provide additional detail on the systems covered in this book and are recommended for readers who wish an in-depth treatment of specific topics.

Final Report, "Assessment of Signals Intelligence (SIGINT)/Electronic Warfare (EW) Requirements to Support USMC Expeditionary Maneuver Warfare," Vol. V: *Surveillance,* **prepared by the Applied Research Laboratory at Penn State University for the U.S. Marine Corps Research University, October 1, 2002.** Despite its SIGINT title, this volume provides extensive details on the design and operation of IMINT technology and systems, including electro-optical, infrared, and hyperspectral systems, as well as information on synthetic aperture radar.

Congressional Budget Office Study, "Alternatives for Military Space Radar," publication no. 1609, January 2007, www.cbo.gov/doc.cfm? index=7691. This report discusses the performance of synthetic aperture radar and the design tradeoffs that must be made in selecting a space-based radar for reconnaissance. It includes a good discussion of how GMTI works.

David Adamy, *EW 101: A First Course in Electronic Warfare* **(Norwood, Mass.: Artech House, 2001).** An excellent tutorial on antennas, receivers, ELINT search, emitter geolocation, and LPI signals.

David Adamy, *EW 102: A Second Course in Electronic Warfare* (Boston, Mass.: Horizon House, 2004). This continuation of Adamy's first book covers radar, electro-optical sensing, infrared sensing, and more advanced geolocation techniques.

Jon C. Leachtenauer and Ronald G. Driggers, *Surveillance and Reconnaissance Imaging Systems: Modeling and Performance Prediction* (Norwood, Mass.: Artech House, 2001). A more technical treatment of electro-optical, infrared, and SAR systems, including a discussion of processing.

Robert Wallace and H. Keith Melton, *Spycraft: The Secret History of the CIA's Spytechs, from Communism to al-Qaeda* (New York: Penguin Group USA, 2008). This text delves into the history of a completely different type of technical collection than covered in this book, specifically the use of technology to support HUMINT operations.

Jonathan Medalia, "Detection of Nuclear Weapons and Materials: Science, Technologies, Observations," Congressional Research Service report, November 6, 2008. This report assesses the rapidly advancing technologies for detecting and tracking nuclear weapons materials, focusing on specific types of uranium and plutonium.

Jayant Sharma, Grant H. Stokes, Curt von Braun, George Zollinger, and Andrew J. Wiseman, "Toward Operational Space-Based Space Surveillance," *Lincoln Laboratory Journal,* 13, no. 2 (2002). This report provides an overview of the challenges and the technologies involved in detecting and tracking satellites from space.

Nicholas L. Johnson, "U.S. Space Surveillance," paper presented at World Space Congress, Washington, D.C., September 1, 1992. While somewhat dated, this remains a very good overview of the ground-based systems used by the United States for space surveillance.

Glossary of Terms

Absolute geolocation accuracy	The closeness of the agreement between a sensor's location of a point or feature with respect to ground coordinates and the true location of that feature, typically expressed as a circular error or linear error.
Absolute radiometric accuracy	The difference between the radiance measured by the sensor and the true radiance of a source. Radiometric accuracy is determined by comparing a calibrated source that can be traced to a radiometric standard.
Absorption	Reduction in the strength of a wave propagating through a medium.
Accuracy	Describes how close a measurement is to the true value of the quantity being measured.
Acoustic intelligence	Intelligence derived from the collection and processing of acoustic phenomena. Also called ACINT.
Adaptive optics	An optical technique that cancels the atmospheric turbulence-induced distortions of an object's image. Adaptive optics uses moveable mirror segments or deformable continuous mirrors to compensate for image degradation.

Along-track	The dimension parallel to the path of a vehicle; for side-looking radars, sometimes called the cross-range or azimuth direction.
Amplitude	Measure of the strength of a signal and in particular the strength or "height" of an electromagnetic wave, measured in units of voltage.
Angular resolution	The minimum angular separation between distinguishable objects observed by a sensor.
Antenna	Device to radiate or receive radiofrequency energy.
Apogee	The point at which an object in orbit around the earth—a satellite or other body—is at the greatest distance from the earth.
Ascending passes	A satellite's travel northward on one side of the earth.
Aspect angle	Description of the geometric orientation in the horizontal plane of an object in the scene.
Atmospheric windows	Wavelengths in the millimeter wave or optical part of the spectrum where the atmosphere is transparent or nearly so.
Attenuation	Decrease in the strength of an EM signal.
Azimuth	The relative position of an object horizontally within the field of view, usually measured from true North.
Azimuth compression	The processing that is done along the azimuth direction to focus a SAR.
Azimuth resolution	The minimum azimuthal separation between distinguishable objects observed by a sensor.
Backscatter	The signal reflected by elements of an illuminated scene back in the direction of the sensor.
Ballistic coefficient	A performance measure for ballistic missile reentry vehicles based on the vehicle's weight, drag, and cross-section; vehicles with a high ballistic coefficient penetrate the atmosphere more quickly than those with a low ballistic coefficient. Also called beta.
Bandwidth	A measure of the span of frequencies that are available in a signal or can be collected by a sensor.
Beamwidth	A measure of the width of the radiation pattern of an antenna.
Beta	Term used to refer to the ballistic coefficient of a reentry vehicle.
Bhangmeter	An optical sensor deployed on satellites to detect the dual flash that characterizes atmospheric nuclear explosions.
Biometrics	The science and technology of measuring and analyzing biological data.

Biometric signature	A biological identifying characteristic, customarily used in reference to humans.
Bistatic radar	A radar with transmitter and receiver widely separated in order to obtain a different signature from that of a monostatic radar or to defeat jamming.
Blackbody	An object that absorbs all incident electromagnetic energy and consequently radiates perfectly; such an object would be completely black, reflecting no energy.
Black program	A name applied to highly compartmented or special access programs.
Blitz	A technique for allocating collection assets to provide relatively brief but intensive coverage of specific targets.
C Band	Microwave radar band between 5250 and 5925 MHz.
Calibration	The process of quantitatively defining the system responses to known, controlled signal inputs.
Change detection	Any technique for observing changes in an image over time.
Charge-coupled devices (CCDs)	The name applied to an array of solid-state devices that detect incoming photons in an image sensor.
Chirp	Frequency modulation applied to a radar pulse for the purpose of obtaining high-range resolution with a long pulse. Often called linear frequency modulation (LFM).
Coherent	A property of a signal such that the signal phase is measurable (for example, over many pulses of a radar).
Coherent change detection (CCD)	Using a synthetic aperture radar to, in effect, overlay two radar images, in order to produce a picture of what changed in the time between the two images. It does this by measuring and storing both the intensity and phase (phase history data) of each image pixel.
Communications intelligence (COMINT)	Intelligence information derived from the intercept of communications by other than the intended recipients.
Contrast	Difference between the tone of two neighboring regions in an image.
Contrast enhancement	A processing technique that involves increasing the tonal distinction between various features in a scene.
Corner reflector	Two or more intersecting flat surfaces that combine to enhance the signal reflected back in the direction of a radar.
Cross-track scanner	Also known as an optical-mechanical or "whiskbroom" scanner; it uses a scanning mirror that projects the image of a surface resolution element onto a single detector.

Data cube	A three-dimensional representation of a hyperspectral image.
Decibel (dB)	A logarithmic measurement of signal power; a doubling of power equates to 3 dB, a halving to −3 dB.
Depression angle	Usually refers to the line of sight from the sensor to a target object as measured from the horizontal plane at the sensor.
Descending pass	The part of a satellite orbit traveling southward.
Detection threshold	The minimum level of signal intensity that a sensor can detect.
Diffuse	Reflection typically made up of many individual reflections of energy having random phase with respect to each other, such as from a natural forest canopy or agricultural field. The term is also used to describe a surface that reflects electromagnetic illumination in this fashion. The opposite term is specular.
Digital image	An image that has been placed in a digital file with brightness values of picture elements (pixels) representing brightness of specific positions within the original scene.
Direction finding (DF)	Measurement of the direction of arrival of a signal.
Distributed scatterers	Elements of a scene consisting of many small scatterers of random location, phase, and reflectivity in each resolution cell. (See Diffuse.)
Doppler	A shift in frequency caused by relative motion along the line of sight between the sensor and the target.
Doppler effect (Doppler shift)	A change in the observed frequency of an acoustic or electromagnetic signal emitted by or reflected from an object, when the object and the observer are in motion relative to each other;
Double bounce	A simple form of multibounce where the electromagnetic energy reflects off two surfaces before returning to the sensor.
Dwell time	Length of time that a sensor can maintain access to a target.
Dynamic range	The ratio of the maximum to the minimum observable signal. The maximum signal is the signal at which the system saturates, while the minimum signal is usually defined as the noise floor.
Edge enhancement	An imagery enhancement technique commonly used in processing images for intelligence, characterized by highlighting the edges of target objects.
Electromagnetic (EM) wave	A wave described by variations in electric and magnetic fields. Light waves, radio waves, and microwaves are examples. All such waves propagate at the speed of light in free space.
Electromagnetic interference (EMI)	An undesired EM signal whose frequency is within the sensor bandwidth. The EMI signal acts to degrade the desired signal quality.

Electronic intelligence (ELINT)	Information derived from the intercept of intentional electromagnetic radiations, primarily radar, that do not fall into the categories of COMINT or FISINT.
Electro-optical (EO) imagers	An imaging sensor that converts incoming light energy to an electrical signal for transmission and storage.
Elevation displacement	Image distortion in a synthetic aperture radar image caused by terrain features in the scene being above (or below) the flat earth reference, and thus closer to (or farther from) the radar than the expected position.
Ellipsometry	Another name for optical polarimetry.
Emissive band	The optical spectrum band extending from mid-wavelength infrared through long wavelength IR and into the far IR region.
Emittance	The ratio of a target's radiance to the radiance emitted from an ideal blackbody at the same temperature.
Estimates of likelihood	Term used to describe the precision with which analytic judgments are expressed in finished intelligence reports.
f number	In optics, the ratio of focal length to aperture diameter.
False alarm	A noise or interfering signal that is mistaken for the desired signal.
False color	An image that depicts a subject in colors that differ from those a faithful full-color photograph would show, usually by shifting the colors in each pixel to longer wavelengths.
False negative	A desired signal that is discarded as interference or noise.
False positive	Another term for false alarm.
Field of regard	The total area that a collection platform is capable of seeing.
Field of view	A defined volume of space that a sensor can see at any instant.
Focal length	In optical systems, the distance between the entrance aperture and the focal plane.
Focal plane	The surface at which an optical image is in focus.
Foreign instrumentation signals intelligence (FISINT)	Information derived from the intercept of foreign instrumentation signals by other than the intended recipients. Foreign instrumentation signals include but are not limited to signals from telemetry, tracking/fusing/arming/firing command systems, and video data links.
Foreshortening	Spatial distortion where terrain slopes facing a synthetic aperture radar's illumination are compressed in range. Foreshortening is a special case of elevation displacement.
Forward-looking infrared (FLIR)	An infrared imaging system designed to operate at night, so called because it is usually mounted on an aircraft or vehicle and looking in the direction of travel.

Framing camera	A camera using conventional optics with a planar array of detectors located in the camera focal plane.
Frequency	Rate of oscillation of a wave, measured in Hertz (oscillations per second).
Frequency difference of arrival (FDOA)	A technique for geolocating an emitter by measuring and comparing the Doppler shifts at different receivers where relative motion exists between the emitter and the receivers.
Frequency division multiplexing	Multiplexing done by allocating a different part of the radio frequency spectrum to each stream of communication.
Frequency hopping	A radar technique where the signal periodically moves to a different frequency (often with each pulse transmitted).
Frequency-independent antenna	An antenna that maintains almost constant beamwidth over a very wide frequency band (the upper frequency limit being several times the lower frequency limit).
Front end	The process that involves collection planning, specifically the development of requirements, collection priorities, collection strategies, and tasking of collectors.
Fully polarimetric	Transmitting and receiving both polarizations simultaneously; used to describe a type of SAR.
Gain	Change in signal level due to processing functions that increase the magnitude of the signal.
Geolocation	The process of pinpointing the location of an object on the earth or in space.
Geolocation accuracy	The accuracy of measuring the location of an object on the earth or in space.
Geophone	A type of microphone used to measure seismic disturbances.
Geospatial intelligence (GEOINT)	The all-source analysis of imagery and geospatial information to describe, assess, and visually depict physical features and geographically referenced activities on the earth.
Geostationary orbit (GEO)	An orbit above earth's equator at an altitude of 35,800 km, where the orbital period is 24 hours, equal to that of the earth's rotation.
Glint	A brief strong radar return, caused when the radar cross-section of a target suddenly becomes very large.
Ground sample distance (GSD)	The distance between the center of adjacent pixels in a sensor image.
Hertz	The standard unit for frequency, equivalent to one cycle per second.

Highly elliptical orbit (HEO)	An extremely elongated orbit characterized by a relatively low-altitude perigee and an extremely high-altitude apogee. These orbits can have the advantage of long dwell times during the approach to and descent from apogee.
Human intelligence (HUMINT)	Intelligence information derived from the use of human beings as both sources and collectors, and where the human being is the primary collection instrument.
Hydrophone	A microphone designed to be used underwater for recording or listening to underwater sound.
Hyperspectral imagery	Optical imagery that uses hundreds of spectral bands.
Image	Mapping of the radar or optical reflectivity of a scene.
Image enhancement	Processing technique used to improve the appearance of the imagery to assist in visual interpretation and analysis.
Imagery intelligence (IMINT)	Intelligence information derived from the collection by visual photography, infrared sensors, lasers, electro-optics, and radar sensors, such as synthetic aperture radar wherein images of objects are reproduced optically or electronically on film, electronic display devices, or in other media.
Imaging radiometer	A sensor that measures the intensity of EM radiation while obtaining an image of the target. It creates, in effect, a "radiometric map."
Imaging spectrometer	A sensor that obtains an image of a target while measuring the spectral characteristics of each object in the image.
Incidence angle	Angle between the line of sight from the sensor to the target and a vertical direction measured from the target surface.
Inclination	In space systems terminology, the angle of a satellite's orbit measured counterclockwise from the equatorial plane.
Incoherent (or noncoherent)	Property of a signal in which the phases of the constituents are not statistically correlated or systematically related in any fashion.
Infrared intelligence (IRINT)	Intelligence information associated with emitted or reflected energy derived from monitoring the electromagnetic infrared spectrum.
Instantaneous field of view (IFOV)	The angular aperture within which one pixel of a sensor is sensitive to electromagnetic radiation, measured in degrees.
Intensity accuracy	The degree to which a sensor can resolve differences in intensity.
Intensity coverage	The range of intensity that a sensor can receive and process linearly. See dynamic range, which has the same meaning.
Intensity resolution	The measure of the difference in signal intensity that can be detected and recorded by a sensor. Also called radiometric resolution.

Interferometer	A sensor that receives EM energy over two or more different paths and deduces information from the coherent interference between the received signals.
Interpretability	The ability to identify and distinguish objects, features, patterns, and textures within an image and to determine their significance.
Inverse synthetic aperture radar (ISAR)	A technique to generate a two-dimensional image of a moving object from a fixed radar location by coherently processing echoes from the object as it moves.
L band	Microwave radar band between 1215 and 1400 MHz.
Layover	Extreme form of elevation displacement or foreshortening in which the top of a reflecting object (such as a mountain) is closer to the radar (in slant range) than are the lower parts of the object. The image of such a feature appears to have fallen over toward the radar.
Linear frequency modulation (LFM)	Modulation on a signal causing it to increase or decrease linearly in frequency over time. Also known as chirp.
Literal information	Information in a form that humans use for communication.
Local sun time	Time measured at a specific point on earth in reference to the sun's position; it can differ from the official time in a time zone by minutes to over an hour.
Low earth orbit (LEO)	Satellite orbits between 200 and 1500 km above the earth's surface.
Magnetic anomaly detector (MAD)	A magnetometer that is used by military forces to detect submarines or in geology to search for minerals by observing the disturbance of the normal earth's magnetic field.
Magnetometer	A device that senses weak changes in the earth's magnetic field.
Measurement and signatures intelligence (MASINT)	Intelligence information obtained by quantitative and qualitative analysis of data derived from specific technical sensors for the purpose of identifying any distinctive features associated with the source, emitter, or sender, and to facilitate subsequent identification and/or measurement of the same.
Medium earth orbit (MEO)	Satellite orbits typically between 10,000 to 20,000 km altitude.
Microwave	An electromagnetic frequency between 1 and 300 GHz.
Motion compensation	Adjustment of a radar system and/or the recorded data to remove effects of radar platform motion, including rotation and translation, and variations in along-track velocity.
Multibounce	A scattering mechanism in which the electromagnetic wave reflects off more than one point before returning to the sensor. The simplest example is double-bounce scattering.

Multifunction	In radar use, a radar that can perform more than one of the four functions of search, track, imaging, and target measurement.
Multilateration	Also known as hyperbolic positioning, it is the process of locating an object by computing the time difference of arrival (TDOA) of a signal at different receivers.
Multipath	Another term for multibounce, usually referring to a radar signal that bounces off multiple surfaces before returning to the radar.
Multiplexing	The combining of independent streams of communication into a single transmission; used to transmit telemetry.
Multispectral imagery	Imagery collected by a single sensor in multiple regions (bands) of the electromagnetic spectrum. Typically used to refer to the collection of fewer than 100 bands, to distinguish it from hyperspectral imagery.
Multispectral scanner	An imaging sensor that scans several spectral bands simultaneously to form multiple images of a scene.
Nadir	A point on the earth's surface directly below the satellite.
National Image Interpretability Rating Scale (NIIRS)	A 10-level rating scale that defines the ability to identify certain features or targets within an image. The NIIRS defines and measures the quality of images and performance of imaging systems.
National technical means (NTM)	A euphemism for satellite collection assets, derived from a term used in the Comprehensive Test Ban Treaty of 1963.
Near real time	Refers to the brief delay caused by automated processing and display between the occurrence of an event and reception of the data at some other location. The term typically describes a delay of a few seconds to a few minutes.
Near-polar orbit	A satellite orbit that passes near the north and south poles.
Noise	Any unwanted or contaminating signal competing with the desired signal. Noise may be generated within the sensor or may enter the sensor from the outside.
Noise figure	A factor that describes the noise level in a receiver relative to that in a theoretically perfect receiver. The noise figure, which is always larger than one, is typically two or more and is usually expressed in decibels.
Nonliteral	Information in a form that is not customarily used for human communication.
Nuclear intelligence (NUCINT)	Intelligence information derived from the collection and analysis of radiation and other effects resulting from radioactive sources.
Nuclear forensics	The collection and analysis of a sample containing nuclear or radioactive material to determine the history or production process of the material.
Operational ELINT (OPELINT)	ELINT that is primarily intended to directly support ongoing military or law enforcement operations.

Optical intelligence (OPINT)	Intelligence information derived from radiometric and spectroscopic exploitation of optical energy (ultraviolet, visible, and near infrared) resulting in a spatial, temporal, or spectral signature of targets.
Orbit cycle	The period of time until a satellite retraces its path, passing over the same point on the earth's surface directly below the satellite (the nadir point) for a second time.
Overhead collection	Term commonly used in intelligence literature to refer to collection from satellites.
Overhead nonimaging infrared (ONIR).	See overhead persistent infrared (OPIR).
Overhead persistent infrared (OPIR).	A term applied to spaceborne sensors that detect and track intense emissions of IR energy over a large area of the earth. Replaces the term overhead nonimaging infrared (ONIR).
P band	The radar band between 420 and 450 MHz.
Panchromatic imagery	Black-and-white imagery that spans an area of the electromagnetic spectrum, typically the visible region.
Parallax	Apparent change in the position of an object due to an actual change in the point of view of observation. Parallax may be used to create stereo viewing of images.
Pattern	The product of analysis (frequently of signatures).
Perigee	The point at which an object in orbit around the earth—a satellite or other body—makes its closest approach to the earth.
Period	Time duration of one cycle of a wave or one cycle of any regularly recurring pattern. Period is inversely equal to frequency.
Phase coding	A type of modulation on a radar pulse caused by periodically changing the phase of the transmitted signal to improve range resolution.
Phase history data (PHD)	The raw data collected by a SAR system prior to range and azimuth compression. Slight differences in frequency, or phase differences, are noted, and the signal intensity and phase differences are recorded to create PHD.
Phased array	A group of antenna elements in which the relative phases of the respective signals feeding the elements are varied in such a way that the main beam of the array is steered in a desired direction.
Photographic intelligence (PHOTINT)	The collected products of photographic interpretation, classified and evaluated for intelligence use.

Photometry	Measurement of the intensity of light emitted from or reflected by an object.
Pitch	Vertical rotation of a sensor platform in a "nose up and down" fashion.
Pixel	Picture element, the smallest element of a digital image.
Polar orbit	A 90-degree inclination orbit, which crosses the equator moving directly north or south and crosses directly over the poles.
Polarimetry	The measurement and interpretation of the polarization of transverse waves, most notably electromagnetic waves such as radio waves and light.
Polarization	Orientation of the electric vector in an electromagnetic wave. In the RF bands, polarization is established by the antenna, which may be adjusted to be different on transmit and on receive.
Post-processing	In IMINT, steps that may be applied to digital image files to adjust selected attributes of an image, such as geometric accuracy or radiometric corrections, including speckle reduction and contrast enhancement.
Precision	A measure of the detail in which a quantity is expressed.
Preprocessing	In IMINT, making radiometric or geometric corrections before the main data analysis and extraction of information are done.
Propagation	The movement of energy in the form of waves through space or other media.
Pulse	A group of waves with a distribution confined to a short interval of time. Such a distribution is described by its time duration and its amplitude or magnitude.
Pulse compression	A technique used in radar and sonar to improve the range resolution and signal-to-noise ratio of the sensor, by modulating the transmitted pulse.
Pulse repetition frequency (PRF)	Rate of recurrence of the pulses transmitted by a radar.
Pulse repetition interval (PRI)	The time interval between successive pulses transmitted by a radar.
Pushbroom imager	An imager that makes use of the motion of a detector array along the ground; the imaging effect resembles the bristles of a broom being pushed along a floor.
Quantization	The process of converting continuous values of information to a finite number of discrete values. It is expressed as a number of bits. A 10-bit quantization means that the measured signal can be represented by a total of 1,024 digital values, from 0 to 1,023.
Quick reaction capability (QRC)	A USAF program designed to suspend normal contract procedures in order to get a weapons system or subsystem into the field rapidly.
Radar	Electromagnetic sensor characterized by transmitting a signal and receiving the reflection from a target; the acronym is derived from radio detection and ranging.

Radar cross-section (RCS)	Measure of radar reflectivity, expressed in terms of the physical size of a hypothetical perfect sphere that would give rise to the same level of reflection as that observed from the sample target.
Radar intelligence (RADINT)	Intelligence information derived from data collected by radar.
Radar resolution cell	A volume defined by range and angular resolution for a radar.
Radiance	A measure of the amount of light energy that is emitted from a given area.
Radiant flux	The total amount of power in a defined optical beam, measured in watts.
Radiation	Act of giving off electromagnetic energy.
Radiometer	A passive sensor that receives and records the electromagnetic energy that is naturally emitted from objects.
Radiometric resolution	The ability of a sensor to distinguish different levels of signal intensity.
Range	Line of sight distance, usually between a sensor and its target.
Range ambiguities	Unwanted echoes that fall into a radar image from ranges that in fact are outside of the intended area of coverage.
Range resolution	In radar, this is the resolution characteristic of the range dimension. Range resolution is fundamentally determined by the radar bandwidth.
Real time	The absence of delay, except for the time required for the transmission by electromagnetic energy, between the occurrence of the event or the transmission of data, and the knowledge of an event, or reception of the data at some other location. Contrasts with near real time, which has an additional delay.
Reconnaissance	Periodic observation of a target area; contrast with surveillance.
Reference emitter	An EM signal from a known location, used as a reference to reduce the geolocation error of the desired target signal.
Reflected infrared	The main infrared component of the solar radiation reflected from the earth's surface.
Reflective band	The UV, visible, near IR (NIR), and short wavelength IR (SWIR) bands.
Reflectivity	Property of illuminated objects to reradiate a portion of the incident energy.
Regional wave	A seismic wave that is sensed relatively close to its source. Compare to teleseismic waves, which are sensed at long distances.
Remote sensing	Sensing, primarily from the electromagnetic spectrum, that is done at long distances (on the order of tens to thousands of kilometers).

Resolution	Refers to the ability of a system to differentiate two signatures—a unit of granularity.
Resolution cell	A three-dimensional volume surrounding each point in a scene. Two separate targets located in the same resolution cell cannot be distinguished.
Retrograde orbit	A satellite orbit having more than 90 degrees inclination. The satellite moves in the opposite direction from the earth's rotation.
Retroreflector	A device that reflects energy, such as a laser light pulse, back to its source.
Revisit time	The time that elapses before a collection asset can sense a target for a second time. This is also called revisit period.
Roll	Rotation of a sensor platform around the flight vector, hence in a "wing up or down" direction.
Roughness	In imagery, the variation of surface height within an imaged resolution cell. A surface appears "rough" to illumination when the height variations become larger than a fraction of the EM wavelength.
S band	The two microwave radar bands between 2,300 and 2,500 MHz and between 2,700 and 3,700 MHz.
Scanner	A sensor with a narrow field of view that sweeps over the terrain to build up and produce a two-dimensional image of the surface.
Scattering matrix	Array of four complex numbers that describe the relationship between the polarization of a wave incident upon a target and the polarization of the backscattered wave.
Scene	The ground area observed by a sensor.
Seismic waves	Waves that travel through the earth (for example, as a result of an earthquake or explosion).
Shadow	In SAR, a region hidden behind an elevated feature in the scene that shows up as black on the SAR image. This region is not illuminated by the radar energy and thus is also not visible in the resulting radar image.
Sidelobes	The parts of an antenna's radiation pattern in any area other than the main lobe.
Signals intelligence (SIGINT)	A category of intelligence comprising communications intelligence (COMINT), electronic intelligence (ELINT), and foreign instrumentation signals intelligence (FISINT).
Signal-to-noise ratio (SNR)	Quantitative basis for comparing the relative level of a desired signal to an unwanted element such as noise. SNR can also be defined as the ratio of the power in a desired signal to the undesirable noise present in the absence of a signal.
Signature	The measurement of the strength, intensity, or state of some physical quantity over space, time, and/or frequency.

Signature library	A database of signatures associated with a specific person or class of objects so that when a signature is identified, it can be associated with a specific person, phenomenon, object, or class of objects in the database.
Smearing	In SAR, image distortion caused by a target accelerating toward or away from the radar.
Space object identification (SOI)	A combination of techniques used to obtain additional information about satellites, reentry vehicles, and space debris.
Spatial accuracy	The accuracy of a sensor's location of a target on the earth or in space.
Spatial coverage	A measure of the area on the earth's surface or the volume of space that a sensor can view in a given time.
Spatial filtering	A processing technique used to enhance (or suppress) specific spatial patterns in an image.
Spatial resolution	Ability of a sensor to resolve or separate two objects spatially, usually stated as a measure of distance on the ground.
Special access program (SAP)	A term used by the DoD and the intelligence community to refer to highly classified programs, usually protected by special classification compartments; also known as a black program.
Speckle	The fluctuation in brightness of a pixel in the image of a scene, usually associated with SAR imagery or laser illumination.
Spectral accuracy	A measure of the accuracy with which a sensor can determine the frequency or wavelength of a signal.
Spectral coverage	A measure of the amount of the electromagnetic spectrum that a sensor can observe.
Spectral resolution	The ability of a sensor to distinguish among energies of varying wavelengths emitted by or reflected from a target.
Spectral response	A measure of the sensitivity of a sensor to different wavelengths of EM radiation.
Spectral signature	A signature created by emission or reflection of electromagnetic energy at specific wavelengths from a target.
Spectrometer	An instrument used to measure the intensity and wavelength of light.
Spectroscope	An optical device that splits incoming light according to its wavelength.
Spectrum analyzer	A device used to examine the spectral composition of an electrical waveform; it is the radiofrequency equivalent of the spectrometer.
Specular reflection	Coherent reflection from a smooth surface in a plane normal to the surface at an angle opposite to the incidence angle. A mirror is a specular reflector.

Spotlight	A mode of SAR operation where the radar antenna is rotated to stay aimed at a target area during flight to increase the integration time and therefore the azimuth resolution.
Spread spectrum	A signal transmission that deliberately uses more frequency bandwidth than needed, for the purpose of avoiding detection, defeating interference, or obtaining more favorable signal reception.
Squint	In SAR, the angle measured from perpendicular (broadside) to the direction of flight (the broadside direction being called zero squint). Forward of broadside (in the direction of flight) is called positive squint; aft of broadside is called negative squint.
Stereograph	A combination of two photographs of the same scene taken from slightly different angles to provide a 3-D view of the scene.
Stereoscope	A device that simultaneously presents the left photograph to the viewer's left eye and the right photograph to the viewer's right eye for the purpose of viewing a 3-D image.
Stovepipe	A term for maintaining a separate collection or analysis process based on organizational, compartmentation, or technical factors.
Strip map	A SAR imaging technique where the antenna points in a fixed direction (normally perpendicular to the direction of aircraft or satellite movement).
Sun-synchronous orbit	A satellite orbit designed so that the satellite passes over a given point on the earth at approximately the same time every day.
Surface-wave radar	A type of over-the-horizon radar that depends on the propagation of EM waves that "bend" along the sea surface instead of traveling line-of-sight.
Surveillance	The continuous observation of a target or target area by visual, aural, electronic, photographic, or other means. Contrast with reconnaissance.
Synoptic coverage	Obtaining sensor coverage of a large region nearly simultaneously.
Synthetic aperture radar (SAR)	A radar that achieves high azimuth resolution by obtaining a set of coherently recorded signals such that the radar is able to function as if it had a very large antenna aperture.
Target	An entity (country, area, object, installation, agency, or person) against which intelligence collection is directed.
Targeting	The process of selecting collection targets and matching the appropriate collection response to them, taking account of requirements and capabilities.
Technical ELINT	RF collection and analysis that is used to assess the capabilities and performance of an electronic system (usually a radar).
Telemetry externals	Changes in a telemetry signal caused by the flight profile of the vehicle.

Telemetry internals	The values of the measurements made by flight instrumentation.
Teleseismic wave	A seismic wave that is recorded far from its source.
Temporal accuracy	The measurement accuracy of a signal's arrival time at a sensor.
Temporal coverage	The duration of a sensor's coverage.
Temporal resolution	The span of time between successive collections against a target. Can refer either to the time that elapses before a collection asset can sense a target for a second time or to the ability to separate two closely spaced events in a signature.
Terminator condition	A satellite observation situation where the ground site is in darkness while the sun illuminates the target.
Thermal imaging	Imagery in the infrared spectrum based on emitted radiation (that is, it does not depend on the presence of an illuminator).
Thermal infrared bands	The MWIR and LWIR bands of the IR spectrum.
Thermogram	An image of relative radiant temperatures.
Time difference of arrival (TDOA)	A measurement of the relative arrival times of a signal at dispersed geographic points, used to geolocate the signal.
Time division multiplexing	Transmitting multiple communications streams where each stream periodically gets to use the entire frequency bandwidth of the transmitter for a short time interval.
Tip-off	Using intelligence from one collection source to cue collection by another source.
Two-color multiview	The technique shows objects that appeared in the first image but have left the scene in the second image, in one color. Objects that have appeared in the scene since the first image are shown in a second color.
Ultraspectral	Measurement of thousands of spectral bands.
Unintentional radiation intelligence (RINT)	Intelligence derived from the collection and analysis of radiofrequency energy unintentionally emitted by devices, equipment, and systems.
Unmanned aeronautical vehicle (UAV)	A powered aeronautical vehicle that does not carry a human operator and can fly autonomously or be piloted remotely. Ballistic or cruise missiles and artillery projectiles are not considered UAVs.
"Valley of death"	Term used to describe the gap between R&D and the creation of a product, so named because most research projects die at this stage.
Van Allen radiation belt	A torus of energetic charged particles around earth, held in place by the earth's magnetic field. The inner belt extends from about 700 to 10,000 km above earth; the weaker outer belt extends from about 3 to 10 earth radii.

Visual magnitude (mv)	Measure of the relative brightness of an object; a first magnitude star, the brightest in the sky, is 100 times as bright as a sixth magnitude star.
Volume scattering	Multiple scattering of EM waves occurring inside a medium such as the canopy of a forest.
Wave	Propagating periodic displacement of an energy field. At any instant of time, a wave is described by its "height" (amplitude) and its "length" (wavelength).
Wavelength	Minimum distance between two events of a recurring feature in a periodic sequence, such as the crests in a wave.
Whiskbroom scanner	An imaging sensor that uses a scanning mirror to create an image using a single detector. Also called a cross-track or optical-mechanical scanner.
Wullenweber	Large circular antenna array used by the military to triangulate HF (3–30 MHz) radio signals; also known as a circularly disposed antenna array (CDAA).
X band	Microwave radar band between 8,500 and 10,680 MHz.
Yaw	Rotation of a sensor platform in the horizontal plane, hence in a "nose right or left" direction.
Zero squint	A condition where a SAR looks exactly broadside to the flight direction.

Index